WARSHIP
VOLUME II

Edited by Antony Preston

Conway Maritime Press
Naval Institute Press

WARSHIP Volume II

Managing Editor Robert Gardiner
Editor Antony Preston
Art Editor Geoff Hunt

© **Conway Maritime Press Ltd 1978**

Second Impression 1980
Third Impression 1984

Published in the UK by
Conway Maritime Press Limited
24 Bride Lane,
Fleet Street,
London EC4Y 8DR

**Published and distributed in the United States of
America by**
The Naval Institute Press,
Annapolis,
Maryland 21402

Library of Congress Catalog No 78-55455
UK ISBN 0 85177 149 1
USA ISBN 0-87021-976-6

Manufactured in the United Kingdom

the Battlecruiser
TIGER
by John A Roberts

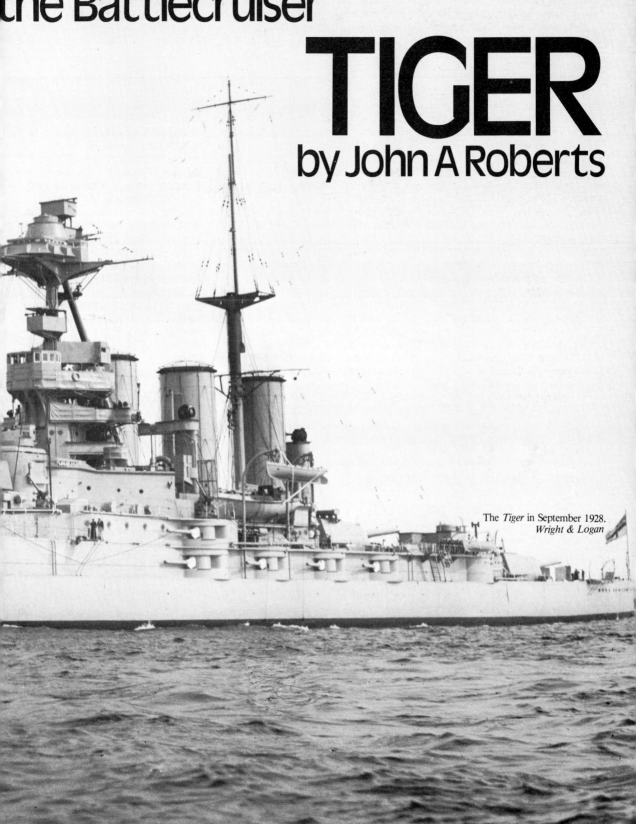

The *Tiger* in September 1928.
Wright & Logan

battlecruiser. The design of the battleships, the *Iron Duke* class, was worked out during the first half of 1911, two main improvements being adopted in the design: an increase in the calibre of the secondary armament guns from 4inch to 6inch to counter the latest types of torpedo craft, and an after torpedo flat providing an additional underwater torpedo tube on each beam. The inclusion of these features in the battlecruiser design was a logical step and this was proposed by the Controller (Third Sea Lord), Rear Admiral C J Briggs, in a memo accompanying three preliminary sketch designs submitted to the Sea Lords in August 1911.[2] The details of these designs with those of the *Queen Mary* are given in Table 1.

Design 'C' was generally similar to *Queen Mary* but owing to the re-positioning of bulkheads necessitated by the provision of an after torpedo flat, it was found convenient to place the after funnel and main mast forward of 'Q' turret. In designs 'A' and 'A1' the turrets were arranged two forward and two aft and a 6inch gun secondary battery was provided. This latter involved an increase in topweight and in order to maintain the level of stability the beam was increased to 90 ft. As the armour protection for the 6inch battery was somewhat better than that for the 4inch battery this modification also

had the effect of improving the ship's protection by adding $8\frac{1}{2}$ ft to the height of the side armour. The belt was further improved by the addition of a strip of armour 3 in thick and 2 ft 6 in deep below the main belt. This, the DNC explained, was regarded with great importance by the Japanese who were fitting similar protection in vessels then under construction in Japan and in the battlecruiser *Kongo* then being constructed by Vickers at Barrow. The Covers give no clue as to the reason for this Japanese innovation, apart from the fact that it was as a result of experience in the Russo-Japanese War. It does seem likely, however, that it was designed to defeat diving shell, or to prevent shells getting under the belt in a heavy swell, or both.

It is worth mentioning here that this is the only evidence in the Ship's Covers of any connection between the designs of *Tiger* and *Kongo*. Claims that the design of *Tiger* was heavily influenced by that of the Japanese ship seem to have been based on the similarity in appearance and the adoption of the same heavy secondary battery whereas, as can be seen from the above, these features resulted from entirely different considerations completely unconnected with the *Kongo*.

The Sea Lords agreed with the Controller's submission regarding

the secondary and torpedo armament and expressed a preference for design 'A1'. But the arcs of fire of the secondary armament were criticised as being restricted, particularly fore and aft. It was suggested that these be improved and, to further improve the general command of the battery, that a 6inch gun be placed on each side of the forecastle deck in the positions occupied by the 12pdr guns in design 'A'. A preference was expressed for the disposition of main armament in design 'C' because 'the two (aft) turrets (in designs 'A' and 'A1') practically form one target when, with sufficient separation, as in 'C', it means the enemy has three separate targets to fire at which complicates his fire control. This is important up to 10 000 yards'. This statement shows a somewhat dated view of naval gunnery; the days when one part of a ship could be aimed at were rapidly fading. However, the argument had some

---

Design A (top) with 6inch gun secondary battery and C (bottom) with 4inch gun secondary battery. Design A1 was much the same as A but did not have the 12pdr guns on the forecastle deck abreast the bridge. The above drawings are based on the verbal descriptions of the designs in the 'Ships Cover' — the actual sketches not being present. The distribution of the secondary battery is assumed, apart from being on the correct deck.

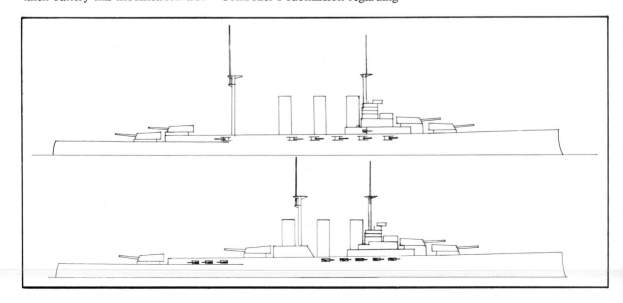

TABLE 1	**A**	**A1**	**C**	**Queen Mary**
LENGTH (PP)	660ft	660ft	660ft	660ft
BEAM	90ft	90ft	89ft	89ft
LOAD DRAUGHT	28ft 6in	28ft 3in	28ft 3in	28ft
DEEP DRAUGHT	32ft 6in	32ft 3in	32ft 3in	32ft 1in
DISPLACEMENT	28450 tons	28100 tons	27250 tons	27000 tons
TPI	101	101	99	99
SHP	80000	79000	76000	75000

LEGEND OF DESIGNS JULY 1911

SPEED	28 knots
FUEL AT LOAD DRAUGHT	1000 tons
COAL CAPACITY	3700 tons
OIL FUEL CAPACITY	1100 Tons
COMPLEMENT	1000 (Queen Mary 999)

ARMAMENT
8—13.5inch/45 cal (80 rpg)
12—6inch/45 cal (150 rpg) A and A1 C and *Queen Mary*
16—4inch/50 cal (150 rpg)
2—1/ pdr (250 r pg) *in A only*
5—Maxim machine guns (5000 rpg)
4—(6 in A1) 3 pdr saluting guns
4—21inch torpedo tubes (2 in *Queen Mary*)
20—21inch torpedoes (14 in   ,,   )
6—14inch torpedoes (for 50ft steam boats)

ARMOUR
MAIN BELT	9, 5 and 4inch
UPPER BELT	6, 5 and 4inch
LOWER BELT	3inch (Not in *Queen Mary* and C)
SECONDARY BATTERY	5inch (A and A1) 3inch (*Queen Mary* and C)
BULKHEADS	4inch
BARBETTES	9 and 8inch
GUNHOUSES	inch
CONNING TOWER	10inch
CONTROL TOWER (AFT)	6inch

PROTECTIVE PLATING
WING BULKHEADS TO
MAGAZINE AND SHELL
ROOMS	$1\frac{1}{2}$ and 1inch
FUNNEL UPTAKES	$1\frac{1}{2}$ and 1inch
DECKS	1inch to 3inch (1inch to $2\frac{1}{2}$inch in *Queen Mary* and C)

WEIGHTS (TONS)
	A	A1	C	Queen Mary
GENERAL EQUIPMENT	820	820	820	805
ARMAMENT	3,860	3,650	3,450	3,352
MACHINERY	5,780	5,720	5,500	5,460
COAL	1,000	1,000	1,000	1,000

ARMOUR & PROTECTIVE
	A	A1	C	Queen Mary
PLATING	7,030	6,980	6,730	6,595
HULL	9,860	9,830	9,6500	9,760
BOARD MARGIN	100	100	100	28
TOTAL	28,450	28,100	27,250	27,000
ESTIMATED COST	£2,235,000	£2,199,000	£2,100,000	£2,085,000

[2]Memo (dated 31 July 1911) and designs were examined initially by First Sea Lord, Admiral Sir A K Wilson, and were then passed on to the Second and Fourth Sea Lords, Vice-Admiral Sir G Le C Egerton and Captain Charles E Madden respectively.

validity in that with the turrets well apart the chances of a single heavy shell or torpedo immobilising both turrets was remote. A few other minor criticisms were made, including the statement that only one mast was required as a second was unnecessary.

To meet these criticisms the First Sea Lord gave verbal instruction for a new sketch design based on 'A1' but incorporating the following modifications:—

a Main armament disposed as in design 'C'.

b Forward 6inch gun embrasures altered to give an arc of fire of 3° across bow.

c An added 6inch gun casemate on each side of the forecastle deck.

On 14 August the new design, designated 'A2', was submitted by the DNC, Sir Phillip Watts, and four days later received Board approval. Criticism was limited to a further request for improvements in the arcs of training of the 6inch guns. The DNC estimated that the 6inch gun casemates would involve an additional weight of 90 tons but the legend of 'A2' was identical to that of 'A1'. However, more detailed calculation of the design resulted in a number of alterations to the legend and on 12 November this document provided the figures shown in Table 2. Under normal circumstances this would have been the end of the basic design stage, but events were developing which were to bring further improvement to the *Tiger*.

1911-12 — THE NEW BOARD

For some time important sections of Parliament, the Press and the Navy had been campaigning for the formation of a Naval War Staff. The attitude of the Admiralty to this idea was to say the least luke-warm. The Agadir crisis of July 1911 brought matters to a head and resulted in the Secretary of State for War, R B Haldane, pressing the Prime Minister for a change at the Admiralty. As a result, on October 25 the Home Secretary, Winston Churchill, exchanged posts with the First Lord, Reginald McKenna. Churchill entered the Admiralty with two main objectives, the formation of a Naval Staff and the appointment of Board of Admiralty of his own choosing. He did not take long; the former took place in January 1912 and the latter was announced in Parliament on 28 November 1911. Admiral Wilson, the First Sea Lord, who was completely opposed to a Naval Staff, was replaced by Admiral Sir Francis Bridgeman and the posts of Second and Fourth Sea Lords were taken by Vice-Admiral Prince Louis of Battenberg and Captain W Pakenham respectively. Admiral Briggs, as Controller and Third Sea Lord, was the only member of the original Board to remain. The new Board took up its duties on 5 December.

One of Churchill's first acts upon hearing of his new appointment was to seek the advice of Admiral Sir John Fisher (First Sea Lord 1905-1910). The two spent three days of discussion together in Reigate Priory and Fisher was 'most of all . . stimulating in all matters related to the design of ships'[3]. Churchill was strongly influenced by the old Admiral's dynamic personality and later events show that he took up several of Fisher's favourite themes. Among these were the desire for ships of high speed and a belief in the advantages of oil fuel over those of coal. Churchill's habit of becoming more involved than was

[3] *The World Crisis, 1911-1918,* Winston Churchill

A rare photograph of *Tiger* in 1915 near the Forth Bridge. The 'TI' on 'Q' and 'A' turrets obviously indicates *Tiger* but the purpose of the triangle on the side of Y turret is not known. The bottom section of the lowered fore topmast can be seen between the legs of the tripod foremast. Note the incomplete sternwalk and the 24inch searchlight on the roof of 'Q' turret, transferred from its normal starboard position on the platform abaft the third funnel.
Imperial War Museum

usual for a Civil Lord soon became apparent. On 20 November he penned the following memo: 'I am making enquiries into the design of this (armoured) cruiser (*Tiger*) which will not be complete for a few days. After this tenders may be invited'.

On 12 December the detailed design and legend of 'A2' was submitted to the Board and approved 'subject to certain modifications to secure additional SHP' — a requirement obviously instigated by Churchill. It was also decided that tenders could be invited but that action regarding the placing of the order would be considered by the Board at a later date. Immediately after this meeting Churchill sent a memo to the Controller asking if the machinery of the *Iron Duke* class and *Tiger* could be adapted to run on oil fuel only. Three days later the DNC

TABLE 2 LEGEND OF DESIGN A2. NOVEMBER 12, 1911

Particulars as those for A1 except as follows:—

BEAM	90ft 6in
DISPLACEMENT	28,200 tons
SHP	82,000
COAL CAPACITY	3,750 tons
OIL CAPACITY	1,150
6 INCH AMMUNITION	200 rpg
CREW	1,109

WEIGHTS

GENERAL EQUIPMENT	840 tons
ARMAMENT	3,600 tons
MACHINERY	5,500 tons
COAL	1,000 tons
ARMOUR & PROTECTIVE PLATING	7,390 tons
HULL	9,720 tons
BOARD MARGIN	100 tons
	28,200 tons

Note: There were also changes to armour arrangement and thicknesses including increasing the secondary battery armour to 6inch thickness.

Tiger as designed, 1911. Bridge and
funnels not yet raised; pole foremast; twin
24 inch searchlights on forward shelter
deck, abreast fore funnel and abreast
torpedo C.T. abaft 3rd funnel; range
finder on roof of torpedo C.T.; boats on
forecastle deck protected by blast screen
from fire of 'Q'turret. Top of masts are
not shown in design drawings and
arrangement is assumed.

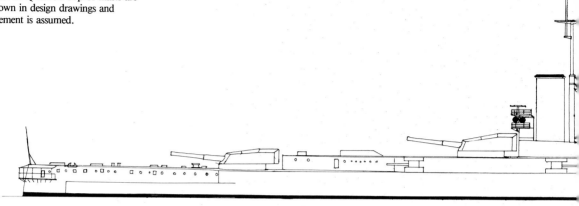

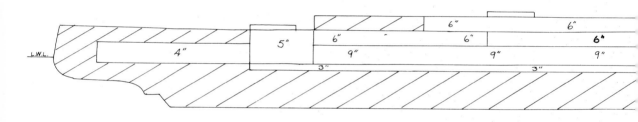

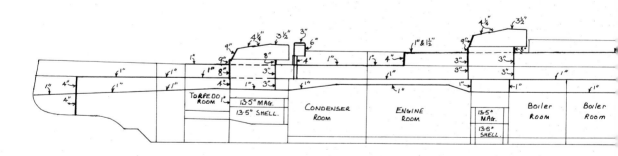

Longitudinal section showing armour
thicknesses (bottom) and hull profile
showing distribution of side armour (top);
shaded area is unprotected.

sent to the Controller two new
sketch designs, 'A2a' and 'A2b',
based on design 'A2'. In 'A2a' the
SHP was increased to 100 000 for a
speed of 29.5 knots which required
an additional 100 tons for
machinery, increasing the
displacement to 28 300 tons and the
draught to 28 ft 4 in. In 'A2b' the
SHP was further increased to 108
000 giving a speed of 30 knots,
adding 350 tons to the machinery

weight and 50 tons to the hull
weight. In addition the fuel capacity
was modified to 2450 tons coal and
2450 tons oil fuel, 450 tons of each
being allowed for at load draught.
This gave a legend displacement of
28 500 tons at a draught of 28 ft 6
in. In answer to Churchill's inquiry
the DNC commented that the
modifications necessary for all-oil
fuel stowage would present no
difficulty, but that to carry the

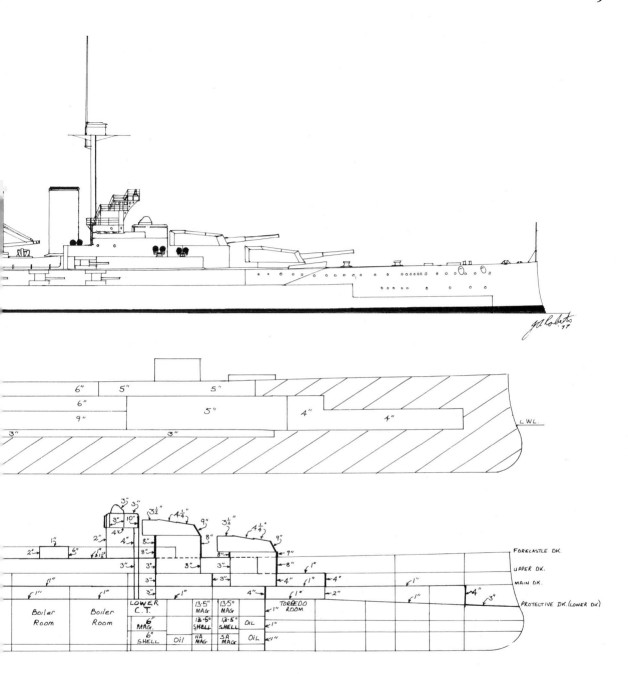

same total amount would require some oil to be carried above the protective deck, which was undesirable. He also pointed out that the loss of protection provided by the coal above this deck would be considerable. The Controller, in submitting the DNC's legends and comments to the Board, expressed a preference for design 'A2b' which would while 'increasing speed and stowage of oil give valuable

experience during construction'. Churchill, and presumably the rest of the Board, approved design 'A2b' on 19 December. Two days later invitations to tender were sent to ten firms.

The Covers provide no clue as to why all-oil stowage was not adopted and the only criticisms noted are those expressed by the DNC. There may of course have been some natural conservatism which required

more careful consideration of all constructional details involved. Care was certainly exercised in the design of the fuel compartments for the completely oil-fired ships of the *Queen Elizabeth* class which were included in the next naval construction programme. A decision was made to increase the oil fuel stowage to 2450 tons and reduce the coal capacity to the same level. The DNC continued to investigate

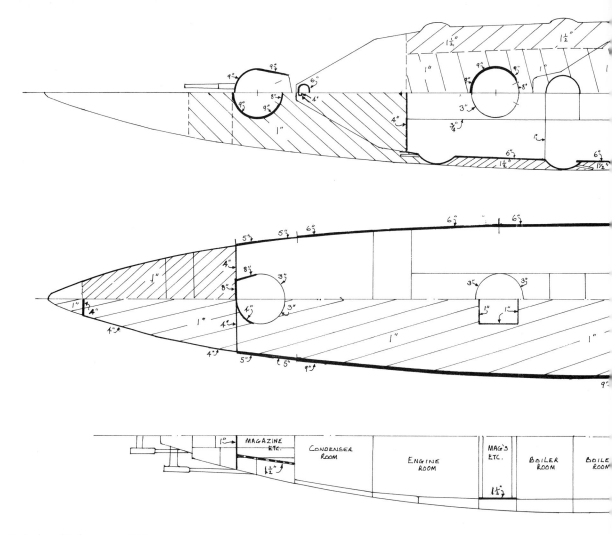

Deck plans showing armour thicknesses.
Shading shows areas of protective plating.

Sections showing armour thicknesses.

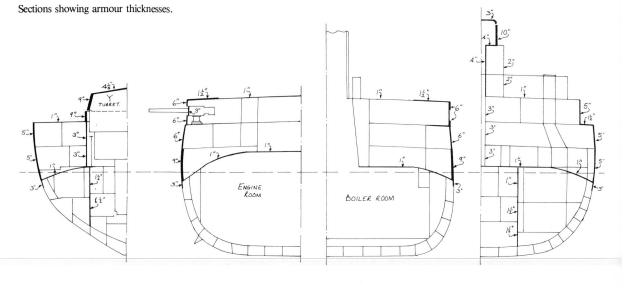

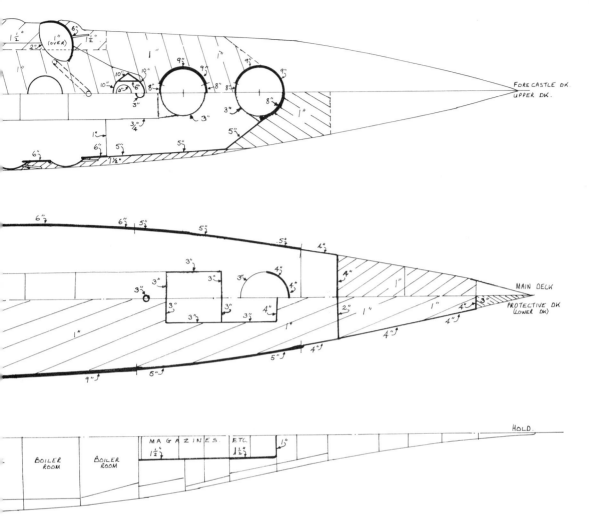

the possibilities of this development and on 20 December proposed to the Controller that the fuel stowage be further increased, principally by utilising the double bottom and other compartments next to the skin plating by fitting them with pipes and valves for use in an emergency.

This was approved on 21 December, the total fuel stowage being increased to an incredible 3480 tons oil and 3340 tons coal. Detailed calculations resulted in a further increase in maximum oil fuel stowage to 3800 tons, giving a total fuel stowage of 7140 tons compared with 4800 tons in the *Queen Mary*. Some of this increase was necessary to provide for the increased fuel consumption of the *Tiger's* more powerful machinery while the remainder served to increase the ship's endurance. But

the ship's full capacity was never employed and the maximum fuel normally carried during the First World War was 3240 tons of coal and 800 tons of oil. Unfortunately I have found no official figures for the *Tiger's* endurance but Parkes [4] gives a fuel consumption of 1245 tons per day at 59 500 HP. This is approximately equal to a speed of 24 knots which would give about 3300 nautical miles with 7140 tons of fuel. The equivalent figure for *Queen Mary* was about 2400 nautical miles.

Two more important modifications were made to the design before the ship was ordered. On 21 December it was decided to increase the height of the funnels to 81 ft above the load water line which added 5 ft to the funnels. This was intended to prevent any

repetition of the smoke interference problems experienced in recently completed capital ships. It was also decided in December or January to fit the ship with anti-rolling tanks. These were athwartship compartments containing free surface water. When the ship was rolling the movement of this water would in theory have had the affect of dampening the movement of the ship. It was intended that these should be fitted in all new capital ships, but in July 1912 it was decided to await the trials of the anti-rolling tanks in the battleship *Conqueror* before proceeding to fit them in other ships. In the case of the *Tiger* the tanks were not fitted. I do not know of results of the *Conqueror* trials, if they were carried out.

[4] *British Battleships 1860-1950* Dr Oscar Parkes

DISPLACEMENT   28,500 tons (load draught)

DIMENSIONS   704ft (oa), 660ft (pp) x 90ft 6in
x 28ft 6in (load, mean) 32ft
(deep, mean)

MACHINERY   Brown-Curtis turbines, 4 shafts, 39
Babcock and Wilcox boilers, 85,000 SHP
=28 knots, 108,000 SHP = 29 knots

FUEL CAPACITY   3340 tons coal, 3800 tons oil fuel

ARMAMENT   8-13.5inch/45 cal Mk V in twin
Mk II mountings (80 rpg)
12—6 inch/45 cal, Mk VII on P VIII
mountings (200 rpg)
6—3pdr saluting guns (166 rpg)
5—0.303 inch Maxim machine guns (5000 rpg)
4—21inch submerged torpedo tubes,
20—21inch Mk II Whitehead torpedoes
6—14inch Mk X torpedoes for steam
boats.

1—12pdr, 8 cwt QF field gun and
carriage (200 rpg)

**ARMOUR
PROTECTIVE
PLATING**   *Belt:* 9inch and 6inch amidships, 5inch
and 4inch forward, 5inch and 4inch aft,
3inch lower belt.

Bulkheads: 4inch and 2inch forward,
4inch aft.

Barbettes: 9inch and 8inch above belt 4inch, 3inch
and 1inch below belt.

Gunhouses: 9inch sides, $4\frac{1}{4}$ and $3\frac{1}{2}$inch
roof.

Conning Tower: 10inch sides, 3inch
roof, 4 inch floor, 2inch base

Conning tower hood and support: 3inch

Communication tube: 4inch and 3inch

Torpedo conning tower (aft): 6inch sides
3inch roof

Torpedo conning tower tube: 4inch

6inch gun battery: 6inch sides, 4inch
aft, 5inch forward.

6inch gun casemates: 6inch side, 2inch
back, 1inch roof.

6inch gun shields: 3inch

Forecastle deck: 1inch and $1\frac{1}{2}$inch
over 6inch gun battery

Upper deck: 1inch over citadel except
under 6inch gun battery.

Main deck: 1inch at ends

Lower deck: 1inch, 3inch at bow.

Protective bulkheads: 1inch and $1\frac{1}{2}$inch
abreast magazines and shell rooms.

TABLE 3   PARTICULARS OF TIGER AS FINALLY DESIGNED 1912

COMPLEMENT   1110

WEIGHTS:

LEGEND CONDITION:

General equipment	845 tons
Armament	3,660 tons
Machinery	5,630 tons
Engineers stores	125 tons
Coal	450 tons
Oil fuel	450 tons
Armour	7,400 tons
Hull	9,580 tons
Margin	100 tons
Water in anti-rolling tanks	250 tons
Total	**28,490 tons**

ORDINARY DEEP CONDITION

Legend displacement		28,490 tons
General equipment	+	125 tons
Coal	+	2,000 tons
Oil fuel	+	2,000 tons
Reserve feed water	+	620 tons
Water in overflow tank	+	80 tons
Water in anti-rolling tanks	+	145 tons
Total		**33,470 tons**

EXTREME DEEP CONDITION

Ordinary deep displacement		33,470 tons
Coal	+	890 tons
Oil fuel	+	1,350 tons
Total		**35,710 tons**

LIGHT CONDITION

Legend displacement		28,490 tons
General equipment	—	237 tons
Engineers stores	—	63 tons
Oil fuel	—	450 tons
Coal	—	450 tons
Water in anti-rolling tanks	—	250 tons
Total		**27,040 tons**

TABLE 4 STABILITY FIGURES FOR TIGER AS DESIGNED

	LIGHT	LEGEND	ORDINARY DEEP	EXTREME DEEP
GM	5ft	4.9ft	6.2ft	6.3ft
Angle of maximum stability	43°	43°	43°	44°
Range	71°		80°	86°

Note: 0.7 ft was taken off the GM in the deep conditions and 0.4ft in legend condition to allow for free surface water in the anti-rolling tanks. The GM as completed was 5ft 2inches in legend condition and 6ft 7inches in deep condition with ranges of 74°and 86° respectively.

1 The *Tiger* late in 1917, Note the aircraft hanger and platform on 'Q' turret, training scales on 'B' and 'Y' turrets and the dark panel painted on the side amidships.

2 The *Tiger* in 1919. Note flagstaff replaced on stern; Carley rafts on 'Q' turret, abreast searchlight towers and bridge structure.

TABLE 5

SPEED	28.38 knots	29.07 knots
SHP	91,103	104,635
RPM	267	278
DISPLACEMENT	28,990 tons	28,790 tons
NUMBER OF RUNS	6	4

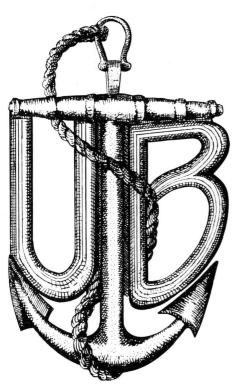

The symbol of the Austro-Hungarian submarine service.
Courtesy of the author

U 4 in Pola harbour, 1917. The operation of the 3.7cm QF gun on the forward edge of the tower was ridiculous: this gun had no recoil but the gunner had to balance on the handrails on the flanks of the tower. The cable clearly visible is a mine deflecting cable, below and less visible is the radio antenna. Note a *Tegetthoff* class battleship in the background.
Dr Aichelburg Collection

AUSTRO-HUNGARIAN SUBMARINES

by Erwin F Sieche

U 1 leaving Pola harbour 1914.
Dr Aichelburg Collection

Although man had tried to invent a submersible ship centuries earlier the accelerating development of technology and the unlimited belief in industrial progress which took place in the second half of the nineteenth century caused a renaissance of the idea. It is interesting that the rich ideas of these inventors were not matched by existing techniques; on the contrary, their inventions caused the development of the technology needed for their realisation.

At the beginning of 1904 the director of Austrian warship construction, Oberingenieur Paul Popper, suggested to the naval-technical committee (MTK = *Marinetechnisches Kommittee,* Pola) the design of a submarine. The development of an Austrian submarine by the MTK turned out to be very complicated due to a great many unsolved technical problems. At the beginning of 1905 the MTK presented a rough design for a single-hull boat with the dimensions 22.1 m x 3.60 m x 4.27 m. The Admiralty doubted the effectiveness of the design and decided to buy three different foreign designs. For every design two boats were to be ordered to be tested against each other, so the A-H navy would evaluate the

specifications for a submarine suitable to their special needs.

THE LAKE BOATS

In 1893 the American Simon Lake lost the competition of the US Navy Ordnance Bureau for a submarine-building contract. His concept of a submarine derived from a boat for peaceful exploring missions. His war-submarine relied on a hand-to-hand fighting system, could roll on wheels on the seabed, and from it divers could exit through a diving chamber to destroy ships and telegraph-cables by explosive charges. Later he incorporated the torpedo in his design, but the basic ideas were still unchanged.

In 1904 Lake's firm was visited by an A-H delegation and in 1906 he came to Pola to finish the contract on the building of *U.1* and *U.2* It was signed on 24 November 1906.

The boats were built to his plans at the naval dockyard, Pola (*Seearsenal* Pola). They had two retractable wheels and a diving chamber under the bow. The diving tanks were located on top of the cylindrical hull. This meant that a heavy ballast keel was necessary to provide vertical stability. As the diving tanks were situated above the waterline, they had to be flooded by pumps. At the first trials this took 14 minutes 37 seconds; later it was speeded up to 8 minutes. When running trials with both boats many technical problems arose. Poisoning

by exhaust fumes and gasoline vapour was a daily problem. As the gasoline engines could not be considered effective under war conditions and did not reach their contract power, the A-H Navy commissioned and paid only for the hulls and the armament. Thereafter new diesel engines were ordered at the Austrian *Maschinenfabrik* Leobersdorf, and until their delivery the original engines were leased for US $4544 per year. The Lake boats had variable-pitch propellers, four pairs of diving rudders which provided a high degree of underwater manoeuvrability. Once a boat was exactly trimmed and balanced it held its depth within a 20 cm oscillation without help from the rudders.

Diving trials showed that the hulls began to crush at 40 m so the trial commission recommended that a diving depth of 40 m should definately not be exceeded. The drop-shaped hull caused a strong bow-wave, and the boats tended to dip their bows under, so the deck and bow casing was rebuilt with a better hydrodynamic shape.

All this leads to the final conclusion that these boats were not sophisticated weapons, but they were exactly what the A-H Navy had ordered: experimental boats to show in extensive trials the reliability of a mass of new technical innovations. Some of these proved to be useless, eg, rolling on wheels on the seabed

Boat No		MTK project	U.1, 2	U. 3,4	5,6,12
TYPE		Austrian design	Lake	Germania	Holland
SYSTEM		single-hull	double-hull,	double-hull internal saddle tanks	single-hull
DSPL. IN METRIC TONS		134.5	229.7	240	240
			248.9 after reconstr. 223.0	300	273
			277.5		
LENGTH	wl	22.6 m	30.48 m	43.2 m	32.1 m (oa.)
HULL	Ø	3.6 m	3.62 m	3.0 m	4.2 m
DRAUGHT		4.37 m	3.85 m	2.75 m	3.9 m
ENGINES			2 gasoline engines tog. 720 HP	2 4-cyl/2-stroke tog. 600 HP	2 6-cyl/gasoline tog. 500 HP
		engines	2 E-engines tog. 200 HP	2 E-engines tog. 200 HP	2 E-engines tog. 230 HP
SPEED		9.5	10.3 kn	12 kn	10.75 kn
		7 kn	6 kn	8.5 kn	8.5 kn
ENDURANCE		950 m/6 kn	950 sm/6 kn	1200 sm/12 kn	800 sm/8.5 kn
			15 sm/5 kn.40 sm/2 kn	40 sm/3 kn	48 sm/6 kn
T-ARMAMENT			2 TT 45 cm/bow 1 TT 45 cm/stern	2 TT 45 cm/bow	2 TT 45 cm/bow
SUPPLY			5 torpedoes	3 torpedoes	4 torpedoes
CREW			18	21	19

18

U 2's conning tower. The tripod on the right of the tower carried the steering wheel during surface manoeuvres, such as when entering harbour. The funnel-like structure on the left is a ventilation mast. Note the primitive type second periscope.
Pawlik Collection

based at Trieste, reconnaissance patrols; 22.12.1917 based at Pola naval base; 11.1.1918 declared obsolete; training boat based at Brioni Island submarine base; ceded as war reparation to Italy 1920; scrapped at Pola.

U.2:
18.7.1907 keel laid; 3.4.1909 launched; 1909-10 trials; 22.6.1911 commissioned; up to 1915 training boat, ie, ten training cruises per month; 24.1.-4.6.1915 refit at Pola, new conning tower; 7.8.1915 based at Trieste, reconnaissance patrols; 11.1.1918 declared obsolete; training boat based at Brioni Island submarine base; ceded as war reparation to Italy 1920; scrapped at Pola.

turned out to be nearly impossible, and today every modern snorkel diver knows more about underwater visibility than the inventor of 1890 who planned underwater-observation bull's eyes.

Operational History of the Lake Boats
U.1:
2.7.1907 keel laid; 10.2.1909

launched; 1910 trials; 5.4.1910 both electric motors damaged through flooding; 15.4.1911 commissioned; 1911-1914 training boat, ie, ten training cruises per month; 13.1.1914 rammed in Fasana Channel by A-H cruiser *St. Georg*, periscope destroyed; end of 1914-early 1915 installation of diesel-engines and new batteries; up to 4.10.1915 training boat; 2.11.1915

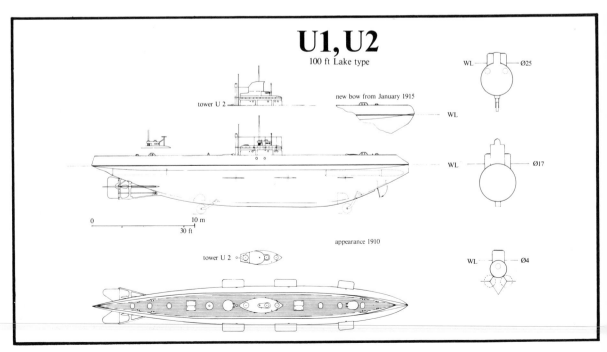

U1, U2

100 ft Lake type

tower U 2

new bow from January 1915

appearance 1910

tower U 2

WL Ø25

WL

WL Ø17

WL Ø4

0   10 m
30 ft

U 4 undated picture, probably taken in Pola Harbour.
Imperial War Museum

THE GERMANIA BOATS

In the growing Imperial German high seas fleet created by Tirpitz there was no place for the concept of submarine warfare. Not until the 1905 official *Torpedoinspektion,* under the direction of Dipl Ing Gustav Berling, did the German Navy begin to develop operational submarines. As other navies already had submarines in service, the *Germaniawerft* at Kiel tried to avoid falling behind by designing submarines for foreign navies.

In March 1904 two A-H naval officers watched the trials of the submarine *Forelle* at Kiel/Eckernförde. At a second contract meeting at the *Germaniawerft* the A-H delegation received the impression that everything was being done to get a building contract but technical questions were deliberately obscured.

The A-H Admiralty therefore refused to purchase Germania-built submarines. So shocked was the *Germaniawerft* that it offered some designs without cost in June 1906. A short time later positive reports on the Germania-built boats for

Czarist Russia reached Austria, and it was decided to buy two boats. Both boats were built at Kiel and towed to Pola via Gibraltar. They were of double-hull type with internal saddle-tanks.

Although the German designers had evaluated the best hull-shape in extensive model trials, these boats had constant trouble with their diving rudders. The rudder fins were changed in size and shape, and finally the bow rudders were removed and a fixed stern flap was installed, but the outbreak of war stopped further experiments. Because of their greater displacement these boats had better seagoing qualities and living conditions than their competitors. Considering that this was one of the first designs of *Germaniawerft* without extensive practical experience, these boats showed a high degree of effectiveness, and *U.4* had the longest operational history of all A-H submarines. This leads to the conclusion that the Germania type was a very modern and well-balanced design.

Operational History of the Germania Boats
U.3:
12.3.1907 keel laid; 20.8.1908 launched; 24.1.1909 arrived at Pola in tow, trials; 12.9.1909 commissioned; 1910-14 training boat, ie ten training cruises per month; 22.8.1914 based at Brioni Island submarine base; 27.9.1914 based at Cattaro naval base, reconnaissance cruises; April 1915 3.7 cm QF gun installed; 10.8.1915 left Cattaro for action north of Brindisi; 12.8.1915 rammed during unsuccessful torpedo attack on Italian armed merchant cruiser *Città di Catania* (3500 BRT; 2 x 12 cm; 6 x 7.5 cm), periscope destroyed, when surfacing shelled by escorting French destroyer *Bisson* and depth-charged, damaged on seabed; 13.8.1915 when surfacing hit by French destroyer, *Bisson* (765 t; 4 x 6.5 cm, 4 TT) and sunk: 7 killed, 14 survivors captured.
U.4:
12.3.1907 keel laid; 20.11.1908 launched; 19.4.1909 arrived at Pola in tow, trials; 29.8.1908

commissioned; 1910-14 training boat, ie ten training cruises per month; 27.9.1914 based at Cattaro naval base, reconnaissance cruises; December 1914 radio equipment installed; 19.2.1915 three Montenegrin captured; April 1915 3.7 cm QF gun installed; 24.5.1915 unsuccessful torpedo attack on Italian *Puglia* type cruiser in the Gulf of Drin; 9.6.1915 British cruiser *Dublin* (5400 t; 8 x 15.2 cm, 4 x 4.7 cm, 2 TT) damaged by torpedo; 18.7.1915 Italian armoured cruiser *Giuseppe Garibaldi* (7350 t; 1 x 25 cm, 2 x 20 cm, 14 x 15 cm, 4 TT) torpedoed off Ragusavecchia (now Cavtat): 53 killed, 525 survivors; 14.5.1915 searched for lost sister *U.3;* 8.11.1915 unsuccessful attack on British *Diamond* type cruiser; 9.12.1915 one Albanian schooner captured in the Gulf of Drin; December 1915 new periscopes and gyro compass installed; 3.1.1916 one Albanian schooner captured; 2.2.1916 French steamer *Jean Bart* (475 BRT) torpedoed and sunk off Cape Laghi; 7.2.1916 unsuccessful attack on British cruiser of *Birmingham* type; 26-27.3.1916 searched for lost A-H submarine *U.24;* 30.3.1916

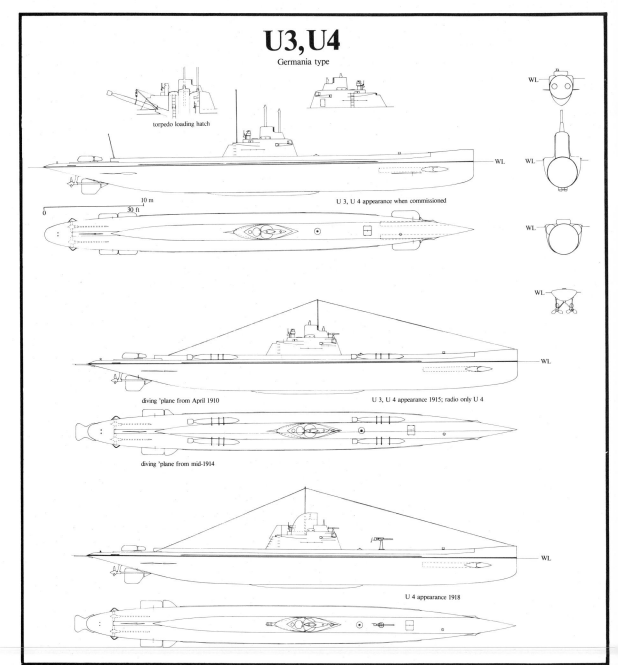

U3, U4

Germania type

torpedo loading hatch

U 3, U 4 appearance when commissioned

10 m
0   30 ft

diving 'plane from April 1910

U 3, U 4 appearance 1915; radio only U 4

diving 'plane from mid-1914

U 4 appearance 1918

British schooner *John Pritchard of Carnar* (271 BRT) sunk with explosive charges off Antipaxos Island; July 1916 7 cm cal/26 gun installed; 2.8.1916 unsuccessful attack on Italian cruiser of *Nino Brixio* type; 5.8.1916 unsuccessfully attacked by enemy submarine with two torpedoes; 12.8.1916 Italian schooner *Ponte Maria* (188 BRT) torpedoed and sunk off Brindisi; 12.8.1916 unsuccessful attack on enemy submarine west of Cape Laghi; 14.8.1916 British steamer *Inverberbie* (4390 BRT) torpedoed and sunk off Cape Nau; 30.5.1917 Italian steamer *Italia* (1305 BRT) torpedoed and sunk off Corfu Island; 19.6.1917 French steamer *Edouarde Corbière* (475 BRT) and Greek steamer *Cefira* (411 BRT) torpedoed and sunk off Taranto; 12.7.1917 French salvage tug *Berthilde* (1500 BRT) torpedoed and sunk off Cape Stilo; September 1917 new bulwark on conning tower fitted; 1.11.1918 final return to Pola; ceded as war reparation to France, scrapped 1920.

THE HOLLAND BOATS
The Irish-American John Paul Holland had designed submarines from the 1890s and earlier. After he won a contract for building submarines for the US Navy in 1893 his company, the Holland Boat Company at Newport, Connecticut, became one of the leading builders of submarines and stayed in the business for decades.

The Fiume-based firm of Whitehead, which had become the developer of the Luppis torpedo, decided to enter the submarine business and bought a licence from Holland to build his submarines. The first two boats were partially assembled in the United States and riveted together at Whitehead's in Fiume which caused a lot of trouble. The third boat was built on speculation and comprised a better development of all mechanical and electrical systems. This unit was named *SS.3* and was offered to the A-H Navy too, but she was refused because of the trials programme. Whitehead offered *SS.3* to the navies of Peru, Portugal, Netherlands, Brazil, Bulgaria and to the A-H Navy a second time. When war broke out Austria bought the unsold boat and provisionally commissioned it as *U.7*. After the end of August 1914 it was definitely commissioned as *U.12*. The Holland type featured a distinctive tear-drop hull bearing a strong resemblance to modern nuclear subs. It had an interesing construction of the torpedo-tube hatches: these were clover-leaf shaped and rotated on a central axis.

Operational History of the Holland boats
U.5:
9.4.1908 keel laid; 10.2.1909 launched; 17.8.1909 towed to Pola for final outfit; 1.4.1910 commissioned, training boat, ie, ten training cruises per month; 1.5.1911 shown to a delegation of Peruvian naval officers; 10.6.1912 trials with a kite balloon to evaluate underwater sighting of hull painting; 22.8.1914 based at Brioni

U 6 in Cattaro Bay, 1915. Note the massive towing hook at the bow.
Dr Aichelburg Collection

Island submarine base; 22.1.1914 based at Cattaro naval base; 3.11.1914 unsuccessful attack on French battleship squadron off Punta Stilo; 6.12.1914 radio receiver and 3.7 cm cal/23 QF gun installed; 27.5.1915 French armoured cruiser *Leon Gambetta* (12 250 t; 4 x 19 cm, 16 x 16 cm, 24 x 4.7 cm; 2 TT) torpedoed and sunk off Santa Maria di Leuca: 648 killed, 173 survivors; 1.6.1915 searched for lost A-H seaplane L 41; 2.7.1915 new 4.7 cm QF gun installed instead of 3.7 cm, complete radio station installed; 5.8.1915 Italian submarine *Nereide* (225/303 t; 3 TT) torpedoed and sunk off Pelagosa Island: 17 killed, no survivors; 29.8.1915 Greek steamer *Cefalonia* (1034 BRT) captured off Durazzo; 26.4.1916 unsuccessful gun attack on merchant convoy in the Otranto Strait; 7.6.1916 unsuccessful attack on Italian *Indomito* type destroyer; 8.6.1916 Italian armed merchant cruiser *Principe Umberto* (7919

BRT) torpedoed and sunk off Linguetta: about 1750 killed, ? survivors; September-November 1917 refit: new conning tower, new gun 7.5 cm cal/30; 16.5.1917 during training cruise in the Fasana Channel struck mine with the stern, sunk: 6 killed, 13 survivors; 20-24.6.1916 raised from 36 m; 22.8.1918 recommissioned after refit; 25.3.1919 transferred to Venice, inspected by British military commissions; ceded as war reparation to Italy 1920; scrapped.

U.6:
21.2.1908 keel laid; 12.6.1909 launched; 1.7.1909 commissioned, training boat, ie ten training cruises per month; 7.11.1910 demonstrated to a Norwegian naval delegation; 26.6.1912 when surfacing after deep diving trial rammed by submarine tender *Pelikan;* 29.12.1914 based at Cattaro naval base; December 1915 installation of 3.7 cm cal/23 QF gun; 23.2.1916 unsuccessful attack on Italian type *Indomito* destroyer;

18.3.1916 French destroyer *Renaudin* (720 t; 2 x 10 cm, 4 x 6.5 cm; 2 TT) torpedoed and sunk off Cape Laghi: ? killed, ? survivors; soon after, unsuccessful attack on French *Bisson* type destroyer; 13.5.1916 trapped in submarine net during break through the Otranto barrage and scuttled by crew: entire crew taken prisoner.

U.12:
1909 keel laid; 14.3.1911 launched; bought by the A-H Navy after war began; 21.8.1914 commissioned; 14.11.1914 3.7 cm cal/23 QF gun installed; 7.12.1914 based at Cattaro naval base; 21.12.1914 French battleship *Jean Bart* (23 470 t; 2 x 30.5 cm, 22 x 13.8 cm, 4 x 4.7 cm, 4 TT) damaged by two torpedoes in the Otranto Strait; 22.3.1915 two Montenegrin schooners captured; 31.3.1916 one Montenegrin schooner captured; 28.6.1916 during refit two additional torpedo tubes installed outboard on the forward casing; about 12.8.1916 sunk by

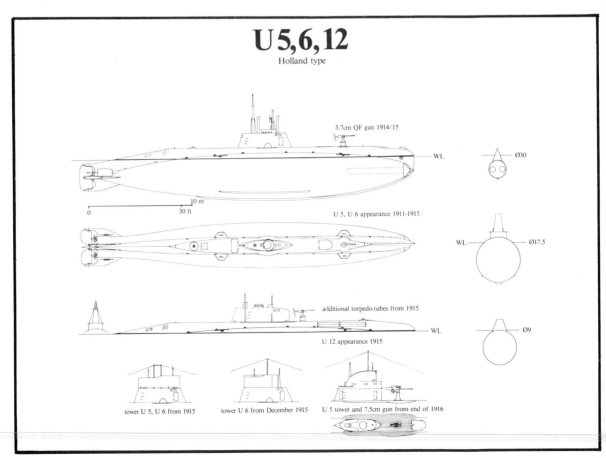

U 5, 6, 12
Holland type

3.7cm QF gun 1914/15

WL

Ø30

U 5, U 6 appearance 1911-1915

0   30 ft |0 m

WL

Ø17.5

additional torpedo-tubes from 1915

U 12 appearance 1915

WL

Ø9

tower U 5, U 6 from 1915   tower U 6 from December 1915   U 5 tower and 7.5cm gun from end of 1916

23

mine when trying to break into the harbour of Venice: entire crew (17) lost; raised by Italy at the end of 1916 and scrapped in the Venice naval arsenal; victims buried at the cemetery of San Michele in Venice.

1 *U 1:* conning tower with embossed pennant number. Note that the towers of the first boats were extremely low.
Dr Aichelburg Collection

2 *U 12* entering Pola harbour, 1914. Note the shape of the tower of this boat which was developed by Whitehead as a private venture and differs slightly from her sister-boats. The base ring for a 3.7cm QF pivot is fixed on deck.
Dr Aichelburg Collection

3 *U 5* in Cattaro Bay, 1915. The bridge is sheltered by a canvas bulwark. The conventional air intakes were later removed.
Dr Aichelburg Collection

1

2

3

SMS U-14 ex Curie

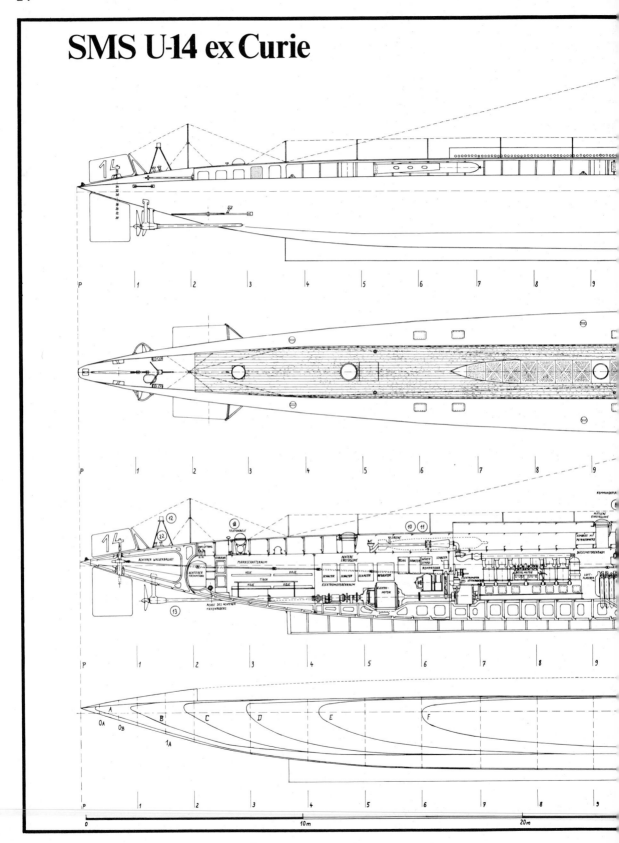

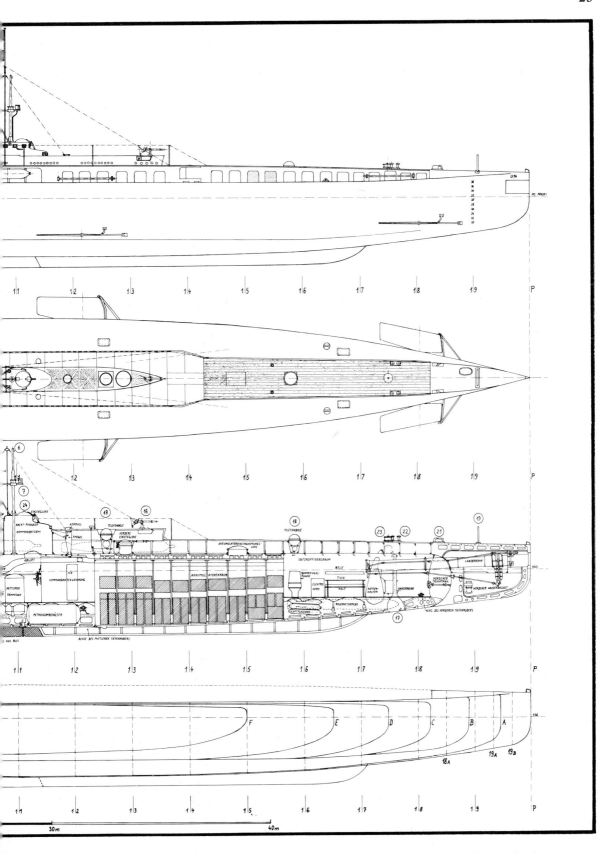

30m

40m

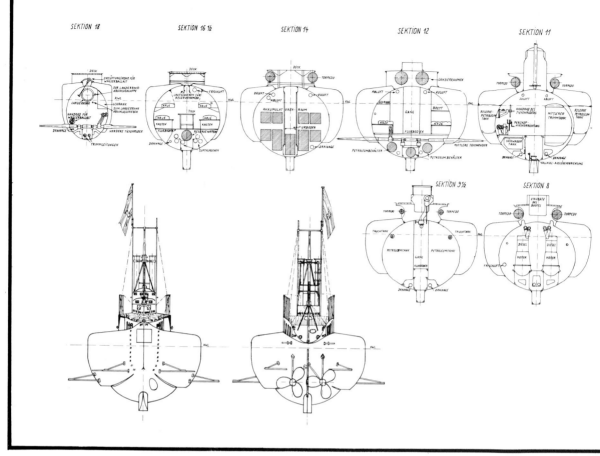

GUN ARMAMENT

As attacks on merchant ships increased, quick-firing guns were installed. From the beginning these were 3.7 cm, later 4.7 cm. *U.5* was upgunned with a German 7 cm/30 cal submarine gun during a major refit.

VARIATIONS IN CONNING TOWERS

For all three types the first intention of the constructors was a real submarine, so they built small, low observation platforms. Later the range of vision turned out to be too short and in addition these towers were very uncomfortable, wet and dangerous for the bridge watches, so all A-H submarines were fitted with bulwarks of different shapes. During major refits some boats received new, higher towers with an enlarged space and protecting bulwarks.

RADIO EQUIPMENT

When the first boats were built radio telegraphy was in its first stage of development too. As the sets became more compact the boats were subsequently equipped with radios.

Note: the antenna-like wires that can be seen on the drawings are 'jumping wires' or mine-deflecting cables; the real antennae were on retractable masts and so thin that one can hardly see them in pictures.

CONCLUSION

Looking at the technology of the first submarines of the A-H Navy, we find trend-setting innovations like variable-pitch propellers, tear-drop hull, diver-locks and retractable ventilation masts (which would have become a real snorkel if it had been developed further). But the difficulties of perfecting these items were not

solved. Also the machinery and the periscopes needed further development, but one must keep in mind that these units were only prototypes. German submarine ratings who visited and examined the early Austrian boats were surprised by their primitive nature and said that they would refuse to make a sortie in such a vessel.

Despite these deficiencies these subs performed admirably and achieved much in the Adriatic war: enemy battleships were forced to leave the Adriatic Sea, and no major action was ever carried against the Yugoslavian coast. The Italian battlefleet left the Adriatic as well and for the whole war remained useless, in safe but remote bases.

Because of the war situation and the alliance, Austria was forced to use German subs and submarine designs with two exceptions: the raised French

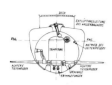
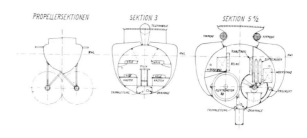
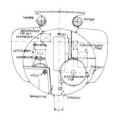

SEKTION 2½   PROPELLERSEKTIONEN   SEKTION 3   SEKTION 5½

SEKTION 6

LANZIERAPPARAT SYSTEM DRCEWIECKI
DROP-COLLAR SYSTEM DRCEWIECKI

ABOVE AND PREVIOUS PAGES:
Details from Friedrich Prasky's superbly
detailed modelmakers' plans of the Austrian
U 14 ex-French *Curie*. Copies of the plan can
be obtained from Mr Prasky at
Feuchterslebengasse 69-71/5, A-1100 Wien,
Austria.

Curie (later the Austrian *U.14*),
and the Whitehead built
Havmanden type.

COLOUR SCHEME
Up to spring 1914 all Austrian
subs were painted light blue-grey,
but submarines could easily be
detected by aeroplanes. On 29
April 1914 trials were carried out
with *U.4* and the seaplane *E.17*.
Dark blue turned out to be the
best underwater colour, but on the
other hand the silhouette above
water was too dark. Because of a
British fleet visit to Pola harbour
(from this occasion dates a
frequently published picture with
the A-H battleship *Erzherzog
Franz Ferdinand* and a 32 ft cutter
with the British White Ensign in
the foreground) the original
painting was restored. After war
broke out all boats were painted
dark blue with a large white
pennant number on the tower.

In spring 1915 the sides of the
towers were painted light grey to
make the boats less visible above
water. Pictures taken in 1915 show
some boats with a multicolour
dazzle painting, but the colour
composition is unknown. From
1916 the boats had no number
painted on their tower. In August
1918 *U.4* and *U.5* had a light grey
hull and tower.

SOURCES AND
ACKNOWLEDGEMENTS
I would like to thank specifically
Dr. Wladimir Aichelburg for
allowing me to use material from
his unpublished manuscript *Die
KuK Unterseebootwaffe 1904-
1918*; without his assistance and
permission this article would not
be so complete. When he
researched the technical and
operational history of the first A-
H subs, it turned out that the few
earlier publications on this subject

were often erroneous because they
did not rely on the official sources
of the Austrian Kriegsarchiv in
Vienna.

A brief article on *U.1* and *U.2*
with my drawing was published in
the Austrian naval magazine
Marine — Gestern, heute (June
1976).

Champions of the

No single class of warship has had more influence on American policies and naval tactics than the 24 *Essex* class fleet carriers. They possessed those factors necessary to insure American dominance of all of the world's oceans: overwhelming numbers, durability, adaptability and good aircraft complement.

Thirty-five years after the commissioning of the first ship, *Essex,* the magnificent *Lexington (CV16)* still sails the oceans. While the majority of the class have been scrapped, a handful are still in reserve and one ship, *Yorktown,* has been made part of a naval and maritime museum in South Carolina. Fortunately, there are a number of groups actively negotiating for the preservation of additional *Essexes.* The most prominent of these groups is Odysseys In Flight Inc., a non-profit organization preparing an aerospace and naval museum complex in the North Eastern United States.

It would take volumes to document adequately the *Essexes'* technical and operational careers. It is the primary purpose of this article to identify the wartime appearances of the *Essex* sisterships which took an active part in the Pacific War. It will also briefly cover all of the units which were completed too late to see any action and a few of the many postwar modifications. For a better understanding of the WW2 *Essexes,* it is necessary to cover the entire class.

This will include prominent gun positions, radars, other visible structural variations and camouflage paint schemes. Practically each *Essex* can be identified by some dominant feature, or arrangement which was unique to that specific ship, at a specific time.

IDENTIFIABLE CHARACTERISTICS

To eliminate repetition, the following list is intended to explain those characteristics which will constantly be referred to:

1 **Short Bow** Ten ships were completed with a near vertical stem. These units carried only a single quadruple 40mm AA mount directly over the stem. The flight deck actually overhung the mount, restricting its field of fire.

2 **The Early Bridge** The first eight units were completed with four quad 40mm mounts on the island, two forward and two aft of the funnel. The foremost mount was sited immediately forward of a rather small and cramped flag bridge.

3 **Off-Centerline Single Quad 40mm On The Fantail** Also carried by the first eight units, this feature was common only to those ships which carried the early bridge.

4 **Hangar Deck Catapult** Never installed on the first two units, it was carried by the third to the eighth completed units, in conjunction with the above three features. The catapult was fixed awthartships on the forward hangar deck, just aft of the fo'csle deck break. The catapult's most noticeable features were the hinged extension arms, on both the port and starboard sides. The port side extension was hinged on an extended outboard platform. The starboard extension arm was flush to the ship's side. Both extension arms were hinged in the 'up' position when not in use. Units carrying a hangar catapult were completed with only one flight deck catapult. When it was removed (from all six units), a

Hornet (CV-12) in dazzle camouflage design 3A, at Pearl Harbor.

Pacific The Essex class carriers

by Lawrence Sowinski

second flight deck catapult was added. Catapults were also known as 'cats'.

5 Starboard Quarter, Hangar Deck Level, Quad 40mm AA Mounts These two mounts were added to the same six ships which carried the hangar deck catapult. Since all the *Essexes* were built on the East Coast of the United States, no unmoveable outboard extensions could be fitted which would not allow passage through the Panama Canal locks. For this purpose the port side (flight deck-edge) elevator was designed to hinge upright.

6 SK Radar Antenna This was the largest antenna carried on the wartime *Essexes*. It was fitted on the first ten units to be completed. Often referred to as a big 'bedspring', it was rectangular in shape. It was sited in three different positions and these tended to depend on the building yard. The first three ships completed at Newport News, Virginia *(CV9, 10 & 11)* carried the SK on top of the tripod mast, in front of the topmast, on the radar platform. The first three units completed at Quincy, Massachussetts *(CV16, 17 & 18)* fitted the SK outboard on the funnel's starboard side, on an extended platform. The last four SK-equipped ships all carried the 'bedspring' on top of the radar platform, but abaft the topmast. The smaller SM dish antenna generally dominated the forward position on the radar platform.

7 SC and SC-2 Radar Antenna This was a comparatively small 'bedspring' antenna. While the SK was higher than it was wider, the SC was wider than higher. Initially, it was close to its base, but was later raised skyward, often on a lattice mast. The majority of the other antennae were too small to deal with individually.

8 Starboard Radio Lattice Masts The first four units *(CV9, 16, 10 & 17)* were completed with five radio masts along the flight deck's starboard side. Three were forward of the island, two aft. All the remaining wartime units carried four (only two forward). Refitted units often had the two after masts removed. All the masts hinged down during flight operations.

9 Outboard Quad 40mm Mounts With the need for increased anti-aircraft fire power, a number of additional medium range AA mounts were installed. Seven mounts were added on outboard extensions; three below the island structure on the starboard side and two on the starboard stern quarter, on the hangar deck, in the same position as the inboard mounts discussed in **5**. The difference was that the outboard mounts were on extended sponsons, with clear fields of fire. The six units with the inboard mounts eventually had them moved outboard. Two outboard quads were added to the flight deck's port quarter. Prior to passage through the Panama Canal, all

seven outboard quad mounts had to be removed.

10 Long Bow Units The remaining 14 sisterships were all long bow units. While the waterline length remained the same, the stem was raked forward in a clipper fashion. As the flare was greatly increased the bow platform could be widened; this improved seakeeping and allowed room for two quad 40mm to be fitted. The flight deck was not lengthened and so both mounts enjoyed a considerably improved field of fire.

11 Later Units The last 15 ships were commissioned with two flight deck catapults and no hangar cat. The port side hangar deck platform remained, but it was used to carry two quad 40mm instead.

These units also carried a number of other modifications: two quad 40mm on an extended fantail platform; an extended flag bridge (the foremost quad 40mm was dropped to make room) and, except for *CV14 and 19,* a large SK-2 dish antenna was fitted in place of the SK. All eight of the early units eventually received most of these modifications.

12 Paint Schemes Three major types of camouflage paint schemes were applied to the wartime ships. The US Navy referred to camouflage schemes as 'measures', and specific types were identified by a code number (12, 21, 32, 33, etc).

Carrier decks and horizontal surfaces were not repainted

Close up of *Lexington*'s (CV-16) radar after her first Puget Sound refit. The SK is the large bedspring between the tripod foremast and the new mainmast. The SC-2 is the smaller bedspring (directly behind the SK) on the raised lattice mast. The SM is on the front of the radar platform, on top of the tripod.

Yorktown (CV-10) was the first unit to carry a hangar catapult. In this view, the catapult extension arm is in the 'down' position. The tubs for the two starboard quarter 40mm quads are just visible under the flight deck.

1
2

32

1 *Ticonderoga* (CV-14) burns and lists after two kamikaze hits on 21 January 1945. Compare her starboard pattern to that carried by *Yorktown*.

2 *Yorktown* (CV-10) after her refit at Puget Sound. All five starboard outboard quad 40s are clearly visible, as is the enlarged fantail sponson. CV-10 remained in dazzle Design 10A till the late spring of '45 at which time she was painted into Ms21.

3 *Intrepid* (CV-11) after her February '45 refit. She was the first *Essex* in Ms12. Unfortunately, the negative is in very poor condition.

1

2

3

when the measures were changed. Flight decks were stained, not painted.

Measure 21 was the only single-color camouflage used by the *Essexes* during WW2. It was an overall solid medium-to-dark blue/gray (known as navy blue). In photographs, it appears as a medium gray (in bright sun) or a dark gray (in overcast skies). The first six *Essexes* were completed in measure 21.

Dazzle Pattern Measures The *Essexes* carried two dazzle measures, but it is difficult for a casual observer to identify one from the other. It was the range of colors which determined which measure was actually carried. The same pattern design could appear on several different ships, with the same color range (measure) or a different color range.

Dazzle measure 33 was carried by five *Essexes* (CV10, 12, 14, 18 and 38). *Hornet* (CV12) carried Design 3A (A for aircraft carrier). The other four ships all were painted in Design 10A. The darkest color

was never darker than navy blue, the lightest was either pale or light gray.

Dazzle measure 32 colors were painted on nine *Essexes* (CV9, 11, 13, 15, 17, 19, 20, 31 and 36). Five separate designs were carried by these nine ships. The lightest color was either light or haze gray. The darkest color was usually dull black, although *CV31* and *36* carried only navy blue).

The dazzle measures were designed to confuse enemy submarines and low-flying torpedo bombers. However, the sudden introduction of *kamikaze* warfare left the carriers somewhat conspicuous to suiciders diving from high angles, and so measure 21 quickly came back into use for want of a better camouflage. Measure 12 was a two-color scheme intended to be more effective than either measure 21 or the dazzle measures. It used a two-tone system of ocean gray (medium) over navy blue (dark).

Instead of discussing each individual ship from start to finish, I have categorized their appearance

changes in chronological order. For those readers unfamiliar with the US Navy practice of hull numbers, keep in mind that these numbers remained the same and did not fluctuate the way most other navies changed pendant numbers.

THE EARLY UNITS
The first two *Essexes* were nearly identical. *Essex (CV9)* completed at Newport News Shipbuilding and Drydock Co, Virginia on 31 December 1942. *Lexington (CV16)* came out of Bethlehem Steel at Quincy, Massachussetts, on 17 March 1943. Both short bow units had early bridges, single fantail quad and five radio masts. The respective position of their large SK antennae enables identification of one from the other. *Essex* carried the bedspring forward on the radar platform, while 'Lex's' was fitted outboard on the funnel. *Essex* also carried a stump mainmast, whereas 'Lex' did not.

Both ships were easily identifiable from the next six units since neither carried hangar catapults or starboard quarter quads.

The next two units were identical to each other, except for the position of the SK antennas.

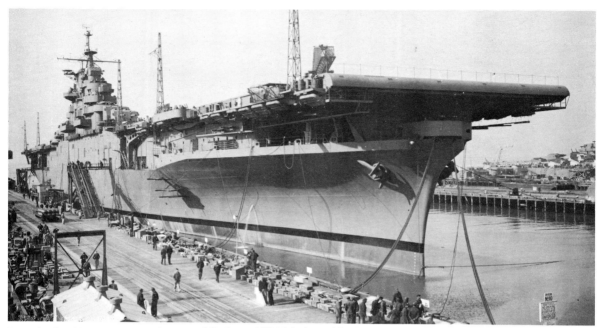

1 *Essex* (CV-9) at Newport News on 19 December 1942. The SK bedspring antenna has yet to be added to the platform on top of the tripod.

2 *Wasp* (CV-18) after her Puget Sound refit. The two port quarter outboard mounts are visible just below the flight deck level.

3 *Lexington* (CV-16) in the Pacific after her January 1944 refit. She was the first of her class to carry the seven outboard quad 40s.

4 *Intrepid* (CV-11) off Norfolk during November '43. Note the single, off centreline quad 40 on the fantail and the two quads along the hangar deck's starboard stern quarter.

36

1 *Hornet* (CV-12) at Ulithi in heavily weathered camouflage. This same starboard pattern (Design 3A) was also worn by *Intrepid* and *Hancock*. The hangar catapult extension arm is in the 'down' position.

2 *Franklin* (CV-13) leaves Norfolk on 4 May 1944 with her port side freshly repainted into Design 3A. Note the new extended flag bridge. The hangar catapult extension arm has been removed.

All photos US official, courtesy of the author

Yorktown (CV10) came out of Newport News (15 April 1943) with her SK in the same position as *Essex*. Out of Quincy came *Bunker Hill (CV17),* matching 'Lex's' SK position 24 May 1943). Both *CV10 & 17* were short bow units with early bridges, stump mainmasts, single fantail quad, five radio masts and measure 21. However, these two carriers introduced the hangar catapult and two quads on the starboard stern quarter.

The fifth unit, *Intrepid (CV11)* was commissioned on 16 August 1943 out of Newport News. She was identical to *Yorktown* except that she initiated the practice of carrying four radio masts; only two were installed forward of the island. When *Intrepid* departed for the Pacific in late November 1943 her SK had been moved from atop the radar platform, down to outboard of the funnel. It will be noted later that her SK would be moved a third and final time, during a 1944 repair and refit.

Quincy completed the sixth *Essex* on 24 November 1943. *Wasp (CV18)* was an exact match for *Intrepid* (with the refitted SK) except for the absence of a stump mainmast; however, she retained this appearance for only a short time.

Hornet (CV12) was commissioned

five days after *Wasp*. Newport News built this, the seventh short-bow *Essex*. While she carried the standard features: early bridge, single fantail quad 40mm, hangar catapult, starboard quarter quad 40mm and only four radio masts, *Hornet* also introduced two new modifications. First, her SK was positioned behind the topmast, on the rear side of the radar platform. This was to become the standard SK position for the next three units, the last units to fit the 'bedspring'. Second, and most important, was the introduction of dazzle camouflage patterns in the *Essex* class, replacing measure 21. *Hornet* painted up into dazzle Design 3A, with measure 33 colors of pale gray, haze gray and navy blue, making CV12 unique. While two and a half more *Essexes* were painted in this same design, only *Hornet* wore the lighter measure 33 colors. Also, only *Hornet* wore this design with all the standard early features, early bridge, hangar cat, etc.

In the Pacific, *Lexington* was damaged by a Japanese aerial torpedo during December 1943. Permanent repairs were made at Puget Sound (Bremerton, Wash) and while there she was fitted with additional AAs. This was to become standard for practically

every *Essex* unit undergoing a refit in Pearl Harbor or on the West Coast. Lex's medium range AA was more than doubled, the number of quad 40mm rising from 8 to 17 mounts. This was a tremendous increase in topside weight, but was considered essential. Seven of these were outboard quad 40mm, two on the port stern quarter and five along the starboard side. She was the only early bridge *Essex* to carry these seven outboard mounts.

Additionally, a platform with two quad 40mm was added in the same position as the port side catapult extension (on the third to eighth units). More radars were added to the island, along with a mainmast.

While units in the Atlantic and Pacific were beginning to paint up in dazzle camouflage, 'Lex' remained in measure 21, and was to become unique because of this; eventually, she would be the only large fleet carrier not in dazzle.

Back in the Atlantic, *Franklin (CV13)* was the eighth unit of the class to be completed, at Newport News on 31 January 1944. Structurally, she was an exact match for *Hornet* except that she carried a noticeably different camouflage, Design 6A. Measure 32 colors were used: light gray, ocean

gray and dull black. This was one of the earliest pattern designs prepared by the Navy's camouflage department, and its port side was very elaborate.

Meanwhile, the *Essex* class in the Pacific began to replace their measure 21 schemes with dazzle patterns. Some time between February and April, *Bunker Hill* painted up Design 6A, probably at Pearl Harbor. She and *Franklin* were the only two *Essexes* to carry this design. Even though both ships were oceans apart, they were now very similar. These dazzle-painted ships could be identified from one another by:
1 *Bunker Hill* carried a stump mainmast, *Franklin* did not
2 *Bunker Hill's* SK was fitted off the funnel, *Franklin's* was abaft the topmast, on the radar platform
3 *Bunker Hill* carried five radio masts, *Franklin* only four.

During March 1944 *Wasp (CV18)* was painted in dazzle Design 10A while still at Boston. *Yorktown* received the same design at about the same time while at Pearl Harbor, and eventually, four *Essexes* would wear this design. *Wasp* was soon in the Pacific alongside *Yorktown*, both could be identified individually as *Wasp* had only four radio masts, no mainmast and the SK outboard, off the funnel.

Another *Essex* carrier fell victim to a Japanese aerial torpedo, during March 1944 after an attack on Truk; *Intrepid* limped back to Pearl Harbor, and then headed for permanent repairs on the West Coast.

In April 1944, *Essex* completed a refit at San Francisco. Of her entire class, she was the only unit to carry dazzle Design 6/10D, the only two-color (light gray and dull black) design carried by any US carrier. Structurally, the flat bridge was extended forward (the island's foremost quad and its director were removed). The stump mainmast was also removed. The radar platform was enlarged and the SC-2 was fitted abaft the topmast. The SK was moved to the funnel. A port side platform was built in the position occupied by the catapult extension (on the six later units). Two quads were added to this platform. At the same time that 'Lex' was having all seven outboard quads added, *Essex* had only two mounts added on the starboard quarter. Incredible as it may sound, both mounts were installed in the obsolete inboard positions, with restricted fields of fire. Even more incredible, *Essex* remained this way for the remainder of the war. She was the only unit of the original eight early *Essex* class never to carry any outboard quads.

The battle of Tsu-Shima

БУЙНЫЙ
Bujnij

by
N J M Campbell

The Russian destroyer *Bujnij* at speed.
CPL W/5/001

Few naval battles, apart from Jutland, have been more often described than the battle of Tsushima, the culminating action of the Russo-Japanese war at sea. Yet no account appreciates the real puzzle of the battle: how the Japanese managed to annihilate the Russian fleet with only 446 12inch shells from their most powerful guns.

THE RUSSO-JAPANESE WAR

The war began on the night of 8/9 February 1904 with a surprise destroyer attack on the Russian ships anchored in the Port Arthur roads. This was a partial success only, but the two best Russian battleships the *Retvisan* and *Tsessarevitch* were put out of action until late May/early June, having to be repaired with the use of cofferdams as there was no dock at Port Arthur that would take them. The night attack was followed up by a rather desultory daylight gunnery action which achieved little. At the outset the main Russian fleet (Vice-Admiral Stark) based on Port Arthur comprised 7 battleships, 1 armoured and 6 light cruisers, of which 4 were large, and 25 destroyers, while 3 armoured and 1 large light cruiser with 10 sea-going and 7 other torpedo boats were at Vladivostock. Including ships that would shortly be available, the Japanese under Vice-Admiral Togo had 6 battleships, 8 armoured and 13 light cruisers, several old ships of which 4 could form part of the main fleet, 19 destroyers and 62 sea-going torpedo boats.

Up to 15 May the Japanese were successful in all the operations off Port Arthur, the most effective being mine-laying. The battleship *Petropavlovsk* blew up on a mine and Makarov, the one notable Russian Admiral who had arrived at Port Arthur on 8 March, was lost with her. The battleship *Pobieda* was damaged by a mine, and other Russian losses from various causes were two light cruisers and three destroyers. But on 15 May two Japanese battleships, the *Hatsuse* and *Yashima,* were lost on Russian mines laid the previous afternoon in a dense fog, and the fast light

cruiser *Yoshino* was sunk in collision. From now on the Japanese heavy ships were used as little as possible near Port Arthur, which had been cut off by the Japanese army on land.

On 23 June, when all the damaged battleships had been repaired, the Russian fleet under Rear Admiral Vitgeft left Port Arthur. But on sighting the Japanese that evening, turned back and with torpedo attacks that night achieved nothing. The battleship *Sevastopol* struck a mine and was out of action for six weeks. On 7 August Japanese 4.7inch guns which had been landed began to shell Port Arthur and three days later Vitgeft took his 6 battleships to sea with 4 light cruisers and 8 destroyers under orders from the Tsar to break through to Vladivostock. The battle that ensued is generally known as 'The Yellow Sea'. Altogether 4 battleships, 4 armoured cruisers, 7 light cruisers, 3 old ships, 1 torpedo-gunboat, 17 destroyers and 30 torpedo boats took part on the Japanese side. For a time the Russians fully held their own, but after more than 5 hours a 12inch shell burst on the *Tsessarevitch's* foremast, killing Vitgeft, and a few minutes later another hit the sighting slit on her CT and jammed the helm hard over, so that the Russian line was thrown into confusion. In the next hour and a half the Japanese inflicted much non-fatal damage, but once again the night torpedo attacks failed, though the battleship *Poltava* was hit by a torpedo that did not explode. This ship, with the battleships *Retvisan, Pobieda, Peresviet, Sevastopol,* the cruiser *Pallada* and three destroyers returned to Port Arthur, while the *Tsessarevitch* and the rest made for various neutral ports where they were interned, except for one destroyer that was driven ashore, and the fast light cruiser *Novik* that made for Vladivostok but was disposed of by two Japanese cruisers in the Soya Straits.

Meanwhile, the three Vladivostok armoured cruisers had come south to meet Vitgeft if he succeeded in breaking out and on 14 August they

1

were engaged off Ulsan by four armoured and two light cruisers under Vice-Admiral Kamimura. The oldest of the Russians the *Rurik,* was sunk and the other two got away, though they took no more part in the war.

The Port Arthur fleet did not sortie again, though the *Sevastopol* came out on 23 August and was damaged by a mine. By 1 October the Japanese had emplaced six 11inch howitzers of French pattern and a further 12 were added during the month. It was not, however, until 5 December, when an observation post was established on 203 Metre Hill that the ships could be disposed of. The *Poltava, Retvisan, Peresviet, Pobieda, Pallada,* and the armoured cruiser *Baryan* that had missed the Yellow Sea battle through mine damage, were sunk in succession by the evening of 8 December, while the *Sevastopol* anchored out of sight beyond the harbour entrance. She was protected by a boom and nets and although 123 torpedoes were fired at her, only one hit, though a number exploded in the nets and

caused some damage. The *Sevastopol* was towed into deep water and scuttled at the surrender of Port Arthur on 2 January 1905. The only important Japanese ship lost in this period of the war was the fast light cruiser *Takasago* mined during 12/13 December.

The major part of the Russian battle Fleet left Libau on 15 October 1904 for the Far East. This was already too late, but two of the most powerful ships had only just been completed. Various reinforcements were subsequently sent, the last on 15 February after Port Arthur had fallen, when the expedition should have been called off.

The whole force finally assembled at Van Phong Bay on the coast of French Indo-China on 9 May 1905. It is outside the scope of this feature to relate the story of the voyage of the various Russian squadrons, but it must be said that, without the use of neutral French harbours, particularly in Madagascar where the main part of the Baltic fleet stayed for eleven weeks, and also without the collier

service chartered from the Hamburg Amerika Company, the Russian force would never have reached the war area. In point of fact the long stay at Madagascar was due to difficulties over the supply of coal and the need to re-negotiate the charter.

The force which left Indo-China comprised 8 battleships, 3 coast-defence ships, 3 old armoured cruisers, 5 light cruisers, 5 auxiliary cruisers (ex-liners), 1 armed yacht, 9 destroyers and a fleet train of 1 repair ship, 2 armed transports, 9 Russian merchant ships, 2 tugs and 2 hospital ships. Among the auxiliary ships which had been intended to accompany the fleet but were prevented by machinery troubles when still in the Baltic, it is of interest to note an ex-liner converted to a balloon ship and the large ice-breaker *Ermak.* The fleet was under the command of Vice-Admiral Rozhestvenski, who seems to have been of no outstanding ability. His main idea was to get to Vladivostok, if possible without a fight, and his battle orders envisaged the use of his cruisers to

2

3

1 The Russian battleship *Poltava*, which had a lucky escape at the Battle of the Yellow Sea, being hit by a torpedo that did not explode.
CPL W/5/002

2 The Japanese cruiser *Hatsuse*, sunk by a mine on 15 May 1904.
Marius Bar

3 The Japanese light cruiser *Yoshino*, the victim of a collision early in the war.
National Maritime Museum

4 The battleship *Petropavlosk*, whose loss to a mine deprived Russia of the services of the distinguished Admiral Makarov, who was killed when she sank.
CPL W/5/003

5 The battleship *Pobieda* was in action at the Yellow Sea and was later sunk at Port Arthur.
CPL W/5/004

4

5

protect the fleet train, his destroyers acting as tenders to the battleships. On the way north 8 of the merchant ships were sent back and 4 of the armed liners were detached to make demonstrations which were quite ineffectual, but the remainder of the fleet train closely accompanied the warships to the end. The Russian battle-line consisted of 12 ships as follows:—

1st Division:
Kniaz Suvarov (Vice-Admiral Rozhestvenski); *Imperator Alexander III; Borodino; Orel;*

2nd Division:
Osliabia (Rear Admiral Felkerzam); *Sissoi Veliki; Navarin; Admiral Nakhimov;*

3rd Division:
Imperator Nikolai I (Rear Admiral Nebogatov); *General-Admiral Graf Apraxin; Admiral Seniavin; Admiral Ushakov.*

THE RUSSIAN SHIPS
The first four ships had been laid down at the St. Petersburg yards in 1899-1901 but not completed until late 1903-1904 and they were not then entirely ready for service. They were high-sided with considerable 'tumblehome' and a nominal displacement of 13 516 tons which was well exceeded. There were four 12inch twin electrically trained French-type turrets fore and aft, and twelve 6inch twin turrets of similar type, three on either beam.

Some of the Russian reinforcements for the Pacific. From left to right: two *Orel* class battleships, the *Sissoi Veliki, Svietlana* and *Almag.*
CPL W/5/005

Twelve of the twenty 3inch were in a main deck battery and the rest in bow and stern casemates. The heavy armour was KC made in Russia or America, with some from Britain. There was a complete belt 11 ft wide and $7\frac{1}{2}$-6 in amidships reduced to $5\frac{3}{4}$-4 in at the ends. The main deck battery was protected by 3 inch armour, and the 12 in turrets had 10 in with $2\frac{1}{2}$ in roofs and 9-7 in bases reduced to 4 in behind the belt. The secondary turrets and bases had 6 in armour with $1\frac{3}{4}$-4 in roofs and the CT 8 in with a 5 in tube. The main deck was 2 in with a 1 in lower deck ($1\frac{1}{4}$ in slopes) and the upper deck over the 3 in battery $2\frac{1}{2}$-$1\frac{1}{2}$ in. There was a $1\frac{1}{4}$ in torpedo bulkhead at a maximum of 6ft 8in inboard. Twenty Belleville boilers in two boiler rooms and two sets of engines gave 16 000 ihp for about $17\frac{1}{2}$ knots.

The *Osliabia,* sister to the *Peresviet* of the Port Arthur fleet, was a thoroughly bad design, built at St Petersburg in 1895-1901. She was also high-sided with a nominal displacement of 12 674 tons and a beam of only $71\frac{1}{2}$ ft. The main armament was only four 10inch twin French-type turrets fore and aft, with eleven 6inch of which one was unprotected in the bows, six in upper deck and four in main deck casemates. Of the twenty 3inch guns, eight were in an unprotected main deck battery. The heavy armour was mainly American Harvey with some KC. Of the $426\frac{1}{2}$ ft waterline, 312 ft was protected by a belt 7 ft 10 in wide and 9 in amidships (5 in lower edge) but reduced to 7 in fore and aft where

there were 4 in bulkheads. Above the belt was 188 ft of 5 in armour to the main deck ending in 4 in bulkheads reaching to the forecastle deck. All the 4 in bulkheads had unarmoured doors. The turrets were 9 in with 5 in bases, the casemates 5 in and the CT 6 in. There was a $2\frac{1}{2}$ in lower armoured deck extending to bow and stern with 3 in slopes, but none of the other decks were over $\frac{1}{2}$ in. Thirty two Belleville boilers in four rooms with three sets of engines gave a designed 14 500 ihp = 18 knots.

The *Sissol Veliki* built in 1892-1896 had a normal displacement of 10 400 tons. There were four 12inch fore-and-aft twin French type turrets, and six 6inch in a main deck battery. The armour was Nickel steel, not Harveyised, with an incomplete belt 16-12 in (4 in lower edge) ending in 9 in bulkheads. The deck was $1\frac{3}{4}$ in over the belt and 3 in below water outside the bulkheads. The armour above the belt was 5 in to the main deck with the same on the battery. The turrets and bases had 12 in armour. Speed was 15.7 knots originally.

The *Navarin* built in 1889-1896 was a low freeboard turret ship of 10 200 tons normal displacement resembling a smaller *Nile* and *Trafalgar.* There were four 12inch fore-and-aft twin turrets, with all-round loading but without individual armour to the turret bases, and eight 6inch on the upper deck. The belt of compound armour was 16-14 in (8 in lower edge) ending in 12 in bulkheads. Above this was a shorter 12 in

upper belt, while the deck was 3 in beyond the belt, 2½ in over the belt outside the upper belt, and 2 in over the latter. The battery had 5 in and the turrets 12 in Nickel steel, not Harveyised. The original speed was about 15½ knots.

The *Nikolai* built in 1885-1891 resembled the British *Sans Pareil* in general layout but had a short higher forecastle. Of 9672 tons displacement, she carried two 12inch in a turret forward, while on the main deck were four 9inch with some protection and eight 6inch with none. There was a complete waterline belt, 14 in max. with 10 in on the turret, the armour being compound. Speed was at most 15 knots originally.

The *Nakhimov* was an old armoured cruiser, launched in 1885 and reconstructed. Of 8500 tons, her armament comprised eight 8inch in fore and aft and beam twin barbettes with ten 6inch. There was a short waterline compound belt of 10-6 in and 8-7 in on the barbettes with a 3 in deck at the belt upper edge amidships and below the waterline at the ends. The original speed had been 17 knots but was only 14 knots in 1904. The *Apraxin, Seniavin* and *Ushakov* were small coast defence ships launched in 1893-96. Their nominal displacement was 4126 tons and the armament four 10inch, (three only in *Apraxin*) in fore-and-aft turrets, with in addition four 4.7inch QF. The 10inch guns were a lower velocity model than those in the *Osliabia*. The thicker armour was Harvey with a partial belt on the waterline of 10 in max. and 8 in on

the turrets, with 2-3 in on the armour deck. Trial speeds were about 16 knots.

The first seven battleships were the only vessels really fit for the battle-line, and of these the *Navarin* had older pattern 12inch guns of low muzzle-velocity. Of the four ships of the *Borodino* class, three had only completed shortly before the first part of the Fleet left Russia, and their trials had been hurried; troubles with the steering occurred on the voyage. A large proportion of the Russian crews was inadequately trained, while the second-in-command, Felkerzam, was in poor health and died four days before the battle with the Japanese was fought. His flag-captain was ordered to lead his division, while Nebogatov, whose ships had been the last to reach Indo-China, never discussed the battle plans with Rozhestvenski.

The cruisers comprised the *Oleg* (Rear Admiral Enkvist), a new 23-knot ship with twelve 6inch guns; the *Aurora,* 20 knots and eight 6inch guns, sister to the *Pallada* of the Port Arthur fleet; the *Svietlana,* 20 knots and six 6inch guns and the *Jemtchug* and *Izumrud,* six 4.7inch guns and of 23-24 knots speed. In addition there were two reconstructed armoured cruisers older than the *Nakhimov,* the *Vladimir Monomakh* and *Dmitri Donskoi,* both with 6inch and 4.7inch guns and a speed of perhaps 15 knots. The armed yacht *Almaz* and the armed liner *Ural,* could make 19 and 20 knots speed but were only lightly gunned. The train limited the fleet speed to 9

knots, but the warships could not have maintained a much higher speed as the *Nikolai,* which was heavily loaded and very foul, had a maximum speed of only 12 knots, and the three ships of the *Ushakov* class were hardly any faster.

Rozhestvenski decided on the most direct route to Vladivostok through the Straits of Korea, and after passing to the north of Luzon and to the east of Formosa, entered the East China Sea. He intended to pass through the eastern half of the Straits of Korea, between the Island of Tsushima and Japan at midday on 27 May, and coaled for the last time on 23 May at sea. It is usually said that the amount of coal taken on was regulated to give the Russian ships their normal load by noon of 26 May, when a battle was expected, but the three small ships of the *Ushakov* type appear to have had a good deal more than their designed quantity. Further reference is made to this point when discussing the fate of the *Borodino* class.

The Russian ships already at Vladivostok took no part in the forthcoming operations. The Japanese had laid extensive minefields off Vladivostok and the large armoured cruiser *Gromoboi* had been seriously damaged by a mine on 23 May. The light cruiser *Bogatyr,* sister to the *Oleg,* had been very badly injured by running ashore in the earlier part of the war and her repair was beyond the resources of Vladivostok. This left only the large armoured cruiser *Rossiya* and some torpedo boats, and they remained inert.

4

ГРОМОБОЙ
Gromoboi

1

2

3

5

1 The fast light cruiser *Novik* which escaped after the battle of the Yellow Sea. While making for Vladivostok, she was intercepted by two Japanese cruisers and sunk in the Soya Straits.
CPL W/5/008

2 The battleship *Sissoi Veliki*, part of the Second Division of Roghestvenski's fleet, was a 10 400 ton vessel completed in 1896.
CPL W/5/009

3 *Navarin* was completed in the same year but construction had commenced as early as 1889. *CPL W/5/010*

4 The battleship *Sevastapol* played an eventful, if ill-fated, part in the war: she struck a mine on 23 June 1904, resulting in a 6 week repair; this was completed just in time for her to sail with the Russian fleet to its defeat at the Yellow Sea. *CPL W/5/011*

5 The armoured cruiser *Gromoboi* was severely damaged by mines off Vladivostock and spent the whole of the war inactive in that port. *CPL W/5/012*

1 The Japanese battleship *Asahi* at Southampton in 1899.
CPL W/5/006

2 The Italian built armoured cruiser *Nisshin* at Port Said in October 1917.
Imperial War Museum

2

THE JAPANESE SHIPS

The Japanese fleet, the ships of which had been given essential re since the fall of Port Arthur, wa concentrated in the Straits of Korea. The heavy ships were bas at Masanpo in southern Korea, while some of the light cruisers a torpedo-craft were at Osaki Bay and Takeshiki in Tsushima. A watch on the Straits of Korea wa maintained by light cruisers reinforced by armed merchant sh and old warships.

The Japanese battle-line, like t Russian, consisted of twelve ship These were organised in two divisions which were to act toget or independently as circumstance indicated. The first comprised th four battleships with two armour cruisers, and the second six armoured cruisers. The order wa as follows:-

1st Division:
Mikasa (Admiral Togo);
*Shikishima; Fuji; Asahi; Kasuga;
Nisshin* (Vice-Admiral Misu).

2nd Division:

Izumo (Vice-Admiral Kamimura);
*Azuma; Tokiwa; Yakumo; Asama;
Iwate* (Rear Admiral Shimamura).

The *Mikasa* had been built by
Vickers in 1898-1902 and had an
actual normal displacement of 14
358 tons. She had four 12inch guns
in fore-and-aft twin turrets, the
mountings by Elswick generally
resembling the British BVI in HMS
Formidable. There were fourteen
6inch, ten in a main deck battery
and four in upper deck casemates,
and twenty 3inch. The heavy
armour was largely KC with a
nearly complete belt 7 ft 8 in wide
ending in a stern 6 in bulkhead. It
was 9 in for 158 ft amidships,
thinning to 7 in by the barbette
bases, at the outside of which were
shallow 12 in bulkheads, and
beyond these the belt reduced to 5½
in and 4 in. The upper belt and
battery armour extended for 158 ft
and was 6 in with angled 6 in
bulkheads to the inner sides of the
barbettes. The battery had 2 in
screens and 1 in longitudinal
bulkheads, and the four casemates
were 6 in with 2 in rear walls. The
turrets were 10-8 in with 3 in roofs
and the barbettes and CT 14 in, the
former reduced to 10 in behind the
6 in bulkheads. The armour deck
was 2 in amidships with 3 in slopes
and 2 in at the ends, but by the
barbettes in the space between the
lines of the 12 in and 6 in
bulkheads, it was curved and 4½ in
thick (1½ in nickel steel on 3 in mild
steel). There was also a 1 in upper
deck over the battery. The 25
Belleville boilers and two sets of
engines gave 16 430 ihp = 18.5
knots on trials.

The *Shikishima* and *Asahi* built
by Thames Ironworks and
Clydebank in 1897-1900 differed in
details from each other, and in
appearance, being respectively three
and two funnelled. Actual normal
displacements were 14 431 and
14 525 tons. The armament was as
in the *Mikasa*, except that the 12 in
mountings resembled the British
BIV in HMS *Glory*, and that the
6inch guns were in eight main deck
and six upper deck casemates. The
heavy armour was Harvey-nickel,
and the 9 in belt extended for 220

ft (224 ft in *Asahi*) and was 8 ft 2
in wide (8 ft in *Asahi*). Shallow-
angled 12 in bulkheads ran to the
barbettes, and beyond these the belt
was reduced to 7 in, 5½ in, 4 in,
extending to stem and stern. The
upper belt reached to the main deck
and was 6 in with 6 in bulkheads.
The turrets were 10-8 in and the
barbettes 14 in reduced to 10 in
behind the 6 in armour. The
casemates were 6 in with 2 in rear
walls and the CT 14 in. The
armour deck was 2½ in with 4 in
slopes amidships, and the main
deck was 1 in here. With machinery
generally similar to that of the
Mikasa, trials gave *Shikishima*
15 355 ihp = 18.6 knots, *Asahi*
15 593 ihp = 18.3 knots.

The *Fuji*, built by Thames
Ironworks in 1894-1897, was of an
older type of 12 450 tlons normal
displacement. Four 12inch guns
were in twin fore-and-aft shielded
barbettes with end-on main and all-
round auxiliary loading, the
mountings resembling the British
BII in HMS *Prince George*. There
were ten 6inch guns, four in main
deck casemates and six in shields on
the upper deck. The heavy armour
was Harvey with a 226 ft x 8 ft
belt, 18 in amidships (8 in lower
edge) reduced to 14 in by the
barbettes and ending in 14-12 in
bulkheads. Above this was 4 in
armour to the main deck with 6 in
bulkheads, while the casemates were
6 in (2 in rear walls). The pear-
shaped barbettes were 14 in,
reduced to 9-4 in behind the 4 in
side, with 6-4 in shields to the
12inch guns. The CT was 14 in and
the armour deck 2½ in at the main
belt upper edge amidships and
below the waterline at the ends. Ten
cylindrical boilers and two sets of
engines gave a forced draught 14
100 ihp = 18.5 knots on trials, but
this was much reduced by the time
of Tsushima.

Of the armoured cruisers, the
Kasuga and *Nisshin* had been built
by Ansaldo in 1902-1904 and
bought by Japan from Argentina.
They were of the *Garibaldi* type,
displacing about 7700 tons normal.
They differed in armament, the

Kasuga having one 10inch forward
and a twin 8inch turret aft while the
Nisshin had twin 8inch fore-and-aft.
Both had fourteen 6inch, ten in a
main deck battery and four in
upper deck shields, as well as ten
3inch. The armour was Terni
Harvey-nickel with a complete belt
about 10 ft wide. This was 6 in
amidships with 4¾ in bulkheads,
and continued to the ends at 4½ in,
3½ in and 3 in. Above this was 170
ft of 6 in armour to the upper
deck, ending in 4¾ in bulkheads.
The main armament had 6-4 in, the
CT 6 in, and the armour deck was
1 in with 1½ in slopes. The upper
deck was 1½ in over the 170 ft of
citadel armour, and beyond this
there was ¾ in at the belt upper
edge. They had cylindrical boilers,
speed was a bare twenty knots and
the *Nisshin* in particular had a
very large turning circle.

The other six armoured cruisers
generally resembled each other. The
Azuma was built at St. Nazaire, the
Yakumo by Vulcan, Stettin, and
the other four by Elswick, the dates
being 1898 to 1901, except for the
Asama and *Tokiwa* in 1896-1899.
Normal displacement was 9300-9750
tons, and all had four 8inch, in
fore-and-aft twin turrets. The
Elswick ships had fourteen 6inch in
six main deck and four upper
casemates, and four upper deck
shields, while the other two had
twelve 6inch, two main deck
casemates being absent; all had
twelve 3inch. The armour was
Harvey or Harvey-nickel in the
Elswick ships and KC in the other
two. The detailed distribution
varied, but in general all had a belt
about 7 ft wide, 7 in amidships and
4-3 in at the ends, rising to the
main deck at the bow. The upper
belt amidships was 5 in, with 6 in
on turrets, and casemates and 14-12
in on the CT. The armour deck was
2 in or 2½ in. The *Asama* and
Tokiwa had cylindrical boilers and
the others Belleville. Speeds were
20-21 knots, the *Azuma* being the
slowest, and the *Tokiwa* with a
trials speed of 22.73 knots
originally, the fastest.

The Japanese had twelve light
cruisers as well as the three
Matsushima's (one 12.6 in, eleven

48

1 The French built armoured cruiser *Azuma*.
   CPL W/5/007

2 The Japanese cruiser *Chitose*.
   Imperial War Museum

or twelve 4.7 in, 16 knots) and the old battleship *Chin Yen* (four short 12 in, four 6 in, originally 14½ knots), and three torpedo gunboats which served as despatch vessels. They also had 21 destroyers and, including local flotillas, 44 torpedo boats, armed respectively with 18 in and 14 in torpedoes having explosive charges of up to 220 and 132 lb.

One of the destroyer divisions was also equipped with mines, and it appears that other torpedo craft would have been used for mining, forming a special detachment under the *Asama,* but this plan was cancelled due to the bad weather. Apart from the *Kasagi* and *Chitose* (4900 and 4760 tons respective normal displacements, two 8inch,

ten 4.7inch, 22½ knots), the light cruisers were of 2450 to 3700 tons, with 6inch and 4.7inch guns and original trial speeds of 18 to 21 knots.

The battle which was fought between these fleets on 27 and 28 May, 1905 is usually known as the Battle of Tsushima, though Togo in his official report, called it the Battle of the Japan Sea. It resulted in the annihilation of the Russian fleet at very small cost to the Japanese. Their war-experienced officers and men were greatly superior to the Russians and Admiral Togo was much the better commander. The Japanese ships in the line of battle were generally better than the Russians and they could maintain a speed of 15 knots,

with a possible 17-18 knots for the 2nd Division, as against a Russian figure of 11-12 knots. On the other hand there were only four Japanese battleships as against seven Russian (excluding the *Nikolai*), and the Japanese had only sixteen 12inch and one 10inch compared with twenty 12inch, six older 12inch and fifteen 10inch guns. Their superiority in 6inch guns was not likely to be important but they had thirty 8inch as against two 9inch and six 8inch of older models on the broadside. With the earlier battles of the war in mind, there was little reason to expect such a complete victory, the relative ease of which was not anticipated by the Japanese.

GUNS IN RUSSIAN LINE OF BATTLE

GUN	Weight (tons)	Bore (cals)	Shells (lb)	MV (fs)	Notes
12inch Obukhov/Canet	42.0-42.7	38.3-38.4	729	2600	*Borodino* class; *Sissoi*
12inch Obukhov/Krupp	55.2	31.9	729	2090	*Navarin*
12inch Obukhov/Krupp	50.6	27	729	1870	*Nikolai*
10inch Obukhov/Canet	27	43.3	496	2550	*Osliabia*
10inch Obukhov/Canet	22.1-22.6	43.5	496	2275	*Apraxin, Ushakov* class
9inch Obukhov/Krupp	21.7	32	277	2325	*Nikolai*
8inch Obukhov/Krupp	13.5	32	193	2300	*Nakhimov*
6inch Obukhov/Canet	5.7	43.5	91	2600	*Borodino* class; *Osliabia, Sissoi*
6inch Obukhov/Brinke	6.3	33.5	91	2300	*Navarin, Nikolai, Nakhimov*
6inch Obukhov wire	5.0				
4.7inch/(120mm) Obukhov/Canet	2.9	43.5	45	2700	*Aprakin, Ushakov* class
3inch/(75mm) Obukhov/Canet	0.9	48.2	10.8	2700	*Borodino* class; *Osliabia*

IN JAPANESE LINE OF BATTLE

12inch Elswick Patterns G,G[1]	48.5-48.9	40.4	850	2400	All four battleships
10inch Elswick Pattern R	30.9	40.35	500	2297	*Kasuga*
8inch Elswick Patterns S,U,W	18.5-19.1	45	250	2480	All eight armoured cruisers
6inch Elswick Pattern various	5.8-6.6	40	100	2300	All battleships and armoured cruisers
3inch Elswick Pattern N	0.6	40	12.5	2210	All but *Fuji*

Note: The Japanese had a considerable reserve of 12inch, as they had purchased 20 spare guns.

THE
Salt Lake City
CLASS
by Norman Friedman

Most accounts of the 'Treaty' cruisers suggest that the 10 000 ton/8inch gun limit imposed at Washington in 1922 was inspired entirely by the characteristics of the new British *Hawkins* class cruisers, which mounted 7.5inch main batteries. The reality, at least in the US case, was rather more complex. American interest in really large cruisers dates from the post-World War I shift from European to Pacific considerations. From 1919 on the most probable enemy was Japan, and the most probable war scenario was a fleet advance across the Pacific towards a decisive battle in Japanese home waters and to accomplish the relief of the Philippines.

At the same time the US concept of cruiser-functions began to shift. Previous cruisers, which had been designated Scouts *(Omahas)* had been intended largely for operations in direct support of the Battle Fleet. However, Pacific warfare would require 'strategic' (as opposed to 'tactical') scouting: reconnaissance on the far side of the Pacific. It

would also require considerable operations on the long trade-routes. At the same time it began to appear that aircraft might well take over most of the fleet scouting function. At a General Board hearing in 1921 one Admiral suggested that the vital cruiser-functions of the future would be:

1 convoy escort against surface raiders.
2 bombardment of lesser enemy bases.
3 driving the enemy's light craft from the sea.

All would require great range and seakeeping ability, ie substantial size.

The question of the 8inch gun was complex. In 1919 the ten light cruisers under construction were to be armed with a high-velocity 6inch/53cal, which would fire the largest shell a man could handle. Indeed, manhandling and individual (broadside) disposition were considered keys to their high rate of fire. The Bureau of Ordnance was interested in a new 8inch/50cal, for future cruisers, but this weapon

could not be loaded by hand and would probably require a turret-mounting. Both power-loading and a multiple mounting were considered very detrimental to a high rate of fire. For example, earlier 8inch/45cal guns mounted in armored cruisers could fire no faster than 12inch turret guns.

Thus a recurrent issue was the 'smothering' effect of rapid 6inch fire versus the smashing effect of individual 8inch hits. Although the 8inch could outrange the smaller gun, it could be argued that its rate of fire would be so slow that few hits would be registered against a rapidly manoeuvering cruiser trying to close the range. In fact hits at very long range would require the complexity of director-control, which in any case would further reduce the rate of fire.

Nor was the evidence from abroad ambiguous. It was true that Britain had built a class of very large cruisers armed with 7.5inch guns, but it could be argued that they had not been particularly successful. Evidence in this direction

Pensacola as refitted at Mare Island, May-June 1945. Note her resemblance to the refitted *Northampton* and *Portland* classes. The large directors are Mk 33s controlling the 5inch secondary battery; superimposed above them are a pair of Mk 35s originally manufactured for the 1850 ton 'leaders', with their single-purpose main batteries. They were later modified for 8inch ballistics, as here.

Both sets of directors employed the small Mk 28 force control radar. At this time *Pensacola* mounted seven quadruple Bofors, as well as eleven twin 20mm machine guns. Her foremast shows SK air search and SG surface search radar; smoke obscures the SP fighter control set on her mainmast, but the array of jamming gear is visible.

52

1 The *Salt Lake City* in dockyard hands, May 1943.
USN

Midships and after superstructure, *Salt Lake City,* May 1943.
USN

Salt Lake City was scheduled for an overhaul similar to *Pensacola*'s, but never received one. Here she is in June, 1944, showing her original very tall foremast with its Mk 22 8inch director (Mk 3 radar); the 5inch director carries the Mk 4 radar system. Her 40mm battery corresponded to that of her sister ship except for the bow mount, which she lacked.

included the completion of one such ship, *Vindictive* as an aircraft carrier, and the evident decision to retreat to more moderate dimensions and 6inch guns in the succeeding 'E' class. Moreover, there were many reports of British dissatisfaction at the cost of the big cruisers, in manpower as well as money. The Royal Navy decision to assign one to the China station was taken as proof that they were not well-liked in the Fleet. It could also be claimed that no foreign power had gone beyond the 6inch gun, although there was one report that Japan was building a 7800 ton cruiser (which, unknown to the US Navy in 1921, would mount 8inch guns) the *Furutaka.*

These issues were resolved in the usual tortuous manner. Postwar Scout design began early in 1919, with priorities essentially unchanged from those which had produced the *Omahas.* The latter were seen as too large for their firepower, which at the time was limited to eight 6inch/53cal, all mounted on the broadside. Thus in February the Preliminary Design section of the Bureau of Construction and Repair (C & R) began a set of sketch designs in two series:

1 Series A, armed as the *Omahas,* but with displacement decreased as much as possible, speed increased towards 37 knots by using machinery designed for a contemporary Destroyer Leader

project. In fact the best that could be done was 36 knots on 6850 tons.

2 Series B, armed with the new 8inch/50cal gun proposed by Ordnance. The initial instruction was to try for four guns, two each fore-and-aft mounted on single turntables with light unarmored enclosures. There were also to be some 5inch rapid-firing guns for protection against destroyers. Quite soon twin 8inch mounts were adopted; a sketch design of March 1919 was presented with the notation that 'this design is believed to be in accordance with the trend of scout or light cruiser design at the present time.' This was an

8100-tonner of 35 knots.

Note that Design B, at least as originally conceived, is not far from that adopted by Japan at this time.

The Scout project was maintained at relatively low priority in view of the large number of *Omahas* not even in service as yet; the preliminary design team was small and the number of tasks large. Work on the Scout lapsed in March and was not resumed until early October. At this time sketch designs were still being prepared largely on the initiative of the designers, *not* on the basis of specific requests from any planning authority (the General Board or perhaps the Office of [the Chief of Naval] operations). In any case, a new series, C, was begun essentially

as an answer to the British *Hawkins* class: seven 8inch/50cal in unarmored turrets; four 5inch/51cal anti-destroyer guns; two triple torpedo-tubes; light side armor (2inch STS splinter armor laid over a 1inch side) over the machinery; a speed of 36 knots; and an endurance of 10000 miles at 10 knots. What was unusual was the arrangement of the battery: a triple mount forward, and two twins (or, for eight guns, one twin and one triple) aft.

However, the preliminary designers were well aware that this large ship did not represent any kind of official policy. They tried, therefore, a series of much smaller unarmored designs: D and E, with five 6inch/53cal and two twin torpedo-tubes, and speeds of 33.5 and 35.25 knots (which cost 5000 and 5750 tons, respectively); and F, 35 knots and six 8inch guns on 6500 tons.

All of these were presented to

Commander Pye, who much later would command the Battle Force in World War II, at the Office of Operations. He appears to have been the first policy planner to have seen the alternative Scout designs, and his view ran contrary to the basic assumptions of the designers. He considered very high speed wasteful (30 knots in a seaway would be enough) and large ships undesirable 'inasmuch as their cost would permit of building not mere than two-thirds of the number of lighter vessels for a given appropriation... further... armor of the thickness practical for scouts was not of sufficient value to warrant the expenditure of the necessary weight. He was very anxious to obtain a large cruising radius...' Of course Pye did not appreciate the fact that large cruising radius and good speed in a seaway — 30 knots would be no mean achievement — in themselves implied considerable size.

Official US Navy plans of *Pensacola* in 1941, showing her arrangement prior to war modification. Note her pronounced sheer.

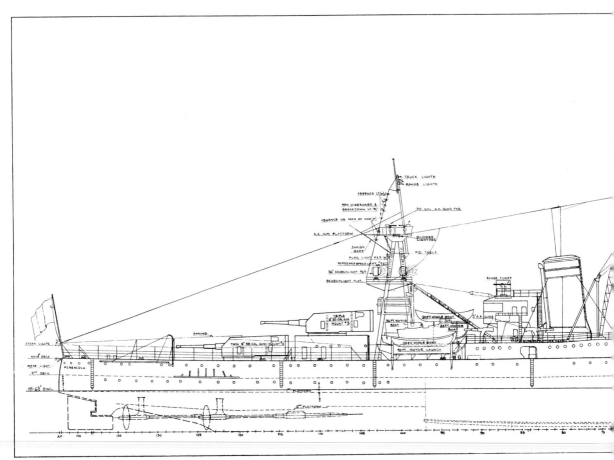

He suggested that Designs D and F be developed, but with reduced speeds. The General Board, responsible for the Characteristics (staff requirements) of new warships, did not share his views, and in March 1920 produced Characteristics calling for deck- and side-armor and for a speed of 35 knots or better. Speed and armor alone would push up displacement, and quite soon a 600 foot hull of about 10 000 tons was now under consideration, for a speed of 35.8 knots, based on Series C.

The General Board's 1920 Characteristics had not produced any ships; in January, 1921 the entire question of Scout armament came up again in the General Board. Admiral Rodgers opened the hearing with a statement that the size of the Pacific Ocean demanded larger ships; and that if the USN wanted to match other navies it would have to go to the 8inch gun. Such ships would be very costly, as the design series had shown: even on 10 000 tons there would be only eight guns and a radius of 8000 nm at 10 knots, where 10 000 would be preferable by far. Moreover, these large ships would have only splinter protection, provided by a 2.5inch deck with 4.5inch slopes and 2.5inch armor at the waterline — and all of that over the machinery only. Magazines would have only deck protection, and turrets and barbettes might well be unarmored. The Bureau of Engineering noted that the full tonnage was required for 35 knots: 'on 7500 it is a tight squeeze to get 32.'

The only question was 6inch vs 8inch guns. Although the 8inch gun could fire to 34 000 yards at 40° elevation, and the 6inch to only about 26 000, it could be argued that few hits would be made outside 24 000, to which a pedestal- (ie broadside)-mounted 6inch could fire (30° elevation). As for penetration, it was true that a 6inch shell could not penetrate a 3inch deck — but neither could an 8inch. It might be true that the heavier shell would behave better at longer ranges, but the lighter one would fire a lot faster, and the Chief of the Bureau of Ordnance went on record as preferring a 6inch cruiser against a *Hawkins*. Commander G J Rowcliff of Ordnance observed:

'It seems to me, Admiral, that in our service the 8inch gun has always been a sort of mongrel type: it is not heavy enough to be effective against an armored ship and has not been light enough to get much rapidity of fire. If we could guarantee for this gun a performance of six to eight shots per minute it might be well to consider it; but I do not believe we can get anything like that, and we believe we can get it from the 6inch gun. It might be different, however, with twin 6inch guns.'

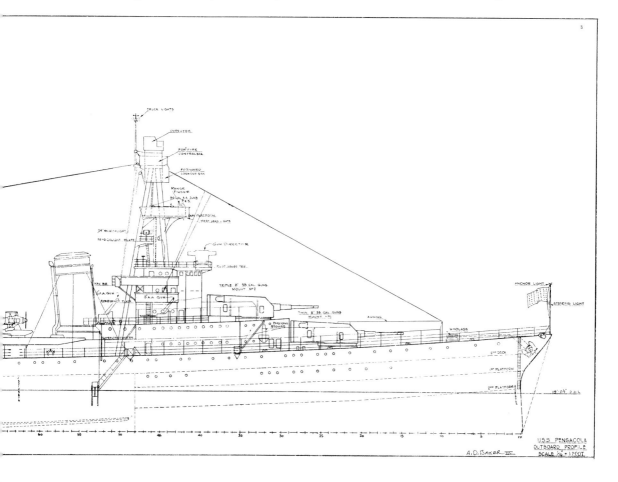

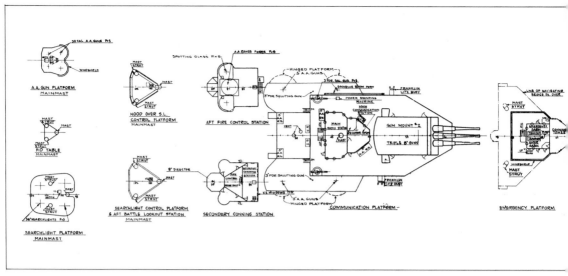

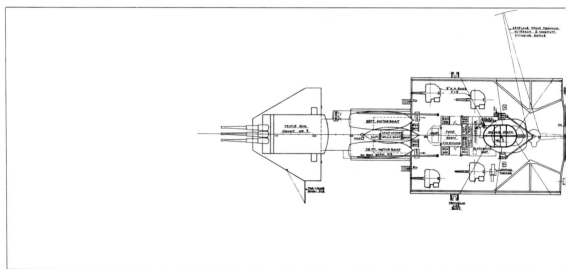

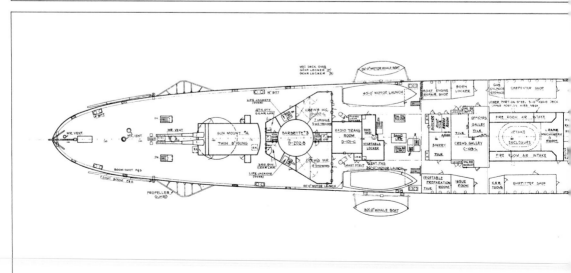

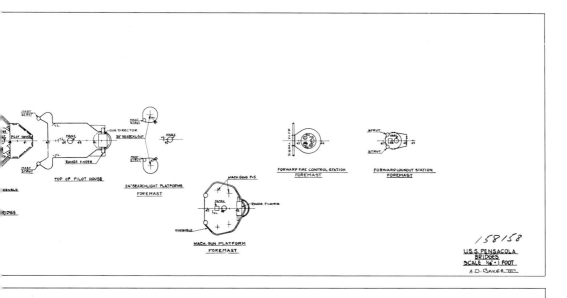

158158

U.S.S. PENSACOLA
BRIDGES
SCALE ⅛" = 1 FOOT
A.D. BAKER III

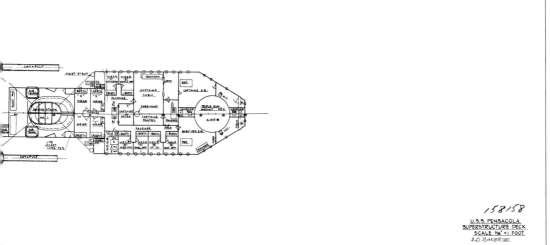

158158

U.S.S. PENSACOLA
SUPERSTRUCTURE DECK
SCALE ⅛" = 1 FOOT
A.D. BAKER III

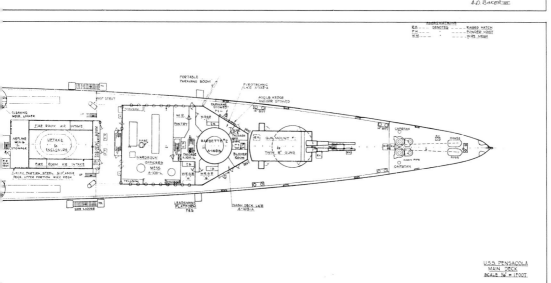

U.S.S. PENSACOLA
MAIN DECK
SCALE ⅛" = 1 FOOT

In fact the multiple 8inch guns were generally rated at three rounds per minute.

It appeared that on 10000 tons the ordnance weights would suffice for eight 8inch or about 16 6inch; but the Bureau of Ordnance was unhappy with broadside mounts, which it considered uneconomical. That meant multiple 6inch mounts on the centerline, and topweight precluded more than two levels. Hence it seemed in 1921 that any 6inch cruiser would have to have 12 guns in four triple mounts (quadruple mounts were not even considered).

In that case the rates of fire of 6inch and 8inch guns might not be so very different. Both batteries would operate by director control and both would require power operation. Now questions of smashing effect per broadside became important. Eight 8inch guns would deliver about 2000 lb of shell, 12 6inch about 1200 lb. Moreover, both C & R and Ordnance had to admit that on 10000 tons armor might be provided which could resist 6inch *but not 8inch* fire, in the form of an inclined deck.

These arguments proved decisive, and in April 1921 the General Board proposed new cruiser Characteristics: 8 8inch guns in splinter-proof mountings, 4 5inch/25cal two triple torpedo-tubes, a speed of 34 knots and a radius of action of 10000 miles at 10 knots. In addition 'without sacrifice of other important features these vessels [are] to be designed to resemble the battlecruiser in silhouette'. Thin armor was envisaged: a 1 inch deck with 1.5 inch slopes, and a 1.5inch belt.

These Characteristics were based on a series of what must have been relatively disappointing design studies. The basic scheme, designated No 1, was progressively modified with reduced speed (a), reduced protection (b), reduced battery (c), and all three reductions (d); and the General Board had to decide that all it could afford was (b):

1 Two views of *Pensacola*, 3 July 1945. This detail view shows clearly the extent to which the forward bridgework was cut down. The jamming gear aft is clearly shown: from the masthead down, the TDY jamming system, SP height-finding radar flanked by IFF antennae; radar intercept and direction finding gear; and, at the base of the mainmast a pair of jammers in large radomes. The ship in the background is the cruiser *Indianapolis* (CA 35), which was lost at the end of July.

2 Note the removal of the starboard catapult, a standard weight-saving measure in US cruisers at the end of World War Two. *Pensacola* and *Salt Lake City* were the only US heavy cruisers without hangars: note the stowage of a spare wing under the port 5inch gun, and of spare wingtip floats (circled) abaft the Mk 51 AA director near the funnel.

Plans and uncredited photos, USN official, by courtesy of A D Baker III

Scheme	l	a	b	c	d
Displacement	12000	10750	10000	11250	8250 tons
Length	635	610	600	625	560 feet
Speed	34.5	*33*	34.5	34.5	*33* knots
Power	125000	96000	118000	122000	88000 shp
8inch guns	8	8	8	*6*	*6*
Deck	3	3	*1*	3	*1* inches
Slopes	4.5	4.5	*1.5*	4.5	*1.5*
Side	5	5	*1.5*	5	*1.5*

In each case radius of action was 8000 nm at 10 knots; reductions are underlined. It was estimated that a 4inch belt and a 2.5 inch deck would provide immunity against 6inch/53cal fire between 11000 and 21000 yards; the combination of 5inch belt and 3 inch deck would resist 8inch fire between 16000 and

21000 yards. All of these designs incorporated a 1inch STS belt extending from the main belt to the bow, the function of which was to prevent the waterline forward from being torn up by penetrating hits: very serious damage forward would slow the ship so much as to doom her. However, main belt protection

was limited to the area over engines and boilers. Placing the magazines below the waterline and below an armored deck was considered adequate protection, and light protection of barbettes and even turrets was considered acceptable.

These, then, were the 10000-ton/8inch gun cruisers which the United States tried successfully to obtain at the Washington Conference. Of course they were not quite what the United States actually built.

The Washington Treaty presented a new problem in cruiser-design. For the first time ships had to be built within a prescribed tonnage limit. Even worse, the tonnage limit was based, not on the usual displacement which included fuel and feed water, but on a new 'standard' measurement which did not. That meant that existing designs had to be re-scaled to give some idea of what could be achieved. For example, 10 000 tons standard was not very far from a 'normal' displacement of about 12 000.

The usual process of feasibility or preliminary design had to be recast to take account of the weight growth common during detailed design and construction; in the post-Treaty series of studies feasibility was reckoned according to the amount of weight margin separating the estimated weights (hull, fittings, battery, armor, machinery, etc) from the 10 000 ton limit. There was really no experience to go by, which is why the first US Treaty designs were completed well within the 10 000 tons.

There was one other new factor. Since the Treaty established a general ceiling on cruisers, it might well be assumed that all of the major naval powers would build 8inch cruisers. In that case protection might not be very useful if it were protection only against 6inch fire — and it might pay to trade heavier armament and higher speed for it. The first US studies, done early in 1923, examined the possibility of mounting 12 8inch guns on a hull with virtually no protection ($\frac{3}{4}$inch STS over magazines, $1\frac{1}{4}$inch over conning tower and steering gear.) A sketch design for 35 knots on 112 000 SHP was rejected because it allowed for only a 133 ton margin. On the other hand a 34 knot type showing a margin of 278 tons was considered acceptable. Ultimately the standard would be a 300 ton margin — but Salt Lake City was completed at 9100 tons, 900 tons within the agreed limit.

By April 1923 the Preliminary Designers were working with alternative batteries of 8, 10, or 12 8inch guns, as a 9 gun three turret arrangement was ruled out from the start. They had concluded that serious protection against 8inch shellfire was impossible 'in view of

the fact that only about 700-900 tons could be reasonably expected under any scheme of Scout Cruiser... having minimum requirements for at least 31 knots and eight 8inch/55cal guns.' This would have meant a $4\frac{3}{4}$inch belt, penetrable at up to 20 000 yards, and a $1\frac{1}{2}$inch deck, penetrable at any range beyond 10 000; there would be no zone of immunity at all. 'Consequently we would not be able to protect between the ranges of 10 000 and 20 000 yards, yet in this range somewhere will be the most probable effective battle range.'

On the other hand, some lesser protection would be worthwhile, against destroyers (5inch/51cal beyond 6000 yards) and 6inch cruisers (6inch/53cal beyond 10 000 yards). It turned out that a 3inch side and $1\frac{1}{2}$inch deck were proof against 5inch shell between 6000 and 15 000 yards and the destroyer would find hitting rather difficult at the latter range and the side would be effective against 6inch shell at 10 000 yards. In a few studies it was shown that protection against 8inch fire would require a reduction in speed to 28 knots, which was entirely unacceptable.

The final design, which became Salt Lake City and Pensacola, was completed at the end of 1925. It called for 10 8inch guns and a speed of 32.5 knots; the emphasis on independent operations at long range shows in a required endurance of 10 000 nm at 15, rather than 10, knots. Armor was set by the destroyer/light cruiser criterion: a main belt 3inches thick, with a 1inch deck amidships. The magazines forward were covered by 4inch side armor and a 1.5inch deck; aft, by the 1.5inch deck and a 3.5inch internal longitudinal bulkhead.

The United States went on to build 16 more 'Treaty' cruisers, each class in turn showing more attention to protection. Ultimately the Salt Lake City and her sister would be condemned as over-gunned, under-protected, and of questionable seakeeping capability in view of their low freeboard. There is no question but that they

were compromises loaded towards firepower, but in view of their evolution it appears that the sacrifices made were greater than need be, largely because of the unknown character of the Treaty environment.

The one great question in their design was the validity of the argument in favor of the 8inch gun US cruiser-evolution shows greater loyalty to this weapon than can be found in any European navy; sometimes it is suggested that the determining factor was somehow bound up with Pacific conditions, since Japan also believed in the big gun.

It is interesting, therefore, to note that a principal argument in favor of the rapid-fire 8inch gun mounted in the Des Moines class at the end of World War II was that it would end the inferiority of 8inch cruisers faced by rapidly manoeuvering light craft. The 8inch gun with bag ammunition never did much better than three rounds per gun per minute. However, the new light cruisers of the Brooklyn and Cleveland types were armed with case ammunition which could be fired much more rapidly, as much as ten rounds per gun per minute. They were turret mounted, but they could deliver the old-fashioned 'smothering' fire. It was enough to make one question the whole logic of heavy cruiser design — enough to make a big light cruiser such as HMS Belfast a logical proposition indeed.

SOURCES

Material for this article is taken from the Preliminary Design files in the US National Archives and in the Washington National Records Center; and from the records of the General Board held by the Operational Archives at the Washington Navy Yard. I am grateful to Charles Wiseman of the Naval Ship Engineering Center for arranging access to the files at the Washington National Records Center, and to Dr Dean Allard and Mrs Kathy Lloyd for their assistance at the Operational Archives.

The origins of the magnetic mine

by Tom Burton

During the early stages of World War II the Germans achieved outstanding results from the use of magnetic influence ground mines against Allied and neutral shipping in British coastal waters, employing surface vessels, submarines and aircraft to lay them. This successful exploitation of an apparently new weapon has often led to the belief that the magnetic mine was a German invention, but it was not. The British designed the first magnetic firing circuit and used it in ground mines laid offensively off the Flanders coast in the summer of 1918, while the Germans did not commence work on a magnetic mine until 1932.

By the beginning of 1916 the moored contact mine had assumed a major role in combating the U-boat menace and during that year considerable British effort was devoted to mine design; as a result, in 1917 the Royal Navy was supplied with its first reliable moored mine, the type H2. Concurrently, thought had been given to the use of influence-firing as opposed to contact-firing circuits and to the provision of a ground mine, and by the middle of 1918 a magnetically-fired ground mine, the Sinker Mk 1(M), began to come forward. An acoustic firing circuit for attachment to the H2 mine was also designed but was never used.

The Sinker Mk 1(M) was, in essence, a truncated concrete cone filled with about 1000 lb of crude TNT and designed to detonate when actuated by the magnetic field of a ship. It was carried on a reinforced concrete trolley fitted with four non-magnetic wheels gauged to travel on any standard ship's mine rail. A wire or chain strop normally secured the mine to the trolley, but this was removed prior to laying so that the two parts could separate on falling from the mine rail.

The speed of descent of the mine was limited to a maximum of six feet per second by means of a canvas parachute attached to the lifting eyes on top of the mine; this released itself after about fifteen minutes' submergence, by means of a soluble sol ammoniac plug.

The gimballed firing unit operated on the dip-needle principle, whereby the field of a magnetic body would move the needle to complete the firing circuit through a detonator in the primer, the necessary electrical energy for the latter sequence being derived from two Helleson dry cells.

Safeguards included a manual safety pin to hold the battery switch in the 'off' position, until removed just before laying; and hydrostatically operated double-pole primer and battery switches in the

firing circuit. The latter switches, held by soluble plugs with a life of about 40 minutes, kept the mine 'safe' until it had come to rest on the bottom and had time to settle.

A clock-operated anti-countermining arrangement was fitted to all mines; and the firing unit chamber could be flooded and the mine rendered 'safe' (or possibly exploded) after a chosen time by means of a soluble plug.

The principal dimensions of the Sinker Mk 1(M) were:

Diameter of shell (max)   3 ft 4 in
Height from trolley rollers 3 ft 10 in
Weight of Sinker   1950 lb (approx)
Weight of trolley   300 lb (approx)

The first order for the manufacture of Sinkers Mk 1(M) was for no fewer than 10 000 but it was hoped at the time to use them defensively, eg at the inshore ends of the Folkestone—Gris Nes Barrage, as well as offensively. It was intended to use both destroyers and coastal motor boats (CMBs) for the latter task, whereas almost any minelayer would be suitable for the former.

As it happened, trials to establish that the Sinker could be used successfully and safely against submerged submarines were not satisfactorily completed by the end of hostilities and the idea of using it in a defensive role came to naught. The employment of CMBs was also discarded, but only because there was insufficient time to construct the necessary storage facility at Dunkirk, whence the CMBs operated against enemy traffic on the Belgian coast.

The actual laying of the Sinkers was carried out by destroyer minelayers; the first such operation taking place in the afternoon of 8 August 1918, when HMS *Abdiel, Vanoc, Venturous, Vanquisher, Tarpon* and *Telemachus* of the 20th Flotilla, laid a total of 234 units about eight miles north of Dunkirk. The units were laid in several separate lines, with individual unit spacing of 300 ft, and the minelayers were escorted by a further eight destroyers. There was no enemy interference and the Germans were apparently unaware of what was going on. Two underwater explosions, presumed to

be prematures, were heard at the time of laying and reported by Captain (D) 20. But as he also reported great activity ashore, with the very distinct sounds of heavy guns and exploding bombs, and it was established later that, in fact, there was very little such activity in the military lines at the time, there was more than a suspicion that the two sources of explosion might well have been confused.

The matter was to be starkly clarified on the next occasion of laying the Sinker. This was on 22 August when the *Abdiel, Venturous, Vanquisher, Tarpon* and *Telemachus* laid a total of 198 units in three lines, about 17 miles north of Zeebrugge. The minelayers on this occasion were supported by monitors as well as destroyers, while several aircraft scouted over the flotilla and to the south-eastward to prevent enemy aerial observation. Once again there was no enemy interference but 98 premature explosions were observed by the minelaying flotilla and no fewer than 131 were reported from other sources, many, doubtless, due to counter-mining. This massive failure was most disappointing, particularly in view of the reported success of the first operation, and the design team was thereafter busily employed in seeking the cause of this instability and a cure for it.

One further test field of 40 units was laid by HMS *Meteor* on 6 September, about 21 miles north-west of Ostend; but 13 premature explosions were observed on this occasion, some of them up to two hours after laying.

The basic faults in design were not rectified in time for the Sinker Mk 1(M) to be laid again before the signing of the Armistice in

November 1918. However, it is known to have been supplied to the British Naval Command at Archangel in April 1919, during the operations against the Bolsheviks. No account has been found of the use to which these mines were put; but the German archives contain such a reference which, whether accurate or not, serves to confirm the Germans' long-time ignorance of the existence of the device.

In a lecture delivered in 1938, on the stage of development of modern German mining materials and their future development, Rear Admiral Ramien (OC Mining and Barrage Experimental Command, Kiel) stated:

'It was not until long after the war that we learned from Russian officers, who were on a visit to Schwinemünde, that the English in their post-war operations against the Russians had employed a non-contact mine, on the compass principle, in Lake Ladoga. Thus for the first time our suspicions were confirmed that some of the hitherto unexplained explosions and losses off the coast of Flanders in the last year of the war were due to non-contact ground mines.'

It is of interest to note that the Germans subsequently discovered the principle on which these British mines worked and employed the same method of firing—with refinements—in the development of their World War II magnetic circuits; whereas the British abandoned the dip-needle principle for the coiled rod, which took account of the rate of change in strength of the magnetic field in the vicinity of the mine, as opposed to the increase in strength.

SINKER Mk 1 (M)
KEY TO DIAGRAM,
AS SHOWN

1. Brass wire reinforcement to base
2. Body of mine — concrete
3. Brass rings to reinforce body
4. Spiral spring to absorb shock on bottoming
5. Primer tube
6. Primer
7. Detonator adaptor
8. Screwed cap to keep detonator in place
9. Detonator
10. Primer switch
11. Combined nuts and lifting eyes
12. Channel connecting primer tube and firing circuit
13. Flooding attachment
14, 14a. Anti-countermining gear
15. Access dome
16. Top cover casting
17. Battery
18. Firing unit
19. Gimbal ring
20. Firing unit chamber
21. Rubber lining to keep TNT away from concrete
22. Brass stays — rubber covered
23. Charge. 1,000lb crude TNT
24. Securing strop

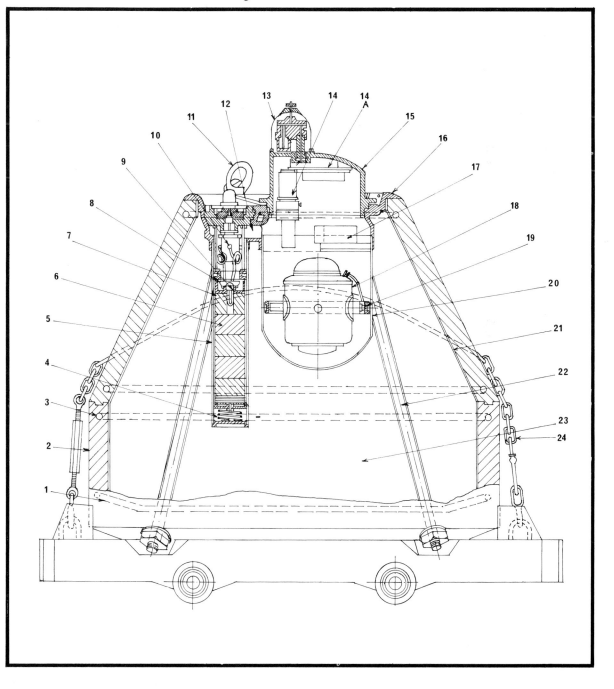

One of the most important parts of the 1936 Naval Treaty was the decision to limit the size of future cruisers to 8000 tons. It was therefore a foregone conclusion that any design of any size would be drawn to that limit. The initial design for the new 8000 ton type were split into two main groups: those with a 6inch main armament, and those with 5.25inch main armament. The 6inch gun designs were produced first, but following the thought that a cruiser with a heavy dual purpose main armament to ward off the increasing threat of air attack was required, a series of alternative schemes were drawn up. Among them was one of 8000 tons with fourteen 5.25inch guns, and a speed of $31\frac{3}{4}$ knots at legend displacement. This particular outline, designated K25G* could well have been chosen to be developed into what was to become the 1937 *Fiji* class programme, had not the argument for the 6inch type prevailed. The drawing shows K25G* as it would have appeared around 1942.

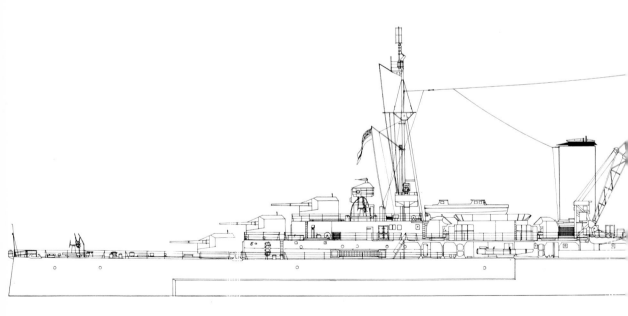

Alan Raven is the co-author of *British Battleships of World War Two* and is currently working on a companion volume on British cruisers.

The 7-Turret Colony class
by Alan Raven

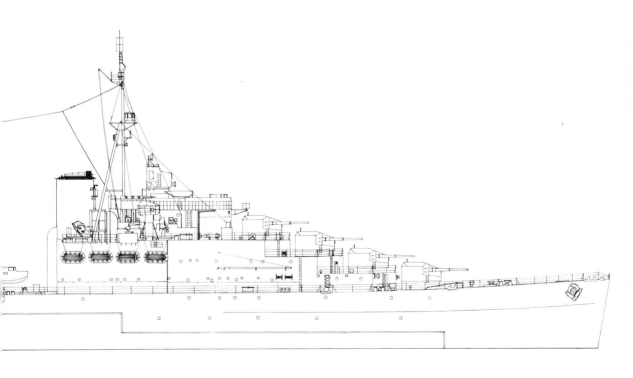

Technical Topics No 4

THE TRANSOM STERN IN THE ROYAL NAVY

By David K Brown

The design of the big battlecruisers of 1920 was severely limited by the number of dry docks which could accept them (see *Warship,* issue 2). Someone at the Admiralty realised that a long, pointed stern, like *Hood's,* only kissed the water and wondered if it would be missed. The Admiralty Experiment Works, Haslar, was asked to test a model of a battlecruiser (43 000 tons, 850 ft length) with the stern cut off in a square transom 30 ft abaft the perpendicular. Further tests were to be made with the transom successively 15 ft and 7½ ft abaft the after perpendicular and finally at the after perpendicular. The resistance of the first three variants was indistinguishable from the original form, only the last extreme cut causing a penalty.

The Superintendent at Haslar (Payne) then indulged in an orgy of cropping; the *Baden, Caradoc* and *Turbinia* models were all given transom sterns. There was a considerable increase in drag for the battleship at all speeds, a slight gain at top speed for the cruiser and a very big gain for *Turbinia.* A transom stern traps a layer of dead water behind it which gives an increased effective length to the ship. Since the economic length for a warship is usually much less than the optimum for hydrodynamic performance at full speed, the transom's gift of effective length without cost is welcome.

Unfortunately, the first large warship built for the Royal Navy

after the First World War was the minelayer *Adventure* and the transom stern fitted to her was not a success. Mines dropped into the dead water behind her transom swung back and broke off their horns on her stern, and she had to be rebuilt with a cruiser stern. This made the transom unpopular and it did not reappear until the *Fiji* class cruisers were built.

Transom sterns only reduce the resistance of ships at fairly high speeds where wavemaking drag is important. At lower speeds, resistance will usually increase and a balance has to be struck which depends on the ship's operating pattern. Tests on an aircraft carrier model with a transom area 3½ per cent of the midship area gave the following results:

Speed (kts)	Change in resistance %
30	4½ reduction
20	4 increase
10	0

For any one speed there will be an optimum size of transom but there is no dramatic change in resistance if this optimum area is slightly exceeded. This is as well since the transom stern has other advantages which often lead the frigate designer into choosing a transom which is bigger than optimum. These are:
1 Increased working area on the quarterdeck
(Particularly useful for helicopter operation)

2 More room for twin rudders and their operating gear
3 Increased buoyancy and waterplane aft which can be useful in designing ships to float after damage
4 Some increase of propulsive efficiency.

On the other hand, all ships get heavier as they grow older and sink deeper into the water. For this reason it is desirable to build a ship with a small transom which will increase through the optimum as the ship grows heavier. As always, the designer must find a happy compromise.

1 The cruiser-minelayer *Adventure,* as completed with the Royal Navy's first transom stern.
CPL W/5/013

Because the transom stern was unsuited to minelaying, it was not employed again until the *Colony* class — clearly demonstrated in this quarter view of *Jamaica* (February 1951)
CPL W/5/014

BOOK REVIEW

Before the Dreadnought — the RN from Nelson to Fisher
by Richard Humble
(Macdonald & Janes)
207pp. 21 illustrations, 4 maps.
£5.95

The very first sentence of this book is encouraging: 'I have always felt that naval historians have been somewhat churlish towards the RN of the 19th century'. Unfortunately Mr Humble is just as churlish towards the warship designer. His book covers life in the Navy, the campaigns of the 19th century after 1815, and developments in ships and guns. For *Warship's* readers this review concentrates on the third section.

Humble asks the question, 'Why did it take so long for new ideas in naval gunnery and warship design to surface?' The best answer was given by Sir Baldwin Walker in 1858, 'It is not in the interest of Great Britain, possessing as she does so large a navy, to adopt any important change in the construction of ships of war which might have the effect of rendering necessary the introduction of a new class of very costly vessels, until such a course is forced upon her by the adoption by foreign powers of formidable ships of a novel character . . .'

This was not 'crusty conservatism' but plain common sense. The Royal Navy's large fleet of conventional ships represented a big investment and it could not afford to render these ships obsolete unnecessarily. The immense industrial power of Great Britain could soon outbuild any

competition, and France's temporary lead in fast wooden battleships with *Le Napoléon* and in armoured ships with *La Gloire* was very soon overtaken by the *Agamemnon* and the *Warrior* respectively. Despite this canny policy the Royal Navy actually led with steamships, iron hulls, screw propellers,[1] steam battleships and turret ships, a record of progress almost ignored by the author. It is time that this simplistic view of a reactionary Admiralty was forgotten.

It is hardly true to say that the last ship built to fight under sail was completed in 1870, as the abandonment of sail was accepted in 1850 and implemented in 1859. Later ships had sails for cruising but fought under steam.

There are a number of minor errors, particularly in the captions to illustrations. On p62 the map dates the Azov expedition as 1854, whereas the text gives it correctly as 1855. The photograph of the *London* following p72 cannot date from 1840; even the RN had not introduced the screw battleship so early!

The statement that for twenty years after 1860 the design of British ironclads dated from before Lissa and Hampton Roads is nonsense. What about *Monarch, Devastation, Inflexible,* not to mention the smaller rams? Was a central battery ship like HMS *Alexandra* identical to the *Warrior* in conception?

HMS *Victory* did not have 64pdr bow chasers (p129); she had 68pdr carronades on the forecastle, but these were close-range weapons, not

chase guns. The 'C' class corvettes (p130) also introduced the armour deck.

Warrior was not the first ironclad in the RN (p136); that title belongs to the floating batteries of 1855. Having complained of *Inflexible's* brig rig, it is strange that the illustration shows her with the late 'military' rig.

On p139 one could add *Georgia* and *Rappahannock* to the list of Confederate raiders built in Britain. Mention, too, of *Scorpion* and *Wivern* might have been made. The *King Edward VII* (p193) mounted four 9.2inch guns, not eight. The Japanese *Kongo* (p199) mounted eight, not ten 14inch guns.

This is a readable book, and the accounts of naval actions seem acceptable, making it even more of a pity that the author accepted the conventional view of technical development and selected his facts to fit this theory. A popular book does not require deep scholarship but it can and should avoid bias and factual error. **David K Brown**

---

[1] Seven screw frigates were ordered before the *Alecto* v. *Rattler* trials (see *Warship* No 1).

Warship Photograph Service

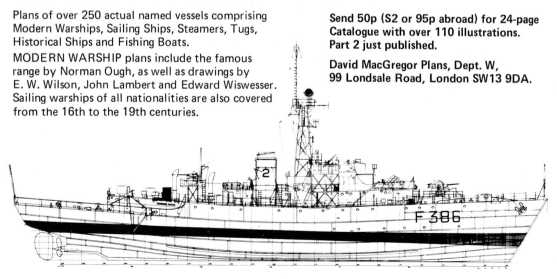

WILLIAM HOVGAARD'S
MODERN HISTORY OF
WARSHIPS

"There are all too few books about modern warships written by naval architects, and so the reappearance of Hovgaard's **Modern History of Warships** is an important event. His unique range of experience was gained at a time when warship design progressed farther and faster than ever before; writing as he did in 1920, Hovgaard was able to describe the hectic pace of development which had culminated in World War 1."

So wrote Anthony Preston in 1971 when we reprinted this standard reference work. However, even the reprint has been out of print for some time and the original is virtually unobtainable, so we have decided to produce a new, but strictly limited edition, distinguished by this handsome dust jacket (right).

The edition will be ready in February 1978 at £12.50, but because it is limited we are taking advance orders now. Do not send payment - just your name and address, or clip the coupon below. You will be invoiced on publication.

WILLIAM HOVGAARD'S
MODERN HISTORY OF
WARSHIPS

NEW BOOKS

CONWAY MARITIME

New Naval Titles

Editorial

This sixth issue of *Warship* manages to ring the changes yet again, going from dreadnoughts to nuclear ships. Nobody who saw the missile cruiser USS *California* at the Queen's Silver Jubilee Review of the Fleet last June could doubt that she is a most formidable fighting ship, and John Jordan has contributed one of his excellent drawings to illustrate his description of the ship. It is interesting to note that the arrival of this big nuclear-powered surface warship caused virtually no stir among the environmental lobby, whereas in many other countries the merest mention of a visit would be the signal for uproar.

Without taking too political a stance on the subject, it seems to me that the threat posed to the environment by a nuclear cruiser is slight, compared to a super-tanker like the *Torrey Canyon*. The danger of radiation is dealt with by heavy shielding and in any case the very nature of the reactor calls for much heavier construction than is found in merchant ships.

From modern ships to a navy which vanished from the scene 60 years ago: those who like dreadnought battleships will be more than pleased to see Friedrich Prasky's magnificent drawings of the *Viribus Unitis*. He has also provided a description and photographs to explain the significance of the drawings. Those who read the late Mr Scheltema de Heere's treatise on these ships in *Warship International* will

appreciate the problems faced by their designers, the political and material difficulties. To judge by her contemporaries in other navies the *Viribus Unitis* was something of a quart packed into a pint pot, and too much was attempted on the displacement, but she was a most interesting ship which combined good looks with an impressive armament.

Three features are carried over from Issue No 5, Lawrence Sowinski's description of the modifications to the *Essex* class carriers, John Roberts' article on the battlecruiser HMS *Tiger,* and Part 2 of John Campbell's detailed account of the Battle of Tsushima. In response to requests from readers of the same author's feature on the *G3* class in earlier issues we asked him to contribute a Technical Topic on cordite. Here at last is a technical explanation of what went wrong with British propellant at Jutland, and how it was corrected. It also provides incidentally an explanation of the method of grading cordite.

Norman Friedman compares British and American radar under the heading of cruiser electronics. It is often forgotten that cruisers are in some ways the best ships to examine for a wide range of fittings; their size, intermediate between battleships and destroyers, meant that they carried surface and AA equipment common to both types. Tom Burton's feature on the British air-laid magnetic mine sheds useful light on the subject, and

taken in conjunction with his earlier feature on the M-sinker, shows that the German Navy's 'secret weapon' of World War II was by no means a total surprise to the RN in September 1939.

John Lambert has provided a feature on the British Type 15 frigates, with one of his first-class drawings of HMS *Rapid*. When she first appeared in 1951 she was hailed as the first 'atom age' warship, but her profile, apparently devoid of armament, evoked nothing but dismay among ship-enthusiasts. Time would show, however, that the Type 15 programme was one of the best measures taken by the Royal Navy to modernise the fleet; the last of the class has only recently been scrapped after a total of more than 30 years' service. They were fast and well-armed for anti-submarine warfare, and what guns they had were provided with adequate fire-control, whereas in their original configuration as destroyers they were quite useless for modern warfare.

The Warship Pictorial for this issue is a brief selection of some of the photographs chosen for the new Conway Maritime Press book *Camera at Sea*. As the captions were provided by some familiar contributors to *Warship* modesty (and space) forbid any detailed description, but it can safely be said that the rest of the photographs in the book are to the same standard.

Antony Preston

5271-45
PLAN VIEW AMIDSHIPS, LOOKING AFT.   (CA-35).
MARE ISLAND, CAL.   12 JULY 1945.

Cruiser Electronics

by Norman Friedman

Norman Friedman is employed in strategic research, which requires familiarity with a wide range of technical developments. His book on US battleships is due for publication later this year, and he is currently working on a volume about naval radar.

USS *Indianapolis* as after her last refit, 12 July 1945 at Mare Island. *Indianapolis* makes an interesting comparison with her near-sister *Louisville.* Her ECM suite is on her foremast, while aft are mounted the big SK air search radar and HF/DF. The small trellis yard, unoccupied in *Louisville,* shows a pair of radar D/F radomes for ECM. Below the HF/DF antenna is an upward-looking ('zenith-search') antenna designed to fill in the blind arc directly over the ship. The foremast shows SG, with the two new IR beacons beside it, and TDY at the foretop (TDY-1a radome just forward of the fore 8inch director). An ECM intercept antenna, resembling a sector of a spoked wheel, is visible just above the forward 5inch director. Note that the starboard catapult has been removed; a spare TDY-1a is bolted down on the deckhouse roof just forward of the break of the forecastle.

USN

In many ways the electronic suit of a modern warship reflects her mission. For example, a comparison of US and British cruiser electronic suits of World War Two suggests differences in the two navies' concepts of cruiser employment, as well as in their approach to electronic technology. This difference however, is filtered through a difference in level of radar sophistication due largely to the fact that Britain had to make the transition from experimental to production systems at a far earlier stage in radar evolution. The size of the US electronic industry may also account for the more rapid evolution of the sets installed in US warships, although there is good evidence that British radar designers were quite as sophisticated as their US counterparts — indeed, the two allies freely exchanged radar information in wartime.

The basic line of radar, and indeed of radio evolution, has been towards shorter and shorter wavelengths, ie, higher and higher frequencies. The shorter the wavelength, the narrower the beam an antenna of fixed size can form. In addition, a narrow beam can 'see' at angles closer to the horizon, since it will suffer less from reflections back from the sea surface. On the other hand, somewhat long wavelength radars (1.5 meters or more) actually benefit from sea reflection to form broader beams (in elevation) to

1

2

7768-42
PLAN VIEW, AFT
MARE ISLAND, CAL. DECEMBER 14, 1942

(CA29)

3

USS *Chicago* (CA 29, December 1942) shows US first-generation systems: the mattress air search set, CXAM on her foremast, and the MK 4 AA gunnery set on her two 5inch directors, fore and aft. In addition she has the Mk 3 main battery gunnery set (one on foretop, one aft on a bracket just above 'X' turret). The next generation is visible in the form of the SG centimetric (10 cm) surface-search set, bracket to the foremast between foretop and 8 inch range-finder. The detail view of her after section shows clearly the difference between the Mk 3 and Mk 4 sets: in effect Mk 3 was the two sections joined horizontally, whereas in Mk 4 they were stacked vertically. In each case switching was used to improve accuracy. In comparison to the British cruisers, note the absence of light AA control radar. The position of SG close to the bridge reflects the centimeter waveguide problem.

USN

HMS *Mauritius* (1942) shows a combination of the first and second periods of British radar development. Her two masts carry the two aerials of her 279 air warning set, distinguishable from the later 281 by its larger dimensions (longer wavelength). The main-battery director forward carries gunnery radar (284): note the *second*, shorter, bar-like aerial on its lower surface. Also in this series was 285, for secondary battery control, an example of which is clearly visible atop the secondary director aft (fishbone-like aerial). Two more would have topped the two forward secondary directors, but they are not clearly visible. The next (centimetric) generation of radars is visible in the Type 273 lantern forward of the bridge, its position determined by the need to keep its waveguides (to the radar office) short. Note that this implied a rather restricted field of view.

MOD by courtesy of Alan Raven

sweep out large volumes of sky. Thus most World War Two naval air search radars operated at long wavelengths, and were correspondingly rather large, whereas it was the advent of 'centimeter-wave' systems (about 9 cm at first; later in the war 3 cm sets were introduced) which made surface search practical. Naturally, shorter wavelengths made fire control systems more effective through their better definition.

Radar began at the upper edge of frequencies achievable at substantial power, since higher frequencies/shorter wavelengths were always desirable. The British, who needed radar more desperately, chose the best they could get at the earliest date: 7 then 3.5 meters. This choice is reflected in the size and poor resolution of the RN air warning sets. The Americans, who could afford to wait to perfect something more ideal, achieved high power at 1.5 meters, and thus managed a narrow beam as well. In radio, higher frequency meant both better information transmission and line-of-sight signals undetectable by an enemy well over the horizon: communications followed radar into higher frequencies. For example, the famous US tactical voice set TBS (often termed 'talk between ships') operated at about 4 meters.

There is one other element of radar evolution which must be recognized here: the 'T-R Box' or duplexer, which allowed the same antenna to transmit and receive. The problem it solves is that a receiver unsensitive to a strong outgoing pulse must yet respond to an echo millions or billions of times weaker. The United States was particularly fortunate in that its radar development team, at the Naval Research Laboratory, succeeded in producing an effective TR box quite early, so that all US seaborne radars used a single antenna. The RN was not so fortunate.

Wavelength (in the reflected *size* of an antenna, measured in wavelengths, which produces a beam of fixed width) and the duplexer are only the *visible* manifestations of radar development, but of course the story is much richer than that. For example, there are the power supplies, development of which permitted far greater detection ranges; display devices such as the PPI (plan-position indicator, the familiar radar 'map'); and there are subtleties of signal-processing to permit a relatively diffuse beam to measure angles very accurately. Typically the latter involves the use of two or more beams at a small angle to each other; the radar switches rapidly from one to the other. When it is pointed directly at the target, the two beams produce equal reflections. Possibly the most visible example of this technique was the US fire control radar commonly used to direct 5inch AA fire: this set's antenna *looks* like two antennas stacked vertically, and that is just what it is. A more subtle example was the US SP 'fighter control' radar, in which the dish antenna spun to produce a slightly off-center beam; in effect this amounted to continuous switching among an infinite series of beams, all at slightly different angles.

In retrospect it seems remarkable that nearly all of the major ideas in radar development were represented by operational sets — many of them naval — by the end of World War Two. The comments above merely suggest the variety of avenues explored in wartime development. From an observer's point of view, the fast pace of radar evolution between 1937 and 1945 meant that sets of radically different appearance often had identical functions. Moreover, in the Royal Navy, unlike the US Navy, sets of apparently obsolete design often remained in service long after their successors had been introduced; this was in large part a consequence of the small size of the British electronics industry, and of the magnitude of its non-naval commitments. For example, many postwar photographs of Royal Navy cruisers show them with radar outfits of 1942 vintage.

Warship electronics may be divided either functionally (surface/air search, fire control, underwater detection, communications) or by type (active, passive, ie, putting out a signal or merely waiting for one to materialize). Long before World War Two, warship electronics consisted of radios for tactical and long-range communication; radio direction finders for both navigation and for the detection of enemy units foolish enough to transmit; and sonar (British ASDIC). At this time the most obvious difference between American and British cruiser electronics was that the Royal Navy fitted asdic. The justification lay in solitary cruiser employment, when a cruiser might find it essential to avoid an enemy submarine upon which it chanced. The US Navy fitted some of its earliest sonars to cruisers, but soon concluded that such units would be unable to make good use of the sets. They would rarely work alone, and even more rarely would they operate at speeds suitable for sonar detection. The sole wartime exception to this policy was the fitting of sonar sets to *Atlanta* class anti-aircraft cruisers. This installation was the subject of some considerable wartime debate;

apparently only once did an *Atlanta* detect an enemy submarine and so cause a Task Force to take evasive action. Wartime proposals to fit other cruisers with sonar foundered on the low probability of use and the inability of the sonar to produce good results at Task Force speeds.

After the war the US Navy experimented with torpedo-detection sonars, some of them intended for linkage to torpedo countermeasures, such as anti-torpedo mortars; but this entire program proved abortive. Sonars did not appear aboard American cruisers until the 'sixties, when a combination of the long range SQS 23 and ASROC or DASH was fitted to the missile cruisers. By then fast submarines were a serious threat to the fast Task Forces these cruisers screened. In addition, the very open formations adopted to reduce the likely damage due to a nuclear attack made it more important that *all* screening ships be sonar-equipped. It is possible that the introduction of the Naval Tactical Data System (NTDS), which permitted automatic exchange of data within a Task Force, made cruiser sonars useful even when the ships carrying them had few or no long-range ASW weapons: thus the program to backfit SQS 23 to the two *Bostons* and to the *Cleveland* class missile conversions. By way of contrast, the three *Chicagos* were completed with ASROC and SQS 23.

As for direction-finding, the major wartime development was its extension to high frequencies (HF/DF), which proved extremely important in the Battle of the Atlantic. U-boats' tactics required considerable signalling, and direction-finder-equipped escorts could often run down surfaced U-boats trying to use their radios. HF/DF was relatively rare in wartime US cruisers, although at least one, USS *Indianapolis,* had an extensive installation. On the other hand, many British cruisers were so fitted, often carrying their HF/DF antennas on stub masts (since *both* topmasts were required for the air search radar).

Radar first appeared in the Royal and US Navies as an aircraft

1 HMS *Gambia,* seen on 27 November 1943, reveals the successful solution of the centimetric waveguide problem: her new 272, in a squatter 'lantern' (as it needed only one antenna rather than the two, stacked vertically, of 273 — the T-R box problem had been solved) was mounted on her foremast, with a far better field of view. The solution to the T-R box problem also shows in the elimination of the lower aerial on her 284, forward. However, note that she still requires two antennas for her air search set, which is now the shorter wave (hence more compact) 281 (double crossed yards just visible on her topmasts). The position before the bridge vacated by the surface search set is filled, here, by a pair of 283 barrage directors (auxiliary sets to permit use of the main battery in AA fire). There was no US equivalent to 283: the US Navy tended to consider its main batteries useless for AA fire. A similar pair of directors was set aft. Not clearly visible are the 282 sets, very similar to 283, mounted atop the 2pdr directors. Both types operated in the same frequency band as the larger gunnery sets; their ill-defined beams were useful mainly for range-finding.

MOD by courtesy of Alan Raven

1

2

USS *Louisville* as refitted, at Mare Island, 10 April 1945. The circles show new modifications. The new Mk 8 Mod 3 (similar to Mk 13) main battery fire control radar, which replaced the earlier Mk 8 'comb' is mounted atop the heavy tripod foremast. On the 5inch director atop the bridge can be seen (at left) a Mk 28 microwave dish, which for the older directors had to stand-in for the heavier Mk 12/22. On the topmast, the small SG surface-search set is flanked by a pair of infra-red beacons (X 2A). From left to right, the foremast yard carries BK antenna (IFF transponder), a TBS antenna; and, on the other side, a VHF antenna and a BN interrogator. Similar antennas are mounted on the mainmast yard. Note the elimination of the starboard catapult.

The mainmast is devoted to jammers (TDY on the topmast, and the fat radome of the centimetric TDY-1a visible just above the cap of the second funnel) and to an SP fighter-control radar.

USN

1

3

2

1 HMS *Swiftsure* (27 November 1944) shows the effects of the widespread introduction of microwave (10 and 3 cm) radars, and of the success of the T-R box (note that now she requires only a single air warning aerial, on the main mast, with IFF interrogator above). She has the new cm main-battery radar (274) and the new height finding/surface search set, 277 (above and abaft the main battery director); but she does not have the 3 cm successor to the secondary-battery radar (275). Atop her foremast she carries the elevating 'cheese' of 293, here difficult to identify because it is vertical and trained fore-and-aft.

MOD by courtesy of Alan Raven

2 HMCS *Ontario* (1945) shows the completion of the shift towards centimetric radar for everything but air and minor fire control. In contrast to *Swiftsure,* she has the new secondary directors, incorporating the distinctive microwave lenses (one to transmit, one to receive) of Type 275. Unlike her near-sister, she has both barrage and light AA directors at the ends; and additional light AA directors are ranged near forward guns and at the base of the after director. Probably the Royal Navy, like the USN, used such devices to control even heavy AA guns against close-in targets showing very high rates of change of bearing. Note that, of all the long-wave gunnery radars, only 282/283 remains. Type 262, the centimetric replacement for 282, did not appear until after the war; and there was no centimetric successor to 283, perhaps in view of the increased capability of the other systems and the decreased efficacy of heavy guns in the face of high speed aircraft.

MOD by courtesy of Alan Raven

3 HMS *Superb* leads cruisers of the Home Fleet in exercises, November 1946. She shows the ultimate RN cruiser radar rig, except that her air search set (on the mainmast) is the long-wave 279. Note the contrast to the set on the *Dido* just abaft her, which still has separate sending and receiving aerials, but has the shorter-wave 281. In contrast to contemporary US cruisers, *Superb* does not have all of her secondary directors on her centerline, and so requires three (one aft); she has only a single main-battery director, forward.

CPL W/6/001

detector. The British sets (79, 279, 281) enjoyed very low definition: in the developed 281 version, the beam was 45 degrees wide (US CXAM of 1940: 14 degrees). It is no surprise that the Royal Navy thought of its aircraft detection radars as air *warning* sets, whereas the US Navy thought of its narrow-beam systems as air *search* sets. The wide beams of the British systems presented a serious problem if their warning were to be translated into data suitable for gunnery, or probably even for fighter control.

In addition the British sets, as introduced, required separate

transmitting and receiving aerials, the former generally being on the mainmast. It may be that the very wide beams of RN air warning sets were found acceptable at first in view of the difficulty of synchronizing the rotation of the two aerials; many photographs of RN warships with the dual antennas show them aimed in very different directions. The Royal Navy did not receive production TR-boxes for these sets until 1943, and indeed many ships carried dual antennas even after the war.

Meanwhile the Royal Navy produced a series of fire control radars of shorter wavelength, such as the 284 for main battery control. Neither 279 nor 284 had a TR-box at first: in 1940 British cruisers required two co-ordinated masthead antennas for air warning, and two 284 antennas per director. Other fire control systems presented similar problems. However, in many cases (such as the 285 secondary-battery set) the two antennas could be mounted side by side, and so they are not obviously distinct.

US radar technology of this period required only one antenna per set, but was not as yet in very large-scale production. It did have the enormous advantage of search sets well adapted to feed data to gunnery equipment or to fighter controllers, a luxury absent from the Royal Navy. Thus a US cruiser of 1942 shows only a big air search

antenna and a surface fire control set roughly equivalent to 284. Soon there were AA fire control systems, such as the famous Mark 4, as well.

Perhaps the single greatest radar development of the war was the British solution of the centimeter-wave (10 cm) radar problem, the beam of which was so well defined that it could be used for surface search. Such systems were very urgently required for ASW, and they were rushed into production in Britain as 271/272/273, which were mounted inside transparent 'lanterns.' These sets still did not solve the problem of poor definition in the air warning sets, although they themselves had very good definition due to their short wavelength.

However, these centimetric sets had their own problem: at first it was very difficult to conduct their signals any great distance. That is why, in many British warships, the radar office is *directly* below the 271 'lantern' even when both are high on a mast. Early US centimetric sets (SG) were mounted directly above the bridge; the air search sets, whose signals were far easier to transmit, could be mounted on a taller mainmast. The solution to the problem shows in the abandonment of these practices in both navies. By 1944, for example, US cruisers typically mounted one SG on each of their two masts, and a big air search set forward.

This did not solve the problem of the imprecision of the British air warning sets, yet it must have seemed that the narrow beams possible with centimetric radar would provide the answer. That was 293, a 3 cm 'cheese' antenna used to obtain a precise bearing corresponding to a crude 281 or 279 bearing. Note that 293 had no US counterpart; but then the standard American air search set, SK, could distinguish two targets only one degree apart. The 293 'cheese' produced a beam very well-defined in *bearing* but very wide in *elevation*. The latter was essential: 279/281 could not give good indications of the altitude of the targets it detected, since its own beam was broad in elevation. Type 293 elevated to keep its broad beam off the sea and so avoid the reflection problem. It might be imagined that 293 in itself would be a useful air search set; but its range was relatively limited (12.5 nm, vs 120 for 281).

Of course, there were also centimetric equivalents to the earlier fire-control radars: 274, for example, in place of 284. US practice was similar; for example, the Mk 13 main battery set of the late war period operated at 3 cm. It replaced the 10 cm 'comb' of Mk 8, which in turn replaced the 40 cm Mk 3. Since antenna dimensions changed very little, each step down in wavelength was a step *up* in accuracy.

All of the search/warning sets mentioned thus far were useful only to give the range and bearing of an aerial target. However, to guide fighter aircraft into the target required also target altitude, which in practice meant an accurate measurement of the angle from the surface to the target. The US Navy deployed the first such 'pencil-beam' height-finding system, SM, aboard carriers in 1943. By 1945 it was common practice to mount a light-weight set of this type (SP) aboard battleships, cruisers, and even radar-picket destroyers. SP might be said to symbolize the extent to which surface ships were integrated with naval aircraft.

The Royal Navy produced no direct equivalent to SM/SP, but it did deploy a narrow-beam radar, 277, which could be elevated to estimate altitude. It could be set at a fixed angle of elevation and rotated to search the horizon. Type 277 was both lighter and simpler than the US sets, and its narrow beam offered some substantial capability for *surface* search operation: it could replace the earlier radar 'lanterns' aboard many British warships. Thus a British light cruiser in 1945 rig shows the full range of centimetric radar systems: 274, 275 (secondary battery) and 262 (light AA) for gunnery, linked to 281 on the main masthead through 293 on the fore masthead; and 277 forward for surface search and height-finding.

A US cruiser of this time shows air and surface search radars, centimetric gunnery and height-finding (fighter-control) radars. In 1945 US warships were also begining to show specialized *zenith-search* sets pointed *up* to cover the blind cone of air search radars over the ship. The Royal Navy deployed no such set, quite probably considering 277 capable of such a role. However, zenith search radars (SS-6 and AN/SPS-4) were staples of the postwar US fleet.

The British radar suit is far more gun-orientated than is the American; 293 had too short a range to be of much value in fighter direction. An alternative formulation would be that, as with sonar, the British systems make far more sense in the context of a cruiser proceeding *outside* the main fleet, ie, without air cover. In such circumstances warning that some raid was en route would be important, but in view of gun range and the relative speeds of ship and attacking aircraft, more precision at long range would be wasted. Ten or twelve miles was quite good enough for 293: AA fire would have little effect until rather shorter ranges were reached. On the other hand, a cruiser vectoring in her element of the Combat Air Patrol would need precision at far greater ranges. Similar considerations apply to missile operations, which is why direct descendents of the US air search sets (eg, SPS 37) survive, whereas the RN had to give up its 281 series after the postwar 960, and accept the US-style 965 in its place.

Shipboard electronics of course includes far more than radar and sonar; in a note of this length it is impossible, unfortunately to provide any detailed account of IFF, which is absolutely vital to radar systems, or of naval communications. The former is visible as a series of subsidiary antennas, some of them so well integrated with the main radars as to be virtually indistinguishable. As for the latter, suffice it to say here that wartime development involved a vast proliferation of radio sets, including special types for ship-to-air and ship-to- (nearby) shore (for amphibious work). Analysis of standard US and RN radio suits, like radar suits, will reflect differences in strategic and tactical outlook; but that is a separate study.

However, it is necessary to mention, if only briefly, the subject of countermeasures. Here the US fleet, faced with Japanese shore defences, ships, and radar-equipped aircraft, appears to have developed a far wider range of devices than did the Royal Navy, whose European enemies tended not to include many equipped with radar. The extensive countermeasures systems aboard US cruisers in 1945 consisted of search receivers to pick up emissions, direction-finders (DBM), and jamming transmitters (TDY). Japanese radar development, like that in the US and the UK, progressed from metric to centimetric wavelengths. The countermeasures devices followed, an evolution visible in their size which, as in radar antennas, reflected the wavelengths on which they operated.

On the other hand the Royal Navy appears to have been far more concerned with the problem of German radio-guided missiles and glide bombs; it fitted many battleships and cruisers with equipment to jam the *radio* command links of these weapons. Once more, this is a reflection of differing operational circumstances.

USS CALIFORNIA
by John Jordan

Anyone who looked out from Stokes Bay on the fleet assembled for last year's Jubilee Spithead Review could not fail to remember the sight of the twin radar towers of the USS *California* rising high above the masts and superstructures of the slim lines of Royal Navy frigates. From close range the impression of size and power was even more striking, a forceful reminder of the undisputed pre-eminence of the United States in the operation of large carrier task-forces in an age when the navies of Europe, for reasons of economy rather than strategy, no longer feel able to remain 'in the business', and have opted for smaller ships to fulfil their reduced strategic aspirations.

California and her sister ship, the *South Carolina*, were designed in the middle 1960s as escorts for the new generation of nuclear-powered strike carriers. US defence planners had realised at a very early stage that it was of little advantage having a nuclear-powered carrier, capable of practically unlimited high-speed operations, at the centre of a task force in which its escorts were in constant need of refuelling, and which for this reason could only maintain high speed for short periods. Nuclear propulsion was just as vital for the escorts. The late 1950s therefore saw the authorization by Congress of the first all-nuclear task-force, comprising the carrier *Enterprise*

(Fiscal Year 1958), the cruiser *Long Beach* (FY57) and the frigate *Bainbridge* (FY56). These three ships, all completed 1961-2 and later joined by the frigate *Truxtun* (in service 1967), operated together throughout the 1960s, proving their value in prolonged operations off the coast of Vietnam and in political forays into the Indian Ocean in support of US foreign policy.

Meanwhile, in Congress, a considerable battle was taking place between the pro-nuclear lobby responsible for the pressure to build these ships, and those who criticised their enormous cost, arguing that for the same financial outlay twice as many fossil-fuelled ships could be built — *Enterprise* cost about 450 million dollars compared with construction costs of less than 230 millions for the later *John F Kennedy*. For several years the anti-nuclear arguments held sway. Planned sister ships of the *Enterprise* were not funded and the only two large carriers completed during this period were the two *America* class ships, which had conventional propulsion. Nevertheless counter-arguments in favour of nuclear power, including lower maintenance costs, less vulnerability to action damage to the propulsion plant because of the absence of boiler

uptakes, and easier 'close-down' in the event of radioactive fall-out, continued to be put forward and eventually won the day.

The result was the authorization of the CVAN *Nimitz* in 1967, together with two frigates (DLGN reclassified as CGN 30 June 1975); *California* in the same year and *South Carolina* in 1968. All three were in service by mid-1975.

The endurance of a task force made up from any combination of these three ships is such that it would be capable of sailing around the world about twenty-five times without refuelling. In the *California*

class this is made possible by a propulsion plant which consists of two geared turbines powered by two pressurised water-cooled DG2 reactors manufactured by General Electric. Two shafts drive the ship at a maximum speed estimated at between 30 and 35 knots.

Both *California* and her sister-ship were built by the Newport News Shipbuilding and Dry Dock Company, now the only yard in the USA capable of building nuclear-powered surface ships. Indeed, such is the technological complexity of these ships that the *Virginia* class cruisers which followed them on to

The general views of *California* used in this article were taken at last year's Jubilee Review, and were kindly supplied by C & S Taylor.

the slips are all at least a year behind schedule owing to an acute shortage of skilled labour. A further indication of their complexity is their cost — 200 million dollars for *California*, 180 millions for her sister.

ARMAMENT

For ships of their size they could hardly be described as over-armed. Indeed from any sort of distance it is difficult to pick out their diminutive guns and launchers. The Mk 13 launcher was originally designed to enable surface-to-air missiles to be launched by much smaller DDGs and DEGs (now FFGs). The Mk 45 5inch gun was also designed as a lightweight mounting and has a remarkably small turret for a 54 cal gun. One Mk13 launcher and one Mk 45 gun are mounted forward with a similar pairing aft. The armament is completed by an Asroc launcher sited just forward of the bridge. All of these weapons except the after 5inch gun are mounted on the Upper Deck, with the magazines inside the hull of the ship. This makes for easier and safer loading arrangements, and the distance of the two SAM launchers from the ship's super-structure gives them excellent arcs.

The missile at present fired from the Mk 13 launcher is the Standard SM-1, an improved version of the original Standard MR missile which besides having double the range of its predecessor (40km approx.) has a horizon-limited surface-to-surface capability. The Standard was the first US missile to have exclusively solid-state all-electric controls — previously these were pneumatic or hydraulically-powered and consequently more prone to failure — and has a dry-storage battery which ensures a reliable power supply even after the missile has been stored for a long period. The SM-1 is comparatively small with a length of only 4.57m — about two thirds that of Soviet missiles of comparable range. This enables 40 missiles to be carried in each of the two magazines.

The Mk 45 5inch gun is a new model delivered to the US Navy in 1974. It was designed to embody improvements over previous models made possible by the latest technology while at the same time being simple, reliable and easy to maintain. This entailed the sacrifice of some of the performance of the Mk 42 mounting which preceded it; upper elevation has been reduced from 85 to 65 degrees, rate of fire from 45 rounds per minute to 20, and the number of ready-service rounds from 40 to 20. The Mk 42, however, had come under heavy criticism following frequent break-downs during fire-support operations off the coast of Vietnam, and it was no doubt thought that a less complex mounting would give greater reliability. Moreover, the Mk 45 has brought other even more significant gains. Its designers have achieved a remarkable reduction in the weight of the mounting from 60 to 25 tons, and a crew reduction from 14 to 6 with none in the turret. The ready-service drum can be fired off by a single man in the gun control centre.

The Asroc launcher is of the standard eight-cell, box-shaped variety. The 4.6m missile — introduced into the US Navy in 1961 — carries alternative payloads of an acoustic homing torpedo (the Mk

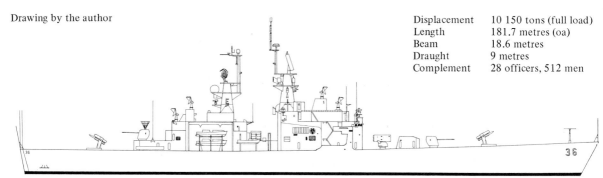

Drawing by the author

Displacement	10 150 tons (full load)
Length	181.7 metres (oa)
Beam	18.6 metres
Draught	9 metres
Complement	28 officers, 512 men

46) or a nuclear depth-charge out to a distance of up to 11km. The large SQS 26CX bow sonar feeds data into a computer which then determines the missile launch angles. After shedding its solid-fuel booster the missile follows a ballistic trajectory to a pre-determined distance from the predicted target position. The torpedo is then parachuted to the surface or the depth-charge dropped into the sea. *California* benefits from a much quicker and simpler method of reloading compared to other ships with the Mk 112 launcher. Missiles are hoisted up from the magazine into the prominent housing forward of the launcher. The launcher is then trained aft and elevated to an angle of about 30 degrees, in which position it is reloaded through the rear doors of the cells.

ELECTRONICS

However, it is not so much these few rather diminutive guns and launchers that constitute the defensive power of the *California* as the remarkable range of electronics provided for the detection and interception of enemy contacts. External evidence of this can be seen in those two massive radar towers with the antennae stepped one above the other.

There are two Mk 74 Missile Fire Control Systems, each comprising two SPG 51D tracker/illuminators with associated computers and control consoles. One pair of trackers is sited on the bridge structure with a further pair on the after super-structure. Initial pointing information is supplied by the large planar SPS 48A three-dimensional radar mounted on the fore-top. This information is received by a computer which then generates a search-pattern for the trackers until acquisition is accomplished. Tracking is then automatic and each SPG 51 radar provides the illumination of the target necessary for the semi-

2

3

4

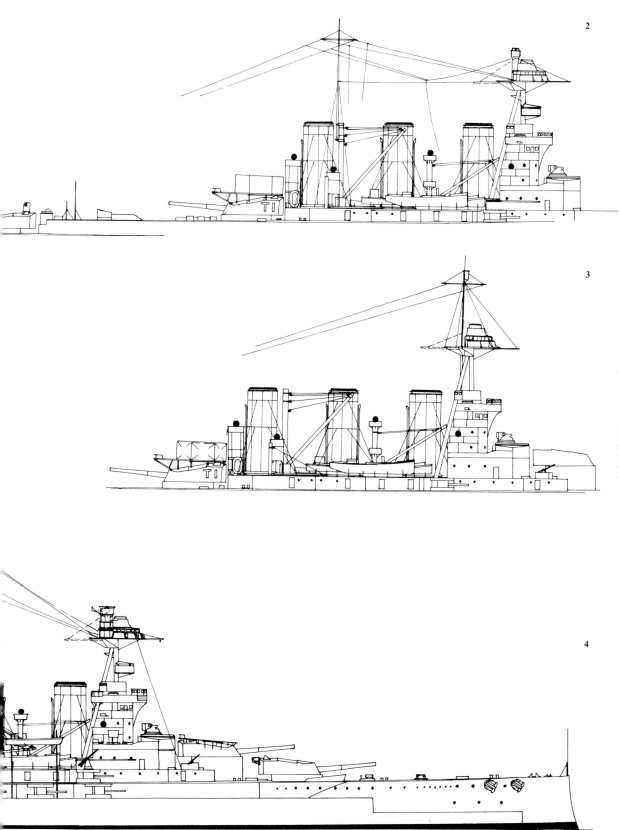

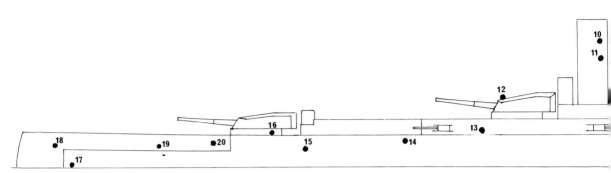

Diagram showing hits on *Tiger* during the
Battle of Jutland (based on drawing in
'The Fighting at Jutland' by Fawcette and
Hooper 1921).
Key:-   S = starboard side
        P = port side

1 5.9inch (P).
2 11inch (P) hit starboard cable holder
penetrated forecastle and detonated in
cable locker flat.
3 Two 11inch (P) burst in sick bay.
4 11inch (P) burst between forecastle and
upper decks causing local damage.
5 12inch (P) hit and cracked A barbette
armour between forecastle and upper
decks.
6 11inch (P) penetrated 5 inch armour
and burst in flour store.
7 11inch (P) hit steaming light, did not
detonate.

8 11inch (P) bounced off without
detonating.
9, 10 and 11 11inch (P) passed through
funnels without detonating.
12 11inch hit roof on Q turret and burst
on centre sighting hood blowing hole in
roof. Killed 3 and wounded several of
gun's crew. Turret temporarily out of
action.
13 11inch (P) penetrated 6inch armour,
upper deck and lower deck and detonated
in ammunition passage over engine room
killing 12 men. Base of shell went through
to engine room and caused minor
damage. Ready use 6inch cordite in
passage caught fire and filled passage and
engine room with dense smoke but speed
not affected.
14 and 15 Two 11inch (P) hit 9inch
armour but did not penetrate. Armour
pushed in about 3inches.

16 11inch (P) penetrated 9inch barbette
armour of Y turret at lower edge level
with upper deck and ended up in centre
of mounting without detonating. Centre
sight setter killed, turret temporarily out
of action.
17 5.9inch (P).
18, 19 and 20 5.9inch (S).
21 12inch (S) detonated on forecastle
deck causing local damage to boats and
structure.

Tiger as completed.

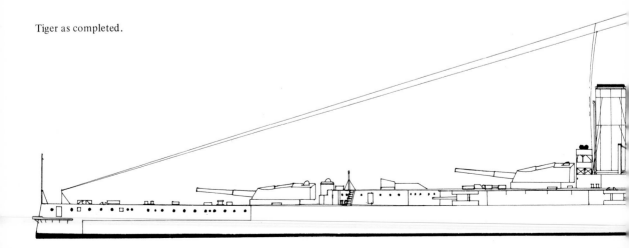

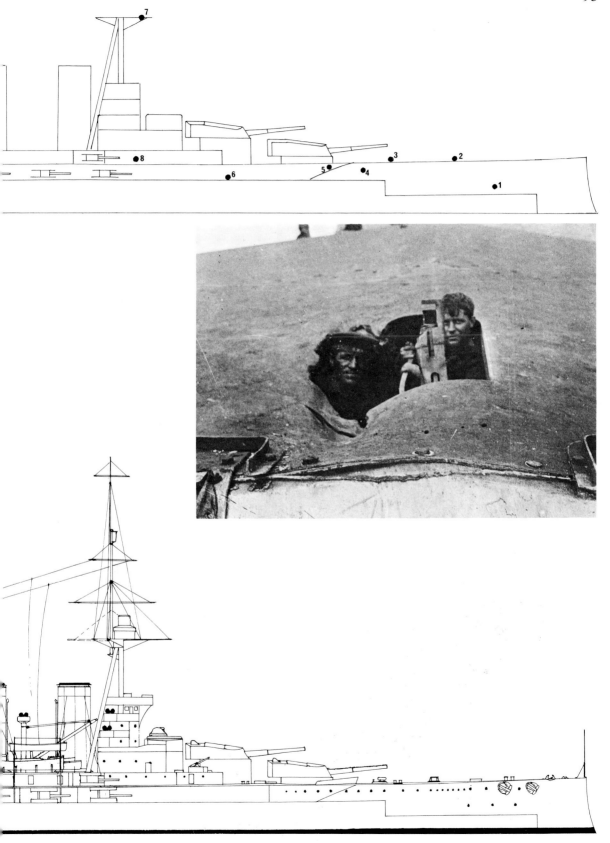

1
2

WAR MODIFICATIONS

After Jutland additional 1inch protective plating was bolted to the existing deck plating around the barbettes to improve the magazine protection. The plating, which totalled 179 tons in weight, was distributed around 'A', 'B' and 'Q' barbettes on the forecastle deck, around 'Y' barbette on the upper deck and around all barbettes on the lower deck. The thicknesses of these decks in those areas then became $2\frac{1}{2}$ in, $2\frac{1}{2}$ in and 2 in respectively. Other plating was worked in as follows:

a 1 in plating bolted to turret roofs; added weight 77 tons.

b Additional protective plating to engine rooms (position not known); weight 24 tons.

c Additional bulkheads fitted in 6inch gun battery; weight 15 tons.

d 1 in plating added to $1\frac{1}{2}$ in screen bulkheads abreast magazines.

Other alterations are shown in the appearance sketches. It was estimated in 1920 that 400 tons had been added to the ship during the war. After 1918 the coal bunkers were modified to reduce the coal stowage to 2660 tons and orders were given that the total fuel carried should not exceed 4900 tons.

POST-WAR SERVICE

From 1919 to 1922 the *Tiger* served in the Battle Cruiser Squadron of the Atlantic Fleet. Between May 1922 and February 1924 she was refitted for service as a sea going gunnery training ship. She was also intended for use as a trials vessel for new gunnery equipment and was fitted with 4 4inch AA guns and an experimental HA control system. Her boilers were modified to burn oil only and fuel stowage was rearranged to provide a capacity of 3394 tons oil and 200 tons coal. Her standard displacement after refit was 28 880 tons and her deep displacement 33 220 tons. She served as a trials and training ship until 1929 during which time she was used to test various items of new gunnery

1 The *Tiger* at Rosyth in 1918 with a US
battleship in the background.

2 *Tiger* immediately after her major refit in
1924. Note the 4inch HA guns and main
director at after end of forecastle deck.

3 Amidships close-up of *Tiger* in 1928.

control equipment. In 1929 she
replaced *Hood* in the Battle cruiser
squadron and was finally paid off
in April 1931 at Devonport. She
was sold for scrap in March 1932
under the terms of the Washington
Treaty.

CONCLUSIONS
Previously published technical
descriptions of the *Tiger* generally
ascribe to her qualities much
beyond her actual value and the
impression given is that she was a
vast improvement over the previous
13.5inch gun battlecruisers. The
actual improvements were:—
a an increase in the depth of side
protection

b an increase in speed
c improved arc of fire for 'Q' turret
d the provision of a 6inch gun
secondary battery.
 The majority of these are
improvements in offensive power
and even the increased depth of side
protection were due mainly to the
decision to fit 6inch guns. Although
these items represent a substantial
advance on the *Queen Mary* design
the *Tiger* retained the basic hull
form and compartmentation of the
earlier ship and in particular the
same armour distribution. Her deck
protection was very weak and the
heaviest of the side armour
protected the machinery
compartments, leaving the

magazines (except for 'Q'
mounting) protected by 6inch
armour only. The 6inch battery
armour improved the protection
amidships but many vulnerable
areas were still open to attack; 'Y'
mounting in particular was just as
vulnerable as in the earlier ships.
Despite all this, however, the *Tiger*
was easily the best of the British
battlecruisers with the exception of
HMS *Hood*.

Champions of the

This close-up of *Randolph* (CV-15) clearly shows two of her outboard quad 40s with the extended flag bridge directly above them.

Pacific The Essex class carriers
by Lawrence Sowinski

INTRODUCTION OF THE LONG BOW

In the Atlantic theatre Quincy completed the ninth *Essex* class carrier on 15 April 1944. *Hancock* (CV-19) was the first long bow *Essex*. She included a number of additional firsts which were worked into her before she was completed. These included: the extended and enlarged flag bridge, two quad 40mm on the fantail, two quads on the lengthened fo'csle and two more mounts on a hangar level platform, on the same site as the former catapult extension on the port side. No starboard quarter quads were installed inboard, nor was the hangar cat fitted; instead, two flight deck catapults were carried. *Hancock's* SK was sitted abaft the topmast and no mainmast was carried. She was dazzle camouflaged in Design 3A (same as CV-12), except that she wore Ms 32 colors of light gray, ocean gray and dull black. *Hancock* was the only long bow unit in Design 3A.

Down at Norfolk, *Franklin* was being modernized before she headed for the Pacific. This included removal of the hangar catapult, the island's foremost quad 40mm, and extension of the flag bridge. A unique change was made in *Franklin's* dazzle pattern; only her port side 6A design was repainted into the simpler 3A design, but with the same colors, while the starboard pattern (6A) remained the same! This has caused some *Franklin* pictures to be miscaptioned as *Intrepid*.

While repairs were being made at San Francisco *Intrepid* was modernized and dazzle-painted in Design 3A. The SK bedspring was moved for a second time, up to the radar platform, abaft the topmast. The hangar catapult was removed and a second cat was added to the flight deck. Two quad 40mm in front of the flag bridge was were removed and the bridge was extended forward. Since *Intrepid* had no need to transit the Panama canal five outboard quad 40mm were added, two off the port quarter and three just under the island's starboard side. When *Intrepid* departed for Pearl Harbor, she wore the same dazzle camouflage design and colors as *Hancock* and *Franklin* (port side only). However, *Intrepid* now presented a unique appearance, since she was the only Design 3A ship to carry any outboard 40mm guns. Only *Intrepid* and later *Yorktown,* carried the very distinctive outboard quads while in dazzle camouflage. They were easy to tell apart since each carried noticeably different pattern designs.

Twenty-three days after *Hancock* commissioned up at Boston, *Ticonderoga* (CV-14) was completed down at Newport News, on 8 May 1944. While she was the tenth *Essex* out of the yards, she was only the second long bow unit to enter service. Structurally, CV-14 was nearly identical to *Hancock,* but her camouflage design made her noticeably different. *Ticonderoga* was the third *Essex* (after CV-10 and 18) to be painted in Design 10A with Ms 33 colors; and was easily recognizable from the two short-hull *Essexes;* she was also the last *Essex* to be completed with an SK bedspring antenna.

Larry Sowinski is a New York modelmaker whose search for accurate information on camouflage drove him to produce a number of fine booklets on the subject — the latest being devoted to carriers. His knowledge of the US photo archives is unsurpassed, and he was largely responsible for the US sections of 'Camera at Sea 1939-1945' (Conway Maritime Press) published this month.

On the West Coast, *Intrepid* departed for Pearl Harbor and two months of training and carrier qualifications. While there, the forward starboard quarter quad was extended outboard for a clearer field of fire; a yard was added to the topmast, and wind and spray deflectors were added to the forward bridges.

After the Battle of the Philippine Sea in June 1944 *Yorktown* steamed for Puget Sound and a much needed overhaul.

The Brooklyn Navy Yard commissioned its first *Essex* class carrier on 6 August 1944; *Bennington* (CV-20) was the 11th unit of the class. She was the first short-bow to complete with those modifications being worked in the early units as they were refitted (and as incorporated into *Hancock* and *Ticonderoga*). *Bennington* was also the first unit to carry an SK-2 dish antenna, outboard off the starboard side of the funnel, and she introduced a new dazzle camouflage, Design 17A. This new pattern design used six colors; designated Ms 32, it used pale gray, light gray, haze gray, ocean gray, navy blue and dull black.

1

1 The long bow *Hancock* (CV-19) with the same dazzle (Design 3A) on her port side as *Intrepid, Franklin* and *Hornet.*

2 *Bennington* (CV-20) in the Atlantic in her six colour dazzle, Design 17A.

On 19 September 1944, Norfolk Navy Yard completed its first *Essex,* the *Shangri La* (CV-38), a long-bow unit and the 12th ship of the class. She introduced the SK-2 dish to the long-bow units, but otherwise was structurally the same as *Hancock* and *Ticonderoga.* Since she wore the same camouflage design (10A) as *Ticonderoga,* the only way to tell them apart was by the different shapes of their SK antennae.

On the Pacific Coast, *Yorktown* completed her overhaul at Puget Sound in September 1944. Still in Design 10A, she was the only dazzle-painted *Essex* to carry all of the outboard quad 40mm *and* two quads on the fantail *(Intrepid* carried only a single fantail quad). *Yorktown's* hangar catapult was removed and two quads were installed on the former catapult platform. A second cat was added to the flight deck and the flag bridge was extended forward. A number of new modifications were also made to *Yorktown,* her SK bedspring was moved from the radar platform to outboard of the funnel, but on the funnel's port

side. *Yorktown* was the only *Essex* with this unusual SK arrangement; CV-10's SC-2 was on a raised lattice mast outboard on the funnel's starboard side. Three of the five radio masts were removed, leaving only the two foremost masts, and a number of whip antennas were installed on the starboard quarter. This radio mast arrangement was to become standard on most of the *Essexes* as they were overhauled.

Randolph (CV-15) was completed by Newport News on 9 October 1944. She was this company's seventh *Essex* class carrier, and two more were still under construction. The long-bow *Randolph* was the 13th *Essex* to be completed, and like *Bennington,* she was also painted up into dazzle Design 17A's six-color patterns. However, her long bow made *Randolph* readily distinguishable, as she incorporated all those features found in *Shangri La.*

After a review of ship camouflage in the Pacific, Design 17A was redrawn to incorporate some new thinking. Thus, *Bon Homme Richard* (CV-31) completed in Design 17A's new three-color patterns. She was commissioned at Brooklyn Navy Yard on 26 November 1944, as the 14th *Essex* class carrier. She was the last short-bow unit to be completed.

Meanwhile, *Bennington* left New York on 12 December 1944, heading for the Pacific. Just before

her departure, she was repainted into Design 17A's three-color pattern and was now very similar t Bon Homme Richard.

Combat reports began to come through about the devastating toll being taken by Japan's desperation weapon, the *kamikaze.* The implications were that suicide plane were singling out carriers with high contrast dazzle patterns. *Kamikaze* tended to come in at high angles, whereas the dazzle-schemes were designed to confuse low-level torpedo bombers. Ms 21 was the b scheme against high angle attackers but this was actually illusory, since the carrier's wake removed any hope of concealment or deception. Carrier men disliked Ms 21 because it was too dark and made a ship much more visible at a greater distance, but despite its continued dislike, Ms 21 was used by the majority of the *Essex* class in the Pacific. Ms 12, a discontinued scheme, was reintroduced in a modified form as a more acceptab compromise between very light schemes, high-contrast patterns and dark paints.

THE LAST YEAR OF THE WAI
Randolph was off the Pacific coast by January 1945. Because of the *kamikaze* threat, she was overhauled at San Francisco and had all seven of the outboard quad 40mm added. Her dazzle design was painted over with Ms 21.

The battered *Intrepid,* with two

kamikaze hits off Leyte, was also at San Francisco, being repaired and repainted in Ms 12. Damaged *Franklin* and exhausted *Bunker Hill* were both being repaired and refitted up at Puget Sound. The *Essex, Lexington* and *Hancock* had also been damaged by *kamikazes* during the Philippine campaign, but all three were repaired at the Ulithi fleet anchorage.

Bennington was hustled out of Pearl Harbor without the benefit of a new paint job or any outboard quad 40mm. Evidently, she was desperately needed to replace the three carriers sent to the West Coast for repairs and refits. The new *Ticonderoga* and refitted *Yorktown* had also just joined the carrier task force at Ulithi.

Meanwhile, Puget Sound got to work on *Franklin* and *Bunker Hill.* Both had their dazzle-schemes painted over with Ms 21, and both received all the outboard quads, and two quad mounts on the fantail and former catapult platform. *Bunker Hill's* flag bridge was extended and hangar cat removed, and both now carried only two radio masts. Whereas *Bunker Hill* retained her original SK, *Franklin* received the new SK-2, fitted outboard of the starboard funnel.

At San Francisco, *Intrepid,* now in Ms 12, had her after starboard quarter inboard quad extended outboard, to match the other four mounts, while two quads were now carried on the fantail. Her four radio masts and SK antenna were left unchanged.

Back in the Atlantic, the Philadelphia Navy Yard completed its first *Essex,* the *Antietam* (CV-36) on 28 January 1945. She was very similar to *Shangri La* and *Randolph,* and the long-bow CV-36 was the fifteenth *Essex* to be completed.

The US Pacific Fleet continued pounding away at Japan's vitals, despite continuous *kamikaze* attacks. *Ticonderoga* was hit by two of them and limped back to the US West Coast (22 January 1945). During February *Intrepid, Franklin* and *Bunker Hill* all rejoined the fleet, but all three soon became casualties again. However, with the return of the three carriers, *Lexington* was released for an overhaul at Puget Sound.

On 11 March 1945, *Randolph* was hit by a *kamikaze* while at anchor in Ulithi lagoon. Her Ms 21 paint did not help much, especially in view of the fact that there were several dazzled *Essexes* nearby. A repair ship took care of the damage without *Randolph* having to move from her anchorage. Just 50 miles off the coast of Japan, the newly returned *Franklin* was preparing a strike against the enemy mainland, when on 15 March 1945 she was hit by a single bomb from a lone aircraft. The flight deck was crowded with fuelled aircraft, armed with bombs and rockets and

the ensuing chain of explosions gutted a major portion of the carrier. Dead in the water, and now completely vulnerable, the carrier was finally towed to safety by the cruiser *Pittsburgh*, and eventually made it back to Brooklyn. The seven outboard 40mm quads had to be cut away so that she could pass through the Panama Canal, but the *Franklin* never saw service again.

Four days later, *Wasp* (still in dazzle design 10A) was damaged by *kamikazes,* and she had to be routed to Puget Sound for a much-needed refit. Her departure left only *Hornet* with an early bridge and a hangar catapult still roaming the Pacific. Okinawa was proving to be costly in men and ships. *Hancock* was hit by *kamikazes* on 1 April 1945, and sailed for repairs and additional AAs at Pearl Harbor. Then on 16 April *Intrepid* was devastated a third time, when the *kamikaze* crashed through the flight deck and partially gutted the hangar. The *Intrepid* was sent back to San Francisco for a third time.

On the same date that *Intrepid* was hit Newport News completed the 16th *Essex* class carrier. The *Boxer* (CV-21) carried all the standard modifications, and was the first long hull to be commissioned in Ms 21. At Philadelphia *Antietam* was repainted into Ms 21 and prepared to depart for the Pacific.

Ticonderoga completed repairs at Puget Sound on 20 April 1945 and was now a very different looking

1 *Boxer* (CV-21) undergoing inclining at Newport News (March '45). Once in the Pacific, the very clean starboard side would be cluttered with five outboard quad 40mm mounts.

2 *Randolph* (CV-15) at San Francisco during '45. The white circles were inked on to the negative original to note additions or changes made during a refit.

3 Close-up of *Bunker Hill's* island, immediately after World War 2. The SK-2 dish is visible in profile. The SM and SC-2 antennas are atop the radar platform. The antenna atop the topmast is a YE aircraft homing beacon.

1

2

1

2

Ticonderoga (CV-14) at Newport News during April '44. She's wearing dazzle design 10A.

Hancock (CV-19) under way in the Pacific with all four radio masts lowered for flight operations.

ship. Dazzle Design 10A was replaced by Ms 21; all seven outboard quad 40s were installed; the two aftermost radio masts were removed and an SK-2 dish replaced the SK bedspring. Except for the fact that she also now carried a mainmast, *Ticonderoga* was a very near match for *Randolph* (also in Ms 21).

On 1 May 1945 *Bunker Hill* was seriously damaged by *kamikazes* off Okinawa. She made it to Puget Sound on her own, but her wartime career was also over as she would not be ready for service until September. *Bon Homme Richard* had been held up at Pearl while all seven outboard quads were added. Since both she and *Intrepid* were in Ms 21 with outboard quads, the only easy means of identification was by the respective SK antennas. *Intrepid* retained the earlier SK bedspring but *Bon Homme Richard* carried the newer SK-2 dish. *Bon Homme Richard* departed Pearl Harbor on 12 May 1945 and headed towards Japan.

Nine days later, *Lexington* completed her overhaul at Puget Sound. I have not discussed AA weapons lighter than 40mm, since single or twin 20mm were not particularly visible. However, *Lex* had a number of Army type .5inch quad AA machine guns added (they fired two over two), whose effectiveness was doubtful. They had to be considered 'last ditch' weapons, whose purpose was to try to blow up or rip apart a *kamikaze* just before it hit the ship. At a distance *Lexington* was now an

exact match for *Bon Homme Richard* since both now had the same heavy and medium AA arrangement, the same SK-2 dish in the same positions and now the same Ms 12 camouflage. *Lex's* mainmast was also removed as was *Bon Homme Richard's*. The only noticeable difference was that *Bon Homme Richard's* upper paint always appeared to be a little darker than *Lex's*.

It's curious that *Lex*, already in Ms 21, was repainted in Ms 12 while many of her sisterships were being repainted in Ms 21 at this same yard, *Wasp* being a good example. *Wasp* completed repairs at Puget Sound on 2 June 1945, with her 10A dazzle design replaced by Ms 21. All the outboard quads were added, as well as additional quads on the fantail and port extension. The two after radio masts and the hangar cat were removed and the flag bridge was extended. However, even at this late date, *Wasp* still retained her SK bedspring, outboard on the funnel's starboard side. This made *Wasp* very similar to *Bunker Hill* (after her January 1945 refit), except that *Bunker Hill* carried a mainmast. Also, the position of the island's forwardmost 40mm director was different. *Bunker Hill's* was mounted on the flight deck between the island and the second 5inch twin mount; *Wasp's* was mounted on the flag bridge's walk-around. Why did *Wasp* retain her SK bedspring while *Lex* had hers replaced by an SK-2? It must have been an equipment shortage.

The Norfolk Navy Yard completed its second *Essex* on 3 June 1945. The long bow *Lake Champlain* (CV-39) was the 17th completed *Essex*. The 'Champ' had the distinction of being the last *Essex* to be completed during WW2; commissioned in Ms 21, she was typical of the late long bow units.

On June 4-5 1945 the fleet was hit by a severe typhoon off Japan. The forward flight decks on both *Bennington* and *Hornet* were bent over the bow. Magnificent *Hornet* had been through it all and yet had come out of it without a scratch from the Japanese. Even with a

crumpled flight deck, she operated a number of aircraft by flying them off the stern. Her damage was no more serious than *Bennington's* but she was also in need of a major overhaul as she still carried only one flight deck catapult, an early bridge and a light array of quad 40s (nine mounts). While *Bennington* went to Leyte for repairs (and repainting in Ms 21) *Hornet* headed for the West Coast and out of the war. Thus departed the last dazzled *Essex* and the last of the early ships of the class.

At Pearl Harbor *Hancock* completed repairs and overhaul on 13 June 1945. Her Ms 32 dazzle camouflage design was replaced by Ms 12's sober scheme, making her the only long bow to wear Ms 12. All seven of the outboard quads were now carried, but she retained the SK bedspring behind the topmast; she was the only long-bow unit to be so rigged.

With repairs completed, *Intrepid* was back in action against the Japanese by 29 June 1945. *Hornet* pulled into San Francisco eight days later to begin her modernization.

I must now pause to bring *Essex* up to this period. Some of the details are sketchy at best; sometime between January and March 1945 *Essex* was repainted into Ms 21, either at Leyte or Ulithi. Also, probably at the same time, her SK bedspring was replaced with an SK-2 dish. This was the only forward base modification of this magnitude made to any *Essex* unit, except for repairs. Thus, by July 1945 *Essex* was a very unusual ship for several reasons. She was the only ship still carrying all five radio lattice masts. Unlike the seven early sisterships, *Essex* never carried any outboard quad 40mm guns. She was also the only unit of the entire class to finish the war with her original single quad 40mm on the fantail, and she was put into mothballs in that condition.

Although *Boxer* reached the Pacific fleet too late to take part in operations she did have all seven of the outboard quad 40mm added, probably at San Diego.

On 15 August 1945, the war in the Pacific ended.

The Viribus Unitis

class
by FRIEDRICH PRASKY

Friedrich Prasky lives in Vienna and his main interest is modelling ships of the old Austro-Hungarian Navy. However, finding that published information was sparce, he undertook his own research and has produced a range of very fine warship plans designed specially for modelmakers. These can be obtained from him at Feuchterslebengasse 69-71/5, A-1100 Vienna, Austria.

Viribus Unitis was one of the four battleships comprising the Austro-Hungarian Empire's first Dreadnought-type design and, because of her short building time of only about twenty-four months, was the first battleship in the world

to go into service with triple turrets. The first Italian Dreadnought, *Dante Alighieri*, also with triple turrets, had been designed and laid down earlier, but she was completed three months after the *Viribus Unitis* had been commissioned.

Viribus Unitis is an unusual name for a battleship — it means 'With United Strength', a motto that expressed the hopes of the Austro-Hungarian Empire, which contained modern Austria, Hungary, Czechoslovakia, parts of Italy, Yugoslavia, Rumania and Poland.

In foreign naval literature the *Viribus Unitis* class are often called the *Tegetthoffs,* for SMS *Tegetthoff* was the first ship of the class laid down, although SMS *Viribus Unitis* was the first ship to be commissioned and became the flagship of the Austro-Hungarian Navy. Articles have been published on these ships but all of them contain errors of fact.

As I am building a model of the *Viribus Unitis* and no model plans were available, I started to draw my own. The necessary information was obtained from the original drawings, the official ship's data book on *Viribus Unitis,* while photos and other documents came from the Austrian State National Archives.

The ships had a cast steel ram bow and six longitudinal frames on both sides of the keel. The lower part of the stern, the rudder trunk and the torpedo-tubes were steel castings which in other ships was made of formed sheet steel. Bow and stern were double plated.

As protection against underwater attack the ships had a double bottom and longitudinal torpedo-bulkheads on both sides. Like most ships of that time, the space between hull and torpedo-bulkhead was too small for the expanding explosion gases of a torpedo. A centreline bulkhead was placed between the engine rooms. The internal subdivision was comparable

with that of English ships but in comparison with German practice was not up to date.

For their heavy armament, with two superimposed triple turrets fore and aft, the ships were too small and had a very low range of stability. Because of hull distortions caused by the weight of the triple turrets the longitudinal frames under the turrets had to be stiffened.

The *Tegetthoff, Viribus Unitis* and *Prinz Eugen,* built in the experienced yard of Stabilimento Tecnico Triestino, were well built, but *Szent Istvan* was built in the Hungarian Danubius yard in Fiume. The yard had no experience of building battleships and that played an important part in the destruction of the ship; the essential factor being the poor quality of the riveting.

In the Austrian State National Archives there are documents concerning investigations on this problem: as early as the gunnery

A pre-war photograph of *Tegetthoff* steaming into Valetta Harbour, Malta.

CPL W/6/001

	Laid down	Launched	Completed	Built
TEGETTHOFF	24 May 1910	31 March 1912	14 July 1913	Stabilimento
VIRIBUS UNITIS	24 July 1910	20 June 1911	5 October 1912	Tecnico,
PRINZ EUGEN	16 January 1912	30 November 1912	8 July 1914	Triestino
SZENT ISTVAN	29 January 1912	17 January 1914	17 November 1915	Danubius yard, Fiume, completed in Poland

Ships Data (from ship's data book for *Viribus Unitis*)

Loa	152.183m
Lwl	151.000m
Breadth	27.336m
Draught	8.234m
Construction Displacement	20 013.55 tons (with 600 tons of coal and 50% consumable goods)
Full Load Displacement	21 595 ton
Designer	Siegfried Popper

Machinery

TEGETTHOFF	12 Yarrow boilers in two boiler rooms. Parsons turbines, four shafts,
VIRIBUS UNITIS	designed output 25 000 SHP.
PRINZ EUGEN	
SZENT ISTVAN	12 Babcock Wilcox boilers in two boiler rooms. AEG turbines, two shafts, designed output 25 000 SHP. Trial speed 20.3 knots. The turrets and all other gear were electrically powered.

Main Armament

12 x 30.5cm/L45 K10 in triple turrets

Elevation	+20°	Charge weight	140kg
Depression	−4°	Pressure	2800 atm
Calibre	305mm	Muzzle velocity	800m/sec
Length of Bore	45 cal	Range	18 000 (1915 20 000m)
Shell weight	450kg	Year of construction	1910

Secondary Armament

12 x 15cm/L50 K10 in barbettes

Elevation	+15°	Charge weight	16.85kg
Depression	−6°	Pressure	2657 atm
Calibre	150mm	Muzzle velocity	880m/sec
Length of bore	50 cal	Range	?
Shell weight	45.5kg	Year of construction	1910

4 x 7cm/L50 K10 anti-torpedo boat and airship gun placed on turrets Nos II and III

Elevation	+90°	Charge weight	1.6kg
Depession	−5°	Pressure	2900 atm
Calibre	66mm	Muzzle velocity	880m/sec
Length of bore	50 cal	Muzzle energy	158mt
Shell weight	4.5kg	Range	?
		Year of construction	1910

A modified type had also been constructed in 1916 with the same ballistic characteristics

12 x 7cm/L50 K10 anti-torpedo boat gun

Elevation	+20°	Charge weight	1.6kg
Depression	−10°	Pressure	2800 atm
Calibre	66mm	Muzzle velocity	850m/sec
Shell weight	4.5kg	Muzzle energy	165.7mt
Length of bore	50 cal	Range	?

trials some of the rivets in the double bottom had been blown out of their holes.

All guns were manufactured at the Skoda Works at Pilsen. The guns of that firm were among the best in the world. The 7cm/L50 guns were easily removeable and their number varied from time to time.

The 7cm/L50 guns mounted on top of the triple turrets could be coupled with the 30.5cm/L45 guns in the turrets to spare 30.5cm ammunition and to save the bore of the heavy guns during gunnery practice.

FATES

Szent Istvan was lost during a raid against the Strait of Otranto, where the Allies had built a strong barrage with permanent nets, minefields and patrolling drifters to stop the Austro-Hungarian and German submarines entering the Mediterranean. The Austro-Hungarians planned to break the barrage with cruisers supported by battleships of the *Viribus Unitis* class.

On the morning of 9 June 1918 at 03.30 near Premuda Island *Szent Istvan* was hit by two torpedoes from the tiny motor torpedo boat of the Italian Commander Luigi Rizzo. The torpedoes struck her on the starboard side near the

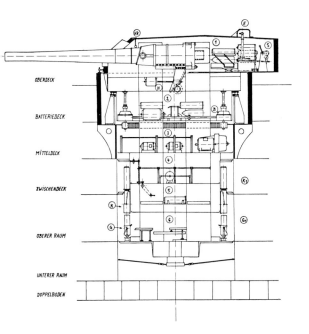

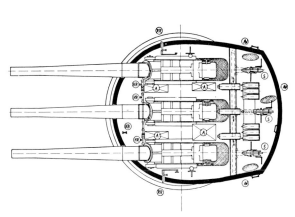

bulkhead between the fore and aft boiler rooms. Water poured into the after boiler room and the ship immediately took a 10° list to starboard. Because of the poor quality of the riveting the bulkheads could not stand the strain and rivets flew out of their holes like bullets. The ship stopped in order to use the steam of the fore boiler room for the pumps, which could discharge 6000 tons of water an hour out of the ship. Some time later the fore boiler room filled and so did the 15cm ammunition store. Counter measures were taken, the turrets swung round to port and *Tegetthoff* tried to take her in tow but without success. The watertight bulkheads broke down one after the other and at 06.05 *Szent Istvan* turned over and finally sank at 06.12 at position 44° 16′N, 14° 13′E. Eighty-nine of her crew died.

Viribus Unitis was sunk in Pola harbour after the breakdown of the Austro-Hungarian Empire. On 31 October 1918 the Austro-Hungarian battle flag was hauled down and the fleet was transferred to the Yugoslav National Council. Captain Jomko Vukovic hoisted the Yugoslav flag on the ship, which was renamed *Yugoslavia(?)*. For the crew the war was finished and there was no more discipline. All the non-Yugoslavian crew members planned to leave the ship for home.

The ship was illuminated and all watertight doors open. In the meantime on the morning of 1 November 1918 two Italian naval officers, Raffaele Rossetti and Raffaele Paolucci, riding a new underwater weapon, a human torpedo called *Mignatta,* succeeded in passing the net barrage of the harbour defence. The *Mignata* was built from a salved German torpedo, but instead of the warhead it carried two mines, each filled with 200 kg of explosives. It was driven by a compressed air engine and ridden by two men. The Italians attached their mines to the hull of the battleship but were seen soon after and taken aboard. They were astonished to find themselves on a Yugoslav ship and informed the Captain that the ship would blow up within 15 minutes. Orders were given to abandon ship, but all discipline was lost and nothing was properly organised or under control.

At 06.30 that morning the mines blew up and the *Viribus Unitis* sank within 15 minutes. About 400 of her crew were lost. The wreck was broken up between 1920 and 1930.

Prinz Eugen was ceded to France and taken to Toulon. She was stripped of all guns and other useful material. In 1922 she was sunk as a target ship by *France* and *Bretagne*.

Tegetthoff went to Italy under the peace treaty of 1920. She was broken up at La Spezia in 1924/25.

Legend

1   gunhouse
2   handling room
3   machine platform
4   crank-handles
5   cartridge platform
6   projectile platform

E   distance meter
S   ram
H   elevation gear
B   turning gear
K   cartridge turntable
G   projectile turntable
K1 cartridge magazine
G1 projectile magazine
A   ammunition hoists
HB, HR, RR   optical equipment
AW cartridge ejecting openings

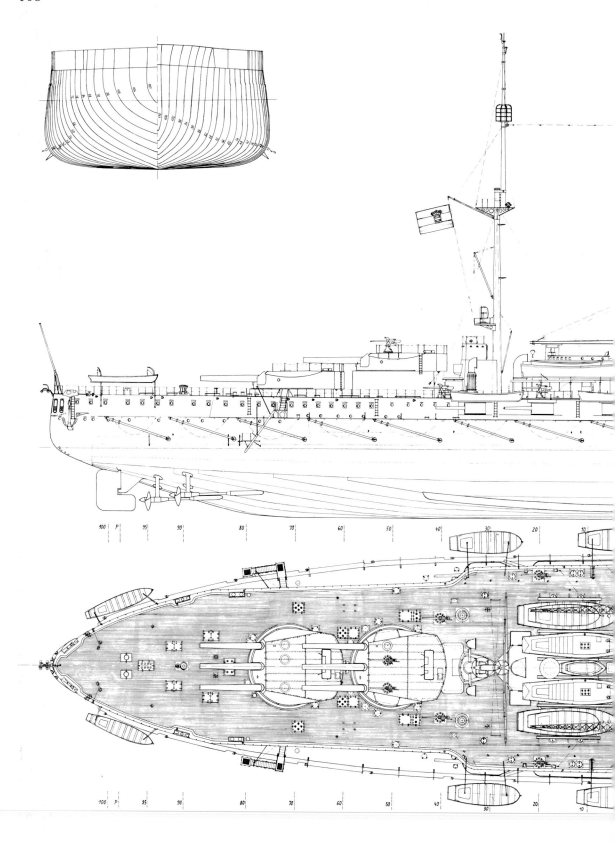

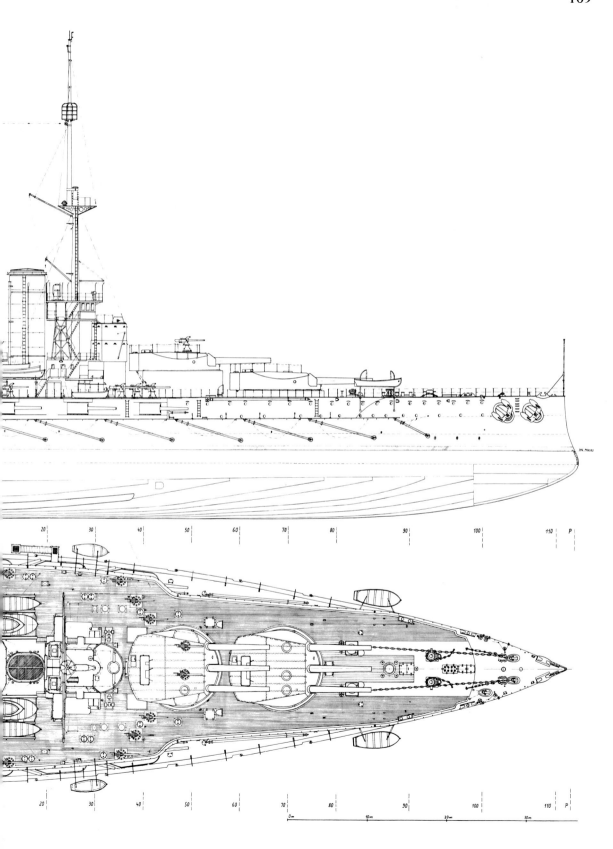

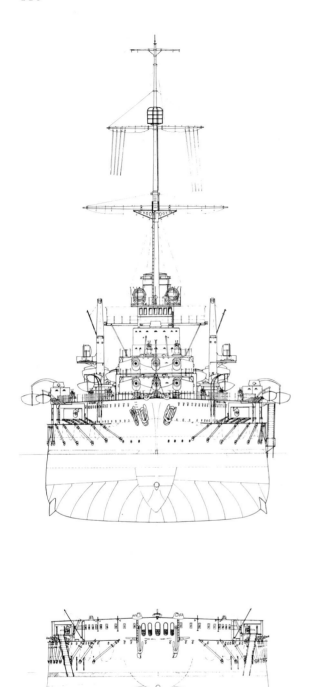

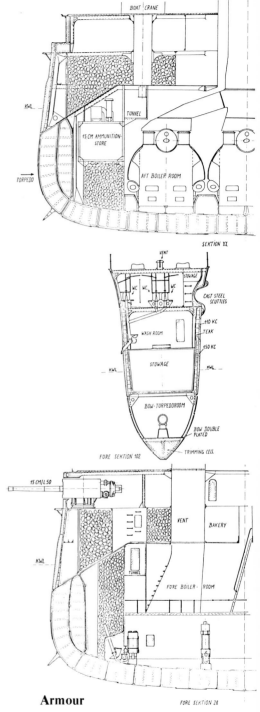

Armour

FORE SEKTION 28

I have copied the armour plans from the ship's data book for *Viribus Unitis*.

I have shown the point at which the torpedo (torpedoes?) hit the *Szent Istvan* at cross section 67 (depth section 22 according to the commande Commodore Seitz). The armour plates were manufactured by the Iron Works at Withowitz: protection against gunfire was quite good.

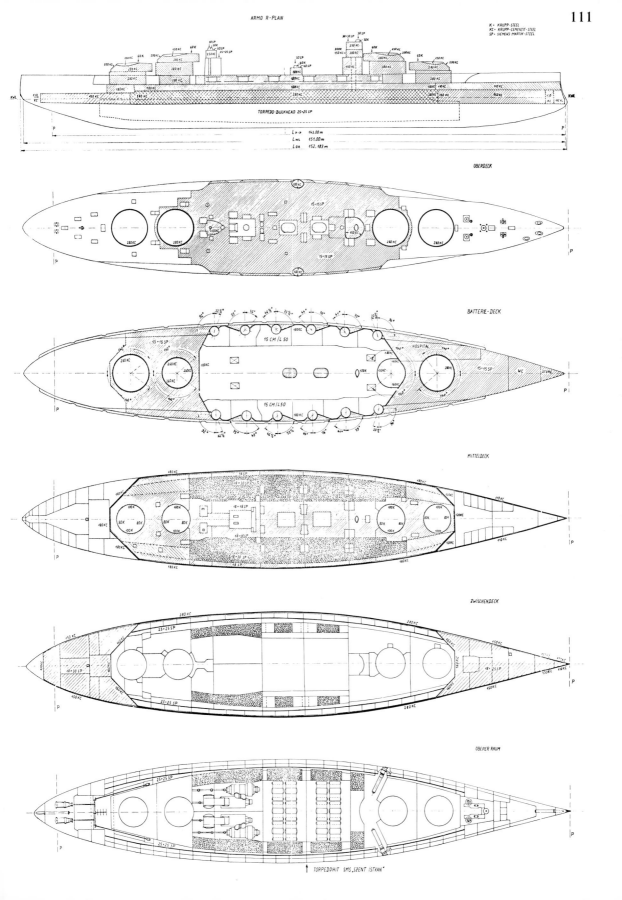

ARMO R-PLAN

K = KRUPP-STEEL
KC = KRUPP-CEMENTIT-STEEL
SP = SIEMENS-MARTIN-STEEL

TORPEDO-BULKHEAD 25+25 SP

L p-p   143.00 m
L wl   151.00 m
L OA   152,183 m

OBERDECK

BATTERIE-DECK

MITTELDECK

ZWISCHENDECK

OBERER RAUM

↑ TORPEDOHIT SMS „SZENT ISTVAN"

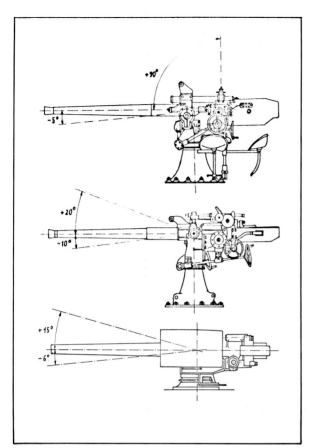

1 7cm/L50 K10 anti torpedoboat and
   airship gun here mounted on a cruiser.
   Collection Pavlik

2 In a 30.5cm/L45 turret of SMS *Prinz Eugen*
   Austrian State National Archives

3 Starboard side turrets III and IV, 7cm/L50,
   stern view, *Prinz Eugen*.
   Austrian State National Archives

4 *Prinz Eugen*, starboard bow view.
   Austrian State National Archives

1

2

3   4

1 *Prinz Eugen,* underwater torpedo tube.
Collection Pavlik

2 SMS *Viribus Unitis,* turbogenerator.
Collection Pavlik

3 *Prinz Eugen,* boiler room
Austrian State National Archives

4 SMS *Viribus Unitis.* Model M1.25,
Heeresgeschichtliches Museum Wien,
one of the best ship models in the world.
Austrian State National Archives

Warship Pictorial

The photo feature in this issue is devoted to some of the illustrations from *Camera at Sea* to be published this month by Conway Maritime Press Ltd. This book was written, edited, designed and produced by the staff and contributors of *Warship,* and is the first of a series of books which we hope to produce for the warship enthusiast. As such we felt it was worthy of notice in the journal.

Camera at Sea is not a pictorial history, but a collection of the very best, most telling, photography of

1

the war at sea. It covers every aspect, from rare action shots to close-up details, and every major participating nation is represented.

This selection shows some of the 275 photographs, mainly drawn from Chapter 2 'Weapons and Equipment', although the larger page size of *Camera at Sea* uses them to far better effect.

The book also includes 16 pages of full colour, costs £12.00 (plus £1.00 postage) and will be available from the publishers from the end of April.

1 The last and most powerful battleship of the German Navy, the *Tirpitz*, completing in the Kriegsmarine Werft yards at Wilhelmshaven in 1940.

2 A quadruple 40mm Bofors mounting Mk II on the US battleship *Arkansas* in 1944. These weapons were virtually doubled versions of the twin Mk I mounting. They were not sophisticated weapons, being designed for rapid production in wartime, but were nevertheless successful. This was in large part due to the provision of a separate, Mk 51, director equipped with a gyro-gunsight to control the mounting by RPC (Remote Power Control).

CPL

3 One of the four twin Mk XIX 4inch gun mountings of the battleship *Resolution* at Gibraltar in 1939. This mounting has been raised by the addition of a circular base between the deck and the base plate, normally the base plate was bolted directly to the deck. The equipment mounted on the box at the right hand rear of the mounting is a fuse setting machine.

CPL

1

2

A minesweeper of the German First Minesweeper Division seen off the Dagö and Ösel Islands, in July 1941.

A view of the Mk VI pom-pom mounting abaft the island superstructure of HMS *Indomitable* in December 1944. This mounting is unusual in that it has an enclosed position for the gunlayer on the right side.

CPL

A twin 20mm Oerlikon Mk V mounting, a weapon first introduced in 1942 and fitted in practically every type of vessel in the Navy. Of particular interest in this photograph is the gyro-gunsight, into which the gunlayer is looking. These were fitted to all types of close range AA weapons during 1944-45, priority being given to ships of the Pacific and Eastern Fleets.

CPL

The USS *Pennsylvania* after refit at the Mare Island Yard in California early in 1942. The ship was not badly damaged at Pearl Harbor and apart from minor repairs the refit was largely concerned with the improvement of her AA defences.

3

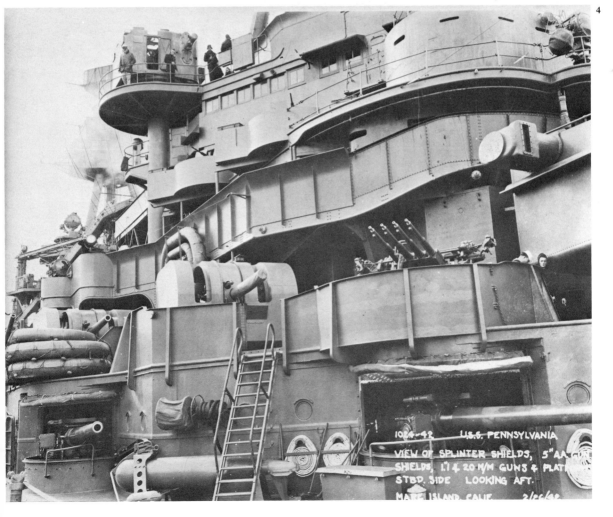

4

1024-42   U.S.S. PENNSYLVANIA
VIEW OF SPLINTER SHIELDS, 5"AA GUN
SHIELDS, 1.1 & 20 M/M GUNS & PLATF
STBD. SIDE   LOOKING AFT.
MARE ISLAND, CALIF.   2/66/42

HMS RAPID
A TYPE 15 FLEET DESTROYER CONVERSION
by John Lambert

John Lambert is a well-known contributor to naval and modelling magazines, specialising in smaller warships and naval guns. This article is the first to incorporate newly released information on the Type 15 'full conversions', and the plans are available from the David Macgregor Plans Service, 99 Lonsdale Road, London SW13. Part 2 will cover the Type 16 'limited conversions' with a full set of plans of 'Terpsichore'.

Rapid in her original conventional fleet destroyer configuration, taken 14 August 1946.

Wright & Logan

A World War Two Fleet Destroyer, HMS *Rapid*, was a unit of the *R* class, one of the 4th Emergency Flotilla, which first commissioned in early 1943. The ninth ship of that name, and utilising the standard emergency war-time construction, the class embodied few innovations.

Built to the dimensions of the previous emergency flotilla, the *Q* class, which gave a length overall of 358ft 3in, length between perpendiculars of 339ft 6in, length along waterline of 348ft, and a beam or breadth of 35ft 8in. She displaced some 2700 tons, and was armed with four single 4.7inch Mk IX guns, on CP XVIII mountings, which fired a 50 lb shell. The anti-

aircraft armament comprised of a four barrelled pom-pom, and four single 20mm Oerlikons. She mounted two quadruple 21inch torpedo-tubes.

The tradition of the officers always berthing aft was broken with the *R* class, when they were placed under the bridge, which helped to prevent the officers on the bridge from being isolated in heavy weather, as in previous classes.

The 4th Emergency Flotilla was ordered on 2 April 1940. *Rapid* was laid down on 16 June 1941, launched on 16 July 1942, and completed on the 20 February the following year. Some delay had occured with the class due to loss of shipyard staff who were engaged in the repair of completed destroyers which had suffered damage in the Norwegian campaign, and during the Dunkirk evacuation.

After commissioning and working up, she was allocated to the 11th Destroyer Flotilla, under Captain Winton (Capt. 'D') in *Rotherham* (Leader) with *Relentless, Redoubt, Racehorse, Rocket* and *Roebuck.*

In February 1944, the 11th Destroyer Flotilla was sent to reinforce the British Eastern Fleet, under Vice-Admiral Somerville, with units of the 16th Flotilla (*P* class), and the 4th (*Q* class).

From the 22-27 July, *Rapid* was part of the force for Operation Crimson, a naval air carrier raid,

and bombardment of Sabang, Sumatra. From the aircraft carriers *Illustrious* and *Victorious*, aircraft carried out the raid on the oil refinery, which was followed by a bombardment from the battleships *Queen Elizabeth, Valiant,* and *Renown*, with the Free French *Richelieu. Rapid* was part of the close escort for this force.

In January 1945 *Rapid* and her sisters were part of Task Force 64, and support for the bombardment for the allied invasion of Ramree Island, off Arakan, Burma. Shortly after the landings there in company with the destroyer *Norman*, and the *River* class frigates *Spey* and *Teviot,* of TF 65, she assisted the landing of 500 marines on Cheduba Island, south of Ramree, then on again to Operation Crocodile, where 120 men were put ashore on the island of Sagu on 30 January. On 19 March, *Rapid* was hit by a Japanese coastal battery, whilst operating off the Andamans.

With the ending of hostilities, the *R*s returned to more peaceable pastimes. Her sisters, *Relentless* and *Rocket,* underwent a long refit and modernisation in Naval dockyards, to up-date them for modern underwater developments. Three units (*Rotherham, Raider* and *Redoubt*) were transferred to the Royal Indian Navy, back to the very waters where they had spent most of their active lives. The remaining *R*s in commission were employed as attendant chase destroyers, attached to our carriers, operating in the Mediterranean.

This was a period of running down in the Royal Navy. New weapons planned during the war were developed and coming into service. The armed forces were being demobilized, and finance was cut back very severely.

Military jet propelled aircraft were now common, with new developments in the pipeline promising faster and heavier aircraft. The development of the submarine had improved in comparison with the designs available in 1945.

By 1945, the German Navy had new types of submarine under construction, with a few in service, on trials and working up. These new designs were capable of much higher underwater speeds, for increased periods of time. With the ending of hostilities, and access to German shipyards, designs and trials data, it was found that the conventionally powered Type XXI U-boats were capable of some 20 knots whilst at periscope depth with the aid of the *schnorchel.* They also produced a higher speed than normal at greater depths, due to much increased battery power, and hull streamlining. Other designs incorporating the new 'Walther' turbine promised an even better underwater performance.

It was realised that the emergency designed frigates, in service in large numbers now, were already obsolete. The *Bay* and *Loch* class frigates could only just match the new high submerged speed, whilst the *Castle* class frigates, and *Modified Flowers,* were simply left behind.

Atomic power for peaceful purposes became readily available. The USA had a design for an atomic powered submarine in the design stage, and due for launching in 1954. If the USA could produce such a weapon, then so could the scientists of the USSR.

In the light of these developments, huge modernisation programmes were put in hand to improve the anti-submarine performance of existing ships. Our own conventionally powered submarines of the *A* and *T* class underwent drastic re-construction to improve their underwater performance.

New weapons systems had been developed. The 'Squid' had been introduced in the last months of the war: an improved ahead throwing weapon, with a much heavier charge, to be replaced in its turn by the improved 'Limbo'. New developments in the field of radar and communications also produced additional problems of electrical power and planning. The plan was to put all the new and modified equipment into a shell that was capable of producing and

The radical nature of the conversion is apparent from this view of *Rapid* taken 10 March 1969, although the weaponry is 'cocooned'.

Navpic

maintaining a high speed in any weather or sea condition.

It was decided to utilise the hulls and engine power of war-built fleet destroyers, and the *R* class was to be the pilot model, to utilise all the new technology. *Rocket* and *Relentless* underwent a long period of re-design at Portsmouth and Devonport naval dockyard, which resulted in a very potent and elegant anti-submarine weapons system.

The conversion to fast anti-submarine frigate involved a considerable re-design. The bridge, mast, superstructure and armament were all removed, and the ship stripped down to her bare hull. The forecastle deck was extended aft, with extensive use made of aluminium to reduce top weight. A new superstructure was built which contained an operations room, asdic control room, and much improved radar display, communications equipment, and accommodation.

The most up to date asdic (now called 'Sonar') was mounted, with early computor control. There were two 'squids' mounted aft, and two short stubby lattice masts gave adequate stowage for all the radar aerials and communications outfits, with much usage of whip aerials.

A revised surface armament was fitted, which comprised a twin 40mm Mk V Bofors mounting forward, and a dual purpose H/A twin 4inch XIX mounting aft, with a H/A director.

1 *Grenville* shows one of the many variations in the bridge structure of these conversions, 9 February 1970.
Navpic

2 A later view of *Grenville* acting as a trials ship, 15 June 1973
Navpic

1

2

The machinery arrangements remained as before. Two Admiralty three drum boilers with superheaters, at a working pressure of 300 lb/sq. inch, driving high pressure, and low pressure Parsons turbines on two shafts of 40 000 SHP giving a sea speed of some 31 knots, and designed for 36.75 knots at maximum power. *(Rapid* as a destroyer, gave 32.7 knots, at 321 revolutions, on builders trials at a displacement of 2460 tons). Provision was made to mount anti-submarine torpedo-tubes. The class's standard outfit of boats consisted of a 25 ft motor cutter, a 27 ft pulling or sailing whaler, a 14ft RNSA sailing dinghy, and aft on the quarter deck, a 16ft fast motor boat.

From these early conversions, some twenty-nine similar units were completed from war built fleet destroyers. The Royal Canadian Navy converted two (*Algonquin* and *Crescent*), and the Royal Australian Navy four, (*Quadrant, Queenborough, Quiberon* and *Quickmatch*).

As the conversions were undertaken over a period of some seven years, there were slight differences in appearance. Over the years these units performed differing duties, with periodic refits. These are apparent from the photographs kindly supplied by Jim Goss of 'Navpic'. Later units were fitted with enclosed frigate type bridges. (*Zest, Ulster* and *Troubridge)*, with some variation in the fitting of the forward gun mounting. *Grenville* and *Undaunted* had helicopter landing platforms built on aft.

We see two views of *Grenville* showing radical equipment changes in a very short period. Her main mast has been plated over, she has a new motor whaler, and the twin 4inch mounting has been deleted and replaced by temporary offices. The A/S weapons have also been removed.

Ulster, seen in September 1969, mounts two 'Limbo's'. Another view shows her in late 1975, slowly being scrapped, having spent part of her service as a training ship for Royal Marines. Her sister *Verulam* had been used as a trials vessel for the testing of new A/S equipment. Only one unit now remains in service. HMS *Ulster* was reduced to the reserve fleet in 1972, but is now retained as a floating classroom for new entries who join the Royal Navy at HMS *Raleigh,* Torpoint.

Other conversions were to end their useful lives as targets for the new guided weapons now in service. *Rapid* herself, along with *Undaunted* and *Whirlwind,* ended her days in this way. But before the end she was given a new lease of life, after some years in the reserve fleet. She was de-cocooned and steamed round to Rosyth Dockyard. Her armament was removed and she became a base training unit for the Engine Room Artificer Apprentices, attached to

HMS *Caledonia.* From early in 1967 she raised steam, taking new members of the 'purple empire' to sea for training. The machinery was operated and maintained under skilled supervision whilst the trainees learned the practice of their theory.

In June 1971, *Rapid's* Commanding Officer, Lt Cdr W Kelly RN, with the agreement of the MOD (Navy) and Cdr C Snell RN of HMS *Cavalier* another surviving war built fleet destroyer, planned a race to prove which was the faster ship.

Rapid was older than *Cavalier* and had seen more arduous war service, but at least her machinery was fully functional. It would appear that *Rapid* was the firm favourite.

On 6 July 1971, a calm day, the two rivals left the Firth of Forth, and sailed north to a start line off the Scottish coast. Both units worked up to full speed, covering a distance of 74 miles in some two hours. Both ships were steaming at about 33 knots, with *Rapid* having a lead of about 100 yards. At that stage, she accidently lifted her safety valve, losing boiler pressure. *Cavalier* slowly caught up, and became the winner by some sixteen yards.

The name *Rapid* dates from 1804. The sixth ship so named was a sloop of 1860, which was broken up in 1881. The seventh was a corvette of 1883, which became a hulk at Gibraltar in 1910. Number eight was a destroyer built in 1916 and sold in 1927, with the latest being our destroyer of 1942. All the ships' battle honours were obtained by this unit: Atlantic 1943; Sabang 1944; Burma 1944-45.

H.M.S. RAPID ~ TYPE 15 CONVERSION.
FAST A/S FRIGATE.

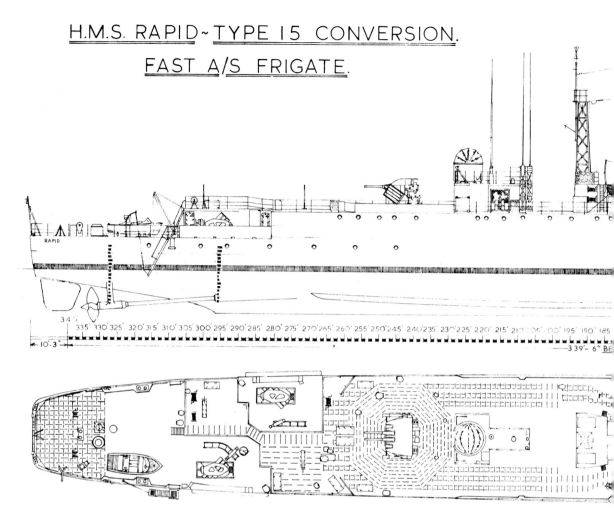

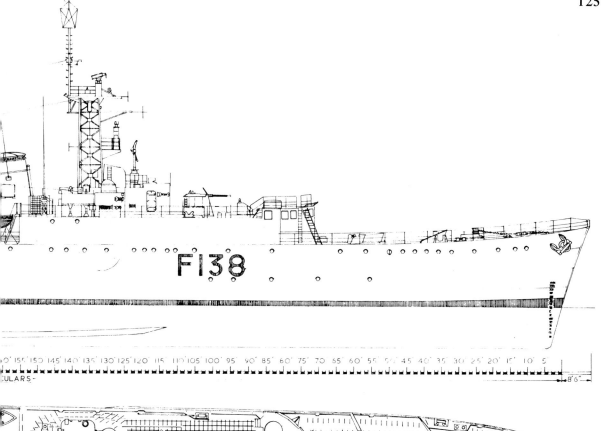

F138

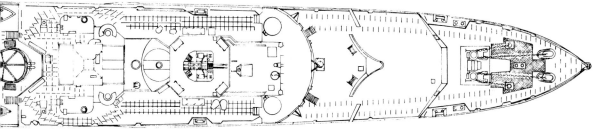

0' 155' 150' 145' 140' 135' 130' 125' 120' 115' 110' 105' 100' 95' 90' 85' 80' 75' 70' 65' 60' 55' 50' 45' 40' 35' 30' 25' 20' 15' 10' 5'

:ULARS — ← 8'6"→

1 *Ulster* (taken 29 September 1969) had the modern 'frigate' bridge fitted in the purpose-built A/S, A/A, A/D and GP frigates.
Navpic

2 An unusual view of *Volage* with a severe list that shows the basic deck layout of the Type 15s.

Navpic (these photos can be obtained from James W Goss, 64 Gains Road, Southsea, Hants PO4 QPL, UK).

FLEET DESTROYERS FULLY CONVERTED TO TYPE 15 FAST A/S FRIGATES

Name	Pennant Number	Class	Converted
ZEST	F 102	Z	Chatham dockyard 1954-56
WAKEFUL	F 159	W	Scotts 1952-53
WHIRLWIND	F 187	W	Palmers 1952-53
WIZARD	F 72	W	Devonport dockyard 1954
WRANGLER	F 157	W	Harland & Wolff, Belfast 1951-52
VENUS	F 50	V	1952
VERULAM	F 29	V	Portsmouth dockyard 1952
VIGILANT	F 93	V	1951-52
VIRAGO	F 76	V	1952
VOLAGE	F 41	V	Whites 1952
GRENVILLE	F 197	U	1953-54
ULSTER	F 83	U	Chatham dockyard 1952-53
ULYSSES	F 17	U	Devonport dockyard 1952-53
UNDAUNTED	F 53	U	Whites 1952-54
UNDINE	F 141	U	1954
URANIA	F 08	U	Harland & Wolff, Liverpool 1953-54
URCHIN	F 196	U	Barclay Curle 1952-54
URSA	F 200	U	Palmer 1952-54
TROUBRIDGE	F 09	T	Portsmouth dockyard & Whites 1955-57
RAPID	F 138	R	Stephens 1952-53
RELENTLESS	F 185	R	Portsmouth dockyard 1952-53
ROCKET	F 191	R	Devonport dockyard 1952-53
ROEBUCK	F 195	R	Devonport dockyard 1952-53
QUADRANT	F 01	Q	Cockatoo Island 1951-57 (RAN)
QUEENBOROUGH	F 02	Q	Cockatoo Island 1951-57 (RAN)
QUIBERON	F 03	Q	Williamstown 1951-57 (RAN)
QUICKMATCH	F 04	Q	Williamstown 1951-57 (RAN)
ALGONQUIN	224	W	Esquimalt dockyard 1954 (RCN)
CRESCENT	226	CR	Esquimalt dockyard 1956 (RCN)

About this intriguing photograph of Grenville Norman Friedman writes:
Her mainmast shows an experimental air search radar, which is now mounted on the cliffs at Portsmouth. Its general form suggests the Type 982 low-level air search set mounted aboard carriers and air direction frigates, which is fed from below and whose reflector curves over, but has very different dimensions. The large roughly triangular box below the reflector is the feed; it may well consist of a series of parallel channels or slots arranged to permit some form of rapid crosswise scanning (eg, Frescan, as in the US SPS 39/52/48). Certainly this structure is *not* the traditional British 'cheese', but its function as feed is suggested strongly by the absence of any dipoles or other radar emitters in the bedspring proper. The small broadside antenna on the stub lattice amidships is reminiscent of many US IFF interrogators, and the combination with what looks like TACAN on the lattice mainmast suggests an experimental air direction system, which would be consistent with a 982-successor. In conclusion this set is probably destined for the new *Invincibles*, combining the functions Types 982 and 965 for low-to-medium level cover (for control of ASW aircraft).

Navpic

The battle of

Tsu-Shima

2

by
N J M Campbell

*John Campbell is a retired
metallurgist who now devotes all his
time to writing. Primarily known as
an expert on ordnance, his
knowledge of the technical side of
naval history is extensive. He is the
author of a Warship Monograph
on the 'Queen Elizabeth' class
(Conway Maritime Press) and a
forthcoming Warship Special on
battlecruisers.*

Rozhestvenski kept his fleet closed
up during the night of 26/27 May,
and Corbett who is critical of the
details of the Japanese watch in his
unpublished account of the battle,
considers that with a little luck, he
would have passed through their
cruiser patrols undetected. The
hospital ship *Orel* was out of
station and this led to her discovery
by the auxiliary cruiser *Shinano
Maru.* This latter ship then located
other units of the Russian fleet and
made the sighting signal by wireless
at 04.50. Other Japanese cruisers
gathered to watch the Russians but
there was much mist and irregular
visibility, and information that the
Russian battleships changed from
their night formation to single line
ahead was never passed to Togo,
who had put to sea at 07.10. There
was a strong WSW wind (Force 5
to 7) in the Straits, and a rough sea
until late in the evening, so that
most of the Japanese torpedo-boats
were sent to take shelter until later
in the day. The 9th TB Division
which had modern 147ft Normand
type boats, recorded that they shot
about like rockets, rolled through
an angle of over 60° and at 15
knots or over seemed almost
submarines. Haze and mist limited
visibility to a distance of 10 000 —
12 000 yds, and objects were often
indistinct at half that distance.

Meanwhile at 09.30
Rozhestvenski signalled his 12 ships
of the battle-line into line ahead
with the *Oleg, Aurora* and *Donskoi*
astern. The fleet train was in a
second line to starboard of the
Oleg, with the *Svietlana, Almaz* and
Ural astern and the *Monomakh* on
the starboard flank. The *Jemtchug*

and *Izumrud,* each with two
destroyers were to starboard of the
Suvarov and *Osliabia* respectively,
and the remaining five destroyers
were with the *Oleg* and *Svietlana.*
At 11.42 the *Ushakov,* or according
to some accounts the *Orel,* opened
fire on the Japanese 3rd Division
(light cruisers) at about 9000 yds,
and the other ships of Nebogatov's
Division also opened fire. About 30
rounds were fired before
Rozhestvenski, whose battle orders
had fixed 6000 yds as the maximum
range, stopped the firing. The
Japanese 3rd Division consisted of
the *Kasagi* (Vice-Admiral Dewa),
Chitose, and the smaller cruisers
Otowa and *Niitaka.* They had
missed contact with the Russians
earlier, going too far to the south,
and were to port of the Russians
and on an East-North-East course
when fire was opened. Only the
Kasagi and *Chitose* replied and the
Japanese drew off into the mist.
Rozhestvenski, for reasons which
are not clear, decided to form his
1st Division into line abreast, or
perhaps his intention was to form
all 12 ships into a single line
abreast. The 1st Division turned in
succession 8 points to starboard
but, instead of then turning
together 8 points to port to form
line abreast, they turned again in
succession thus forming a second
line ahead, to starboard of the
other eight ships. It is not certain
whether the manoeuvre was
misunderstood by the *Alexander,*
astern of the *Suvarov* or if it was
annulled by Rozhestvenski, as his
ships had become visible to the
Japanese on entering a less misty
area. At any rate the line of four

Russian ships turned somewhat to port and increased speed to take station again ahead of the other eight and at 14.08 when the battle began in earnest, all but the *Orel* which was to starboard of the *Osliabia* had got back into the van.

THE BATTLE: FIRST STAGE

At 13.39 Togo, who was then about 10 miles NW of Okinoshima, sighted the Russian fleet, faintly discernible to the SW in the mist which now allowed visibility to 14 000 — 16 000 yds. The Russian course was NE by N and Togo followed by Kamimura, steered NW by N and then W. At 13.57 the Russians bore S by W 10 000 — 14 000 yds off. The Japanese note that the greyish-yellow funnels of the Russian ships were very easy to see and a good aiming mark, and the Russian painting, which incorporated blackish hulls and funnel tops with these funnels, was certainly at a disadvantage as compared with the Japanese uniform grey colour. At 14.02 Togo altered course to SW by S and it appeared that he intended to pass the Russian fleet on a reverse course, but at 14.05 he turned his Division in succession to port on to an ENE course to press the Russian van. At this time the leading Russians were steaming nearly NE by N and bore S by E at about 8500 — 9000 yds range, and at 14.08 when only the *Mikasa* had settled on her new course and the *Shikishima* was about to do so, the *Suvarov* opened from her fore turret at 7400 yds, the shot falling 20 yds astern of the *Mikasa,* and other leading Russian ships immediately followed, concentrating on the two leading Japanese.

In thus turning his ships at a fixed point within range of the Russian van, Togo ran some risk but it was less than it might seem at first sight. The bearings were such that initially the Russian after turrets could not train, the last five ships of their line were out of range, and the *Orel* was on the beam of the *Osliabia* which had to slow to allow her to get ahead. The two Japanese ships were thus under the fire of ten 12inch and two 10inch guns only, and it was

improbable that at over 7000 yds they would all find the range at once. Kamimura's Division following Togo, would have run more risk but he turned a little to starboard before making his turn to port which was thus made at a greater distance from the Russians and by that time the fire of the leading Japanese ships was beginning to take effect.

The *Mikasa* opened fire on the *Suvarov* at 14.10 at 7000 yds and as they steadied on the new course, the other ships of Togo's and Kamimura's divisions followed so that by 14.20 all were firing. The *Iwate* and possibly the *Kasuga* and *Nisshin* had in fact opened fire

before turning. Initially the *Mikasa, Asahi* and *Azuma* fired at the *Suvarov,* and the rest at the *Osliabia,* easy to identify by her three funnels, but targets were altered and of the battleships, the *Fuji* changed to the *Suvarov* soon after 14.20. The Russians mostly fired at the *Mikasa* and also at some of the armoured cruisers. The rough seas washed into windward main deck gun-ports and gave a good deal of motion to the ships making it difficult to lay the guns. However the Japanese quickly found the range and maintained a highly accurate but usually slow fire. The Russian shooting too, was good in the early stages of the

action. The courses of the two fleets were roughly parallel and to the north of east but the Japanese were doing 15 knots as compared to the Russian 10 and the latter were gradually forced to starboard. The range was mostly 5500 — 6500 yds and not below 4700 — 5000 yds. Rozhestvenski apparently considered an attempt to get to closer range, but it does not seem that it was ever made. By 14.35 Togo was steering due E and by 14.43 ESE and four minutes later a little further to the south, threatening to cross the 'T' of the Russian line.

By this time the Russians were in grave trouble. At about 14.18 the *Osliabia* had been hit by a heavy shell on or below the waterline forward which made a large hole and caused very serious flooding. Another shell pierced the armour amidships and entered a coal bunker, and here again serious flooding occurred. The ship took a heavy list to port and was down by the head, and counter-flooding and hole-stopping attempts were unsuccessful. In addition the fore turret had been hit and put out of action and she was badly on fire so that the *Shikishima* at 14.40 could not lay her guns on the *Osliabia* for smoke. At 14.50 the *Osliabia* turned to starboard out of line and at almost the same time was hit again on the waterline by two heavy shells, one of which made a second huge hole close to the first bad hit.

The *Suvarov* was frequently hit early in the action and by 14.20 was on fire. This apparently started from the fore chart-house and became very violent. By 14.35 Rozhestvenski and her captain had been wounded by splinters entering the conning-tower and at 14.40 the *Suvarov* was temporarily hidden from the Japanese in smoke. Rozhestvenski was again wounded and flames drove into the conning-tower, making it untenable, and the ship had to be directed from lower fighting stations. A 4-point turn to starboard had been ordered but the helm jammed so that the turn could not be stopped and at about 14.52 the *Suvarov* turned out of the line and continued round to starboard until she could be steered by her engines. There had been a large explosion in the after 12inch turret which ceased firing, and the after funnel had fallen, but her condition was not as critical as the *Osliabia's*.

These two ships were the main Japanese targets, but visibility was frequently impaired by mist and smoke; at about 14.35 Togo's division reported that they could only see the battle-flags at the Russian trucks: and other ships were also engaged. According to the British observer in the *Asahi*, the *Alexander* was hit several times early in the action, and she was also soon on fire. After the *Suvarov* was hidden in smoke at 14.40, she became the target for several ships and seems to have been badly on fire. The *Borodino* had a bad hit at about 14.30 according to the British observer in *Asahi*. For a short time she subsequently left the line, perhaps due to a machinery or steering defect, and with the *Orel* and *Osliabia* masked each other's fire. The *Borodino* seems to have regained her station at 14.50 or a little after. The *Orel* was certainly hit a number of times in this phase of the battle but her injuries were not vital. The *Sissoi* or perhaps the *Navarin* were set on fire but do not seem to have been badly hit up to 14.50, and the ships astern of them do not appear to have been engaged by the Japanese except that the *Iwate* fired at the *Nikolai* for a time.

1 Admiral Togo's flagship, the battleship *Mikasa.*

Photo by courtesy of Antony Preston

2 *Asama,* a British built 'Elswick' armoured cruiser in pre-war livery.

CPL W/6/002

3 The Japanese armoured cruiser *Iwate,* built on the Tyne 1899-1901.

CPL W/6/003

The *Mikasa* had been hit by six 12inch and nineteen 6inch shells between 14.10 and 14.50 but her fighting power was virtually unaffected. Of these hits, five 12inch and fourteen 6inch had been made between 14.10 and 14.25. A few unimportant hits had been made on the other three battleships, while the *Kasuga* had one 12inch hit at 14.33, and at 14.40 the right fore 8inch gun in *Nisshin* was cut in two by a 12inch shell. All Kamimura's armoured cruisers had been hit and the *Azuma's* 8inch gun right aft had been put out of action by a 12inch shell at 14.50, but the only ship seriously affected was the *Asama.* At 14.28 a 12inch shell had struck her on the starboard quarter, and the shock of impact had put the steering gear temporarily out of action. At the time she was turning to port and she thus fell out of the line. Repairs were completed in six minutes but the other Japanese ships had vanished in the mist and the *Asama* put on full speed to rejoin them. For a time the Russian ships fired heavily at her but no serious hits were made until 15.00, shortly before she made contact with the Japanese again.

When the *Suvarov* turned to starboard and left the line, the *Alexander* at first followed her, but then led on an easterly course, until at 14.55 her captain turned suddenly to port and headed northwards followed by the other ships. This manoeuvre caused Togo to turn his division 8 points to port together at 14.57, and a further 8 points together at 15.05, thus coming into line ahead in reverse order, the *Nisshin* leading on a

WNW course, to block the Russian northward movement. Kamimura however, seeing that the Russians were becoming disordered and apparently about to turn to starboard, continued on the previous course at an increased speed of 17 knots, masking the fire of Togo's ships as he passed across their sterns, and it was not until 15.10 that he turned 8 points to port in succession, followed by another 8 points to port at 15.16.

In this period the range was reduced, Kamimura's division closing to about 3300 yds which had increased by the time his turn was made. His main target was apparently the *Alexander* but the *Sissoi* and probably *Navarin* were fired at, as well as the *Osliabia*. The latter was now sinking with an increasing list. The sea entered her main deck ports and then the bases of her funnels, and by 15.10 the *Osliabia* had gone down without capsizing, her deck nearly vertical. Russian destroyers rescued 385 survivors but 514 were lost.

Most of Togo's division ceased fire while making their turns, but a number of 12inch hits were made on the Japanese, of which the most important were one on the *Fuji* at 15.00 and two on the isolated *Asama* at the same time. The hit on the *Fuji* pierced the after barbette shield and burst inside, causing a cordite fire and putting the right gun out of action. The *Asama* was hit by two 12inch shells on the starboard side aft, 5 ft above water. These caused serious flooding and her draught was presently increased to 5 ft over the proper figure aft.

So far no torpedo attacks had been made though 17 Japanese destroyers were on the disengaged side of the battle divisions, and the four equipped with mines, had recently joined them. At 15.06 however, the torpedo-gunboat *Chihaya* attached to Kamimura's division, fired two 14inch torpedoes at 2700 yds at a ship which seems to have been the *Orel*. Neither hit, as might be expected. At about this time the *Jemtchug* steamed towards the rear of Kamimura's division and the head of Togo's, but was driven off by the *Iwate, Nisshin* and *Kasuga* at about 3300 yds

before she could launch her torpedoes.

THE SECOND STAGE
Togo did not yet know that the *Osliabia* had sunk, though ships of Kamimura's division had seen her go down, the *Iwate* mistaking her for a *Jemtchug* class cruiser. He must however have known that victory was assured provided the Russian fleet did not escape northwards in the mist and fog. The next 2½ hours of the battle were governed by Russian efforts to break through to the North and the Japanese countermoves. The visibility had deteriorated as much smoke combined with the mist and for the most part did not exceed 6000 or 7000 yds at best.

The Japanese were now steaming approximately WNW with Togo's division leading in reverse order. The *Asama* soon made contact again and at 15.15 took station ahead of the *Nisshin*. The Russian fleet had been in disorder since 15.00 or a little after, and the details of the movements of the various ships are not known. The *Alexander* broke off her northward advance and turned sharply to starboard, and the surviving three ships of the Russian 2nd Division fell astern so that Nebogatov's 3rd Division took their station next to the *Orel*. Togo opened fire on the Russians, who were now on the port side of the Japanese, at 15.07, Kamimura's division joining in at 15.20. The ranges varied from 5000 — 6000 yds down to 3000 or less to the main body of the Russian ships, while the *Suvarov* which was to the westward of the other Russian ships, was engaged at 15.20 for a time by the *Shikishima,* and apparently the *Mikasa*, at under 2500 yds. At 15.35 she suddenly appeared out of the fog on the port beam of Kamimura's ships and was engaged for five minutes by all five at down to 2000 yds or less. Apart from the *Suvarov,* the Japanese targets cannot be all identified and they were frequently obscured in mist and smoke. The leading Russian ship, believed to be still the *Alexander* (though according to some accounts she fell out temporarily and the *Borodino* led)

was engaged by the *Mikasa* and other ships, and the *Sissoi,* at which the *Fuji* reported firing for a time, also appears to have been attacked. The *Mikasa* fired an 18inch torpedo at 15.21 at a ship which seems to have been the *Suvarov* and at about 15.35 the *Yakumo* and the *Azuma* each fired one 18inch at her. None of these three torpedoes hit.

By 15.30 the Russians were vanishing in the mist on the port quarter of Togo's division, and he ordered the *Nisshin* to alter course 4 points to port. At 15.42 he turned simultaneously 8 points to port, and then again at 15.49, thus bringing the *Mikasa* back to the lead on a North-Easterly course. At 15.47 Kamimura turned his division in line ahead to starboard and took up a position on Togo's port bow. The Russian ships, apart from the *Suvarov* had meanwhile steamed SE from about 15.30 and then at 15.40 turned approximately NNE, so that another encounter was imminent.

It seems likely that the *Alexander* received much of the damage, which was eventually to prove fatal, in the action described above. At 15.25 the *Izumo* reported that her target, which was probably the *Alexander* had a considerable list to port, and by about 15.40 it appears that she was no longer leading the Russian line. The *Sissoi* and *Orel* were also probably damaged, while the *Suvarov* was in a bad way. Her fore 12inch turret was put out of action, Rozhestvenski was again seriously wounded and unconscious, and the British observer in the *Azuma* reported that she was down by the bow with a heavy list to port, with no foremast or after funnel and only a ragged half of the fore funnel left. He adds that she was one mass of thick grey smoke from forecastle to mainmast, but still firing some after guns. At 15.39 the torpedo gunboat *Chihaya* closed the *Suvarov* to 1750 yds and fired two 14inch torpedoes, one of which was claimed as a hit, though the *Suvarov's* condition showed no visible change. At 15.45 the 5th Destroyer Division also attacked the *Suvarov* at 450 to 900 yds, and five 18inch torpedoes were fired. It seems probable that no hits were made. The *Chihaya* was hit by a shell just above the waterline and had to make emergency repairs, and the destroyer division leader had a 3inch shell in one boiler. These shells may have come from other Russian battleships, rather than the *Suvarov*.

Of the Japanese armoured ships the *Mikasa* was hit by a 12inch shell as were the *Shikishima*, *Fuji* and *Nisshin*. Hits were also made on most of Kamimura's division but no very important damage was caused to any of the Japanese armoured ships in this phase of the battle.

THIRD STAGE

At 15.55 Togo caught sight of the Russian main force again, now bearing East by South and 7500 — 8000 yds away, and at 16.01 the *Mikasa* opened fire at the third Russian ship, at a range of 7100 yds. The other ships of the 1st Division, as well as the 2nd Division ahead, opened within the next few minutes, and the *Mikasa* changed to the leading ship at 16.03. The Russians were now apparently in the order: *Borodino, Orel, Alexander, Nikolai, Apraxin, Seniavin, Sissoi, Navarin, Nakhimov, Ushakov,* the last named having a large shell hole forward. The Russian line was gradually forced southward and by 16.24 the Japanese were steering approximately east. In a few minutes the Russians headed southwards and disappeared in the mist.

The *Suvarov* meanwhile had steamed to the North-East and once more found herself between the two fleets. The *Mikasa* opened a heavy fire on her at 16.08, and other ships of Togo's division followed at a range which fell from 6100 to 2200 yds. Some of Kamimura's ships also fired at her and the Japanese 1st Division reported that tongues of flame were issuing from main-deck gun-ports, and that she resembled an island volcano in eruption. At about 16.30 the British observer in *Asahi* saw a 12inch shell burst between decks, close to the after 6inch turret. Flames spouted 50 ft from the side, the stump of her main-topmast fell and at the same instant there was a considerable explosion. Until then

Shiranui, a Japanese destroyer of the Murakumo class, which were built by Thornycroft and were similar to the '30-knotters' built by that company for the Royal Navy.

CPL W/6/004

she was still occasionally firing from an after turret, but now only one or two of the stern 3inch guns still fired. She showed no signs of sinking however, and the British observer in the *Azuma* thought that she was less down by the bow at 16.20 than $\frac{3}{4}$ hour previously. The *Mikasa* had fired an 18inch torpedo at 16.18 and another at 16.24, while the *Shikishima* fired one at 16.32 but none hit.

Apart from the *Suvarov* it is impossible to identify the Japanese targets, and ranges appear to have been always over 4000 yds to the main body of the Russian ships. It cannot be stated with any certainty how much damage was done to them in this period of the action, but the *Alexander* was undoubtedly the ship in worst state, other than the *Suvarov*.

The *Mikasa* was hit by a 12inch shell at 16.15, and the *Nisshin* by a heavy shell at 16.05 which sent splinters into the conning-tower and wounded Vice-Admiral Misu. Some of the 2nd Division were also hit, and the unlucky *Asama*, which had sighted her own Division at about 15.50 and steamed ahead on the disengaged side of the 1st Division to regain her proper station. She was so slowed by her previous damage aft and by a 6inch shell through the base of the after funnel, which reduced the boiler furnace-draught, that she did not take station astern of the *Iwate* until 17.05. Apart from the Russian hits, the right fore 12inch gun failed in *Shikishima* at 16.15, and the turret roof was damaged and the left gun also put out of action for a time.

At 16.35 Togo turned his division 8 points to port simultaneously, to forestall any attempt to escape North round the Japanese rear, but no such movements developed and at 16.43 he turned 8 points together to starboard back into line ahead. The Russians had now completely vanished in smoke and haze and at 16.51 Togo altered course to due South. Meanwhile Kamimura in the van, had altered course to approximately SE at 16.35 and to nearly due S at 16.42, but fearing to lose touch with Togo, he turned back onto a North-Westerly course at 16.47. At this time he heard firing far to the South, and soon, seeing that Togo's division had turned onto a Southward course, he again turned in that direction and took station on the port bow of the 1st division.

TORPEDO ATTACKS ON THE SUVAROV

At 16.43 Togo had ordered the 4th Destroyer Division to attack and they made for the *Suvarov* at 18 knots. This division which was to accomplish more in the battle than any other destroyer division, was the one fitted for minelaying and each destroyer carried eight mines with 100 lb charges in addition to her usual armament of two 18inch torpedo-tubes and four torpedoes. The division comprised the *Asagiri* and *Murasame*, built in Japan, and the *Asashio* and *Shirakumo*, built by Thornycroft. All four were 375ton boats with designed speeds of 29-31 knots, but a ricochet had hit the *Murasame* at 14.10 and reduced her speed to 20 knots. The *Suvarov* was blazing with flames

shooting out of the upper deck and sides but was still steaming roughly WNW at about 10 knots and was sufficiently under control to turn her head quickly to starboard when the destroyers were seen on the port side.

At 17.05 the *Asagiri* and *Murasame* each fired one torpedo at 650 yds and the *Asashio* immediately followed with two, but the rough seas striking the sides of the torpedoes as they entered the water, made them inaccurate. The *Asagiri* and *Murasame* again attacked on an opposite course at 350 yds and though the *Asagiri's* torpedo misfired, that launched by the *Murasame* hit the *Suvarov* on the port quarter. She suddenly listed about 10° but showed no signs of sinking, and although only one shell hit the *Asagiri* without causing much damage, the fire of the *Suvarov's* one or two remaining 8inch guns was reinforced by that of other Russian ships. As a result the *Shirakumo* did not fire any torpedoes, nor did the 3rd Destroyer Division, which had been intended to make a subsequent attack; this division was fired at by Russian ships at 3300 yds.

CRUISER FIGHTING
Under Togo's plan, his 12 light cruisers, with the three *Matsushima* class and the *Chin-Yen* which comprised Vice-Admiral Kataoka's 5th Division, were to attack the Russian cruisers and fleet train to the rear of their battleships. This action had been going on since about 14.45, though Kataoka's ships did not engage for two hours, and its details are not relevant to

the major fight between the armoured ships. It must be noted however that from about 14.10 to 14.20 some of the Japanese light cruisers had fired at the leading Russian battleships at 6000 — 9000 yds, and that at about 16.45 some of the Russian battleships driven South in the main action, engaged the Japanese light cruisers for 15 or 20 minutes at about 4500 — 9000 yds without doing very much damage. The *Takachiho* which had been repairing previous damage and was separated from the other light cruisers had a brush with Russian battleships at 17.20 when the range was 9400 yds, and Kataoka's 5th Division may also have had a short engagement with them at about 17.10.

FOURTH STAGE
Since 16.51 Togo had been steaming South and at 17.00 two *Borodino* class battleships were sighted to the South-West on a northerly course. The Russian ships opened fire at 7200 yds to which the *Mikasa* immediately replied and the other ships of the 1st Division followed. The *Fuji* reported a range of 5200 yds at 17.07 but this then increased, and the Russians disappeared in the mist soon afterwards. Togo did not turn North after them at this stage, but continued to the South firing at various targets dimly seen through the mist. The armed liner *Ural* disabled and abandoned in the cruiser-fighting previously was the most visible of these. The Japanese were now facing the evening sun, and conditions were probably better from the Russian line as the *Nisshin*

was hit by a 12inch shell at 17.20 which cut the left after 8inch gun in two. Why Togo did not immediately turn after the *Borodino* class ships is not clear, but by 17.28 he concluded that the main body of the Russians were to the North of him, and turned his division on to a NNW course. In point of fact the Russian battleships, led by the *Borodino* and *Orel*, had turned on to a North-Westerly course, and Togo had been steaming in roughly the opposite direction.

Meanwhile Kamimura's division ahead, had fired at various targets in the mist and fog, and hearing firing on the starboard bow, had altered course in that direction. His ships intervened in fighting between the Japanese and Russian cruisers, and soon after 17.30 went in chase of some of the latter to the South-West, thus parting company with Togo's division for the time being.

Since the attack of the 4th Destroyer Division, the *Suvarov* seems to have steamed Southward at 4-5 knots and the Russian destroyer *Buiny* crowded with survivors from the *Osliabia* at about 17.30 or a little later, took off Rozhestvenski, who was only intermittently conscious, and also some of his staff. Nebogatov was apparently never formally notified that the command had passed to him, though he received Rozhestvenski's orders to make for Vladivostok on a course N 23° E. The destroyer *Biedovy* is said to have been sent to take off the rest of the *Suvarov's* crew but this was never done.

1 The Japanese destroyer *Asashio* which like
Shiranui was built by Thornycroft, but to a
later design.
IWM

2 The Russian protected cruiser *Oleg*.
CPL W/6/005

THE LAST TWO HOURS
Though much damage had been
inflicted on the Russian battleships
at small cost to his own, Togo
cannot have felt very satisfied with
the position at 17.30, but the last
two hours of the daylight battle
were to end in the assurance of a
great victory. During this period of
the battle the 1st and 2nd Japanese
Divisions were not in company until
the end and Kamimura's ships

contributed little to the action with
the main Russian force.

After Togo's turn at 17.28, his
division maintained a generally
NNW course until 17.52. They fire
at the derelict *Ural* and at the repa
ship *Kamchatka,* which was also
disabled, and both the *Mikasa* and
Shikishima fired a torpedo at the
Ural, the latter of which hit at 240
yds, and in a few minutes the *Ural*
went down. At 17.52 Togo altered

1

2

course to WNW, but sighting some Russian destroyers which appeared to be intending an attack, he temporarily turned to the NE at 17.56 until they were driven off by the *Mikasa's* fire. At 17.57 two *Borodino* class battleships were seen in the WNW, steaming Northwards and 6900 yds away, and at 18.00 Togo turned onto a NNW course again and opened fire.

The Russian fleet had now re-formed with the cruisers and destroyers, as well as the surviving fleet train, on the disengaged side. The armoured ships were in order as follows: *Borodino, Orel, Nikolai, Apraxin, Seniavin, Alexander, Sissoi, Navarin, Ushakov, Nakhimov.* The *Alexander* was to starboard of the *Seniavin* and there were gaps between the *Orel* and *Nikolai* and between the *Seniavin* and *Sissoi*₁. At first the Japanese concentrated on the *Borodino* and the range fell slowly to 6000 yds at 18.25. The setting sun was shining on the sea, and the fall of shot could not be seen so that the Japanese firing became slower. Soon conditions for the Japanese apparently improved and at 18.33 the *Mikasa* noted a good many hits on the *Borodino*. She was hidden in smoke and some ships changed target to the *Orel* which was shooting accurately, the spray from her near-misses often drenching the bridges of the Japanese ships. The Russians had begun to edge off to the westward, and the range had risen to 7200 yds at 18.42 causing the Japanese to turn onto a NW course at 18.45. The Russians however turned further to port and the range gradually increased so that the Japanese 6inch guns ceased firing, the main armament continuing a slow and accurate fire.

Although the *Borodino* was the principal target, the *Mikasa* reporting her on fire at 18.40 and Captain Pakenham, the British observer in the *Asahi* seeing a very conspicuous hit at 18.57 when the range was 8400 yds, the first ship to fall out was the *Alexander*. The Japanese state that the 1st Division fired only at the *Borodino* and *Orel* in this action, except that the *Kasuga* occasionally fired at other ships, and though it is possible that targets were mistaken and that the *Alexander* was fired at for a short time when the Russian line first turned away westward, it seems likely that her falling out was as a result of continued flooding from injuries received in the earlier part of the battle. Russian witnesses in other ships say that her bows were nearly destroyed and there was a huge hole in the port side forward. A very large fire was also raging on the boat deck, and the *Alexander* began to fall astern, flying the distress signal, and with a heavy list to port. She temporarily recovered and returned to the line astern of the *Seniavin,* but shortly before 19.00 again turned out of the line to port, and at 19.00 or a few minutes after, suddenly capsized and sank with all hands.

The *Borodino's* end was not to be long delayed. At 19.04 the *Mikasa* reported that her mainmast had fallen and that there was a large fire, and at 19.18 when the range was 9000 yds two 12inch shells fired by the *Shikishima* hit. Pakenham relates that flame burst from her after battery and leaping to a height of at least 30ft, at once gained possession of the whole breadth of the ship and seemed to be working forward rapidly. Her after turret was now silent. It was already twilight and after a few more shots, the *Mikasa* turned due north at 19.23 and ceased fire. As the *Fuji* reached the turning point her last 12inch shot produced the sensation of the day. In Pakenham's words:

> Entering the upper part of the *Borodino* near the foremost broadside turret, it burst, and an immense column of smoke, ruddied on its underside by the glare from the explosion and from the fire abaft, spurted to the height of her funnel tops. From every opening in engine-rooms and stokeholds steam rushed and in two or three minutes, the ship from foremast to stern was wrapped in fiercely whirling spirals of smoke and vapour, gaily illumined by frequent tall shafts of flame. It was evident that the conflagration had reached a stage where it could defy

control, and that the vessel's fighting days were numbered, though even so it was not realised how near was the end. Though sudden, this was not dramatic. While all watched, the unfortunate ship disappeared, her departure only marked by a roar not greatly louder than that of one of her own bursting shells, and, until dispersed by the wind, by a great increase in volume of the dense cloud that brooded over the place she had occupied. It is doubtful whether any in the Japanese fleet saw her go, as little but the outline of her stem had been visible for some minutes.

It seems certain that the final hit caused a magazine explosion which sank the *Borodino*. There is some difference in the various reports as to the exact time when she sank, but it was probably at 19.30. Only one man was saved from her crew of 855.

The remaining Russian ships made off to the south-west, while at 19.28 Togo ordered the Japanese fleet to go north and fixed Utsuryo To on the north side of the Island of Matsushima for the rendezvous next morning. The wind had now somewhat fallen, but there was still a good deal of swell and in the fading twilight the Japanese torpedo craft could be seen coming up from North, South and East through heavy seas.

In this last action of the daylight battle, further hits were also made on the *Orel*, but she was not vitally injured. In the Japanese ships, the right fore 12inch gun in *Mikasa* failed at 18.04 from a premature, and as in *Shikishima* previously, the turret roof was damaged and the left gun put out of action until 18.40. The *Mikasa* was also hit by a 12inch shell at 18.45 and by a 6inch at 18.26 which disabled one 6inch gun permanently. A 12inch shell hit the left fore 8inch gun in the *Nisshin* at about 19.00 and cut the gun in two, but otherwise there was no important damage to Togo's division in the phase of the battle.

---

¹According to some the *Ushakov* was astern of the *Seniavin* which does not seem likely. The *Navarin* may have been ahead of the *Sissoi*.

²Though some accounts say there were four survivors from a total of 840.

The development of a British air-laid ground mine

by Tom Burton

Tom Burton is an authority on mine-warfare and the author of a Profile on HMS 'Abdiel'. He is currently working for the Admiralty.

Following the unsatisfactory performance of the British Sinker Mk I (M), laid off the Flanders coast in the late summer of 1918, research into magnetic firing circuits, for torpedo war-heads as well as for mines, continued in the succeeding years. As a result of this research work, in 1931 it was decided that the dip-needle firing principle for mine circuits should be abandoned for a new system, which incorporated a mu-metal detector rod and relied for firing on the rate of change, as opposed to the increase in strength of the magnetic field in the vicinity of the mine.

Up to as late as 1936, all development effort was devoted to the production of a moored magnetic mine, for use mainly as a defensive anti-submarine weapon, and no serious thought was given to the design of a magnetic ground mine with which to attack an enemy at base, very probably from the air. This now very apparent error in policy arose from a misinterpretation of the vast fund of mining experience gained by Great Britain during World War I. For want of a proper analysis of the results obtained and ignoring subsequent advances in anti-submarine techniques, the proficiency of the moored mine as an anti-submarine weapon was greatly over-emphasised. Thus it came about that, with only a very small design staff available, first priority was given to the perfection of a mine which would be laid in deep water rather than shallow, and offensive mining was considered of secondary importance to the laying of large defensive minefields around the shores of Great Britain.

Happily, if rather late in the day, a Staff Requirement for an air-laid magnetic ground mine was issued in 1936. The requirement was for a mine suitable for carriage in the same dropping gear as that used with the 18inch torpedo, and containing as much explosive as possible within an overall weight of 1500 lb. Dropping requirements stipulated that the mine be suitable for laying in a minimum depth of water of five fathoms, from as great a height as possible and without a parachute; the use of a parachute was to be considered at a later date. The magnetic sensitivity was to be the maximum attainable. It would be acceptable if the mine fired against a destroyer steaming at eight knots in ten fathoms, and it was desirable to obtain a sensitivity greatly in excess of the destructive radius of the charge. Provision was to be made for adequate safety in handling and laying, and the mine was to become active within 15 minutes of entering the water. Any special devices which would increase the enemy's sweeping problem without unduly complicating the design were to be incorporated.

During the next three years the mine — known as the M Type E — was developed in close co-operation with the Royal Aircraft Establishment at Farnborough, and it was determined that the dimensions of the mine shell should be 18 in diameter x 113 in length.

To ensure ballistic stability in flight through the air a tail unit 50 in long was added, arrangements being made for it to disengage from the mine on impact with the water. Additionally, in order to decelerate the mine rapidly after entry into the water, it was given a flat nose inclined at 70° to the axis, which caused the mine to turn from its trajectory path and ease itself to the bottom. To prevent any ill-effect during the flight, a wooden fairing was fitted over the inclined nose, perpendicular to the axis; the fairing broke away on impact with the water.

Initial dropping trials were carried out during May 1938, when inert-filled mines were released from a Swordfish aircraft at a speed of 100 knots, from a height of approximately 100 feet and into six fathoms of water. In these trials the mine's ballistic and entry performances were satisfactory, but some structural weaknesses were exposed, necessitating modifications to the main body and tail unit. The next series of drops covered release from heights of 100 to 900 ft, at speeds of 100 to 150 knots and revealed a weakness in the rear section, due to stress caused by the turning of the mine on entry into the water, when released from heights above 200 ft.

New rear sections were manufactured and trials carried out early in 1939 showed that the mine could be released from aircraft at speeds around 100 knots and from heights of from 400 to 700 ft, into five fathoms of water, with reasonable expectation that no damage would result to the shell or components.

In July 1939 an experimental order was placed for 30 mines, with an additional 120 for emergency use, and at the same time the Air Ministry was given the characteristics of the mine. In the course of subsequent discussion between the Naval and Air Staffs, at which the whole question of air mining was considered, it soon became apparent that the Beaufort torpedo-bomber earmarked by Coastal Command for mine-laying had too short a range to reach many of the enemy-controlled areas where such operations were most desirable, and it was therefore decided to employ, in addition, Hampden aircraft of Bomber Command.

This decision necessitated some redesign of the mine to allow it to be laid from not less than 500 ft at a speed of 150 knots, and work was therefore put in hand to produce a parachute drogue attachment. At the same time the rear section of the mine was modified to take either a tail unit or a parachute attachment, which latter would also free itself when the mine hit the water. Successful trials of this new arrangement were not completed until the middle of March 1940.

On the outbreak of war in September 1939 the need for a mine such as this, for use in enemy

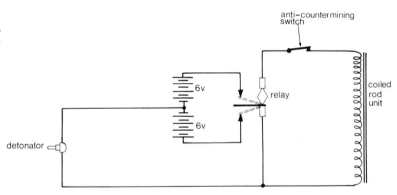

1	Nose Fairing	7	Detachable Tail
2	C.R. Unit	8	Release Mechanism
3	Primer	9	Rubber Diaphragm
4	Detonator Holder	10	Rear Section
5	A.C. Switch	11	Hydrostatic Switch
6	Relay	12	Forward Section

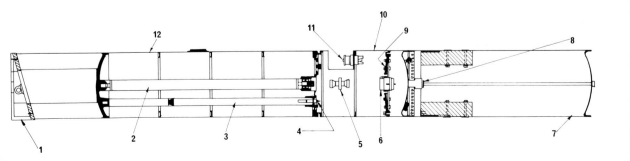

waters where surface minelayers could not operate, became urgent. Consequently, although trials data were considered to be incomplete, contracts for the manufacture of the mine in quantity were placed in the autumn of that year. The firms concerned were J I Thornycroft & Co of Southampton, who had carried out all previous work in regard to the provision of experimental mines; J & E Hall & Co Ltd of Dartford; and B T H Co Ltd of Rugby.

The A Mk 1, as the first production mine was known, in its final form weighed about 2000 lb overall, including 750 lb of amatol in the charge; the diameter of the mine was 18 in, and the length 170 in when fitted with a tail, and 121 in when fitted with a parachute. The single-contact firing circuit initially installed could be activated only after the closing of a hydrostatic switch, which was itself operated both mechanically (just before laying) and by means of a soluble plug (after immersion). In the 'safe' position the hydrostatic switch provided a double break in the detonator circuit and a short-circuit across the relay. An anti-countermining switch was also incorporated.

The operation of the activated firing circuit was simple. On the approach of a target, an electrical current was induced in the coiled rod by virtue of the change in the local magnetic field. This current was sufficient to operate the 30 micro-amp relay, causing it to make contact on one side or the other, and so allowing current to pass from one of the 6-volt batteries through the electric detonator. In practice the relay incorporated a six-second delay in order to attain the best firing position relative to the target, ie under the after portion of the ship.

Mines fitted with parachutes were at first considered unsafe for carriage outside the fuselage; Swordfish and Beaufort aircraft therefore used the tailed version. No aircraft could carry more than one mine until February 1942, when multi-mine-carrying aircraft of Bomber Command were first used.

In April 1940 sufficient A Mk 1 mines became available for an acceptable level of laying to be maintained with the few aircraft then allocated to that duty. The first British aerial minelaying operation was carried out on the night 13-14 April, when Hampdens of No 5 Group, Bomber Command, laid 13 mines in the Great and Little Belts. This was the first of a sustained trickle of operations in an air mining campaign which was to reach vast proportions as the war progressed, in which new mines and many sophisticated devices played a leading role in the overall attack on the enemy's shipping.

Technical Topics No 5

CORDITE

by John Campbell

This term has been widely used in Britain for any type of solid propellant excluding gunpowder, but where accompanied by additional classification as in 'Cordite MD' or 'Cordite SC' it has a precise meaning and it is now customary to limit the use of the word in this way and to replace it otherwise by 'propellant'. Manufacture of Cordite Mark I began in 1889, three years after Vielle in France and Duttenhoffer in Germany had produced the first usable propellant from gelatinised nitrocellulose. For 40 years previously attempts had been made to employ nitrocellulose as a propellant, but it was not until the nitrocellulose was dissolved in a solvent, later usually acetone, which was then removed, that success was achieved. In 1888 Nobel introduced 'Ballistite' with 40-50 per cent Nitroglycerin and the balance Nitrocellulose. This was unusual for the period as the Nitroglycerin served as the solvent for the Nitrocellulose, which was of low Nitrogen content. It had greatly increased energy per unit weight, and was less liable to moisture absorption than the straight nitrocellulose propellant. France, Russia and USA favoured the latter, but Britain, Germany and most other countries preferred a propellant with Nitroglycerin, though acetone was used as the solvent for the high nitrogen nitrocellulose.

Cordite Mark I had the composition 58 per cent Nitroglycerin, 37 per cent Nitrocellulose (13.1 per cent Nitrogen) 5 per cent Petroleum Jelly (Vaseline). The latter, originally present as a lubricant, served as a moderately efficient stabiliser, as the unsaturated hydrocarbons which it contained would react with the decomposition products, to which all except perhaps the purest and most carefully made nitrocellulose was liable. Cordite Mark I produced exceedingly hot and erosive gases, and it was soon clear that the search for high energy per unit weight had gone too far. It was made in thin cylindrical or cord form, the different sizes being known by a number indicating the diameter of the extrusion die in .01 of an inch — thus Cordite 50 for 12inch Mark VIII and IX guns, Cordite 30 for 6inch QF, Cordite 5 for the Hotchkiss 3pdr. It is now clear that a mistake was made in choosing solid cylindrical grain form, and it would have been better to adopt a tubular form with roughly constant surface area while burning, as was done in Germany.

For all this, Cordite Mark I was a great advance over the brown powder which it replaced. This material known as 'Prismatic Brown' (Pr Br) or with different processing 'Slow Burning Cocoa' (SBC), was developed by Rottweil of Dünaberg and instead of the usual 75 per cent Potassium Nitrate, 15 per cent Alder or Willow charcoal, 10 per cent Sulphur in black powder, it contained 79 per cent Potassium Nitrate, 18 per cent Rye straw charred by superheated steam and only 3 per cent Sulphur. It was slower burning and less damaging to guns than black powder, but its rate of burning was extremely sensitive to moisture content. The charges were also enormous, 630lbs for the standard 13.5inch Marks I to IV, and 960lbs for the 15.25inch in eight 120lb bags — the largest charge ever used in any ship — while the Cordite Mark I charge for the 13.5inch was only 187½lbs. For 6inch guns, EXE in composition essentially $\frac{2}{3}$ brown and $\frac{1}{3}$ black powder had been in favour, but the heavy smoke produced by gunpowder charges was impossible for the larger QF guns, and as Cordite Mark I was relatively 'Smokeless', a term often applied to such propellants at one time, the first issues to the Royal Navy in 1893 were for 6inch, 4.7inch, 6pdr and 3pdr QF guns, while the first size 50 for 12inch guns was supplied in May 1895.

The excessive heat of the gases from Cordite Mark I were reduced in Cordite MD, the first few batches of which were delivered in 1901. This contained 30 per cent Nitroglycerin, 65 per cent Nitrocellulose (average 13.1 per cent N) 5 per cent Petroleum Jelly and the calories per gram on burning (water as liquid) were reduced from 1270 to 1020, a very high figure by present standards but indicating much less erosive gas than with Cordite Mark I. The grain form was unchanged, though tube was used in the 4inch QF Mark III, and usual sizes were MD45 for heavy guns, and 37, 26, 19, 11, 8, 4¼ for 9.2inch to 3pdr. Cordite MD was a stiff and hard colloid and though it was hoped to use MD55 in the 12inch Mark XI, it was found impossible to remove all the volatile solvent in production. The shrinkage in drying was also great, as MD45 could finish at 0.34inch diameter. If properly and carefully made Cordite MD was a reasonably satisfactory propellant, and with its variant MC (qv below) remained standard in the Navy until 1927. Charges had to be increased in weight as compared to Mark I, figures for the 12inch Mark IX being 246 and 211 lbs, but the reduced erosion of the gun was far more important.

Very serious trouble due to instability of the nitrocellulose in Cordite MD occurred in the 1914-18 War. It had been known since before nitrocellulose was used as a propellant, that unless it was correctly made from pure raw material, devastating explosions could occur spontaneously, and this was emphasised by a long series of incidents in the ships of several navies, of which the most notorious prior to 1914 were those in the French battleships *Iéna* and *Liberté*. Testing, safe life and storage procedures had of course been laid down, but in November 1914 the *Bulwark* and in December 1915 the *Natal* were destroyed by internal explosions. The former accident may perhaps have been due to gross carelessness with fused Lyddite shell, but there is little doubt that spontaneous explosion of the nitrocellulose in cordite MD was the cause of the latter. Necessary precautions tend to be reduced or overlooked in the interests of wartime production, and by the beginning of 1917 there were indications that an increase in the safety margin against spontaneous ignition in Cordite MD was highly desirable. Thus from April 1917 clean carded cotton sliver was to be used as the source material for the nitrocellulose instead of cotton waste, the nitrating time was to be 2½ hours and not shorter, to lessen the chances of unstable compounds being formed and resident inspectors were to watch all stages of manufacture. It should be explained that low Nitrogen Nitrocelluloses are made by adjusting the initial composition of the nitrating acid, and that the use of wood cellulose as a raw material was of much later date. Other improvements were the addition of a little chalk as a stabiliser, and the use of cracked petroleum jelly to increase the quantity of unsaturated hydrocarbons (hence Cordite MC) both of which had been shown to be desirable in pre-war experiments.

6000 tons of propellant were to be withdrawn and replaced by materials made by the new method, but this was too late to prevent HMS *Vanguard* blowing up on 9 July 1917 in the worst of all such disasters to British ships. After this catastrophe the supply of new propellant was hastened and by March 1918 all the Grand Fleet, and six months later all ships, had their old outfits replaced. The magazine explosion and fire which led to the scuttling of the *Glatton* in September 1918 was primarily due to the presence of hot boiler ash and clinker against the magazine bulkhead! Later work in the 1920s showed that iron pyrites, a common constitutent of some coals and of such things as cinder paths, could have a devastating effect on the stability of nitrocellulose if small particles were present as an impurity, a by no means impossible occurrence. The Sulphur in the pyrites would slowly oxodise to sulphuric acid which corroded the Nitro-cellulose with considerable localised evolution of heat sufficient to cause spontaneous ignition, as the poor thermal conductivity of the propellant assisted the development of high local temperatures.

Meanwhile, an important advance had been made in Germany with RPC/12, a solventless propellant in general use in the High Seas Fleet in the First World War. In this nitrocellulose of 11.7 — 12.1 per cent Nitrogen content was dissolved in a mixture of Nitroglycerin and 'Centralite' (symmetrical Diethyl Diphenyl Urea). This non-volatile solvent was not removed, and the 'Centralite' was also an excellent stabiliser. The composition of RPC/12 varied a little, being 'hotter' for smaller calibres, and was within the range 25-29 per cent Nitroglycerin, 64-68 per cent Nitrocellulose, 4-7 per cent Centralite with 0.25 per cent Magnesium Oxide, and 0.1 per cent Graphite.

In addition to improved stabilisation from the 'Centralite' the non-removal of solvent gave much better dimensional accuracy. The material was, however, very stiff to extrude and needed much higher pressure than the Cordite MD type.

The British propellant of this type, Cordite SC, introduced in the Navy in 1927, and in use till after the Second World War, was of rather different composition: 41 per cent Nitroglycerin, 50 per cent Nitrocellulose and 9 per cent Diethyl Diphenyl Urea known as 'Carbamite' in Britain. It was still a hot propellant, though the calories/gram figure was about $4\frac{1}{2}$ per cent down on Cordite MD. For most guns it was made in cord form, the size being now indicated in 1/1000th of an inch. Typical sizes were 280 or 300 in heavy guns, 205 in 8inch 150 in Mark 6inch and 103, 061 or 048 in various 4inch guns. Larger sizes could be made if required, the 14inch Mark VII at Dover using SC 500 for cross-Channel firing, while variants in tube form were used in such guns

as the 6pdr Hotchkiss and 2pdr Mark VIII.

The British Navy at last had a satisfactory stable Cordite, its performance in accelerated corrosion tests far surpassing that of Cordite MC, but a cooler propellant was desirable and SC also gave a bright muzzle flash in most guns. The Germans achieved cooler propellants by replacing Nitroglycerin with Diethylene Glycol Dinitrate in RPC/38 and RIC/40, but in the British Navy SC was retained unless flashlessness was desired. The requirement for this last is that the products of the charge should be cool enough not to ignite when meeting the oxygen of the outside air at the gun muzzle, a deceptively simple requirement, and hardest to meet in large high velocity guns. In point of fact service flashless charges were not provided in the British Navy for guns over 5inch, though flashlessness was a requirement for the 16inch Mark IV intended for the redesigned *Lion* class, a project abandoned after the Second World War.

Various additions such as Potassium Sulphate or Cryolite reduce muzzle flash, and in the United States flashless propellants for a number of guns were made from Nitrocellulose, Dinitrotoluene and Dibutyl Phthalate and these found considerable use in Britain during the the Second World War. A better type of propellant was based on Nitroguanidine, a substance investigated to some extent before the 1914-1918 war. A propellant of this type was approved for reduced charges for naval star shells in 1931-1932. This contained 55 per cent Nitroguanidine, 21 per cent Nitroglycerin, 16.5 per cent Nitrocellulose (12.2 per cent Nitrogen), 7.5 per cent Carbamite and the calories/gram figure was about 750, which necessitated larger charges than with SC. Though flash was absent or greatly reduced, smoke was considerably increased and the extreme resistance to accidental ignition was accompanied by the need for large igniters in the charge. Since then much development work

has been done in propellants of this kind which have very largely or entirely replaced the older types and similarly cord has been supplanted by various forms of tubular grain.

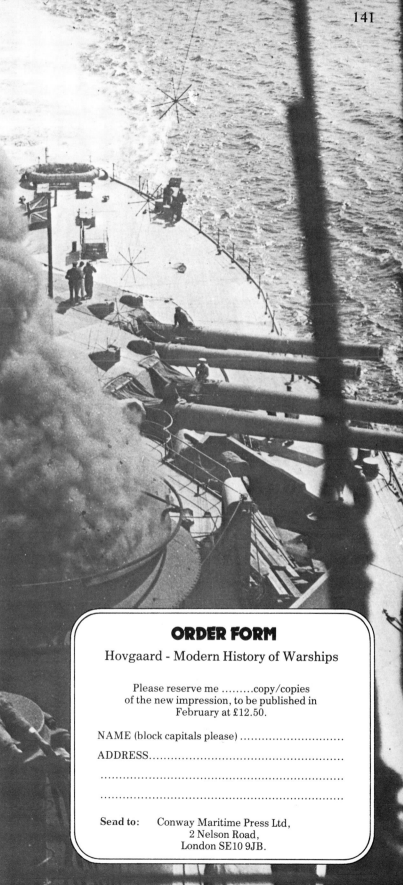

NEW BOOKS

CONWAY MARITIME

New Naval Titles

CAMERA AT SEA 1939-1945 edited by the staff of 'Warship'

A remarkable collection of the very best photography of the war at sea - ships, weapons, equipment, personnel and action shots, many of them never before published. The photos are reproduced large for maximum detail, and the book includes 16 pages of full colour.

The captions were written by an international team of naval experts, including David Brown, Aldo Fraccaroli, Jacques Mordal, Antony Preston, Alan Raven, John Roberts and Anthony Watts.

12¼" × 8", 192 pages, 274 photos (24 in full colour) **Available April** £12.00 (plus 75p post and packing)

WARSHIP VOLUME 1 edited by Antony Preston

The hard-backed annual volume of the first four issues of **Warship**. Subjects covered range from the *Lexington* (CV-2) to the *Kiev*, from Italian battleships to *Flower* class corvettes, and from British destroyer appearance to German battleship armour schemes. Over 40 articles, 100 plans and diagrams and 200 photographs.

Available April £9.50 (plus 50p post and packing)

WARSHIP 'SPECIALS'

Available shortly, this new series is devoted to technical and historical aspects of warships. Written by acknowledged authorities, they are designed to provide the essential in-depth information and pictorial reference for all model-makers, wargamers and enthusiasts. The first two titles are **Battlecruisers** by John Campbell and **Super-Destroyers** edited by Antony Preston, which covers the big destroyer leaders of the Second World War.

9½" × 7¼", 260 pages, over 100 plans and line drawings, 200 photos.

Available May £2.50 (plus 30p post and packing)

MODERN HISTORY OF WARSHIPS by William Hovgaard

A new limited edition of this classic work on the development of the warship from 1860 to 1920, covering all ship types and every major navy. 9½" × 6", 500 pages, 210 plans and diagrams and 6 folding plates. **Available late February** £12.50 (plus 50p post and packing)

. . . Also

MODEL SHIPWRIGHT 24 Edited by John Bowen.

The latest edition of the only quarterly devoted to scale ship modelling of the highest quality.

Available June £2.25 (including postage) or only £7 for a full annual subscription. (In North America, available from S.M.A., 38 Hartford Avenue, Wethersfield, Connecticut 06109, at $4.50 or $18.00 respectively.)

Please add the post and packing if ordering direct from:
Dept. WS
CONWAY MARITIME PRESS LTD
2 NELSON ROAD
GREENWICH
LONDON SE10 9JB
UK
(Tel: 01-858 7211)

NEW BOOKS

CONWAY MARITIME

New Sailing Ship and Modelmaking Titles

SAILING SHIPS ON OLD POSTCARDS
[Segelschiffe auf alten postkarten] by Jürgen Meyer
A magnificent collection of 610 postcards, depicting European sailing ships of the 19th and 20th centuries. Issued in this country for the first time, it is an unusual and delightful reference - a genuine collector's item. 10½" × 12", 200 pages. **Available March £25.00 [plus £1.00 post and packing]**

The following three books are acknowledged by modelmakers and enthusiasts to be classics in their field, and originals are now expensive collectors' items. They contain unique and detailed information and are illustrated in depth with plans, drawings and photographs. These large format reprints are designed to preserve the clarity and detail of the original illustrations and to make them available once more at a reasonable price.

SHIPS OF THE PAST by Charles G Davis
A study in a degree of detail to satisfy the most exacting modelmaker - of a range of local sailing craft, schooner, packet ships and naval frigates. Appendix on sources for plans.
10¾" × 8¼", 188 pages, 43 photos, 33 plans and 55 line drawings.
Available March £5.50 (plus 50p post and packing)

THE FRIGATE CONSTITUTION and other Historic Ships by F Alexander Magoun
An anatomy of the construction of the oldest warship still afloat, by the man who drew up the plans for her reconstruction. A full set of plans are included, and the book also covers a Viking longship, *Santa Maria, Mayflower,* the clipper *Flying Cloud* and the schooner *Bluenose*
10¾" × 8¼", 156 pages, 30 photos, 16 plans and 63 line drawings.
Available March £5.50 (plus 50p postage and packing)

THE BALTIMORE CLIPPER by Howard Chappelle
The definitive study of the privateering, smuggling, slaving and blockade-running schooners that were built first and foremost for speed. Many detailed plans by the author, who was probably the most eminent authority on sailing craft in the world.
10¾" × 8¼", 200 pages, 36 photos and 48 plans. **Available March** £5.50 (plus 50p post and packing)

. . . Also
WARSHIP 6 edited by Antony Preston
The latest issue of this popular quarterly journal devoted to the design, development and service history of combat ships.

Available April £2.25 per copy (including postage) or £9.00 for an annual subscription.

Please add the post and packing if ordering direct from:
Dept. WS
CONWAY MARITIME PRESS LTD.
2 NELSON ROAD
GREENWICH
London SE10 9JB
UK
(Tel: 01-858 7211)

144

USS *Laub* (DD-613): an enclosed base ring
5inch/38 cal mount. The history of this
most successful DP weapon is detailed by
Norman Friedman in the next issue of this
journal.

USN

Editorial

In *Warship 7* we start a new two-part article on the famous *Capitani Romani* light cruisers of the Italian Navy, written by Elio Andò. Signor Andò is well known to ship-lovers for his distinctive drawings of warships seen as jacket-illustrations on the official histories of the Italian Navy, the *Orizzonte Mare* series and elsewhere. The text is accompanied by a magnificent drawing of this very handsome class.

The *Capitani Romani,* whose names commemorated that Imperial Roman past constantly recalled by Mussolini, were a well-considered reply to the French *contre-torpilleurs,* small and ultra-fast (41 knots) cruisers as against over-sized destroyers. As a result the Italians had a type of ship which could also serve as a convoy escort, with good AA and torpedo-armament. The best tribute to them is that the *San Giorgio* (formerly the *Pompeo Magno*) is still in service with the *Marina Militare* as a training ship, two reconstructions later.

A French contributor, Pierre Hervieux, has written an account of the Japanese B-series of large aircraft-carrying submarines. Just why and how the Imperial Navy's submarine policy should have failed so disastrously has never been clear. Whereas the surface fleet and the naval air arm had no problem in identifying its objectives, the submarine command was misled about which targets were worthwhile. As a result the US Navy was saved the additional burden of elaborate precautions to secure its supply-lines across the Pacific, and could concentrate its ASW resources on the protection of naval forces. Instead of reversing the priorities the Japanese high command then switched its highly trained submarine force to the task of carrying supplies to outlying Army garrisons, a diversion of effort which frittered away the resources even faster.

Peter Elliot, author of the book *Allied Escorts of World War II* has written about the production of escorts by Allied shipyards. The output of frigates, corvettes and DEs from American, British and Canadian yards matched their achievements in mercantile building, but it is interesting to see how widely the average building times could vary. Organization of the yard and supply of components was just as important as size, and quite small yards often did better than the bigger yards, which may have had a bigger workload of repairs.

Norman Friedman describes that uniquely successful American gun, the 5in/38cal, which is still very much in evidence 40 years after coming into service. The combination of a robust gun-mounting and a well-designed fire control system gave USN ships a great advantage in medium-range defence, and it is interesting to note that in 1942 the Admiralty considered arming British destroyers with 5in/38s, which explains why HMS *Delhi,* the only British AA ship with that gun, was so rearmed.

Peter Hodges, author of books on the *Tribal* and *Battle* class destroyers, has written about changes to the *Leander* class frigates. If ever there was a flexible design it is the Type 12 hull, which progressed from the original *Whitby* class of 1950-55 through the *Rothesay* to the *Leander* series, now in the middle of their half-life refits. Nor is that the end of the story, for the Dutch are rearming their *Leanders* with Harpoon missiles and OTO-Melara 76mm guns, and the Indian Navy is expanding the design to allow a Sea King helicopter to be embarked.

John Lambert has followed his drawing of a Type 15 frigate with an equally good one of HMS *Terpsichore.* The Type 16 conversions were quicker and cheaper than the full Type 15, and always looked like destroyers.

Warship has not previously dealt with personalities, but David K Brown in this issue explains the importance of William Froude in the history of warship design. Froude was a good example of the Victorian polymath, who turned his hand to anything; he designed a machine to print graph paper, and from scratch perfected the science of tank-testing ship models. His work has saved untold millions by obviating the need for full-scale trials and enabling the naval architect to investigate the drawbacks of a hull-form before building the ship.

Antony Preston

Capitani Romani
PART I – DESIGN AND CONSTRUCTION

by ELIO ANDO

Elio Andò is a civil engineer who commands the Gorizia fire brigade. He is also a Midshipman in the Reserve and an official technical artist to the Italian Navy. A number of his monographs on Italian warships have been published, and he is illustrator of several more. The greater part of the photos used in this article are from his own collection but some were kindly supplied by E Bagnasco and F Bargoni.

Scipione Africano on her sea trials 18 April 1943. Note the typical Italian camouflage of light grey and dark grey, both greys having a bluish tinge.

DESIGN HISTORY

The *Capitani Romani* can be considered the Italian reply to the large, fast French destoyers of the *Le Terrible* and *Mogador* classes. The Italian Navy decided to build them in 1937, placing the project in the hands of Generals Alfano and Pugliese of the Marine Engineers (*Genio Navale*).

Initially they appear to derive from the *Condottieri* type cruisers of the *Alberico da Barbiano* (1925) class, but they in fact abandoned their larger, antiquated design, becoming more compact, low lying, and warlike in appearance.

They were first classified as 'ocean scouts' (*esploratori oceanici*), because of their high speed, extensive range and a larger displacement than the other 'scouts'. These characteristics equipped them for open sea missions rather than for action in the Mediterranean. However, a scout cannot be defined either in terms of tonnage or of armament, but essentially by the task assigned to it: that is, scouting work in bad weather conditions such as fog, something which in the 1930s could not be tackled by aircraft. However by the end of the decade extensive experience of aerial scouting with increasingly sophisticated machines, not to mention the appearance of radar, meant that the sea scouts' contribution was no longer needed. The units rated as scouts therefore were reclassified: the larger craft became light cruisers and the smaller craft, destroyers. These modifications also applied to the *Capitani Romani*, which were classified, according to their displacement and armament as light cruisers, although their protection was ultimately removed.

In the planning stage maximum displacement was intended to be 3400 long tons standard; protection was minimal and limited to the most vital parts, the conning tower and the machinery; maximum speed was to be around 41 knots. Armament consisted of eight guns of 135mm/45 (5.3inch), six 65mm/64 AA, eight 20mm/65 or 20mm/70 machine guns, eight 533mm torpedo tubes and one aircraft without catapult or hangar.

It was immediately evident that no protection would be possible in order to maintain both the armament and speed required of the vessels. Even though the superstructure, apart from the vital parts, was built almost entirely of light alloys, standard displacement exceeded design displacement by about 350 tons. The aircraft was omitted, and also the 65mm/64 guns which were not ready at that time; in their place eight 37mm/54 MGs were adopted.

Twelve units in all were planned, which was the same number as the original 'scouts' — later classified as destroyers — of the *Navigatori*

class. The choice of names was unique in Italian naval tradition, but the sentiment was similar to that of all the light cruisers, which were named after Renaissance or modern leaders: the new, small cruisers took the names of men who built up the greatness of Imperial Rome.

They were all laid down in 1939 in the major Italian shipyards: *Attilio Regolo, Scipione Africano, Caio Mario* and *Claudio Tiberio* in the Odero Terni Orlando shipyard in Livorno; *Cornelio Silla* and *Paolo Emilio* in the Ansaldo shipyard at Genoa-Sestri; *Pompeo Magno* and *Ottaviano Augusto* in the Navali Riuniti shipyard at Ancona; *Claudio Druso* and

Vipsanio Agrippa in the Tirreno yards at Riva Trigos; *Giulio Germanico* in the Navalmeccanica yards at Castellammare di Stabia and *Ulpio Traiano* in the Navali Riuniti yards at Palermo.

HULL AND SUPERSTRUCTURE
Nickel steel plates were used in the construction of the hull, varying in thickness from 7 to 14mm. Extensive use was made in the superstructure of a light aluminium alloy called *Maral*, in order to save weight. High tensile steel was used for the parts subject to high stress.

The hull was streamlined, with no foc'sle and with a pronounced sheer forward. The stem was straight from the keel to a point

well above the waterline and then flared out to meet the upper deck. The transom stern had a curved profile as far as the waterline, which gradually flattened out below to meet the keel. The framing was mainly longitudinal in the central section, and transverse at the bow and stern.

Forward a full width superstructure broke the continuous line of the upper deck, and extended beyond the long bridge structure to form the shelter deck for the superfiring 135mm 'B' turret. The bridge was built up of three square 'boxes' surmounted by the rangefinder and Primary Fire Control Director Tower (1° DT-*Direttore del Tiro*).

1 2

Directly abaft this was the tripod mast, which originally in the *Regolo* was a single pole. Tripod legs were fitted to the platform intended to carry the rotating antennae of the EC/3 ter *Gufo* radar set. The straight funnel was of elliptical cross section. The crane on the deckhouse, used for torpedoes and boats, was of a new design, and had a capacity of 5 tons. The after funnel also had an elliptical cross section, but was shorter and surrounded by four machine gun positions, with two searchlight/signalling projectors abreast.

The after superstructure contained the emergency command position, with the tower of the Secondary Fire Control Director (1°DT).

There was no armoured conning tower but protection for the forebridge against aerial machine gun fire was provided, on all sides and on the upper part, by 15mm armour plates. All the navigation equipment for the ship was concentrated on the forebridge, as were the repeaters for the machinery and the communications network. At the base of the bridge ahead of the fore funnel the flagdeck (*stazione segnali*) was located.

There were three steering positions, one hydraulic and power-assisted on the forebridge, and two aft, one with mechanised steering and the other hand-worked. The rudder was semi-balanced with electro-hydraulic steering gear. It had a surface area of 15.72 sq metres and the maximum angle of the helm was 40°.

There was no damage control centre: the ship was divided into three areas, the central section (comprising the machinery), the bow and stern sections which extended to the respective collision bulkheads. Each area was organised separately as regards emergency procedure, the more important bulkheads being strengthened. Piping for the fire-fighting system was limited to the central area. There were three 50 tons per hour pumps, two in the forward, and

The launch of *Attilio Regolo* at Livorno, 28 September 1939. Note the aperture in the stem for the paravane boom.

Protected by booms, the *Attilio Regolo* fitting out.

one in the after machinery spaces. However the main bilge system applied to the whole ship, and consisted of six electric pumps with 31 ejectors. The fire-fighting equipment also included 74 foam fire extinguishers, 21 carbon dioxide extinguishers, 36 oxygen respirators and 18 asbestos suits.

The ships carried two bower anchors of the Ansaldo 3 ton type (3.5 ton Hall type in the units built at Ancona); they were worked by two capstans powered by interchangeable electric motors, each of 55 hp (Italian): the chain cable had a breaking strain of 8 tons.

MACHINERY

The Naval Planning Committee (*Comitato Progetti Navi*) was responsible for designing the machinery. It was based round two geared turbine units, each generating a projected power of 55 000 hp. Each unit contained auxiliary machinery, turbines and two boilers and was set up independently, with no communication between them. The forward unit was connected to the starboard propeller and the after unit to the port propeller.

Each engine consisted of a Belluzzo type high pressure turbine, and two Belluzzo type low pressure turbines (Parsons type for the Ancona units), operating via single reduction gearing. The low pressure turbines worked independently through two condensers. The high pressure turbine consisted of one two-speed rotor and a group of three rotors for high power. Placed in between were eleven single rotors which were designed for getting under way, but these were cut out when the ship *l* as at full speed. The low pressure turbines, running in parallel had nine ordinary rotors for forward movement and one double rotor and two single (or simple) ones for reverse.

The four oil-fired Thornycroft water-tube boilers, with superheaters, were positioned in pairs on the forward end of each turbine unit, and in case of breakdown, they were capable of single connection. The boiler furnaces were provided with 12

Table 1

'CAPITANI ROMANI' Class (8+4 units)

	Builders	Laid down	Launched	Completed
ATTILIO REGOLO	O.T.O. — Livorno	28-9-39	28-8-40	14-5-42
CAIO MARIO	O.T.O. — Livorno	28-9-39	17-8-41	—
CORNELIO SILLA	Ansaldo — Genova	12-10-39	28-6-41	—
GIULIO GERMANICO	Navalmecc Castellamare	11-5-40	20-7-41	—
OTTAVIANO AUGUSTO	C.N.R. — Ancona	23-9-39	31-5-42	—
POMPEO MAGNO	C.N.R. — Ancona	23-9-39	28-8-41	24-6-43
SCIPIONE AFRICANO	O.T.O. — Livorno	28-9-39	12-1-41	23-4-43
ULPIO TRAIANO	C.N.R. — Palermo	23-9-39-	30-11-42 demolished	—
CLAUDIO DRUSO	C.d.T. — Riva Trigoso	27-9-39	from 16-12-41	
CLAUDIO TIBERIO	O.T.O. — Livorno	16-9-40	from 24-11-41	
PAOLO EMILIO	Ansaldo — Genova	12-10-39	from 20-10-41	
VIPSANIO AGRIPPA	C.D.T. — Riva Trigoso	?-10-39	from 1-7-41	

Displacement: 3 745 t standard; 5 035 t at normal Load; 5 420 t at full Load.
Dimensions: 142.18m; (overall) and 138.74m (between perpendiculars) Length; 14,4m beam; 4,06m draft (at standard displacement).
Machinery: Belluzzo and Parsons types geared turbines in two groups; 108.000 SHP approx. (110 000 italian HP); four boilers Thornycroft type; 1 400 t fuel oil; 150 t Water for boilers, reserve.
Speed: 41 knots (more than 43 knots best sea speed in wartime).
Autonomy: 3 000 miles (approx.) at 25 knots.
Armour: hull — ; conning tower 15mm; gun turrets 6-20mm.
Armament: 8-5,3 inch/45 cal. (135/45); 8-37mm/5A AA; 8-20mm/70 AA; 8-21 inch t.tubes (T.l.s. 533mm); equipped for minelaying (40-136 mines).
Complement: 18 officers + 400 petty officers and seamen.

sprayers and the boilers operated at a pressure of 29kg per square centimetre. The water supply came from four main and four auxiliary electric pumps. To ensure the running of various services on board when in port, two small auxiliary Tyrsa type boilers were fired. One was situated near the after funnel and one next to the steering gear.

There were two fixed pitch three-bladed propellers, each 4.2m in diameter and weighing 12 tons. When steaming forward the right hand propeller rotated clockwise and the left hand one anticlockwise. At full power — 110 000 hp (Italian) or 108 482 shp the propellers reached 320 rpm, 3140 rpm for the high pressure turbines and 2190 for the low pressure turbines. All the completed units attained 41 knots at their trials. On wartime missions and when displacement was markedly increased, they maintained and even exceeded this performance, but with some difficulty. The machinery station was situated on the upper deck on the port side of the midship's deckhouse directly abaft the forward torpedo tubes. All the machinery monitoring equipment was directed into this station.

Preparation for getting under way, depending whether the boilers were cold or fired, took 6 or 3 hours in normal conditions, 4 or 2 hours in an emergency and 3 or 1 hours in exceptional circumstances. Electricity for all services on board was provided by two generators, placed ahead and abaft the machinery, by means of one turbo-alternator and one diesel alternator per generator, producing 230 volts AC.

ARMAMENT

Main armament consisted of eight 135/45 guns, Ansaldo and OTO type 1938, in four twin turrets. (Italian designation for turrets, 1, 2

Pompeo Magno (in camouflage) and *Ottaviano Augusto* in advanced stages of completion at Ancona early in 1943.

The EC/3ter 'Gulf' radar set of *Scipione Africano*.

The compact bridge of *Pompeo Magno:* the rangefinder is sited below the primary Director Control Tower.

1

2

3

3, 4, corresponds to the British A, B, X, Y.) Turret armour was between 10 and 20mm (front) and 6mm on the sides and the top. The guns were in independent sleeves, but at extreme ranges the dispersal of the fall of shot was only adequate. This problem was a common one with Italian naval artillery, because of the wide tolerances allowed in munitions testing. However, the 135/45 could be used, with suitable ammunition to lay down an AA barrage.

Secondary armament, in place of the planned 65/64s which proved to be too long in the development stage, consisted of eight 37/54 AA Breda 1932 MGs in single mountings, arranged four to each side, three on the forward superstructure and the fourth abreast the emergency command position. The 37/54 machine guns, generally mounted in pairs, performed well in action, particularly in low level anti-aircraft fire such as against torpedo planes.

Around the after funnel, in four twin mountings were eight 20/70

Scottie and OM 1941 MGs on modified RM 35 type mounts. The performance of these guns was almost equivalent to the 20/65 Bredas more frequently found in Italian units. Some 8mm and 6.5mm moveable MGs were fitted, usually on the forecastle and quarterdeck.

The torpedo tubes, in quadruple mountings of a new type, had two tubes placed close together above two lower ones which were farther apart. There were eight torpedoes (Si 270/533.4 x 7.2 Type M) plus four reserves, each weighing 1715kg with the following speed in knots (distances in metres): 49±1 (4000), 38±1 (8000), 30±1 (12 000). The quadruple mountings could be trained at fixed angles of 60°, 90° and 120°, to port and starboard. They did not enjoy a high rate of success, as they broke down frequently.

100kg depth charges completed the armament, eight of them on quadruple racks, eight in reserve, and a further eight on rails.

Special rails could be placed on

the main deck to lay mines of various types which would vary in number depending on whether the torpedo tubes and No 4 135mm turret were to be used. Maximum mine stowage was 114 (40) P2000 type, 136 (52) Elia type and 130 (48) Bollo type — but with this number it was not possible to train the torpedo tubes or No 4 turret. The figures in brackets indicate the maximum number of mines that could be transported with the full armament unencumbered.

AMMUNITION

Ammunition was stored in four magazines, 1 and 2 corresponding to the respective 135mm turrets forward, and 3 and 4 aft. It was intended to provide a flooding system and roller shutters and Kingston hatches. Each 135mm turret was supplied by two hoists fitted with a continuous belt for the vertical transfer of ammunition from the magazine to the handling chamber, where two angled hoists which revolved with the turret lifted the ammunition to the gun house. Each hoist cage carried three

Trial firing of a torpedo from *Pompeo Magno*'s quadruple tubes.

Pompeo Magno: view aft from the bridge showing the twin 20/70s and single 37/54.

2

Table 2

Particulars of the guns and machine guns

	5.3 inch	37/54	20/70
Constructor and year	Ansaldo e O.T.O. 1938	Breda 1932	Scottie O.M. 1941
Weight of mounting in Kg.	—	1.500	2.300
Muzzle velocity in m/sec	825	800	840
Maximum elevation	+45°	+80°	+100°
Maximum depression	— 5°	—10°	— 10°
Maximum range, as a naval weapon, in metres	19 600	7 800	6 100
Maximum range, as an AA weapon, in metres	—	5 000	2 500
Round per minute (each barrel)	6	120	220

charges and three shells at a rate of 12 elevations per minute when electrically powered, and six when worked manually.

The 37/54 and 20/70 machine guns were also supplied, electrically or manually, by vertical hoists.

Total magazine stowage amounted to:
135/45: 1280 flashless shells *(VR: — vampa ridotta) — 440 AP* projectiles; *756* HE shells with *OBO* detonators; 84 anti-aircraft barrage with *OMTP* detonating fuses; plus 260 star shells, half of which were *VR.*
37/54: 12 000 rounds 10 800 with proximity fuses *(AD)* and 1200 without.
20/70: 19 200 rounds.

FIRE CONTROL

Firing was controlled by completely stabilized San Giorgio apparatus. The Primary Fire Control Director tower rotated on top of the bridge, and the Secondary Fire Control Director on the deckhouse abaft the second funnel. Both were supplied with optical sights for target indication.

The main firing control room, of RM 1 type, situated in the forward superstructure supplied the two stations with firing information. Three rangefinders measuring four metres at base fed data into this room. Two of them were housed together in the base of the primary DCT and the third in the secondary DCT aft. There were also two

stations for night and searchlight firing situated on the wings of the bridge, comprising general look-out sights for night firing. These two stations, connected to the primary DCT and to the sighting positions of the secondary DCT, were also used to lauch the torpedoes. An inclinometer, situated in the primary DCT completed the range of equipment.

The circuits for the firing system led into a central switchboard, which the Primary or Secondary DCT could switch to four positions:
1 All 135 turrets following the Primary DCT.
2 All 135 turrets following the Secondary DCT.
3 All 135 turrets attuned to night

apparatus for visual direction.
4 All forward turrets attuned to the Primary DCT, and all after turrets to the Secondary DCT.

AC electric wiring for the fire control system was led along both sides of the hull and was divided so as to ensure normal functioning even when one side was damaged. The optical target indication system was based on six sights, three on each side of the bridge wings, which transmitted the bearings to the target indication sights. The two night look-out positions, also in the bridge wings, functioned as sights for night fighting.

PARAVANES AND SMOKE DISCHARGERS

Passive minesweeping defence for the ship was provided by two type C paravanes, carried on the forward superstructure and handled by means of a sliding pole on the starboard side of the bow. They swept an area 60 metres wide and about 10 metres in depth on each side. The ship could free herself of the paravanes by increasing speed, paying out the safety cables into the sea and waiting for the tow ropes to break.

Smoke-screens could be provided by two smoke dischargers per funnel, connected to smoke channels, operated from a control panel situated beside each funnel. Right aft on the quarterdeck was a hydrochlorine discharger, used to conceal the ship when stationary.

ELECTRONICS

Towards the end of the 1930s Italy was eager to participate in radar research. However, the war came before she was able to use it, because the scientists had insufficient funds or because the support of the military authorities and politicians was grudging. Far more serious was the fact that Italy

Attilio Regolo as completed, Livorno 1942
All photos by courtesy of the author

was unaware of British use of radar until after the night encounter of Matapan. Furthermore she did not know that the Germans had been using radar on board their ships since 1939.

The navy received a German De Te (Decimeter Telegraphen) 'Seetakt' which was installed for experimental purposes on the old torpedo boat, *Carini*. Meanwhile, research continued at fever pitch on an Italian set, the *EC/3 ter Gufo*, but it was not until April 1942 that results comparable to the German ones were obtained. In the summer of 1943 about 15 units, including battleships, cruisers and destroyers, were supplied with *Seetakt* or *Gufo*.

Of the *Capitani Romani*, all three units in operation were supplied with a tripod mast, but *Pompeo* never in fact carried radar. The only ocasion when Italian radar was used effectively by the units was on the night of 17 July 1943, when

Scipione Africano encountered four English motor torpedo boats.

A 1935 SCAM echosounder set was then installed; the receiver was placed in the charthouse and the transducer between No 2 magazine and the forward boiler room.

CAMOUFLAGE
The Italian units entered the war with uniform, light grey colouring. In March 1941 two experimental schemes were introduced, each for a different purpose. The light cruiser *Duca D'Aosta* was given a double herring-bone design in order to disturb rangefinding. The heavy cruiser *Fiume* was painted in blotches of two colours, to alter the apparent shape of the ship.

Around the summer of 1942 all the units' camouflage schemes showed areas of light and dark grey, both ash-coloured and slightly blue-tinted, separated by straight or curved lines.

Regolo, Scipione and *Pompeo* were already camouflaged when they went into service. On the forecastle they carried the diagonal red and white stripes common to all the Italian units for the purpose of aerial recognition. During the period when Italy joined the Allies, after 8 September 1943, the three units adopted a typical Allied colouring of dark grey deck and light grey superstructure.

(Part 2, in the next issue, will cover their operational careers.)

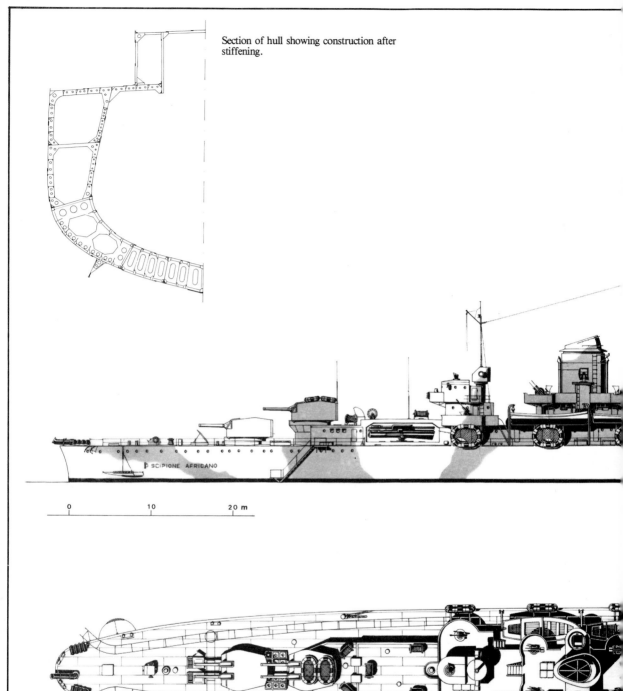

Section of hull showing construction after stiffening.

SCIPIONE AFRICANO

0   10   20 m

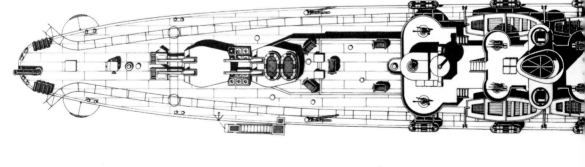

E. ANDO'

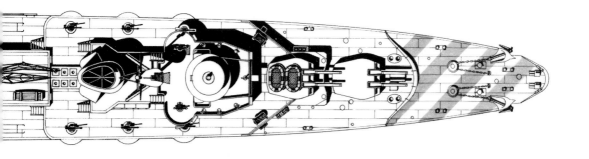

Leander class
FRIGATE CONVERSIONS
by Peter Hodges

Naiad with the 'igloo' cover over the Ikara launcher. The Seacat Director is repositioned centrally abaft the main mast to control either of the two Seacat launchers. The A/S Mk 10 triple barrelled motar is in its designed 'stow' position which keeps the muzzle below flight deck level.

A good deal of water has flowed under the bridges of the *Leander* class frigates since they first joined the Fleet and these notes are intended to bring the reader up to date with the latest developments.

The *Leander* building programme was spread between the laying down of the name-ship in April 1959 and the completion of the 26th, *Ariadne,* in February 1973. With such a time span, many changes were introduced to individual ship-fits, even before the major conversions began.

The class building was split into three stages of 10, 6 and 10 ships,

each stage having slightly different boilers, and the last having increased beam. The latter are generally referred to as the Broad-beam' *Leanders.*

The equipment fits of one stage tended to overlap the next, so that (as the table shows) the Seacat missile system was introduced after the seventh ship of stage 1, and (although neither in the table nor externally detectable) an improved version of the Medium Range (Gunnery) System was introduced with the fourth ship of stage 2. Looking again at the table, it will be noted that the first 7 ships had a

40mm close range armament instead of the intended Seacat system and that not all had the Variable Depth Sonar fit. Some, indeed, ran without a 'Wasp' helicopter when they first commissioned.

The first Seacat-fitted *Leander* was *Naiad* with GWS 20, followed by *Arethusa,* nominally the first with GWS 22, but actually overtaken by *Cleopatra* whilst building. *Arethusa's* GWS 22 was low-set on the hangar roof, and

thus she became an odd-man-out amongst the subsequent GWS 22-fiited members of the class, whose directors are sited on a raised platform.

In clarification of the designations GWS 20 and GWS 22 it is worthwhile to digress for the moment from the *Leander* class and discuss the broad outline of the Seacat systems.

GWS 20

The first Seacat system was designated as Guided Weapon System Mk 20 and was initially designed for simple and rapid installation 'across the board' as a Bofors replacement for close range AA defence.

Although the GWS 20 system met the requirements of simplicity (it has been called the poor man's missile system), the design of the GWS 20 director placed a heavy responsibility on the Seacat aimer. The director itself is hand-worked, and initially is simply unlocked and pushed around to the designated bearing by the Director Officer ('Officer' defines a task rather than a rank) who stands outside the rotating structure. He receives bearing information from the ship's

	Stage	After Armament	As normal Leanders		Ikara/ Exocet	
			VDS Well	VDS Fit		
LEANDER	1	B	●	●	I	AS IKARA LEANDER
DIDO		B	●	●	I	**For'd** 1 x IKARA launcher 2 x 40mm Bofors
PENELOPE		B	see text		E	**Mid** 2 x 8-barrelled rocket launcher 1 x Seacat Director
AJAX		B	●		I	2 x Seacat Launcher
AURORA		B	●	●	I	1 x Triple A/S Mortor Mk 10 1 x V.D.S.
GALATEA		B	●		I	
EURYALUS		B	●		I	
NAIAD		20	●	●	I	
ARETHUSA		L22	●	●	I	
CLEOPATRA		H22	●	●	E	
PHOEBE	2	H22			E	AS EXOCET LEANDER
MINERVA			●			**For'd** 2 x Twin EXOCET Launcher 2 x 40mm Bofors
SIRIUS			●			1 x Seacat Director 1 x Seacat Launcher
JUNO			●			2 x 8-barrelled rocket Launcher
ARGONAUT			●			**Mid** 2 x Seacat Launcher
DANAE			●			1 x Seacat Director
ANDROMEDA	3	H22	●			AS STANDARD LEANDER
CHARYBDIS			●	●		**For'd** 2 x 4.5inch 2 x 20mm Oerlikon
HERMOINE			●	●		1 x MRS 3 Director
JUPITER			●	●		**Mid** 2 x 8-barrelled rocket launcher
BACCHANTE			●	●		**Aft** 1 x Seacat launcher
SCYLLA						1 x Seacat Director
ACHILLES						1 x Triple A/S Mortor Mk 10
DIOMEDE						1 x VDS (see table)
APOLLO						
ARIADNE						

Notes
1. B=40mm Bofors; 20=GWS 20; L22=Low set GWS 22 Director H22=High GWS 22 Director.
2. Penelope ran as a Sonar Trial Ship before evaluating Sea Wolf.

G.W.S. 20 DIRECTOR

A. Director officer's indicator and control panel
B. Hood ribs
C. Aimer's independent binocular frame
D. Aimer's binoculars
E. Aimer's right hand 'pistol grip'
F. Aimer's cab windshield
G. Director officer's platform
H. Housing locking bolt
I. Director officer's training locking brake
J. Director officer's firing pistol
K. Link rod locking brake
L. Combined training push-bar and locking brake hand-grip

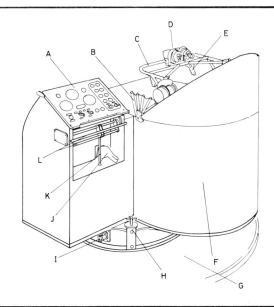

Weapon Direction System by conventional indicator transmissions and alignment is achieved by matching pointers. The rotating structure is then locked to this bearing. Within it, the Seacat aimer sits behind a bowed frame equipped with a left and right hand pistol grip. The frame carries his aimer's binoculars and is capable of being elevated and also of being traversed by hand within the director structure over a limited arc to the left and right of the designated bearing.

One pistol grip has a miniature joystick operated by the aimer's thumb and this, through the radio command guidance link, actuates the control surfaces of the missile during its flight, so that the aimer visually steers the missile towards the target. Therefore he has three concurrent tasks: first, constantly to track the target and keep it in his binocular line of sight; second, to counteract ship movement in roll, pitch and yaw by applying his own 'stabilisation'; and third, superimposed upon the first two, to steer the missile with his thumb joystick.

This was the system fitted in *Naiad* — and it currently appears in the *Rothesay* class; the AD frigates *Salisbury* and *Lincoln*; and the assault ships *Fearless* and *Intrepid*.

GWS 21

To overcome the target acquisition and tracking problems inherent in GWS 20, its successor was introduced as an intermediate system while the finalised version was being developed. Known as GWS 21, it employs the same launcher, computer and radio guidance link but with a different director.

The director owes its origins to the twin 40mm STAAG mounting, a totally self-contained weapon system embracing automatic target acquisition and radar 'lock-on' target tracking. The radar and prediction components of the STAAG were later built in to a drum shaped director known as the Close Range Blind Fire Director (or CRBFD) and, with minor changes to suit their particular ballistics, it was capable of controlling independent Bofors mountings (including the 6-barrelled Mk 6); twin 4inch Mk 19 (in the Type 15 AS frigates); or 4.5inch Mk 6 (in the *Daring* class destroyers and *Cat* class Type 41 AA frigates).

The straight CRBFD was next modified to become the director of the MRS 8 system. Although its appearance was virtually unchanged, its built-in prediction units were removed and replaced by a between-decks computer which

might be either a Single Ballistic Unit or a Dual Ballistic Unit. The former provided a continuous fire control solution for one calibre of gun and appeared, for example, controlling twin 40mm Bofors Mk 5 mountings in *Hermes* on first-fit; the latter was capable of controlling two different calibres at the same time, its biggest application being in *Belfast* on modernisation. Here it was linked to her 40mm Bofors and twin 4inch Mk 19 mountings.

Not only did the DBU provide continuous deflections for each calibre, but also automatic commencement of fire. Thus, as the target was tracked-in, the 4inch would automatically open fire as it reached their greatest future range capability followed, as the range closed, by the Bofors.

The automatic target acquisition and radar lock-on tracking capability needed to improve the Seacat system therefore already existed in the family of CRBFD's and MRS 8 directors; and as they became obsolete in the original form, they were further modified to become the GWS 21 director.

Trials on this improved system were carried out on the *Daring* class destroyer *Decoy* and it was subsequently fitted in the four *Battle* class ships *Aisne*, *Agincourt*, *Barrosa* and *Corunna* on their conversion to the Air Direction rôle. The Type 81 frigate *Zulu,* alone among the *Tribal* class, had two 'sided' systems at first-fit, but subsequently all *Tribals* received two systems at long refit, replacing their existing single 40mm Bofors. Elsewhere, sided GWS 21 systems appeared in the first four *County* class ships *Devonshire, Hampshire, Kent* and *London.*

GWS 22

Meanwhile work was progressing on the development of GWS 22 which was envisaged as the standard Seacat system, rather as Medium Range System Mk 3 (usually referred to as 'Missus Three') became the standard gun fire control system. Indeed the GWS 22 director closely resembles that of MRS 3 — from which it was developed — and employs a similar radar with a very much greater maximum range than the outdated radar Type 262 of the CRBFD family.

STAGE 1

Of the ten ships of Stage 1, only *Cleopatra* was built with the standard GWS 22, while *Penelope,* already lacking the Variable Depth Sonar, was withdrawn from normal frigate duties to become first a Sonar Trials ship and latterly a test-bed for the Seawolf system (GWS 25). In the first phase of her special duties she ran with a packaged director and twin 4.5 Mk 6; omitted the 965 aerial on the mainmast, and had her VDS well plated in. Later, as the Seawolf trials ship, she lost her 4.5inch mounting altogether, had extensive structures built on to the flight deck area and reverted to the conventional VDS well, but without the sonar.

With *Penelope* engaged in trials and *Cleopatra* already fitted with the standard GWS 22 system there remained eight Stage 1 ships, all approaching Long Refit, and all needing modernisation to a greater or lesser degree. The post-war new construction programme of specialised frigates had been abandoned in favour of a general purpose ship that was to be all things to all men. This scheme reached fruition with the *Leanders*; but their overall building

1

2

G.W.S. 22 DIRECTOR

A. Aimer's hood
B. Aimer's binoculars
C. Cine-camera mounting bracket
D. Aerial reflector
E. Conically scanning aerial
F. Forced lubrication pump
G. Electrical training motor
H. Fixed director base
I. Revolving structure
J. Radar and electronic cabinets

The Sonar 199 Towed Body. The gantry, which functions as a pantograph, is initially lifted from its inboard stowed position by a pair of hydraulic jacks. As it passed top dead centre the weight of the assembly is taken by the tipping winch cables, seen here passing over sheaves near the deck edge. The Towed Body is held into the saddle by a hydraulic locking bolt and the gantry totally immerses it before it is launched. Notice the anti-cavitation faring attached to the towing cable.

Andromeda, a third group *Leander*, in June 1977. She has recently been taken in hand at the Devonport frigate complex for the first major refit to a member of her group, a refit which is reported to include the installation of the 'Seawolf' point defence missile system.

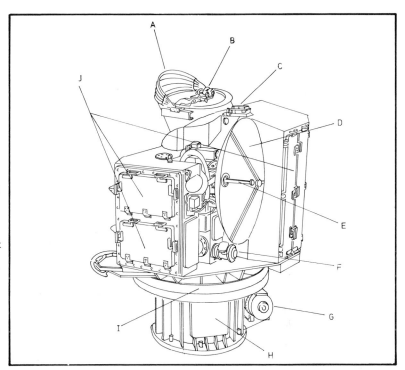

programme had scarcely been completed, when the specialist ship concept was re-introduced, by the decision to replace the twin 4.5inch by the Ikara AS missile system in eight of the Stage 1 ships.

The Ikara Conversion

The transformation has been undertaken by Devonport Dockyard in their newly created Frigate Complex but, exceptionally, *Arethusa* was taken in hand at Portsmouth where, when she was open to the public during the 1977 Navy Days, one could see what the conversion entails.

Forward, the twin 4.5inch Mk 6 with its associated shell room, magazine, MRS 3 director and fire control system disappear. The forward superstructure is extended by a box shaped missile handling compartment leading to a drum shaped spray shield surrounding the Ikara launcher. The spray shield extends up the slope of the fo'c'sle deck over the original site of the second breakwater and the launcher, set in its well, is protected in the non-action state by a large 'pram-hood' ribbed cover, power operated to fold forward.

The position occupied by the MRS 3 director on the bridge roof is taken up by the Ikara Guidance Aerial in a tracker-head under a 'thimble' dome. Sponsons have been built out abreast the foremast trunk to port and starboard carrying single electric-powered 40mm Mk 9 mountings for surface gunfire 'police' duties. (These replace the single 20mm Oerlikons fitted for the same purpose at the time of the Malayasian confrontation with Indonesia, to give ships equipped with 4.5inch and missile systems a close quarter 'junk bashing' capability.)

Two additional platforms on the foremast trunk project towards the starboard bow and port quarter for (but not always with) the satellite communication system aerials, and a new athwartship 'flying bridge' abaft the funnel has a whip aerial at each extremity. In this general boat deck area there are 8-barrelled rocket launchers to port and starboard with an independent 2 inch rocket flare launcher mounted co-axially above them.

A small IFF radar scanner has replaced the original early warning radar Type 965 aerial on the short trunk mainmast and abaft it, the launcher deck (which is also the hangar roof) has been completely redesigned for the new Seacat system. This — GWS 22B — has a director on the centre line immediately abaft the mainmast controlling either of two Seacat launchers, sited to port and starboard at the after-most corners of the launcher deck. The arrangement much improves Seacat arcs that were earlier restricted by the asymetrical positioning of the director to starboard and the single launcher to port.

The flight deck and AS mortar Mk 10 remain as first fitted, but those Stage 1 ships not equipped with the VDS system in the first instance (see Table column 5) have been given it to complete their specialist AS weaponry. In some cases, existing VDS fits from later *Leanders* were removed and transferred to make up the required numbers.

By and large, the Ikara conversion has produced a frigate with an over-bearing of AS weaponry — AS mortar and AS helicopter *and* Ikara — at the expense of all save close range weapons. The 'wooding' of the Seacat director by the mainmast

The converted *Arethusa,* fitted for, but not with the Satellite Communicator System (SCOT) aerials. Note the collapsed forward RAS 'mast' and the RAS platform abaft the Ikara shield. Her A/S Mk 10 mortar is in the "ceremonial" stowed position, rolled upright and pitched forward.

IKARA 'LEANDER' — FIG.1

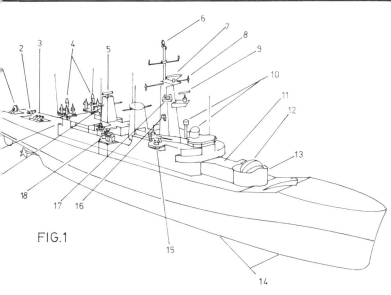

FIG.1

1. V.D.S gantry.
2. Towed U/W decoy winch.
3. Triple A/S Mortar Mk. 10.
4. Port and starboard Seacat launchers.
5. I F F.
6. E W Aerial.
7. Medium Range Surveillance/ Weapon Direction Radar.
8. U H F.
9. Navigation/Helicopter landing control Radar.
10. Ikara tracker/guidance aerials.
11. Ikara handling room.
12. Ikara launcher hood.
13. Spray shield.
14. Attack and search sonars.
15. 40mm. Bofors (p & s).
16. E.W. aerial.
17. Satellite Communication system aerial base (p & s).
18. 8-barrelled decoy rocket launcher/ co-axial rocket flare launcher.
19. G W S 22 B Director abaft mainmast trunk.
20. A/S helicopter flight deck.

leaves only 40mm Bofors to cover the wide forward arcs so that the Ikara's must rely on others to protect them from above water threats.

THE EXOCET *LEANDERS*

None of the six ships of Stage 2 had the VDS fit (although five had the associated well); only the last three had the improved gunnery fire control; and two ships were left over from Stage 1 — *Penelope* and *Cleopatra*. This rather hybrid batch of ships form what will eventually become the Exocet octet. Two — *Cleopatra* and *Phoebe* — had already emerged from Devonport yard at the time of writing, the former in later 1975 and the latter in April 1977. Again the changes are extensive, but provide a better balance of weaponry.

The twin 4.5inch is replaced by four Exocet launchers set in two pairs on platforms built-up forward of the existing bridge front. Unlike Ikara, these are one shot launchers, and have no in-ship reloads, so that from an overall loading and top weight point of view, original and

additional equipment has been fitted or retained, over and above the Ikara *Leanders*.

The MRS 3 director has been directly replaced by a GWS 22D director, controlling a single Seacat launcher on the fo'c'sle to cover the forward arcs. The foremast is topped by a new aerial and a 'junk bashing' capability is provided by two single Mk 9 Bofors. Satellite communication system aerial bases are sited to port and starboard on sponsons projecting from the Emergency Compass Platform.

The 965 aerial and IFF remain on the mainmast and abaft it the two sided Seacat launchers, although positioned like the Ikara's, are more comprehensively controlled. Each has its own computer and radio command guidance link to which the centre-line director can be switched for fully automatic control. Each launcher also has a secondary hand-worked director allowing effectively, full GWS 22 system control to one, and GWS 20 style control of the other. The switchery not only

allows the director proper to take on the major threat on either beam, leaving its junior opposite partner to cover the back door, but also provides for two independent systems should the principal director be knocked out.

In the hangar below the launcher deck, the ships have been made ready to accept the Lynx helicopter, and the flight deck areas has been substantially increased by the removal of the AS mortar Mk 10, and the plating-over of its mortar well. This ship-borne AS weapon has been more than replaced by above water AS torpedo-tubes, mounted at boat deck level abaft the rocket launchers on a widened shelter deck.

Altogether, the Exocet *Leander* looks a much better bet than the Ikara — not least by the retention of 965 and Seacat coverage on the forward arcs — but may yet find herself a long way from home with the four Exocet shots expended and more surface targets looming large on the horizon. Like the Ikara *Leanders*, the Stage 2 ships are

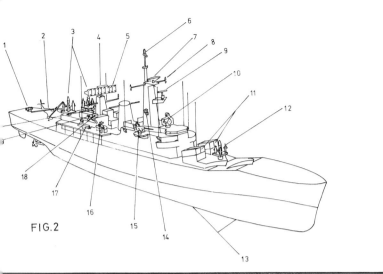

FIG.2

EXOCET 'LEANDER' — FIG.2

1. Towed U/W Decoy winch.
2. 'Lynx' A/S Helicopter.
3. Seacat launcher, port and starboard.
4. I F F.
5. 965 Long Range Surveillance.
6. E W.
7. Medium Range Surveillance/Weapon Direction.
8. U H F.
9. Navigation/Helicopter landing control.
10. G W S. 22D Director.
11. Exocet.
12. Forward Seacat.
13. Search and Attack Sonars.
14. E.W. port and starboard.
15. 40mm. port and starboard.
16. Multi-barrel Decoy and flare rocket launcher.
17. Triple A/S Torpedo tubes, port and starboard.
18. Satellite Communication System aerial base, port and starboard.
19. Secondary after Seacat director, port and starboard.
20. G W S. 22C Director abaft mainmast trunk.

doubtless to form part of a mutually supporting force.

HMS *Cleopatra* is the only *Leander* named after a historical rather than mythological character and is one of the intended eight Exocet conversions. Note the doubled-up breakwater on the fo'c'sle, the forward Seacat launcher and the efflux baffles abaft the Exocet cannisters. There are single Mk 9 40mm Bofors abreast the foremast, which is topped by a 'dunces cap' EW aerial. SCOT aerials are fitted on a flying bridge in this group of frigates and the support for the after Seacat Director is a wide compartment housing the independant control consoles for the two Seacat systems. Triple torpedo tubes are carried on a new shelter deck, which also holds the 8-barrelled decoy rocket launchers, and there is no longer a mortar or Sonar 199 well. Floodlighting booms have been rigged on the portside.

STAGE 3

The remaining ten conventional *Leanders* are all comparatively new, and their future beyond Major Refit can only be conjectural. Half might be Ikara-ed (five have VDS wells), but this entails a Canadian-developed sonar and an Australian-developed AS missile system. Giving Exocet to the other half would equally entail further purchases from the French but in any event, the stalwart twin 4.5inch must surely be ending its useful life.

If a gun-ship is still required, the new 4.5inch Mk 8 could conceivably replace the 4.5inch Mk 6 in all ten ships; but the Type 21 frigates and the Type 42 destroyers (plus, of course, *Bristol*) have a 4.5inch Mk 8 and there may be no requirement for more gun-ships by the time the Stage 3 *Leanders* reach modernisation.

My own view is that they will be brought towards the equipment fit of the new Type 22 frigates with Seawolf; Exocet on the fo'c'sle; 40mm 'junk-bashers' on the bridge wings; decoy rocket launchers; Lynx helicopter operating from an enlarged flight deck (as in the stage two ships) and AS torpedo-tubes. Only time will tell whether the guess is inspired or otherwise.

1. The new triple A/S torpedo tube mounting which unlike the obsolete above-water 21 inch, has no cut-away "lip-end" and has a power operated end cap.

2. *Naiad* in November 1977. Note that the SCOT domes have anti-icing rubber 'overshoes' fitted.

3. The Satellite Communication System (SCOT) aerials on HMS *Naiad*, angled out from the foremast. One of the Ikara tracking aerials can just be seen on the extreme right of the photograph.

4. The newly introduced 'head-lamp' Electronic Warfare jammer aerial. It is fully stabilised and can "look" in any direction. It features as part of the Ikara conversion (but not of the Exocet) and is being fitted elsewere in other classes.

1

2

3

4

The American 5 inch/38 dual purpose gun

by Norman Friedman

The US 5inch 38 calibre DP gun was probably the single most successful medium-calibre naval weapon of World War II. In stark contrast to the single-purpose destroyer guns of other navies, it symbolized US attention to the combination of air and surface threats. It was, to be sure, not as powerful as the DP guns some other navies mounted aboard their capital ships; but it was heavy enough, and yet could be mounted on all classes of combatants from destroyer up. The Royal Navy, by way of contrast, used four calibres — 4, 4.5, 4.7, and 5.25inch — to do the same set of jobs. Other navies were even less economical.

Certainly the gun was popular within the US Navy. Typically, the newer automatic 5inch/54 was considered far less satisfactory in robustness, reliability, even accuracy: 'I'd prefer a 5inch/38 in a fight any day.' Nor is its day over. Although the last 5inch/38 mounts were manufactured during World War II, such prodigious numbers were built that they were installed on new ships as late as the 1960s (*Brooke* and *Garcia* class frigates and the *Hamilton* class Coast Guard cutters — not to mention Danish *Peder Skram* class frigates).

Perhaps as significant as the widespread installation of the 5inch/38 was the fact that its existence, and the significance accorded air defense by the USN, combined to inspire the design of fire control gear which made heavy AA fire practical even from a rolling, pitching, destroyer. In consequence many US destroyers of war and late prewar construction were not markedly inferior in anti-aircraft effect to converted British AA cruisers — a point brought home by the rearmament of HMS *Delhi* with five single 5inch/38 (and, it must be admitted, two rather than the standard one DP director) in 1942.

The 5inch/38 was a direct descendant of the US 5inch/25 heavy AA gun, a weapon specified in 1921 for the AA batteries of American battleships. It differed from contemporary foreign heavy anti-aircraft guns in its low muzzle velocity, 2200 feet per second,

which was accepted beause:
1 American AA doctrine was most concerned with laying down a barrage of shell bursts ahead of and around level bombers, to throw off their aim. There was little expectation of hitting except on a statistical basis. It followed that rate of fire was paramount; and the highest rate of fire *plus* the greatest weight of fragments (for a large lethal radius) demanded a minimum powder charge, for a minimum net weight of ammunition to handle: hand-loading was assumed. In particular, hand-loading limited the unit ammunition weight to about 100 pounds. In fact the light weight permitted movement of the shell by *hand* into a *power* rammer, which in turn guaranteed a very high rate of fire. Power ramming in turn required a rigid powder casing.
2 AA fire at rapidly moving aircraft also demanded handiness in the gun mount, which in turn meant a short-barrelled gun with a limited moment of inertia (resistance to turning). Ease of rapid elevation also militated against barrel length, not to mention the heavy counterweights required to balance long-barrelled guns whose trunnions were located near their breeches; this in turn was required in order to keep the breech within reach of the loaders.

The latter consideration also translated into relatively low gun power, as a high-powered weapon would require a long recoil and hence either a very high mount (to fire at high angles) or else the structural complication of a gun-pit.

The limit on total ammunition weight, taking into account a 54-pound shell, limited the powder charge to 9.5 pounds (compared to 23.8 for the contemporary 5inch/51 single-purpose surface-fire weapon) and muzzle velocity to 2200 (vice 3150) feet per second. On the other hand, the 5inch/25 was often credited with a rate of fire of 15 or 20 rounds per minute, using a power rammer. The much heavier 5inch/51, which could not use power ramming because its powder was bagged, made about 9 rounds per minute under comparable circumstances.

Accuracy was another matter.

USS *Downes* (DD-375), rebuilt late in the war, showing the right hand side of the enclosed pedestal mounts. The inside of the bank of fuze-setters can just be made out below the breech of No 2 gun.

172

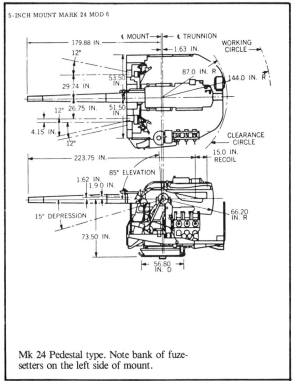

5-INCH MOUNT MARK 24 MOD 6

Mk 24 Pedestal type. Note bank of fuze-setters on the left side of mount.

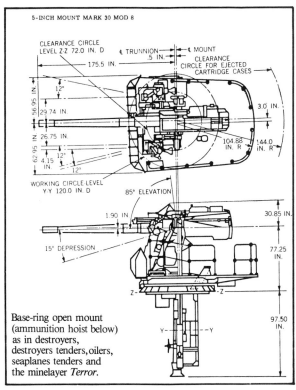

5-INCH MOUNT MARK 30 MOD 8

Base-ring open mount (ammunition hoist below) as in destroyers, destroyers tenders, oilers, seaplanes tenders and the minelayer *Terror*.

Because of its low velocity, the 5inch/25 shell had to follow a highly curved trajectory if it was to achieve any great range, whereas the 5inch/51 followed an extremely flat trajectory. Thus the bare statement that maximum ranges were, respectively, 14 000 and 20 000 yards does not tell the whole story. Another measure of interest is *danger space,* in effect the allowable miss distance given a target of standard height: a shell moving within the danger space will still pass through the target.

Average spotting errors at 5000 yards were 185; at 5500, 200; at 6000, 240, and at 6500, 375 yards. At 6780 yards, for the ten highest-scoring destroyers (1928-1929 Long Range Battle Practice), 80% had errors beyond 60 yards, and 60% beyond 120 yards. It followed that one salvo of high-velocity (2900 ft/sec) 4inch/50 would make 96% hits with 60 yard plotting errors and 80% at 120. But under the same circumstances the 5inch/25 would make, respectively, 80 and 40. It was etimated that at 6000 yards a 4inch gun would make 1.6 times as many hits as would the 5inch/25.

Generally the low-velocity gun was credited with half the danger space of the high velocity; it would have to gain 60 yards in fire control accuracy to make up the difference.

As for handiness, a 1930 study suggested that the 5inch/51 had about three times the moment of inertia (for train) of the 5inch/25.

These figures give some idea of the sacrifices entailed in the pure AA gun. In the mid-1920s they were considered perfectly reasonable; battleships were armed with highly accurate 5inch/51s for surface fire against attacking destroyers, and with rapidly-firing 5inch/25s to stop level bombers. It was recognized that dive bombers would require something new and work was proceeding, albeit rather slowly, on a multiple machine cannon (which would become the notorious 1.1inch) to hose down the sky in front of a dive bomber.

However, when the 5inch/25 was installed in battleships, their officers began to think of it as a dual purpose gun; they began to fire it in the annual *surface* gunnery practice. At the same time the first of the new Treaty cruisers were begun. In

these ships the only guns other than slow-firing (3 rounds per minute) 8inch were 5inch/25s, which would have to counter enemy destroyer attacks as well as air attacks. The idea of dual purpose operation began to be accepted, and in fact dual purpose secondary batteries were specified for a series of battleships designed in the United States in 1928, against the end of the ban on new battleship construction scheduled for 1931. 5. and then 5.4inch guns were projected; and this design project survived the demise of the battleship studies after the London Conference of 1930.

What finally pushed the US Navy to a new gun was the destroyer problem. The United States ended World War I with an enormous mass of 'flush deck' destroyers, most of them armed with 4inch/50 single-purpose guns. A few were armed with (and the rest of the *Clemson* class designed with provision for) the heavy 5inch/51, as a counter to German U-cruisers; and others had a twin 4inch/50. The existence of this vast force dissuaded Congress from buying

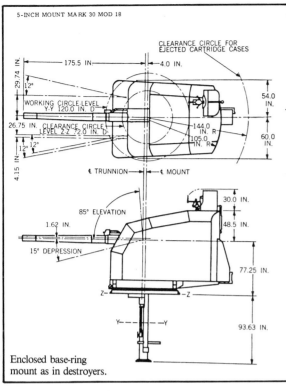

5-INCH MOUNT MARK 30 MOD 18

Enclosed base-ring mount as in destroyers.

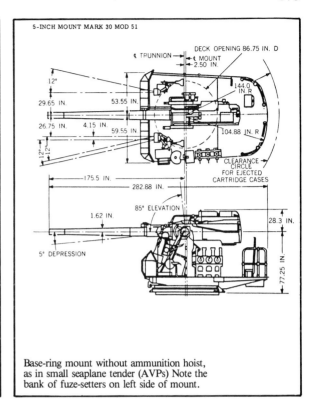

5-INCH MOUNT MARK 30 MOD 51

Base-ring mount without ammunition hoist, as in small seaplane tender (AVPs) Note the bank of fuze-setters on left side of mount.

any new destroyers; but foreign navies did begin new programs during the 1920s. Generally the new ships outgunned the US craft: the Royal and Italian Navies chose the 4.7inch gun, France the 5.1 (5.5 in some craft). Japan, the most probable future opponent, was credited with a 4.7, although in fact her new destroyers had 5inch guns. Sketch designs for new American destroyers generally showed either 5inch/25 or 5inch/51 guns, but the issue was not really discussed in great depth in view of the improbability that Congress would authorize new construction. However, by 1930 the obsolescence of existing destroyers seemed so patent that the senior Navy council, the General Board, was hopeful that new ones would be built. Even in the absence of new destroyers, the Board was interested in rearming the existing force of *Clemsons,* 87 of which had 4inch guns on mountings stressed for 5inch.

It began to canvass the Fleet, the Office of Naval Operations, and the technical Bureaux. The existing 4inch gun found many supporters,

but it had shown a lack of effect in test firings against four old US Yangtse gunboats. Fuzes were not sensitive enough, and fragmentation appeared poor. Although the Bureau of Ordnance promised a better shell, these results must have told. Fleet Training expected 6-8 rounds per minute for the 4inch/50.

The 5inch/51 was generally conceded to be awkward to handle, too few had been mounted in destroyers for any accurate estimate of the rate of fire to be made. Battleships could fire 9 rounds per minute, but they were very steady gun platforms. Fleet Training was impressed with the accuracy of the long gun, but noted that its shells had small bursting charges (1.7 vs 5.63 pounds for the 5inch/25).

The 5inch/25 fired much faster, and at *short* ranges would probably achieve a high percentage of hits. Fleet Training was inclined to feel that its poor trajectory would be an important factor only at ranges too long for effective control. In addition, it promised high-angle fire — although effective AA fire would require eleborate fire control mechanisms, and might be negated

by the motion of the destroyer.

Others differed in their opinions. Some felt that the twin 4inch/50 was the best means towards a high volume of fire — although recent writers have suggested that it was rather overcrowded. The 5inch/25 was derided as too heavy (twice the current 4inch/50 mount) and some officers suspected, wrongly, that a new weapon of intermediate calibre (4.5 and 4.7inches were both mentioned) would be far lighter.

As for AA fire, the DP gun was seen as a means of protecting the battle line against heavy bombers; but against dive bombers or torpedo planes the key weapon would be a machine cannon or machine gun. In fact, some noted that the French Navy had retreated from a 2.9inch AA cannon to a 37mm triple automatic weapon.

In the end, the 5inch/25 was a better gun than the older 5inch/51, but not so much better as to make the case clear. Tests of the 5inch/25 aboard the destroyer *Gilmer* showed that the high rate of fire could indeed be maintained in a seaway, even though at low elevations the breech of the gun was at the height of a man's shoulders and so less than suitable for quick loading. A major objection to the 5inch/25, its need for an anti-actuated power rammer which might easily be disabled in action, was overcome.

Rearmament of existing destroyers was, however, rejected on the grounds of cost and of the short life remaining to them: new guns would go into the new destroyers finally in prospect.

The General Board remained unhappy about the low velocity and called for a compromise: a gun moved slightly towards the surface role, a dual-purpose weapon. Its length of about 40 calibres was set by the muzzle velocity required, about 2600 feet per second. In fact design refinements led to the 38-calibre length actually selected. The prototype gun, the 5inch/38 Mk A, was a 5inch/51 Mk 9 cut down in length. It had been built as a submarine gun, and unlike the destroyer and battleship models used semi-fixed ammunition, in which the metal cartridge case was loaded separately from the projectile. The same scheme was adopted for the new dual-purpose gun; it had the great advantage of suitability for power-ramming and hence a high rate of fire. In addition the use of a cartridge case permitted, in both 5inch/25 and the new 5inch/38, the use of a sliding wedge breechblock, a mechanism of particular simplicity.

The new gun and its mount were essentially enlarged versions of the 5inch/25, including the inconveniently high breech. However, five were mounted in each of eight new *Farragut* class destroyers, with a new dual-purpose director (Mk 28). It might almost be said that the destroyers received so elaborate an installation largely because their guns had an AA capability; and that in turn was a consequence of their ancestry and of the fact that a primary value in AA gun development had been rate of fire.

In fact not all of the new destroyers were given an AA capability. The 1850 ton *Porters* were completed with twin *single-purpose* mounts which elevated only to 35 degrees. In their case there

was just enough weight for twin mounts but not for twin DP mounts: the *Porters* and their half-sisters of the *Somers* class were the only US destroyers of the World War II period with single purpose guns. The General Board Hearings on the Characteristics of the big destroyers give no impression of any great struggle over the DP capability, even though the provision of specialized fire controls cannot have been inexpensive.

Indeed, in 1936 proposals were made to switch to single-purpose guns as a means of saving weight. By this time the value of heavy AA on destroyers had been appreciated, and it was justified by an analysis of the probable course of a Pacific campaign. In particular the War Plans Division suspected that Japan, limited by Treaty to a numerically inferior battle line (10:15) would try to wear down the US battle line prior to a fleet engagement, using those arms — aircraft and submarines — not limited by Treaty. It followed that US destroyers should not sacrifice their AAW and ASW qualities, that the sacrifices entailed by a dual-purpose main battery were well worth while. This sacrifice included the financial burden of continued development and large-scale procurement of advanced AA fire controls, culminating in the Mark 37. The mature systems incorporated a 'stable element' which could sense ship motion, and remote power control to correct gun position automatically and continuously.

However, there remained one major change in the destroyer gun. The 5inch/38 pedestal mount was at the limit of turning masses easily manhandled. It incorporated no shell hoist; instead there was a fixed hoist or scuttle on deck, from which rounds could be passed to a rack of three fuze-setters on the rotating mount (AA shells used time fuzes) and then to the high breech. At low angles loading was still difficult, whereas at very high angles power-ramming was required.

A new base-ring mount first appeared in the *Craven* (DD 380) class of 1937. It was now possible

to place the shell and powder hoists on the axis of the mount, so that shells and cartridges could be passed directly to the gun at any angle of train; rate of fire was now as much as 15 to 22 rounds per minute. Fuzes were set in the hoist. In addition, with no need for shells or powder to be passed from deck to mount, the mount could be completely enclosed. These improvements cost considerable weight: an unshielded Mk 30 Mod 1 weighted 33 500 lb, compared to 29 260 for the pedestal Mk 21 Mod 0, and 20 200 for the 5inch/25 Mk 19 Mod 2. With an ⅛inch shield, Mk 30 Mod 6 weighted 41 700 lb, and was not at all amenable to hand training. Power drives were not well liked because they seemed an unnecessary source of vulnerability, particularly since a ship just hit and thus without auxiliary power might need her AA battery particularly badly. However, the advantages of higher rate of fire and much better fragment protection outweighted this disadvantage; and the single enclosed gun could just barely be manhandled.

Not so the twin. The DP twin mount had a history nearly as convoluted as that of the 5inch/38 itself. In 1930, at the same time the General Board was investigating destroyer guns, it began to consider the vulnerability of cruiser secondary batteries to fragments and strafing attacks. The obvious solution seemed to be some kind of shield, and it was proposed that the 5inch/25 guns be paired to economize on shield weight. The cruisers *Wichita, Helena,* and *St Louis* were, therefore, designed with twin enclosed 5inch/25 mounts. However, *Wichita* proved weight-critical and, in view of the advantages of the single 5inch/38 over even a twin 5inch/25, the former was substituted for the latter in 1936. That left only the two light cruisers, for which a special twin 5inch/25 would have to be developed. They were not so close to overweight as was the heavy cruiser, and so could receive twin 5inch/38 on a one-for-one basis. Theirs were the first US twin 5inch/38 DP mounts, and a

USS *Aylwin* (DD-355) in March 1942, showing the bulge (on the left side only) for a bank of fuze-setters on the enclosed pedestal mounts forward.

modified design went into production for the secondary batteries of capital ships, cruisers, even destroyers. There were many variations; for example, with shields of varying thicknesses. All greatly outweighted the older single-purpose twin: for example, with 0.125 inch shields, the Mk 38 used in destroyers weighed 95 700 lb, the older Mk 22 of the 1850-tonners, about 70 000. It is no great surprise that these ships were rearmed with two twin and one single dual purpose 5inch/38 (plus one twin or quadruple Bofors) in place of their former four twins (about 238 000 lb of DP plus 15 000 or 25 000 lb of Bofors — plus fire controls — versus 280 000 lb of SP 5inch/38).

There was one other type of mount. The Mark 37, a base ring mount without hoist or shield, was evolved for merchant ships and auxiliaries which could not accept elaborate installations: it was produced in place of a pedestal type probably in order to achieve a higher rate of production through commonality of parts with other base-ring types. Fire control arrangements were primitive: there was no provision for remote control (although there was allowance for future addition of follow-the-pointer indicators for a fire control system), and the usual gun sights were omitted in favor of open sights with provision for the addition of a simple telescope. Development was approved by the CNO on 5 May 1942. Over 1600 were installed aboard merchant ships.

Enormous numbers were produced. Beginning in 1939, the Navy drew private manufacturers into the 5inch gun program, looking towards rapid industrial mobilization. A contract for 20 single mounts was let to the General Electric Company, and 10 to the Goss Printing Press Company. The Northern Pump Company was brought into the program in view of the total monthly capacity of 5 for GE, and 12 for Goss: 700 were ordered in 1940, for delivery within three years. In fact Northern Pump (later Northern/Ordnance) built 955 within 16 months, but this rate might be explained in part by wartime rates of working. Other large-scale producers included the Consolidated Steel Co, the Continental Gun Co, Fisher Body Co, and the Herring-Hall-Marvin Safe Co. Production did not actually catch up with requirements until November 1941. Thus, between 1 July 1940 and 30 November 1941, 118 single mounts were built against a requirement for 140 (63 twins against 66 required).

According to the Bureau of Ordnance history, production totals were

a Single (base ring) through 1 November 1945: 2168.
b Single Mk 37 through 1 July 1945: 3298.
c Twin through 1 August 1945: 1257. (It was planned to terminate twin production at 1357).

It is not clear whether these figures include guns produced

before 1 July 1940, but those numbers are in any case quite small. On that date there were 315 single, 52 twin SP, and eight twin DP 5inch/38 in the Fleet.

How successful was the 5inch/38? The US Navy liked it well enough, but that only meant that it was reliable and effective — there was no rival with which to compare it. Royal Navy, cursed with the lack of any DP gun at the outbreak of war, liked it very much and at one point considered wholesale importation of 5inch/38s for new destroyers. The RN actually did import a large number of the Mk 37 directors developed for, and because of, the 5inch/38. Japan developed her own 5inch guns, some of them for high angle fire — and one of them 40 calibres long — but in the end found a high velocity 3.9inch/65 more attractive for AA work. France tried to develop dual purpose heavy AA guns (5.1 and then 6inch) but her

efforts appear to have failed through over-ambition.

Just before the war, the Navy had been embroiled in an internal debate over the character of the next DP gun; and much of the thinking had been directed towards a greater anti-surface capability, even at some cost in rate of fire. At the same time there was concern that bombers might operate above the effective ceiling of the 5inch/38. At the time this was absurd, but during the war the Germans were able to drop guided bombs from great altitudes with considerable precision, as the Allied fleets learned to their cost at Salerno. A cruiser, Savannah, was rearmed with twin 5inch/38 (in place of her 5inch/25) precisely because of this 'guided missile' danger (1944) and further conversions were considered. Even the 5inch/38 could not be entirely satisfactory, but the successor adopted in 1939 had not yet appeared.

That was the 5inch/54, in effect a scaled-up 5inch/38. It had originally been approved, in twin mounts, as the secondary battery of the Montana class battleships; it was inferior to the 5inch/38 in rate of fire, though not in weight of shell (79 lb vs 55), but it would be far more effective against the big Japanese destroyers. It was also adopted for the Midway class carriers for the same kind of reason: a carrier, as envisaged in 1942, needed some insurance against the possibility of a sudden encounter with enemy light forces at night or in bad weather. Eventually single 5inch/54 mounts went to sea aboard the Midways, and after the war a faster firing automatic version (Mark 42) appeared. It is the gun those who lovingly remember the old 5inch/38 know too well for its high rate of fire — when its high rate of jamming does not interfere.

enham (DD-397) showing open base-ring
ounts aft.

SS Mahan (DD-364) at Mare Island in June
44, showing a relatively cramped gun-shield
d details of the sliding-wedge breech block.
ote the Mk 33 5inch director with its new
k 22 radar dish.

SS Downes (DD-375) after 5inch on open
destal mounts.
ll photos USN

2

HMS TERPSICHORE

A TYPE 16 FAST ANTI-SUBMARINE FRIGATE OF 1953

by John Lambert

Terpsichore in February 1955. Still very much a destroyer in overall layout including a set of torpedo-tubes aft, but the armament is much reduced and the new enclosed bridge is an obvious modification.

H.M.S. *Terpsichore* was the fifth ship of that name to serve in the Royal Navy. The first was a prize of 20 guns, taken in 1760 and sold in 1766. The second was a fifth rate of 1785, to be broken up in 1830. Number three was a corvette of 1847, broken up in 1866, and the fourth, a cruiser, built in 1890 and sold in 1914. The last ship to carry the name *Terpsichore* (the muse of dancing) is the subject for this issue, a Fleet Destroyer of 1943, modernised as a fast anti-submarine frigate in 1953.

DESIGN

A unit of the 6th War Emergency Flotilla, or *T* class, the flotilla was ordered on the 14 March 1941, and comprised of HM ships *Troubridge* (leader), *Teazer, Tenacious, Termagant, Tumult, Tuscan,* and the last to complete, *Terpsichore.*

The class were of standard RN destroyer design, being repeats of the previous *S* class, and having a modified *Tribal* class bow, to improve seakeeping and reduce spray forward, which increased their overall length to 362 ft 9 in (339 ft 6 in BP), and a beam of 35 ft 9 in.

Terpsichore was built at Dumbarton, by William Denny and Bros Ltd. She was laid down on 25 November 1941, launched on 17 June 1943, and completed on 20 January 1944, a building time of 25 months 26 days.

Her main machinery was the same as specified to the earlier *J* class, the standard well proven design produced pre-war. Two Admiralty 3-drum boilers with 'Melesco' superheaters, having working pressure of 300 lb/sq inch, driving two Parsons SR geared turbines of 40 000 shp to give 36 knots at standard condition, and 32 knots at deep load, at 350 rpm. On her trials, at a displacement of 2299 tons, *Terpsichore* reached 32,28 knots, with an indicated 41 141 shp at 325.4 rpm.

The early units of the class (*Troubridge, Tumult, Tuscan* and *Tyrian*) were completed with tripod foremasts. The later built ships were completed with the new lattice masts, giving improved aerial layout for radar. Type 272 search radar in its distinctive lantern was fitted on a short lattice mast amidships, and HF/DF and a pole mast aft for type 291 air warning radar.

As completed she carried six twin 20mm Oerlikons in powered mountings, with the whole class mounting four of the newly introduced dual purpose 4.7inch Mark XXII mountings, with a maximum elevation of 55° as their main armament. The class carried two sets of quadruple 21inch torpedo-tubes. (*Tumult* had her forward set deleted for a trial period, and replaced by two single 21inch tubes, angled out from her centre line). They also carried four depth charge throwers, and short rails, with a normal complement of 70 charges.

H.M.S. TERPSICHORE ~ TYPE 16 CONVERSION
FAST A/S FRIGATE

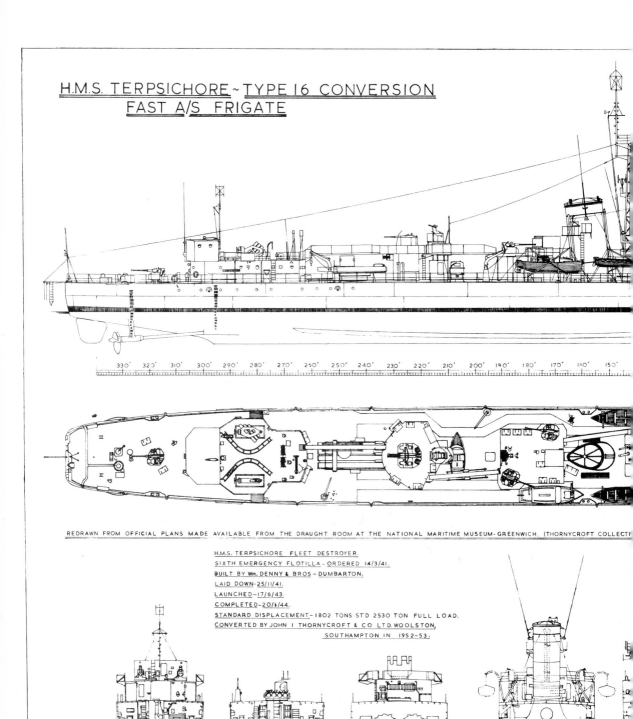

330′ 320′ 310′ 300′ 290′ 280′ 270′ 250′ 250′ 240′ 230′ 220′ 210′ 200′ 190′ 180′ 170′ 160′ 150′

REDRAWN FROM OFFICIAL PLANS MADE AVAILABLE FROM THE DRAUGHT ROOM AT THE NATIONAL MARITIME MUSEUM - GREENWICH. (THORNYCROFT COLLECTI

H.M.S. TERPSICHORE FLEET DESTROYER.
SIXTH EMERGENCY FLOTILLA - ORDERED 14/3/41.
BUILT BY Wm. DENNY & BROS - DUMBARTON.
LAID DOWN - 25/11/41.
LAUNCHED - 17/6/43.
COMPLETED - 20/1/44.
STANDARD DISPLACEMENT - 1802 TONS STD 2530 TON FULL LOAD.
CONVERTED BY JOHN I THORNYCROFT & CO LTD. WOOLSTON,
                SOUTHAMPTON IN 1952-53.

FRAME 72½   FRAME 65.   FRAME 60.   FRAME 48.

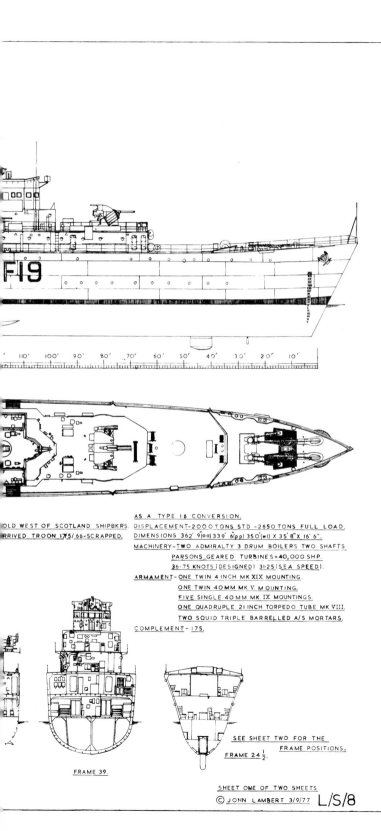

F19

110' 100' 90' 80' 70' 60' 50' 40' 30' 20' 10'

OLD WEST OF SCOTLAND SHIPBKRS.
RRIVED TROON 17/5/66-SCRAPPED.

AS A TYPE 16 CONVERSION.
DISPLACEMENT-2000 TONS STD -2650 TONS FULL LOAD.
DIMENSIONS 362' 9"(oa) 339' 6"(pp) 35 0'(wl) X 35' 8" X 16' 6".
MACHINERY-TWO ADMIRALTY 3 DRUM BOILERS TWO SHAFTS
PARSONS GEARED TURBINES=40,000 SHP.
36·75 KNOTS (DESIGNED) 31·25 (SEA SPEED).
ARMAMENT-ONE TWIN 4 INCH MK XIX MOUNTING.
ONE TWIN 40 MM MK V. MOUNTING.
FIVE SINGLE 40MM MK IX MOUNTINGS.
ONE QUADRUPLE 21 INCH TORPEDO TUBE MK VIII.
TWO SQUID TRIPLE BARRELLED A/S MORTARS.
COMPLEMENT - 175.

FRAME 39.

SEE SHEET TWO FOR THE
FRAME POSITIONS.
FRAME 24½.

SHEET ONE OF TWO SHEETS
© JOHN LAMBERT 3/9/77 L/S/8

WAR SERVICE

After normal trials and working up period, she joined her sisters for a short exercise period, prior to the flotilla being sent to the Mediterranean. On the 15 August *Terpsichire,* with HMS *Ramillies* and cruisers in operation 'Dragoon' was part of the escort force giving fire support to troops during the landing on the French Mediterranean coast on the 'Baie de Cavalaire'.

On 19 September, whilst operating off the North coast of Crete in company with *Troubridge* (L) and the Polish destroyer *Garland,* the German submarine *U 407* was forced to the surface by depth charge attack, and was subsequently rammed and sunk by the *Garland.*

Later that month the 24th Destroyer Flotilla, under Captain Firth RN in *Troubridge,* was further East in the Aegean as part of the covering force to seven RN escort carriers, supplying air strikes during the allied occupation of the Greek Islands and part of the mainland. There were many engagements with small axis naval units, and the shelling of enemy shore positions.

The *T* class were then withdrawn from the Mediterranean to proceed to the United Kingdom for short refits, to equip them for service in the Far East and Pacific fleets in allied operations with the US task forces, and to join their close sisters of the *V, P, Q* and *U* classes on that station. The modifications were mainly to improve the ships' air defence against Japanese kamakaze attacks. This entailed replacing, where possible, the twin 20mm Oerlikon mountings with single 40mm Bofors, which gave their AA fire greater stopping power. The depth charge complement was decreased by half to partly compensate for the additional topweight.

The refitted *T*s joined their new operation areas in April/May 1945. From the 12 to 17 June, *Terpsichore* with four of her sisters

H.M.S. TERPSICHORE SHEET TWO
DETAIL

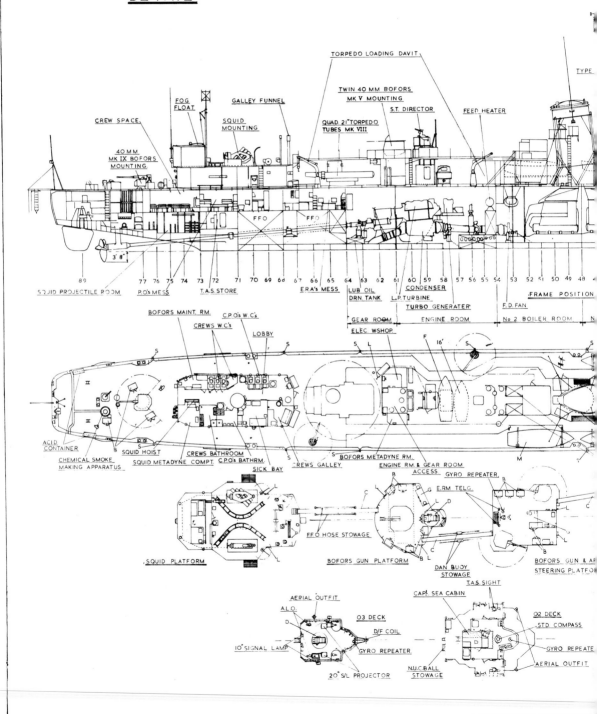

TORPEDO LOADING DAVIT

TWIN 40 MM BOFORS
MK V MOUNTING

S.T. DIRECTOR

FEED HEATER

TYPE

FOG
FLOAT

GALLEY FUNNEL

QUAD 21" TORPEDO
TUBES MK VIII

SQUID
MOUNTING

CREW SPACE.

40 MM
MK IX BOFORS
MOUNTING.

FFO   FFO

3' 8"

89   77 76 75 74 73 72   71 70 69 68   67 66 65 64 63 62   61 60 59 58   57 56 55 54   53   52 51 50 49 48

SQUID PROJECTILE ROOM   P.O's MESS   T.A.S. STORE   E.R.A's MESS   LUB OIL   CONDENSER   FRAME POSITION
                                                                                              DRN. TANK   L.P. TURBINE
                                                                                                           TURBO GENERATER
        BOFORS MAINT. RM.   C.P.O's W.C's   F.D. FAN
                                                                              GEAR ROOM   ENGINE ROOM   No 2 BOILER ROOM   N
        CREWS W.C's   ELEC. WSHOP.
                        LOBBY

                                                                                             F   16'   S
S   S   S   S L   S L   S   S

                                                                                                                                                 M

ACID
CONTAINER   B   SQUID HOIST   CREWS BATHROOM   S   BOFORS METADYNE RM.
    CHEMICAL SMOKE   SQUID METADYNE COMPT. C.P.O's BATHRM.   CREWS GALLEY   ENGINE RM. & GEAR ROOM
    MAKING APPARATUS   SICK BAY   ACCESS   GYRO REPEATER
                                                                                                                           B
                                                                                             E.RM. TELG.
                                                                                                          G

                                                                           FFO HOSE STOWAGE
                                                                                                     L D
                                                                                                    B L
SQUID PLATFORM   BOFORS GUN PLATFORM   DAN BUOY   BOFORS GUN & AF
                                                                           STOWAGE   STEERING PLATFO

                                                                                      T.A.S. SIGHT
                        AERIAL OUTFIT   CAPT. SEA CABIN
                A.L.O.
                                    O3 DECK   O2 DECK
                                                                                         STD COMPASS
                                         D/F COIL
10" SIGNAL LAMP   GYRO REPEATE
                                    GYRO REPEATER
                                                        N.U.C. BALL   AERIAL OUTFIT
                20° S/L PROJECTOR   STOWAGE

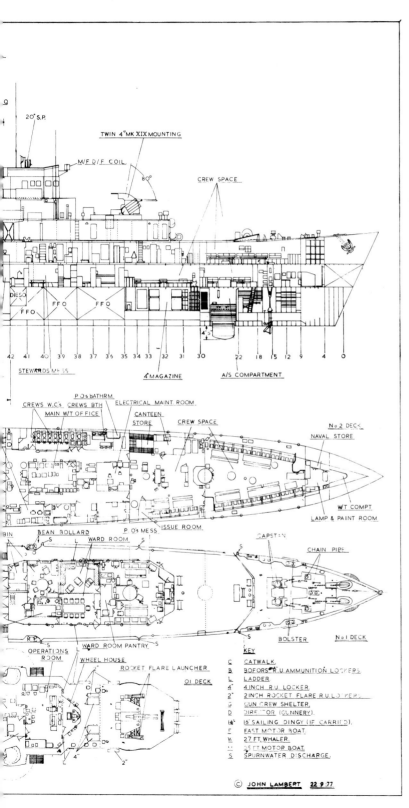

20° S.P.

TWIN 4"MK XIX MOUNTING

M/F D/F COIL

80°

CREW SPACE

DIESO   FFO   FFO

FFO

42 41 40 39 38 37 36 35 34 33 32 31 30   22 18 15 12 9   4   0

STEWARDS MESS   4"MAGAZINE   A/S COMPARTMENT

P. O's BATHRM
CREWS W.C's   CREWS BTH   ELECTRICAL MAINT. ROOM.
MAIN W/T OFFICE   CANTEEN
                              STORE   CREW SPACE   No 2 DECK
                                                                            NAVAL STORE

                                                                            WT COMPT
                                                                            LAMP & PAINT ROOM

BIN   P. O's MESS   ISSUE ROOM.
     BEAN BOLLARD   WARD ROOM.   S   CAPSTEN
                  S   CHAIN PIPE

                                                              BOLSTER   No 1 DECK
OPERATIONS   S   WARD ROOM PANTRY   S   KEY
ROOM
        WHEEL HOUSE   C   CATWALK,
           ROCKET FLARE LAUNCHER   B   BOFORS R.U. AMMUNITION LOCKERS,
                                        OI DECK   L   LADDER
                                                           4' 4INCH R.U. LOCKER.
                                                           2' 2INCH ROCKET FLARE R.U.D KEPS,
                                                           G   GUN CREW SHELTER.
                                                           D   DIRECTOR (GUNNERY).
                                                           16' 16' SAILING DINGY (IF CARRIED).
                                                           F   FAST MOTOR BOAT.
                                                           W   27 FT. WHALER.
                                                               35 FT. MOTOR BOAT.
                                                           S   SPURNWATER DISCHARGE.

© JOHN LAMBERT 22.9.77

was engaged as part of the escort for the raid by carrier based aircraft from the carriers Implacable and the escort carrier *Ruler on Truk*.

The following month, with the carriers *Formidable, Victorious,* and *Implacable* and other heavy units she joined Task Force 37 for raids by British carrier based aircraft on the Tokyo-Yokohama area. After regrouping and refuelling, other raids were carried out on 9 August with the 6inch gun cruisers *Gambia* and *Newfoundland,* and the destroyers *Termagant, Tenacious,* and *Terpsichore*, against targets on North Honshu and Hokkaido, shelling Kamaishi, on the Island of Honshu.

On the 11 and 12 August, with refuelling of the group completed, Task force 37 returned to the Island of Manus, to re-ammunition and re-store and to re-form Task Group 38.5 for the main thrust: the invasion of the Japanese mainland. By the end of August however, with the dropping of the two atomic bombs which resulted in the unconditional surrender of that nation, the huge allied fleet was present for the occupation and the return of allied prisoners-of-war.

In company with most of the other war built fleet destroyers, the *T*s returned to the United Kingdom and with the resumption of peace time conditions and the run down of the three armed services, were reduced to reserve.

POST-WAR CONVERSION
Improved weapons systems that were under development towards the end of the war gradually came into service. Many new naval projects were discovered during the allied occupation of Germany in particular new submarines were examined and trials carried out to establish their performance. These new designs were found to be capable of a much improved underwater speed, particularly whilst travelling at periscope depth, with the 'schnorkel' mast raised, in order that the diesel engines could propel the ship at up to 15 knots. The battery capacity had also

increased threefold, to produce the same high speed at increased depths, and it was realised that contemporary Allied anti-submarine units, built in large numbers towards the end of the war, were virtually obsolete.

This information, in company with modern technology, proved that the USSR was capable of building a modern submarine fleet from the knowledge gained by her occupation of Germany and her access to personal and secret material.

Huge modernisation programmes were set in motion on both sides of the Atlantic to improve the performance of existing ships. British conventionally powered submarines of the *A* and *T* classes were improved by streamlining the hull contours and building in much increased battery power. 'Snort' (as 'schnorkel' are known in the RN) masts were fitted and the hulls improved by the removal of all guns and external torpedo-tubes, and redesigned 'fins' replaced the old conning towers.

The war built anti-submarine frigates were incapable of hunting and catching the modern submarine: *Castle* class frigates could manage just $16\frac{1}{2}$ knots on their single screw, and the larger twin screw, *Lock, River,* and *Improved Black Swan* classes were only capable of a service speed of 19 knots.

New construction to fill this requirement was in the planning stage but the design and building would take at least five years. The construction of the *Whitby* class (Type 12) and the utility *Blackwood* class would not join the fleet until 1956 at the earliest. A simple fast anti-submarine unit was required to fill the gap until the construction of the more sophisticated A/S units were completed. Therefore, the modernisation of the vast numbers of modern fleet destroyers laid up in reserve was authorised. The larger proportion (24 ships) were to undergo a full A/S frigate conversion, taking up to two years or more — the Type 15 (see the previous issue of *Warship*). A cheaper, simpler form of modernisation was also authorised,

taking less time, but producing a useful fast anti-submarine unit, and still retaining a reasonable anti-aircraft protection. The ten units so converted were known as Type 16, or 'limited' conversions.

With the exception of *Troubridge,* which underwent a full Type 15 conversion starting at the Royal Dockyard, Portsmouth in 1955 (but was completed by J Samuel White & Co Ltd, at Cowes, Isle of Wight, on 29 July 1957) all the *T* class were given limited conversions. Similar reconstruction was carried out on the older war built destroyers *Orwell, Paladin* and *Petard.*

Terpsichore was brought out of reserve and underwent her conversion in the hands of John I Thorneycroft & Co Ltd, at their Woolston works near Southport between 1952-53.

I have drawn her as completed at this period, which produced an elegant looking warship. As can be seen her whole armament has been completely revised. Forward in 'B' gun position is a single D/P twin 4inch Mark XIX mounting, with rocket flare launches in position on each side. Her close range armament comprises of a twin 40mm Bofors Mark V mounting amidships, with a good arc of fire, and five single 40mm Bofors Mark IX mountings. One on each of the bridge wings, two on the after steering platform aft of the single funnel, and a single mounting aft on the quarter deck. Unlike the Type 15 full conversions, she retains a quadruple set if 21inch torpedo-tubes aft.

For anti-submarine warfare, two 3-barrelled 'squid' ahead throwing mortars were mounted aft on a platform, situated almost directly above the projectile room and connected by hydraulic hoist and reload gear. Her main asdic dome, aft of frame 22, was lowered 4 ft 6 in below the hull when in use, and on frame 15 was the type 147P depth finding sonar. She was fitted with the new frigate type enclosed bridge, with a M/F D/F frame fitted in front. H/F D/F was carried at the masthead, and an impressive radar display was carried.

Her power plant remained as before, and she retained much the same performance as previously. Her new complement was reduced to 175 officers and men.

Terpsichore remained in service until 1965, until she was sold to the West of Scotland Shipbreakers, arriving at Troon on 17 May 1966 for scrapping.

Her battle Honours:—
Martinique 1795, Teneriffe 1797, Jawa 1806, Adriatic 1944, South of France 1944, Aegean 1944.

My drawings of *Terpsichore* on two sheets are available from the David MacGregor Plans Service, 99 Lonsdale Road, London SW13.

1 *Tenacious,* April 1952.

2 *Teazer,* February 1959.

3 *Termagant,* June 1953. Note that she still has an open bridge.
All photos Wright & Logan

1

2

3

The battle of Tsu-Shima

3

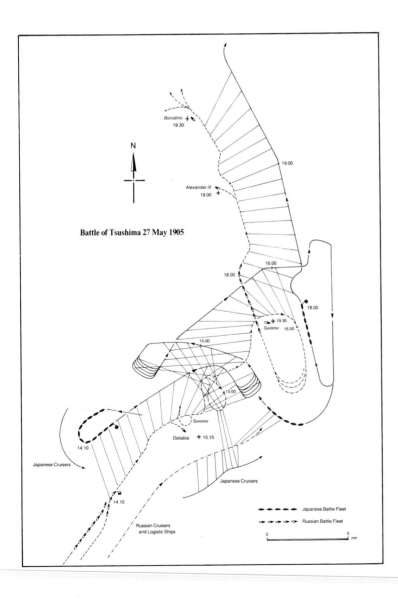

Battle of Tsushima 27 May 1905

N

Borodino +
19.30

19.00

Alexander III +
19.00

16.00

18.00

18.00

+ 19.30
Suvorov 16.00

15.00

15.00

Suvorov

Osliabia + 15.15

14.10

Japanese Cruisers

14.10

Japanese Cruisers

Japanese Battle Fleet

Russian Battle Fleet

Russian Cruisers
and Logistic Ships

0   5
                         nm

The movements of Kamimura's division and the end of the *Suvarov* remain to be described. Shortly after 17.30 Kamimura had chased some Russian cruisers to the south-west but they altered course to the north-westward and Kamimura was actually following them on an outside curve, which was latterly somewhat divergent, and he could not catch them. At 18.03 he abandoned the chase and turned towards the estimated position of Togo's division. The details of his course alterations need not be related, and after passing the disabled *Suvarov* and *Kamchatka*, at which some of his ships fired, Kamimura at about 18.30 sighted the rear of the Russian line at about 12 000 yards range on the port bow, and according to the report of his division, temporarily on a southward course. The *Tokiwa* reported sighting one *Borodino* class (*Alexander*), with the *Sissoi*, *Navarin* and *Nakhimov,* and it seems that these three latter ships temporarily turned southward and then on to a north-westerly course at a greater distance from Togo's division than the rest of the Russian battleships. The southward turn was apparently made shortly after the *Alexander* first fell out of the line.

The *Tokiwa* was the first to open fire and by 18.50 other armoured cruisers had followed with a slow fire at about 8000-9000 yards. Conditions of visibility were not good and except at 19.15 when the three leading armoured cruisers fired at a *Jemtchug* class cruiser,

by N J M Campbell

Maps from *Atlas of Naval Warfare* by Helmut Pemsel (Arms and Armour Press, 1977) reproduced by kind permission of the publishers.

Note that the transliteration of some of the ship names is different from that adopted in the article.

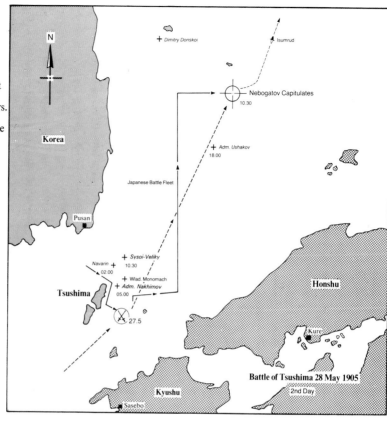

Battle of Tsushima 28 May 1905
2nd Day

targets are not identified in the reports. By 19.30 firing ceased and at 20.08 *Kamimura* rejoined Togo's division. It is doubtful if the Russians were much damaged in this action by the Japanese 2nd Division, and the *Izumo* was hit by a 12inch shell at 19.10 which might have caused considerable injuries if it had burst.

The *Suvarov* was now near the disabled repair ship *Kamchatka*. She was a complete wreck, still blazing, with flames out of most scuttles and ports, but still steaming slowly, though not under control, and able to fire two or three small stern guns. As noted above, Kamimura's ships had fired a few rounds at her and from about 18.30 most of the Japanese light cruisers were firing at her and the *Kamchatka* at ranges down to 1300 yards. The *Kasagi* had, however, been compelled to make for shelter by a hit below the waterline, received earlier in the battle, and the *Chitose* had accompanied her, so that none of the light cruisers had heavier guns than 6inch. At 18.48 Kataoka's 5th Division, without the *Matsushima,* which had had a steering-gear breakdown, engaged the *Suvarov* and *Kamchatka* at 3800-4900 yards, aided by one light cruiser division, the others having steamed North. Kataoka's ships had heavy guns, and Corbett says that 12.6inch shells kept bursting on the *Suvarov,* but this is not supported by the Japanese ammunition returns, which gave the heavy projectile

expenditure for the entire battle as:- *Itsukushima* two 12.6inch; *Chin-Yen* five 12inch; *Hashidate* nil; and *Matsushima* (temporarily absent), three 12.6inch. The failure to make more use of the heavy guns in this division may have been due to the difficulty of working the older-pattern barbette mountings in rough seas.

The *Kamchatka* sank at 19.00 or soon afterwards, but the *Suvarov* was still under way as before. Kataoka had at this time a number of torpedo-boats in company, and the 11th Division of four 128 ft Schichau type boats attacked at 19.20. They ran in at 20 knots to 300-350 yards without being fired at, and launched seven 14inch torpedoes of which two or three hit. One torpedo was thought by the attackers to have exploded a magazine as black and yellow fumes poured out. The *Suvarov* heeled over to port and then capsized. For a short time she floated bottom up and at 19.30 or just before, her bows lifted high in

the air and she slid rapidly out of sight. Except for the few taken off with Rozhestvenski, there were no survivors and 928 were lost with her.

Thus by 19.30 Togo had achieved a great victory; the *Suvarov, Alexander, Borodino* and *Osliabia* sunk. The *Sissoi* and *Navarin* were seriously damaged near the waterline, and the *Orel* much battered. The other five Russian ships in the line did not count for much in any case, but all except the *Seniavin* were damaged to some extent. In the Japanese armoured ships three 12inch and four 8inch guns were out of action, but only the *Asama* had been seriously damaged.

During the night, the Japanese torpedo craft were to attack the surviving Russian ships. At dusk the swell was high enough to cause torpedo-boats to roll through 50° or 60°, but this dropped during the night. Salt spray which had covered the boats during the day had impaired the eyesight of the crews.

The attacks were made as follows:-

1st and 2nd Destroyer Divisions (totalling 9 boats) and the 9th Torpedo-boat Division (4 boats) originally to the northward, between 20.10 and 21.20.

3rd and 5th destroyer Divisions (8 boats), originally to the East, between 20.30 and 21.15 with one isolated attack at 22.30.

1st, 10th, 15th, 17th, 18th Torpedo-boat Divisions (20 boats), originally to the South, between 21.10 and 22.10.

Of the other Japanese torpedo-craft, the 4th Destroyer Division (4 boats) did not attack until later and the 14th, 19th and 20th Torpedo-boat Divisions (11 boats) never located the Russian ships. The one serviceable boat of the 16th Division located a target after 01.00 on the 28th but was driven off before she could fire torpedoes. The 11th Division (4 boats), which had attacked the *Suvarov* at 19.20, returned to base for more torpedoes, and the 5th Torpedo-boat Division (four older boats) based on the Japanese coast, never found any Russian ships.

The Japanese attacks were somewhat confused from so many torpedo craft working independently, and there was no detailed plan of attack. 2 destroyers and 4 torpedo-boats of the attacking divisions never found a target, and in addition 3 destroyers and 3 torpedo-boats were involved in collisions, in which one torpedo-boat (*No 69*) was sunk. As one destroyer had made an attack before collision, the total number which actually fired torpedoes in these attacks was 13 destroyers and 17 torpedo-boats. These launched respectively, 23 — 18inch and 31 — 14inch torpedoes at ranges of about 200 to 650 or exceptionally 900 yards, and made three hits. A number of the Japanese torpedo craft were hit by Russian projectiles from rifle bullets upwards, and some were damaged but only two torpedo boats were sunk, after they had made attacks. (*Nos 34* and *35*).

The Russians had been steaming in a south-westerly direction at nightfall but at about 20.30 Nebogatov, who now commanded the Russian fleet, altered course to N 23°E as previously ordered by the seriously wounded Rozhestvenski. The ships in company with the *Nikolai* were the *Orel, Apraxin, Seniavin* and the cruiser *Izumrud*. According to Nebogativ their speed was a little over 11 knots, and he had forbidden the use of any searchlights. He states that the *Nikolai* was attacked once unsuccessfully, but otherwise these ships appear to have escaped the Japanese. Some of the vessels astern used their searchlights and in so doing gave their positions away to the attacking torpedo craft. The *Nakhimov* was torpedoed in the earlier part of the attack, it is said by a destroyer which was mistaken for a Russian. She was hit on the starboard bow and though later attacks were avoided, she had to stop engines to make temporary repairs. Finally the *Nakhimov* made stern first for the nearest land, and reached the east coast of Tsushima at 07.00 on the 28th.

The old cruiser *Vladimir Monomakh* is also said to have mistaken her attacker for a Russian destroyer. She was hit by a torpedo on the starboard side forward and also made for the coast of Tsushima. The *Navarin* had been seriously damaged near the waterline aft during the daylight battle and, according to a survivor, by 21.00 on the 27th her stern had settled so much that water on the upper deck reached the after 12inch turret. She was forced to stop and was then hit by a torpedo from a boat which had crept right under her stern. She was not completely disabled, however, and seems to have got under way again.

Enkvist with the *Oleg, Aurora* and *Jemtchug* stated that several unsuccessful attacks were made on these three cruisers, but as all were 3-funnelled and only two destroyers report firing torpedoes at 3-funnel ships, this statement is open to doubt. There is unfortunately insufficient evidence to decide what Japanese torpedo craft attacked any particular Russian ship or to assign the three hits made with any certainty. So far the torpedo attacks had met with very limited success, but the 4th Destroyer Division, employing both their mines and torpedoes, were later to achieve a remarkable result. The *Murasame* had to return to base at 23.30 as she was taking water aboard from the ricochet hit noted previously, but the other three saw a Russian ship at about 02.00 next morning, about 600 yards away on their starboard bow. Their recognition signals were unanswered and each dropped her mines, 24 in all, about 300 yards ahead of the Russian ship. In a minute or two a dull thud and loud explosion were heard. This ship was the *Navarin*, whose few survivors thought that she had been torpedoed again. An explosion seemed to heave up the whole stern and then there was another to starboard amidships, and

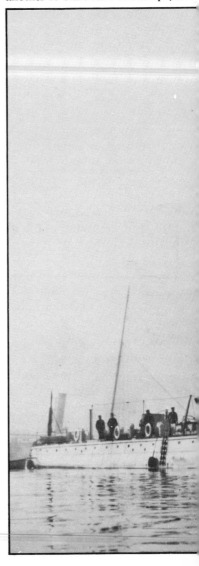

Russian destroyers, including the *Bodry* (left) and *Bezuprechny* which fought at Tsushima. *CPL W/7/001*

The Japanese destroyer *Akatsuki*. *IWM*

1

2

2-я Тихоокеанская эскадра. № 12.
Крейсеръ I ранга „ДМИТРІЙ ДОНСКОЙ".

Dmitri Donskoi

1
2

KASAGI JAP

The *Dimitri Donskoi*.
CPL W/7/002

The Japanese cruiser *Kasagi*.
CPL W/7/003

A 6inch/40 mounting on the quarterdeck of
the Japanese protected cruiser *Suma* of 1892.
CPL W/7/004

Russian naval officers aboard the *Alexander
II*.
CPL W/7/005

she capsized and sank. Only three were saved from her crew of 674.

The 4th Destroyer Division sped on and at about 14.40 came up with the *Sissoi,* at which each of the three fired a torpedo in passing. One hit right aft, wrecking the rudder, but the *Sissoi* was able to steer by her engines. She had however been seriously damaged forward near the waterline during the daylight battle, and steamed for the coast of Tsushima.

Meanwhile Togo and Kamimura proceeded North, untroubled by any attacks from the Russian destroyers. The *Asama*'s flooding aft increased during ther night, and she had to stop for 50 minutes at 06.30 but was then able to continue. On the morning of 28 May, the ships with Nebogatov were located to the South of the main Japanese force. They comprised the *Nikolai, Orel, Apraxin* and *Seniavin* with the cruiser *Izumrud*. The Japanese steamed to attack them and opened fire at 10.34 at about 8000 yards. After a few shots, their firing became general but the Russian ships did not reply. One or two hits were made on the *Nikolai* and it was then seen that the Russians had surrendered and firing ceased by 10.50. The fast *Izumrud* had previously made off and got away. The rights and wrongs of this surrender cannot be discussed here but the position of Nebogatov's squadron was quite hopeless. Of the four ships only the *Orel* was of any real value to the Japanese.

Of the Russian ships off Tsushima, the *Nakhimov* was taken by a Japanese destroyer and an auxiliary cruiser but her crew had opened the sea-valves and she sank at 09.00. The *Sissoi* surrendered to three auxiliary cruisers and the Japanese attempted to take her in tow, but here again valves had been opened, and she went down at 11.00. The old cruiser *Vladimir Monomakh* also surrendered, and kept afloat until 14.30 when she sank.

The *Ushakov* alone remained of the 12 ships originally in the Russian line of battle. She had fallen far astern during the night from damage received in the daylight actions, but had not used her searchlights and had avoided torpedo attack. She was sighted to the South on the afternoon of the 28th and the *Iwate* and *Yakumo* overtook her at 17.00 and called on her to surrender. This was ignored and at 17.30 the action began at 9800 yards. In a little over 20 minutes the *Ushakov*'s guns were silenced and she had apparently stopped her engines. At 18.07 there was an explosion, thought by the Japanese to be from scuttling charges, and in three minutes she went down. Neither Japanese ship was hit in this action in which they fired 89 — 8inch and 278 — 6inch shells.

Of the Russian light cruisers, Enkvist broke away to the South during the night of the 27th and the *Oleg, Aurora* and *Jemtchug* were eventually interned at Manila. The *Izumrud* got away when Nebogatov surrendered, but was wrecked on the coast North of Vladivostok, and the *Svietlana* was sunk on the 28th

by the Japanese light cruisers *Otowa* and *Niitaka*. The fate of the old *Vladimir Monomakh* has already been noted, and the *Dmitri Donskoi,* after engaging Japanese light cruisers on the evening of the 28th, was attacked early that night off Matsushima by four Japanese destroyers which fired eight 18inch torpedoes at 350-550 yards, apparently without success; she was abandoned and scuttled soon after daybreak on the 29th.

The armed liner *Ural*, repair ship *Kamchatka* and ocean tug *Russ* were sunk on the 27th and the hospital ships *Orel* and *Kostroma* captured. The armed transport *Irtish* badly damaged on the 27th, was run ashore on the Japanese coast, and the transport *Korea* and ocean tug *Svir* escaped to Shanghai where they were interned. The armed transport *Anadyr* was missing for 45 days and then turned up in Madagascar from whence she returned to Russia.

Of the nine Russian destroyers

the *Buistry, Bezuprechny* and *Gromky* were sunk or driven ashore by the Japanese. The *Buiny* was scuttled and the *Biedovy* to which Rozhestvenski had been transferred, surrendered. The *Blestiashchy* was abandoned in a sinking condition and scuttled and the *Bodry,* short of fuel, drifted about the Yellow Sea until found by a British steamer on 4 June and towed to Shanghai where she was interned. Only the *Grosny* and *Bravy* with the armed yacht *Almaz* reached Vladivostok.

The Russian casualties were 4830 killed or drowned, 5917 taken prisoner, of whom many were wounded, and 1862 interned; a total of 12 609. Another 1227 escaped to Vladivostok or Madagascar. The Japanese had 117 killed and 583 wounded, and only three torpedo-boats were sunk. Victory could scarcely have been more complete.

The Russian cruiser Diana.
CPL W/7/006

ДІАНА
Diana interned /05

ESCORT SHIP PRODUCTION IN WWII

by Peter Elliott

Peter Elliott has recently completed a full analysis of the building times of all Allied escort ships built during Worl War II ('Allied Escort Ships of World War II') and hence of the comparative production achievements of the four major Allied shipbuilding countries: UK, USA, Canada and Australia. This research appears to be the first of its kind to be published, and the results show up some interesting trends.

In the first part of this article I will deal with the larger escort types: frigates, destroyer escorts, and sloops; in the second part, the smaller types will be analysed: corvettes, PCs/PCEs, fleet minesweepers and trawlers.

The individual statistics in this study need to be accepted with caution. There are undoubtedly a number of suspect dates, even in official records in UK, USA, Canada and Australia (the primary sources of information) and especially in the later war years; the amount of prefabrication done outside the builder's yard heavily affected the period on the slipway, and so the building time. Some of the US destroyer escort times are most affected by this, due to mass production methods.

The production figures of escort ships built by the Allies during the war show a massive effort covering some 4000 warships, and whether individual yard building times were faster or slower takes nothing away from this magnificent achievement. Conversely, the slower building times in all four countries were surprisingly similar, running to about 20 months.

PEAK PERIOD
For the larger escorts, designed in 1941/42 from earlier war experience, the great peak of high rates of production and quick individual building times came from the end of 1942 to the first half of 1944; in the second half of 1943 alone, 512 new escorts in all were launched.

Then towards the end of 1943 the Allies agreed to cut the escort building programme back, and from mid-1944 onwards fast individual times were still being recorded, but the proportion of slower times was rising fast. This cutback was in order to switch the emphasis to building landing craft, and especially the big LSTs, since the rising number of new frigates and DEs was giving the Allied escorts growing supremacy in both the Atlantic and Pacific.

WAR LOSSES
For the RN the war losses were significant. In 1944-45, the RN's annual rate of loss of war-built escorts alone was running at about 10 per cent of the new construction rate, great as it was, and the annual rate of loss was still rising in 1945.

The RCN also increased in this period, but the USN did not experience such a high loss rate. The U-boat campaign and the English Channel and North Sea operations of 1944-45 seem to have been more damaging to escorts than the Pacific war.

1 The final destroyer armament configuration, with single 5inch aft, one quadruple and two twin Bofors, and two single Oerlikons on the fantail. Compare this with the RN's North Atlantic armament pattern for *Loch* class frigates.
US BuShips

2 Destroyer escort *Swasey* (DE-248) being launched sideways at a shipyard in Houston, Texas, March 1943.
US BuShips

Table 1: COMPARATIVE BUILDING TIMES
This chart compares the fastest and slowest times for each class, in months and days

Class	1940	1941	1942	1943	1943	1944	1945
RN BLACK SWAN							
Fastest	17.8	19.3	15.13	11.24	15.15		
Slowest	19.6	19.10		23.10	23.5		
RN HUNT							
Fastest	9.0	10.25	10.16				
Slowest	19.4	26.29	20.23				
RN RIVER							
Fastest			9.7	7.5	8.10		
Slowest			16.21	22.17	24.17		
RCN RIVER							
Fastest				5.21	5.3		
Slowest				17.20	15.21		
RAN RIVER							
Fastest				16.8	20.20	22.23	
Slowest					21.27	24.15	
RN LOCK/BAY							
Fastest				10.1	7.25	8.25	
Slowest					13.2	17.10	
USN PF							
Fastest				5.0	5.14	14.5	
Slowest				9.6	18.7	21.8	
USN DE TYPES							
EVARTS TYPE							
Fastest			12.6	3.3	3.27		
Slowest				21.20	13.14		
BUCKLEY TYPE							
Fastest				1.23	3.2		
Slowest				10.20	13.21		
EDSALL TYPE							
Fastest				3.25	3.7		
Slowest				11.18	15.30		
BOSTWICK TYPE							
Fastest				3.11	3.8		
Slowest				11.24	15.30		
RUDDEROW TYPE							
Fastest					2.7		
Slowest					10.26		
JC BUTLER TYPE							
Fastest				3.7	4.18	10.6	
Slowest					11.27	25.6	

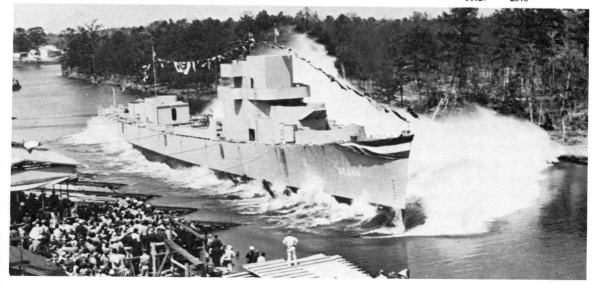

UK

The *River* class (RN, RCN and RAN) was designed in the UK and put into production there and in Canada and Australia. The USN picked it up, improved on the design and produced it as the PF (Patrol Frigate) class.

The design was intended for production in yards not used to naval specifications, and very successful it was. Mass production methods had not been introduced in 1942 in the UK, when this class emerged, but some creditable building times were achieved by the five yards mainly involved.

In 1942, 6 of the 13 ships completed took between 10 and 12 months each. In 1943, of 30 completed, 2 took 8 months, and 11 were completed in under 12. In 1944, the fastest time was 9 months, but 9 out of 15 were completed in under a year.

CANADA

Five yards were involved in the class programme here and the overall building times were rather faster than in the UK. During the 1943-44 period, of the 60 ships completed in Canada, 2 were completed in 6 months, 3 more in 8, 5 more in 9, and a further 27 in under a year. Note that third class was built about a year later than in the UK, and the numbers cancelled at 96 showed that the programme would have run full blast into 1945.

The specification had been improved, too; most of the RCN ships had a twin 4inch mounting forward, in place of the single gun of the UK-built ships, and full naval motor boats and whalers were added.

AUSTRALIA

The numbers built in Australia were comparatively small, and the completion dates were later than those in Europe so that the slowdown and cancellation decision had its effect. Overall building times were longer for this reason, but again the original *River* class specification was improved, to resemble the later RN *Bay* class, with twin 4inch mountings and single 40mm Bofors.

UNITED STATES

The PF class retained a strong resemblance to the RN's *River* class in hull and layout (the first two *Rivers* built in Canada were transferred to the USN as the first two units of the PF class), but many items were changed to current USN design to take advantage of the mass production programme by then in full swing.

Thus the 4inch guns gave way to a DE layout of three single 3inch/50 calibre guns, with two twin Bofors mountings aft, and American radar and other electronics mounted on a pole mast rather than a tripod.

American mass production came through in the building times. Though not quite as impressive as the DE results, the eight shipyards participating produced 12 ships in under 5 months, a further 16 in 6 months, a further 11 in 7 months, and 8 more in 8 months. The two fastest yards produced 30 ships between them in under 8 months each!

The slowdown in 1944-45 shows through here, too, and overall building times for the class fluctuated (Table 2).

Building times by navy for this class shown an interesting pattern (Table 3).

1 *Outremont,* a Canadian *River* class frigate, showing how units built in Canada approached the UK-built *Bay* class in armament.
Public Archives of Canada

2 *Meon,* a *River* class frigate converted to a headquarters ship for assault landings. Six of the class were so converted and proved the best for this job.
Wright & Logan

TABLE 2: PF BUILDING TIMES (IN MONTHS AND DAYS)

	Shortest	Longest
To end 1943	2.0	9.6
First half 1944	5.14	13.16
Second half 1944	9.15	18.7
First half 1945	14.5	21.8

TABLE 3: COMPARATIVE SPEEDS OF CONSTRUCTION

Completed in months	5	6	7	8	9	10	11	12
RN RIVER				2	7	7	10	7
RCN RIVER		2	1	2	5	10	7	10
RAN RIVER								
USN PF	9	16	11	8	3	5	3	5

1

2

1

2

3

1 *Asheville* (PF-1) a *River* class frigate built in Canada for the RN, but transferred to the USN as the first unit of the PF class. She has both British and American radar, but American 3inch guns.
USN

2 *Helmsdale*, showing how the *River* class would have been converted to Squid mortars. Armament had been removed, as this was a postwar shot (1952).
Wright & Logan

3 The famous *England* (DE-635), which sank 6 Japanese submarines in a few days. She represents the standard *Buckley* type of destroyer escort.
US BuShips

Loch/Bay class (RN and RCN) was the main mass production class for the RN and was planned to produce fast building times, even approaching some of the fastest DE times. But by the time the first ships were completed the production cutback had already been put into effect and no startling results were achieved. Indeed, the overall building times were deliberately kept slow as the European war approached its end, and only the few *Bay* class units for the Pacific were hurried through.

Naval shipyards came back into the picture in the UK for this class, including Harland & Wolff (11 built, 19 cancelled), Swan Hunter and John Brown. Smith's Dock, originators of all the major RN escort classes during the war, remained as the lead yard on design and drawings, but also built 5, with 11 cancelled.

Black Swan and Hunt classes (RN) classes kept to naval specifications and naval builders, but they were not designed for mass production, so no very fast times were turned out. the *Black Swan* class had a fastest time of $11\frac{1}{2}$ months in 1943, rising to $15\frac{1}{2}$ months in 1944, while the *Hunt* class averaged 15 months each, though some came out in 10.

THE AMERICAN DESTROYER ESCORTS

Not only was the overall number built (nearly 500) fantastic, but the American shipyards achieved magnificently fast building times, with welded mass production methods on a far grander scale than was possible in the UK or Canada. The DEs may be grouped into 353 built by seven shipyards achieving the fastest times, making an interesting comparison (Table 4) with the *River* class.

TABLE 4: US DEs

	2	3	4	5	6
Completion in months					
Seven fastest yards	2	7	49	75	90

Of the 138 units built in shipyards unable to achieve such fast building times overall periods of 7 to 10 months were still quite common.

Yards were specially laid out for mass production, and those yards not achieving the faster times were generally those with smaller numbers of the class on their books. The finest example of organisation came from the Bethlehem-Hingham yard near Boston, which turned out 75 turbo-electric DEs all in 4-6 months each. Of the overall total of DEs built, no less than 222 were completed in under 6 months.

Ships were often laid down in pairs and even four at a time. Philadelphia Navy Yard laid down 7 together on 22 February 1943 but they were completed one month apart consecutively, as the construction programme was cut back. There were three yards which laid down two ships on the same day and completed them on the same day later, and many DEs were launched in pairs, while Philadelphia (again) launched six of the TE type on 29 May 1943, with five other examples of four at a time. It is hard from the records to analyse the number of building slips in operation in the yards, but at Bethlehem-Hingham there must have been at least 12 berths at the height of the production race.

DE PROGRAMME CUTBACKS

In December 1943, in line with the other allies, the DE programme was cut in half. No less than 447 units were cancelled, mostly of the two latter types (*Rudderow* 187 and *John C Butler* 211), while those ships completed after 1943 were slowed down considerably.

Of the cancelled ships, most had been ordered from the five yards producing the fastest building times. No less than 120, all of the *Rudderow* type, were cancelled from the Bethlehem-Hingham yard alone. The number of shipyards participating in the 'second 500' was reduced from 16 to 11; of the five yards which dropped out, their total of DEs produced was 63 out of the overall total of 491. Part of this reorganisation stemmed from naval construction programmes; Bethlehem-Quincy, having produced the fastest DE building time of all — 1 month 29 days with DE 682 — dropped out of the DE programme, but also built 4 carriers, 17 cruisers, 45 LSTs, and 3 destroyers!

CONVERSIONS AND DESIGN PROGRESSION

These did affect the capacity of the yards to produce fast times. Alterations in specification could produce sudden delays, and the secret of the great DE programme was undoubtedly the concentration on one basic type, with modifications only to the armament, though this in itself was impressive.

In the UK, there was some dilemma as to whether to convert the ships already completed to the anti-submarine Squid mortar, once this had proved its worth in 1944. Plans were in fact agreed to convert the *River* class from Hedgehog to Squid, but in fact only *Helmsdale* was converted, as the European war came to an end.

The Pacific war in 1945 demanded RN and RCN escorts capable of long distances away from base and heavy anti-aircraft defence; hence the rather hurried *Bay* class, and the planned conversion of many RN and RCN *River* class units to include a twin 4inch mounting multiple Bofors and new radar.

River class frigate *Prestonian* alongside the frigate fitting out quay at Levis, Quebec, in 1944. Three other ships of the class are in the background.
Public Archives of Canada

JAPANESE B TYPE SUBMARINES AT WAR 1
by PIERRE HERVIEUX

The Japanese Navy had great hopes for its submarine fleet. When War began on 7 December 1941, 58 submarines were operational, as well as a few midget submarines not included in this study. The Japanese concept of submarine warfare was to use squadrons of these vessels as part of a battle fleet and it was with this in mind that experiments were started to find the submarine best suited to this role. The design of the first big Japanese submarines, *I-1* class (Type J 1), was directly developed from the German cruiser-type of submarine. During hostilities 119 units were launched (103 of them being completed) in the Japanese shipyards, but the transport submarines built specifically for this purpose are not included, and only the submarines armed with torpedoes and Kaitens are covered.

The tonnage of many Japanese submarines was bigger than that of the German U-boats. The Germans thought that big submarines were not handy. The Japanese, often impressed by sheer size, built the biggest battleships, aircraft carriers and submarines, but their submarines had inferior equipment to the American counterparts. In fact the modest achievement of the Japanese submarines was due to the inferiority of their technology, a judgement which is confirmed by

Admiral S Fukutome, former Commander of the Japanese combined forces:

'Our submarines, built and equipped with inferior weapons [to those of the Americans] were counter-attacked before they could approach their target or get away. Many of them knew they were in contact with the enemy only when attacked by him!'

If there were many big submarines, it was not without reason, for they had two important roles:
1 The destruction of enemy naval forces;
2 Reconnaissance, using the small planes carried on board and launched with a catapult.

Their main target was enemy aircraft carriers, then battleships, cruisers and only occasionally . . . merchant ships. The German captains, in contrast, were free to make their own choice of targets. It was the same with torpedoes; whereas the Germans could fire as many torpedoes as needed, the Japanese could only launch a full bow-salvo of torpedoes against aircraft carriers and battleships. A maximum of three were authorised to sink a cruiser, only one for a destroyer or a merchant ship, and in the last category it depended how big she was! That is why at the beginning of the war many Allied

merchant ships were attacked by Japanese submarines with gunfire and were only damaged. To reinforce their troops on Guadalcanal, and later in the war in other areas, Japanese fleet submarines were used as transports and also to evacuate surrounded garrisons. Many of them had their main gun removed and carried only two torpedoes! As regards radar, the Japanese submarines were greatly inferior to their American counterparts. A few months after the start of the war, the American submarines received air-warning and surface-warning radars, whereas the first combat action involving a Japanese submarine equipped with radar did not take place until May 1944. This submarine, the *I-44,* was attacked by night, being on the surface, by an American destroyer, and her radar revealed nothing. Nevertheless she succeeded in escaping, although slightly damaged by depth charges. It is therefore easy to understand what Captain Hashimoto, who sank the *Indianapolis* in *I-58*, meant:

'If we had had radars like the American ones, the result of the war could have been quite different'.

JAPANESE B-TYPE SUBMARINES

This study deals with three classes of Japanese submarines, the *I-15,*

I-40 and *I-54* classes which had the same dimensions, but had different displacements, horsepower, speed and number of torpedoes carried.

THE *I-15* CLASS (TYPE B 1)

Developed from the earlier KD 6 cruiser type submarines, these vessels were a highly specialised scouting class. In comparison with preceding classes the hull and conning tower on the *I-15* class was very streamlined, the seaplane hangar being a smooth rounded fairing extending forward as part of the conning tower.

Although designed to mount four 25mm AA, they were completed with a single twin 25mm AA mount on the conning tower, and the 5.5inch gun aft of the conning tower. An exception to this was *I-17*, in which the hangar and catapult were placed aft of the conning tower whilst the 5.5inch gun was placed forward of it.

The performance of this class was much the same as that of the A and C types, with a radius of action of 16000 sea miles at 16 knots cruising speed on the surface and 96 sea miles at 3 knots submerged. The operational range was 90 days and the diving depth 325ft.

During the war some vessels were modified by the removal of the catapult and hangar, their place being taken by a 5.5inch gun. The vessels so converted were reclassed as attack submarines.

At the end of 1944, *I-36* and *I-37* were modified to enable them to carry Kaiten submarines. The 5.5inch gun aft of the conning tower and the hangar and catapult were removed. Thus modified they were able to carry four Kaitens, but *I-36* was later refitted to carry six. Out of this fairly large class only *I-36* survived the war, being surrendered at Kure. In September 1945 she was taken to Sasebo and later sunk by the United States Navy off Goto Island. The exact date of loss of *I-23* and *I-26* is unknown, but it is thought that the dates given are fairly accurate.

Submarines of this class achieved some outstanding successes against warships, as was intended by Imperial Headquarters, but their

PARTICULARS

DISPLACEMENT:	2198 tons standard (2584/3654 tons normal; surfaced/submerged)
Length:	108.66m (oa) 356.50ft
	102.41 (CWL) 336ft
Beam:	9.29m 30.50ft
Draught:	5.10m 16.75ft
Machinery:	2 shaft Diesel/Electric motors, HP 12400/2000=23.50/8 knots
Armament:	1 5.5inch, 2 25mm AA (1 x 2) guns
	6 21inch (bow) TT and 17 torpedoes
	1 aircraft
Complement:	about 100

successes against merchant shipping far outweighed this.

INDIVIDUAL FATES

I-15 built by Kure Navy Yard, launched in 1939, commissioned in September 1940. She missed the US battleship *Washington*, 27 October 1942. She did not sink any ships for, according to a Japanese source, on 15 Sept 1942 she did not fire any torpedoes and the US destroyer *O'Brien* was in fact hit by *I-19*. *I-15* was sunk by the American destroyer *McCalla* off the Solomon Islands, 2 Nov 1942.

I-17 built by Yokosuka Navy Yard, launched on 19 July 1939, commissioned in Jan 1941.
1 She sank the American tanker *Emidio* (launched 1921, 6912 tons), in the Pacific, 40°N/125°W, 20 Dec 1941.
2 She damaged the American tanker *Larry Doheny (1921, 7038 tons), in the Pacific, 40°N/125°W,* 23 Dec 1941.
3 She unsuccessfully attacked the American tanker *William H Berg* (1937, 8289 tons), off San Francisco, 37°25N/123°28W, 28 Feb 1942.
4 She sank the Panamanian tanker ship *Stanvac Manila* (1941, 10169 tons), in the Pacific, 23°45S/166°30E, 23 May 1943; two American motor torpedo boats were embarked aboard the tanker and were also lost *(PT 165* and *PT 173)*.
I-17 was sunk by the New Zealand armed naval trawler *Tui* and US Navy aircraft, 40 miles south east of Noumea Bay, 19 Aug 1943.

I-19 built by Mitsubishi at Kobe,

launched in 1939, commissioned in April 1941.
1 She damaged the American tanker *H M Storey* (1921, 10763 tons), in the Pacific, 34°35N/120°45W, 22 Dec 1941.
2 She damaged the American cargo ship *Absaroka* (1918, 5695 tons), off California, 34°N/121°W, 24 Dec 1941.
3 On 15 September 1942, in the Pacific:
a) at 14.45 hrs she sank the American aircraft carrier *Wasp* (1939, 14700 tons), 12°25S/164°08E;
b) at 14.52 hrs she damaged the American battleship *North Carolina* (1940, 38000 tons), 12°S/164°E;
c) at 14.54 hrs she damaged the American destroyer *O'Brien* (1939, 1620 tons), 12°S/164°E, which sank on 19 October 1942 on her way back to the States.
4 She sank the American cargo ship *Phoebe A Hearst* (1943, 7176 tons), in the Pacific, 20°07S/177°35W, 30 April 1943.
5 She damaged the American cargo ship *William Williams* (1942, 7181 tons), in the Pacific 20°09S/178°04W, 2 May 1943.
6 She sank the American cargo ship *William K Vanderbilt* (1942, 7181 tons), in the Pacific 18°41S/175°07E, 16 May 1943.
7 She damaged the American cargo ship *M H de Young* (1943, 7176 tons), which then became a total loss off Fiji, 21°50S/175°10E, 13 August 1943. *I-19* was probably sunk by American Navy Aircraft off the Gilbert Islands, 18 Oct 1943.

I-21 built by Kawasaki at Kobe, launched in 1939, commissioned in July 1941.

One of the most successful of the B-1 type, *I 26* in November 1941, shortly after commissioning. She sank the cruiser *Juneau* and damaged the carrier *Saratoga*.
IWM by courtesy of Anthony J Watts

1 She sank the American tanker *Montebello* (1921, 8272 tons), in the Pacific, 35°30N/121°15W, 23 Dec 1941.
2 She damaged the American tanker *Idaho* (1919, 6418 tons), in the Pacific, 35°N/121°W, 23 Dec 1941.
3 She sank the American cargo ship *John Adams* (1942, 7180 tons), in the Pacific, 22°30S/164°35E, 5 May 1942.
4 She sank the Greek cargo ship *Chloe* (1928, 4641 tons), in the Pacific, 22+59S/166°29E, 6 May 1942.
5 She sank the Panamanian cargo ship *Guatemala* (1920, 5527 tons), in the Pacific, 33°40S/152°04E, 11 June 1942.
6 She sank the American destroyer *Porter* (1935, 1850 tons) in the Pacific, 08°32S/167°17E, 26 Oct 1942.
7 She damaged the American cargo ship *Edgar Allen Poe* (1942, 7176 tons), in the Pacific, off Noumea, 56 miles south east of Amedee Point, 9 Nov 1942.
8 She damaged the American tanker *Mobilube* (1939, 10 222 tons), which then became a total loss, in the Pacific, 33°56S/152°09E, 18 Jan 1943.
9 She sank the Australian cargo ship *Kalingo* (1927, 2051 tons), in the Pacific, 34°07S/153°15E, 18 Jan 1943.
10 She damaged the American cargo ship *Peter H Burnett* (1942, 7176 tons), in the Pacific, which then became a total loss, 32°54S/159°32E, 22 Jan 1943.
11 She sank the British cargo ship *Iron Knight* (1937, 4812 tons), in the Pacific, 30°51S/150°38E, 7 Feb 1943.

12 She sank the American cargo ship *Starr King* (1942, 7176 tons), in the Pacific, 34°15S/154°20E, 9 Feb 1943.
13 She sank the American cargo ship *Cape San Juan* (1943, 6711 tons), in the Pacific, 22°08S/178°06W, 11 Nov 1943.
I-21 was sunk by aircraft from US carrier *Chenago* off the Gilbert Islands, 29 Nov 1943.

I-23 built by Yokosuka Navy Yard, launched in 1939, commissioned in Sept 1941.
1 She damaged the American tanker *Agwi World* (1921, 6771 tons), in the Pacific, 37°N/122°W, 20 Dec 1941.
2 She damaged the American cargo ship *Dorothy Philips* (1918, 2119 tons), in the Pacific, Monterey Bay, 24 Dec 1941.
I-23 disappeared after 14 Feb 1942, probably lost on 26 Feb 1942.

I-25 built by Mitsubishi at Kobe, launched in 1940, commissioned in Oct 1941.
1 She damaged the American tanker *Connecticut (1938, 8684 tons), in the Pacific, 10 miles West of Columbia, 27 Dec 1941.*
2 She damaged the British cargo ship *Fort Camosun* (1942, 7126 tons), in the Pacific, 47°22N/125°30W, 20 June 1942.
3 She sank the American tanker *Camden* (1921, 6653 tons), in the Pacific, 43°43N/124°54W, 4 Oct 1942.
4 She sank the American tanker *Larry Doheny* (1921, 7038 tons) in the Pacific, 41°30N/125°22W, 6 Oct 1942.
5 She sank the Soviet submarine *L-16* (1939, 1040 tons), in the Pacific,

46°41N/138°56E, 11 Oct 1942.
6 She sank the American tanker *H M Storey* (1921, 10 763 tons), in the Pacific, 17°20S/173°30E, 17 Mar 1943.
I-25 was sunk by the US destroyer *Ellet* off New Hebrides, 3 Sept 1943.

I-26, built by Kure Navy Yard, launched in 1940, commissioned in Nov 1941.
1 She sank the American cargo ship *Cynthia Olson* (1919, 2140 tons), in the Pacific, 34°N/145°W, 7 Dec 1941.
2 She sank the American cargo ship *Coast Trader* (1920, 3286 tons), in the Pacific, 48°15N/125°40W, 7 June 1942.
3 She damaged the American aircraft carrier *Saratoga* (1925, 36 000 tons), in the Pacific, 10°34S/164°18E, 31 Aug 1942.
4 She sank the American light cruiser *Juneau* (1941, 6000 tons), in the Pacific, 10°34S/164°04E, 13 Nov 1942.
5 She sank the Yugoslavian cargo ship *Recina* (1930, 4732 tons), in the Pacific, 37°24S/150°19E, 11 April 1943
6 She sank the Australian cargo ship *Kowarra* (1916, 2125 tons), in the Pacific, 24°26S/153°44E, 24 April 1943.
7 She damaged the American cargo ship *Robert F Hoke* (1943, 7176 tons), in the Indian Ocean, 20°00N/59°25E, 28 Dec 1943, the ship was beached and completely lost on 5 Jan 1944.
8 She damaged the British tanker *Tornus* (1936, 8054 tons), in the Indian Ocean, 19°45N/59°10E, 31 Dec 1943.
9 She sank the American cargo ship

Albert Gallatin (1942, 7176 tons), in the Indian Ocean, 21°21N/59°58E, 2 Jan 1944.

10 She sank the American tanker *H D Collier* (1938, 8298 tons), in the Indian Ocean, 21°30N/66°11E, 13 March 1944.

11 She sank the Norwegian tanker *Grena* (1934, 8117 tons), in the Indian Ocean, 20°48N/59°38E, 21 March 1944.

12 She sank the American cargo ship *Richard Hovey* (1948, 7176 tons), in the Indian Ocean, 16°40N/64°30E, 29 March 1944.

I-26 went missing 27 Oct 1944, off Leyte, exact cause and date of loss unknown.

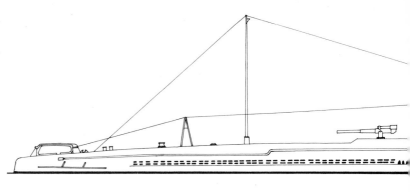

I-27 built by Sasebo Navy Yard, launched in 1941, commissioned in Feb 1942.

1 She damaged the Australian cargo ship *Barwon* (1939, 4239 tons), in the Pacific, 45 miles south east of the Island of Yabo, 4 June 1942.

2 She sank the Australian cargo ship *Iron Crown,* (1922, 3353 tons), 38°17S/149°44E, 4 June 1942.

3 She sank the British cargo ship *Ocean Vintage* (1942, 7174 tons), in the Indian Ocean, 21°37N/60°06E, 22 Oct 1942.

4 She sank the British cargo ship *Fort Mumford* (1942, 7132 tons), in the Indian Ocean, 10°N/71°E, 20 March 1943.

5 She sank the Dutch cargo ship *Berakit* (1924, 6608 tons), Indian Ocean, 03°40N/75°20E, 7 May 1943.

6 She sank the American cargo ship *Montanan* (1917, 4898 tons), Indian Ocean, 17°54N/58°09E, 3 June 1943.

7 She sank the British tanker *British Venture* (1930, 4696 tons), Indian Ocean, 25°13N/58°02E, 24 June 1943.

8 She sank the Norwegian cargo ship *Dah Pu* (1922, 1974 tons), Indian Ocean, in Muscat Harbour, 28 June 1943.

9 She damaged the American cargo ship *Alcoa Prospector* (1941, 6797 tons), Indian Ocean, 24°21N/59°04E, 5 July 1943.

10 She damaged the American cargo ship *Lyman Stewart* (1943, 7176 tons), Indian Ocean, 03°30N/75°00E, 7 Sept 1943.

11 She sank the British cargo ship

Larchbank (1925, 5151 tons), Indian Ocean, 07°38N/74°00E, 9 Sept 1943.

12 She sank the British cargo ship *Sambo* (1943, 7219 tons) Indian Ocean, 12°28N/43°31E, 10 Nov 1943.

13 She sank the British cargo ship *Sam Bridge* (1943, 7219 tons), Indian Ocean, 11°25N/47°25E, 18 Nov 1943.

14 She sank the Greek cargo ship *Athinia Livanos* (1936, 4824 tons). Indian Ocean, 12°20N/44°00E, 29 Nov 1943.

15 She sank the Greek cargo ship *Nitsa* (1915, 4732 tons), Indian Ocean, 11°42N/45°32E, 2 Dec 1943.

16 She damaged the British cargo ship *Fort Camosun* (1942, 7126 tons), Indian Ocean, 11°23N/46°03E, 3 Dec 1943 (already damaged by *I-25,* in the Pacific 20 June 1942).

17 She sank the British cargo ship *Khedive Ismail* (1922, 7513 tons), Indian Ocean, 00°57N/72°16E, 12 Feb 1944.

I-27 was sunk by British destroyers *Paladin* and *Petard,* 60 miles north west of Addu Atoll, 12 Feb 1944.

I-28 built by Mitsubishi at Kobe, launched in 1941, commissioned in Feb 1942.

She did not sink or damage any ship and was sunk by the American submarine *Tautog,* 45 miles south east of Truk, 17 May 1942.

I-29 built by Yokosuka Navy Yard, launched in 1941, commissioned in Feb 1942.

1 She damaged the Soviet cargo ship *Uelen* (1913, 5135 tons), Pacific, 50 miles south east of Newcastle, 16 May 1942.

2 She sank the British cargo ship *Gazcon* (1932, 4224 tons), Indian Ocean, 13°01N/50°41E, 1 Sept 1942.

3 She sank the British cargo ship *Haresfield* (1919, 5299 tons), Indian Ocean, 13°05N/54°35E, 9 Sept 1942.

4 She sank the British cargo ship *Ocean Honour* (1942, 7174 tons), Indian Ocean, 12°48N/50°50E, 16 Sept 1942.

5 She sank the American cargo ship *Paul Luckenbach* (1913, 6606 tons), Indian Ocean, 10°03N/63°42E, 22 Sept 1942.

6 She sank the British cargo ship *Tilawa* (1924, 10 006 tons), Indian Ocean, 07°36N/61°08E, 23 Nov 1942.

7 She sank the Norwegian tanker *Belita* (1933, 6323 tons), Indian Ocean, 11°29N/55°00E, 3 Dec 1942.

8 She sank the British cargo ship *Rahmani* (1928, 5463 tons), Indian Ocean, 14°52N/52°06E, 12 July 1943.

I-29 was sunk by the American submarine *Sawfish,* in the Balintang Channel, 26 July 1944.

I-30 built by the Kure Navy Yard, launched in 1941, commissioned in Feb 1942.

She did not sink or damage any ship and was sunk by mine off Singapore, 13 Oct 1942.

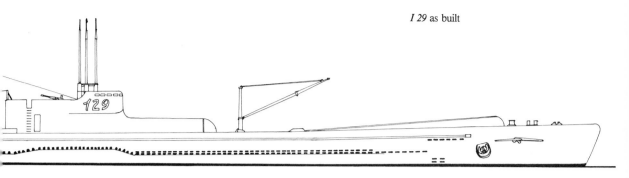

I 29 as built

I-31 built by Yokosuka Navy Yard, launched in 1941, commissioned in May 1942.

She did not sink or damage any ship. In the Pacific, she missed the American battleship *Pennsylvania* twice, 13 and 14 May 1943, off Ottu and afterwards went missing.

I-32 built by Sasebo Navy Yard, launched in 1942, commissioned in April 1942.

She did not sink or damage any ship. Was sunk by American *D E Manlove* and *SC1135*, 50 miles south of Wotge, 24 March 1944.

I-33 built by Mitsubishi at Kobe, launched in 1942, commissioned June 1942.

During her first sortie at sea she sank accidentally on 3 October 1942, off Truk. Was salved repaired and during her first trial sank again, being lost with her crew of 104 men, 13 June 1944 off Matsumiya.

I-34 built by Sasebo Navy Yard, launched in 1942, commissioned in Aug 1942.

She did not sink or damage any ship. Was sunk by the British submarine *Taurus* off Penang Island, 13 Nov 1943.

I-35 built by Mitsubishi at Kobe, launched in 1942, commissioned in Aug 1942.

She did not sink or damage any ship. In the Pacific, north of Attu, she missed the US light cruiser *Santa Fe* 16 May 1943. She was sunk by the US destroyer *Frazier* and *Meade* off Tarawa Atoll, 22 Nov 1943.

I-36 built by Yokosuka Navy Yard, launched in1942, commissioned in Sept 1942.

1 One of her Kaitens sank the US landing craft *LCI 600* (1943, 246 tons), off Ulithi, Pacific, 11 Jan 1945. on the same day the US ammunition ship *Mazama* was missed by another Kaiten from *I-36*. On 29 April 1945, the American destroyer *Ring Gold* was missed by one of her Kaitens, off Okinawa.

2 *I-36* damaged the American LST repair ship *Endymion* (ex *LST 513*, 1943, 1653 tons), with a torpeodo off Saipan, 22 June 1945. With Kaitens, she missed the American transport *Antares* and a tanker ship, off Saipan, 28 June 1945.

Surrendered at Kure in August 1945, she was scuttled by the US Navy off Goto Island, 1 April 1946.

I-37 built by Kure Navy Yard, launched in 1942, commissioned in March 1943.

1 She sank the British tanker *San Ernesto* (1939, 8078 tons), Indian Ocean, 09°18S/80°20E, 15 June 1943.

2 She sank the American cargo ship *Henry Knox* (1942, 7176 tons), Indian Ocean, 00°00N/70°15E, 19 June 1943.

3 She sank the Greek cargo ship *Fane Romeni* (190, 3404 tons), Indian Ocean, 16°21S/40°04E, 23 October 1943.

4 She sank the Norwegian tanker ship *Scotia* (1939, 9972 tons), Indian Ocean, 00°00S/69°03E, 27 Nov 1943.

5 She sank the British tanker *British Chivalry* (1929, 7118 tons), Indian Ocean, 00°50S/68°00E, 22 Feb 1944.

6 She sank the British cargo ship *Sutlej* (1940, 5189 tons), Indian Ocean, 08°00S/70°00E, 26 Feb 1944.

7 She sank the British cargo ship *Ascot* (1942, 7005 tons), Indian Ocean, 05°00S/63°00E, 29 Feb 1944.

I-37 was sunk by the American destroyer *Conklin* and destroyer escort *McCoy Reynolds,* off Palau, Pacific, 19 Nov 1944.

I-38 built by Sasebo Navy Yard, launched in 1942, commissioned in Jan. 1943.

She did not sink or damage any ship. Was sunk by the American destroyer *Nicholas,* 85 miles south of Yap, Pacific, 12 Nov 1944.

I-39 built by Sasebo Navy Yard, launched in 1942, commissioned in April 1943.

She sank the American fleet tug *Navajo* (1939, 1280 tons), Pacific, east of New Hebrides, 11 Sept 1943.

I-39 was sunk by the American destroyer *Boyd,* off Gilbert Islands, Pacific, 26 Nov 1943.

Champions of the
The Essex class carriers
by Lawrence Sowinski

Bon Homme Richard (CV-31) on 28 March 1952. The SK-2 dish is easily recognizable. Unlike most WWII *Essexes* she never had her after two radio lattic masts replaced by whip antennae.

Pacific

POSTWAR

Hornet completed her refit at San Francisco on 7 September 1945. She now looked like the modernized *Lexington*. Dazzle design 3A was overpainted with Ms 12, the flat bridge extended and the hangar catapult removed. A second cat was added to the flight deck. All necessary modifications were made to bring the number of quad 40mm from nine up to 17 mounts. Her SK was replaced by an SK-2 dish, but it remained in the same position — on top of the radar platform, abaft the topmast. *Hornet* was the only *Essex* to carry the dish on top of the tripod. All other units carried the dish outboard of the funnel.

During the same month, *Bunker Hill* was back at sea and took part in 'Operation Magic Carpet', bringing the boys back home. Late in September *Randolph* transited the Panama Canal to take part in the European 'Magic Carpet', and to fit through the locks all seven of her outboard quads had to be removed.

With the arrival of peace the pace of construction was considerably slackened, and *Princeton* (CV-37) did not therefore complete at Philadelphia until 18 November 1945. She was followed by *Tarawa* (CV-40) on December 8, at Norfolk. They were the 18th and 19th members of the *Essex* class to be completed, and instead of peacetime haze gray, both were painted in Ms 21, with the standard long-hull configuration. The next four units' completions were stretched out through 1946. Another unit was held up, while two more units were scapped incomplete.

Kearsarge (CV-33) was the 20th unit, completed at Brooklyn on 2 March 1946, followed by Newport News' *Leyte* (CV-32) on April 11. Quincy's *Philippine Sea* (CV-47) was commissionedon May 11. The Philadelphia Navy Yard commissioned the last *Essex* (to what I will call the 'wartime appearance') on 3 November 1946. This was the 23rd sistership to be completed, the *Valley Forge* (CV-45). The 24th and last ship,

Oriskany (CV-34) was under construction at the Brooklyn Navy Yard, but it was decided to suspend further work pending review of World War 2 combat experience and new ideas.

The end of the war brought tremendous global responsibilities to the US Navy and it is fortunate that there were plenty of brand new carriers to meet the call. Therefore, as the new *Essexes* were completed in late 1945 and 1946, the war-weary *Essexes* were put into mothballs during 1947-48. During the late 1940s the public heard nothing of *Essex, Yorktown, Intrepid, Lexington* or *Wasp*. Instead, names like *Boxer, Leyte, Valley Forge, Tarawa* and

Philippine Sea became familiar.

The big *Midways* also took much of the publicity because of their immense size. Despite massive advances in technology and aircraft size, the US Navy could maintain undisputed control of all of the world's oceans — if it so chose.

KOREA TO TODAY

Oriskany (CV-34) was finally commissioned on 25 September 1950, three months after the invasion of South Korea. She was very different, compared to her 23 earlier sisterships. Despite serious weight problems caused by overloading (especially high up in the ship), the original *Essex* design was well up the task of being

1 *Boxer* (CV-20) off Korea during 1951. Except for some new radars and enclosed bridges, she is little changed from her 'as completed' appearance.

2 *Oriskany* (CVA-34) as first completed to a modernized design. Twin 3inch mounts replaced all of the obsolete quad 40mm mounts. She is shown as she appeared in 1953.

1 2

converted to the modernized *Oriskany* design (SCB-27A). Modernized *Essexes* were able to handle atom bombers and the heaviest of jeÜs, all éf which aere unheard of at the time of the original *Essex* designs, back in 1939.

The umodified *Essexes* proved to be highly effective during the Korean hostilities, when Banshee and Panther jets were able to operate off their flight decks. Meanwhile, most of the wartime *Essexes* in mothballs were being given a new lease of life by undergoing modernization under the SCB-27A program. Thus *Essex* was a brand new ship by January 1951, *Intrepid* by June 1954, etc.

Bon Homme Richard was taken out of mothballs and rushed to Korea without any modifications. As such, she was the only active short-bow *Essex,* but still entirely in her WW2 appearance. This included the tubs for all seven of the outboard quad 40mm added at Pearl in 1945, although some of the mounts had been removed.

While most of the *Essexes* completed post-war were not noticeably different during this period, there were two exceptions. *Princeton* had served in the Pacific after WW2, but it was not until the Korean conflict that she had four outboard quad 40mms added, two on the port quarter and two under the island (starboard). This made *Princeton* unique.

.ØØ *Antietam* also came out of Brooklyn with an angled flight deck (a British invention), being completed during December 1952. She was the only unmodified *Essex* to carry this feature, and was the test ship. The angled deck aould eventually be worked into all the modernized *Essexes* (SCB-27A) except for *Lake Champlain*.

Of the nine long-bow *Essexes* completed between 1945 and 1946, only *Lake Champlain* and *Kearsarge* were converted into modern attack carriers (SCB-27A). The other seven units were downgraded and eventually scrapped. Thus, because of modernizations, the earliest *Essexes*

also had the longest lives. Only the *Franklin* and *Bunker Hill* were scrapped in their WW2 appearance.

Age affects the greatest and most powerful, whether they are ships or men. The *Essex* class were the undisputed champions of WW2, and it is hard to believe that they were still powerful contenders as late as 1975. The security of their presence and numbers is now forever gone. We shall all miss them.

The photographs are all official US Navy. Most of the dazzle camouflage pictures are 'out takes' from **Camouflage 2, Fleet Carriers** *by Larry Sowinski and Tom Walkowiak.* **Ships Data 7, USS Yorktown** *by Norman Friedman, was especially useful in the preparation of this article.*

Intrepid (CV-11) after her 1954 SCB-27A modernization. She is carrying twin engine bombers which were designed to carry atom bombs. The after elevator was originally fitted in the middle of the flight deck, but was moved moved to the starboard side (outboard) to enable more continuous flight operations.

The world's oldest aircraft carrier is also the world's oldest operating carrier. *Lexington* (CVT-16) is almost 35 years old and still going strong. Attempts are also being made to preserve 'The Lady *Lex*'.

William Froude
by David K Brown

It is doubtful whether anyone has ever had such an influence on the shape of ships as did William Froude. The principles of hydrodynamics and the techniques of model testing which he developed are as useful today as when they were developed in the 1960s.

William was born in 1810 at Dartington Parsonage, one of eight brilliant children of the Reverend R H Froude and Margaret (*nee* Spedding). His brothers included James Anthony, the historian, and Richard Hurrel who was one of the leaders of the Oxford Movement and was to become his brother's tutor at Oriel. William graduated in 1832 with a first in Maths and a third in Classics, but his heart was already in sailing, chemistry and mechanics.

He then became a pupil of H R Palmer, the engineer of the London docks, working also on the SE London railway. In 1837 Froude moved on to become I K Brunel's assistant and life long friend, working on the Bath and Exeter section of the Great Western Railway. He soon became well known as a railway engineer but this phase of his life was a short one.

In 1839 William married Katherine Holdsworth and a few years later gave up full time work to look after his ailing father. For nearly 20 years this brilliant man seems to have been comparatively inactive, though he kept in touch with Brunel and acted as a consultant from time to time. He

helped solve the problems of launching the *Great Eastern* and on her completion went to sea to study rolling. His mathematical work on the rolling of ships was to stand for a hundred years. Froude also seems to have been to sea in some of the early screw warships and he refers to experiments with self-propelled models.

By the 1860s William Froude had acquired a considerable reputation as a theoretical naval architect and was elected to a committee of the British Association studying the performance of steam ships. It must be realised that at the time there was no way at all of estimating the power required to drive a ship at a given speed. Attempts to predict performance from models and from existing ships alike had given rise to embarrassing and expensive mistakes.

The committee recommended a series of trials in which actual ships were to be towed to measure the drag of different hull forms at different speeds. Froude dissented from the majority view, pointing out that the cost and difficulty of such trials would limit the number of measurements to such an extent that the data would be insufficient to derive design rules. Against the overwhelming view of the profession, Froude believed that model tests could be used to give useful results. Ironically, only one trial was actually carried out and that with William Froude in charge. By the time that HMS *Greyhound* was towed by HMS *Active* in 1871, the object of the trial was to verify

Froude's modelling proposals.

Many men had tried to predict the resistance of ships from that of models and, with one exception, the results were nonsense. These early workers had failed to realise that the resistance to motion of a floating body has more than one component and these componenets of resistance obey different laws. Only Colonel Beaufoy, working under the auspices of the Society for the Improvement of Naval Architecture at the end of the eighteenth century had discovered, during experiments in Greenland dock, Deptford, that resistance due to friction behaved differently from the rest of ship resistance.

During the autumn of 1867, William Froude carried out a series of experiments in a creek at Dartmouth with models of two different shapes which he called *Swan* and *Raven* (now on show at the Science Museum). For each shape, there were 3ft, 6ft, and 12ft models and he observed that when models of either form were run at speeds scaled in proportion to the square root of their length, then the wave pattern on the water surface was similar, scaled to the model length. It was then possible for Froude to show that the part of the resistance associated with wavemaking was proportional to the weight of the model when run at this 'corresponding' speed. This result is known as Froude's Law (though the French mathematician Reech had also derived it in the 1830s), and is the basis of all model tests used to estimate the speed and power of ships.

One of the tanks at the present Admiralty Experimental establishment at Haslar.
CPL W/7/007

On 24 April 1868, Froude wrote to Edward Reed, the Chief Constructor, proposing that an experiment tank be built and outlining a two year programme of work. After due deliberation, in February 1870, their Lordships approved the expenditure of £2000 to build a tank in the grounds of Froude's house, Chelston Cross, Torquay and to run it for two years. Froude himself gave his services free but his son, Edmund, was given a salary of £3-3-0 a week as the assistant. Prominent in the programme of work was the measurement of the drag of flat planks of various sizes and with different surface finishes. Froude suggested that the frictional resistance of a ship was the same as that of a plank of the same length and area when moving at the same speed. Though this assumption is now known to be inexact it is accurate enough for most purposes.

The first experiment in the new tank was run in March 1872 with a model of HMS *Greyhound* and soon the basic truth and value of Froude's great and simple ideas was apparent. The resistance of a ship is obtained from a model test as follows:

1. Total resistance of model is measured. The frictional resistance is calculated using data from plank tests and this is subtracted from the total to give the 'residuary' resistance.
2. The residuary resistance of the ship is equal to that of the model multiplied by the ratio of their weights.
3. The frictional resistance in the ship is calculated from plant results and added to the residuary to give the total resistance.

The full scale trial of the *Greyhound* confirmed this approach though William had to study the effect of shallow water and of the slipstream of the towing ship before he got agreement with his model results. Confident, now, in the accuracy of his testing procedures, for the first time ever it was possible to make rational comparisons between one form and another.

Soon it became clear that the interaction between the hull and the propeller was of prime importance in powering estimates and Froude made a remarkable dynamometer to record the rotational speed, power and thrust of model propellers. It was built in 1873, with a wooden frame, brass pulleys and leather bootlaces, and, transferred to Haslar in 1886 it continued to give good service until replaced in 1938. This dynamometer was not the last

of Froude's equipment to remain in service as his graph paper machine was in use well into the 1960s. Both these items, and many others are on display in the Froudes' museum at Haslar (which may be visited on prior application to the Chief Superintendent AMTE(H)).

In the next seven years Froude was to change the shape of the Royal Navy. He was able to show that shorter, fatter ships were more appropriate to the relatively slow speeds of the day. His work included studies of the torpedo-tube and ram arrangement for the *Polyphemus,* which foreshadowed the bulbous bow, sorting out problems with the propellors of *Iris* and tests with Ramus' unsuccessful rocket-driven ram.

In 1878 William Froude became ill and took a voyage for the benefit of his health to South Africa where he died on 4 May 1879. He was succeded at the tank, to be known as the Admiralty Experiment Works, by his son Edmund, who was to remain in charge for another 40 years, developing and extending his father's work. The Froude tradition was passed round the world by men trained at Torquay or Haslar, who used equipment designed by the Froudes.

NEW WARSHIP TITLES
Conway Maritime Press

CONWAY MARITIME PRESS LTD, 2 NELSON ROAD, GREENWICH, LONDON SE10 9JB

CAMERA AT SEA 1939 - 1945 edited by the staff of 'Warship'

A remarkable collection of the very best photography of the war at sea — ships, weapons, equipment, personnel and action shots, many never before published. The photos are reproduced large for maximum detail, and the book includes 16 pages of full colour. The captions were written by well-known contributors to 'Warship' including Aldo Fraccaroli, Antony Preston, Alan Raven, John Roberts and Larry Sowinski.
192 pages (12¼" x 8"), 274 photos. Casebound with full colour jacket. June £12.00 (plus 75p postage)

BATTLECRUISERS By John Campbell

The first in a series of 'Warship Specials' - in the same format as a single issue of *Warship*, they employ the same combination of an authoritative text and a high proportion of illustration. *Battlecruisers* covers both British and German ships of the WW1 period, their design and service history, including the most detailed information on battle damage ever published.
72 pages (9½" x 7¼"), 55 photos, 30 line drawings. July 1978 £2.50 (plus 30p postage)

SUPER DESTROYERS edited by Antony Preston

This, the second 'Warship Special', covers the big destroyer leaders built between the wars for the navies of Britain, Germany, France, Italy, Japan and the USA. *72 pages (9½" x 7¼"), 70 half-tones, 30 line illustrations. September 1978 £2.50 (plus 30p postage)*

FORTHCOMING

SCALE MODEL WARSHIPS edited by John Bowen

In the same series as the highly successful *Scale Model Sailing Ships*, this book adopts the same approach and format, with 9 highly skilled modelmakers each discussing particular aspects of the hobby, from research sources, through the construction of the hull, decks and superstructure, to gun mountings and deck fittings. There are specialist chapters on working models and radio control, miniatures and plastic models.
192 pages (9½" x 7¼"), 150 photos and 120 plans and diagrams. Casebound with full colour jacket. October 1978 £7.50 (plus 50p postage)

BATTLESHIP DESIGN AND DEVELOPMENT 1906 - 1945 by Norman Friedman

Many books have been devoted to the history or technical details of battleships, but this is the first layman's guide to the design process, the factors which governed the development of capital ships, and the reasons *why* battleships were built in a particular way: essential reading for anyone seeking a deeper understanding of the most impressive warships in history.
160 pages (10" x 8"), over 150 illustrations. Casebound with full colour jacket. November 1978 £8.50 (plus 50p postage)

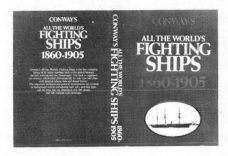

CONWAY'S ALL THE WORLD'S FIGHTING SHIPS 1860 - 1905

The first complete listing of all major warships built in the period between the first ironclad and the *Dreadnought*. The book is organised by country, sub-divided chronologically by ship type and class, with detailed tabular data and design history. The important technical and political developments are covered in background articles on major navies and ship types and the class lists are illustrated with 400 photos and 500 constant scale drawings.
384 pages approx. (12" x 8½"). Casebound with jacket. January 1979 £18.95 for first three months of publication, £24.00 thereafter (plus £1 postage)

Warship Photograph Service

As part of the service to readers WARSHIP has come to a special arrangement with the Popperfoto/ Conway Picture Libraries to make available any of their photographs used in the journal. These are credited 'CPL' after the captions and include a reference number for ordering prints. Please note that no other photos from these libraries are available to the general public, and that only two sizes of prints can be supplied.

This offer stands until further notice, although this advertisement may not appear in every issue.

RATES (per print, post free)

	UK	plus 8% VAT
A. Full plate, 6" x 8" (162 x 203mm)	£0.50p	4p
B. Continental postcard, 4" x 6" (102 x 162mm)	£0.12p	1p

OVERSEAS RATES (VAT does not apply, includes airmail postage to Europe or airmail printed paper rate elsewhere)

	US & Canada	Australia & NZ	Germany	France
A.	$2.00	$1.65	DM3.50	Fr 15
B.	$0.50	$0.45	DM1.00	Fr 4

Other rates on application

ORDERING
When ordering please quote your name and address in block capitals, the number, size (A or B), and reference numbers of the prints required. Payment by cheque, postal or International Money Order, crossed and made payable to Conway Maritime Press Ltd, and endorsed 'A/C Payee'.

NAUTICAL HISTORICAL RECORD SERIES

304 pages
305 x 255 mm

FAST FIGHTING BOATS by Harald Fock

Design, construction and use, 1875 - 1945, of boats of all navies capable of eighteen knots and over. Virtually every variation drawn and/or photographed including remarkable advance projects from the German navy.

A definitive survey, fairly technical and comprehensive but readable too, containing about 400 plans and photos plus 16 appendices. Prince £19.50 net.

Uniform with this volume:

THE DHOW Clifford W. Hawkins
An illustrated history of the dhow, its construction and use, and containing some magnificent colour plates. 12 pages of colour and over 120 b/w plates.
144 pages, 305 x 255 mm.   Price £18.50 net

FAST SAILING SHIPS David MacGregor
Text and illustrated analysis of design and construction of fast ships between 1775 and 1875, with 302 plans, photos and engravings.
7 colour plates
316 pages, 305 x 255 mm.   Price £18.50 ne

Please send for full list

NAUTICAL PUBLISHING COMPANY LTD. Nautical House, Lymington, Hampshire SO4 9BA.   Lymington (0590) 72578

217

Frontispiece: The forward turrets and bridge of the Italian cruiser *Scipione Africano*, May 1944.
Elio Andò Collection

THE K CLASS
STEAM SUBMARINES
By JOHN LAMBERT

HM Submarine *K3*.

At the outbreak of the Great War on 4 August 1914 the Royal Navy was considered to be the most powerful and efficient in the world. However the senior service was woefully short of modern ocean going submarines. Of the 64 units in commission only 17 were capable of operations beyond our own coastline. The remaining units were of obsolete design and up to ten years old.

The German Navy, however, was composed of some 28 modern ocean going submarines already in service with some seventy others under consruction. These U-boats, skillfully employed, were to produce far reaching changes in the Royal Navy and to set new standards in modern warfare.

The early months of the war were catastrophic in losses to the British, including many cruisers torpedoed with great loss of life.

These unexpected sinkings led to an order stopping the movement of allied shipping in the Channel, and restricting the sailing of troop transports to France, except from ports in the West country.

With rumours and suppositions rife, the German U-boats were very soon credited with a much exaggerated performance. Lord Fisher was recalled as First Sea Lord on 30 October and, on the express orders of Winston Churchill, he was immediately faced with the problem of improving our anti-submarine defences and the rapid production of new submarines of improved design and performance. He was appalled to find that the Royal Navy had 12 less submarines in service than on his retirement in January 1910.

With his customary energy he set about cutting red tape and producing results. Ten days later

Fisher placed orders with twelve British shipbuilders for 38 submarines, and within another few days ordered a further 6 units, and 10 from the United States. (These were to become the *H* class.) This vast building programme produced the *E, F,* and *G* class boats, the mainstay of the submarine service during the Great War.

Rumours about U-boats continued and the loss of the battleship HMS *Formidable* on New Year's Day 1915 aggravated the stories. The U-boat was said to have kept pace with the battleship in a Force 9 gale. On 4 January, Fisher wrote to Jellicoe, 'We can't touch their submarines. We know that two of them have gone 19 knots on the surface . . .' Therefore he ordered the Director of Naval Construction (DNC), Sir Eustace Tennyson-d'Eyncourt, to design immediately a submarine capable of

at least 20 knots on the surface.

FLEET SUBMARINE DESIGNS

It had long been the hope of senior officers that the submarine could take part in grand strategy and assist in a fleet action. They felt that the battle fleet should have its own flotilla of submarines, capable of working with the larger capital ship at a surface speed of 21 knots. With these submarines in the van the British Admirals could use them as surprise weapons to hit the enemy as his fleet deployed or retreated, slowing down the enemy fleet and enabling the big guns of the main British fleet to destroy it in the relulting confusion.

Commodore Keyes, who had charge of submarines, shared the dream. In 1913 during exercises he tried the idea against opposing fleets. Four submarines, a mile apart, deployed behind the forward

THE 'K' CLASS

No	Builders	Commissioned	Fate
K 1	Portsmouth Dyd	May 1917	Sank after a collision with K 4, 17.11.17 off the coast of Denmark
K 2	Portsmouth Dyd	Feb 1917	Scrapped 1926
K 3	Vickers	Aug 1916	Scrapped 1921
K 4	Vickers	Jan 1917	Sank in collision with K 6, 31.1.18 off May Island
K 5	Portsmouth Dyd	May 1917	Lost 120 miles off Scilly Isles 20.1.21
K 6	Devonport Dyd	June 1917	Scrapped 1926
K 7	Devonport Dyd	July 1917	Scrapped 1919
K 8	Vickers	March 1917	Scrapped 1923
K 9	Vickers	May 1917	Scrapped 1926
K 10	Vickers	June 1917	Scrapped 1921
K 11	Armstrong	Feb 1917	Scrapped 1921
K 12	Armstrong	Aug 1917	Scrapped 1926
K 13	Fairfields	Jan 1917	Sank on trials 29.1.17. Raised and renumbered K 22
K 14	Fairfields	May 1917	Scrapped 1926
K 15	Scotts	May 1918	Sank in Portsmouth harbour 25.6.21. Raised and scrapped in 1924
K 16	Beardmores	May 1918	Scrapped 1924
K 17	Vickers	March 1917	Sank in collision with *Fearless* off May Island 31.1.18
K 18	Vickers	April 1918	Became *M 1*
K 19	Vickers	Nov 1919	Became *M 2*
K 20	Armstrong	1920	Became *M 3*
K 21	Armstrong	Cancelled	Incomplete hull sold 1921
K 22	K 13 refitted by Fairfields	Oct 1917	Scrapped 1926
K 23	Armstrong	Cancelled	
K 24	Armstrong	Cancelled	
K 25	Armstrong	Cancelled	
K 26	Vickers & Chatham Dyd	May 1923	Scrapped 1931
K 27	Vickers	Cancelled	
K 28	Vickers	Cancelled	

Another view of *K3* in her original configuration, getting underway at Scapa Flow.

screen of cruisers, the idea being that the cruisers should locate the enemy, and he would then direct the submarines to dive and attack as the opportunity arrived. However this exercise had to be carried out at 14 knots, the maximum speed of the surface submarines. Nevertheless, the trial was deemed to be a success, although the submariners were not very enthusiastic at charging about so close to ships of their own side, with all the additional risks of collision.

By the end of January 1915, the DNC had designed a diesel powered submarine utilising three engines as fitted to the submarine of the *E* class and on 29 January Fisher authorised the construction of eight of these new units, the *J* class, at Portsmouth, Devonport and Pembroke dockyards. By February 1915 problems between Lord Fisher and Commodore Keyes led to his replacement by Commodore Sydney Hall, who had previously commanded that branch of the service from 1906 to 1910. By April Fisher had to be informed that the *J*'s would not be able to exceed 19 knots, 2 knots too slow for fleet work.

Jellicoe, Beatty and Hall, with others whose opinion Lord Fisher trusted, repeatedly impressed on him the requirement for 21 knots. It was felt that, with their superiority in diesel engine development, Germany would soon equip her navy with fleet submarines, if they were not already under construction. The Grand Fleet must also have this weapon no matter the cost. The firm of Vickers stated that they were unable to produce additional power from existing diesel engine designs, and proposed and submitted drawings for a steam-driven submarine.

STEAM SUBMARINES

The idea of using steam turbines for surface power on submarines was not new, but it was fraught with technical problems. In 1913 two experimental submarines had been designed and were then under development and trial. The *Nautilus,* built by Vickers, was powered by Italian Fiat engines, whilst the firm of Scotts, who were not satisfied with the reliability of the foreign engines, suggested utilising steam turbines, which were reliable and had ample power for a high surface speed. The novelty of the power source in Scott's *Swordfish* was kept strictly secret. The French Navy also had a steam powered submarine in service, the *Archimede.*

In early 1913 the DNC had produced another design for a steam driven submarine — a giant displacing some 1700 tons, and larger than many destroyers, being 338ft long. The armament was to be four 21inch torpedo-tubes, four similar beam tubes and two guns for surface action.

The problems were again examined and the various designs compared. *Swordfish* was giving trouble due to condensation and other problems, but they were sure the engineering was sound. The best ideas from all the designs were incorporated into an up-dated version of d'Eyncourt's 1913 design. The new design was to have seven power sources: two steam turbines, four electric motors, and an auxiliary diesel engine as a standby. Another modification was the introduction of a communicating passage alongside the boiler room. The torpedo armament was uprated, from the eight original 21inch torpedo-tubes, to ten 18inch tubes, two additional mounts being fitted in the funnel superstructure for surface use at night.

THE *K* CLASS

Lord Fisher sanctioned four of the new submarines, and drawings were sent to Vickers asking for the earliest delivery in conditions of utmost secrecy. Two of the boats were to be constructed in Portsmouth. On 18 June 1915, the Admiralty contracts department accepted Vickers costs of about £300 000 for each unit, and the work was put in hand. Thus the *K* class was born.

Twelve *K*'s were ordered during 1915 and 7 more during 1916. The Royal Navy was committed to 21 revolutionary new warships, of an untried design, costing more than £6 000 000.

I have drawn the layout of the submarines *K 3, K 4, K 8, K 9, K 10,* and *K 17* from the as fitted drawings supplied by the National Maritime Museum at Greenwich. As can be seen from the photographs there are minor differences in appearance between the ships constructed in different shipyards. 338ft long overall with a beam of 26ft 8ins, they displaced some 1880 tons on the surface and 2560 tons when submerged. Two steam turbines of 10 500 shp gave a maximum speed of almost 25 knots on the surface, and their four electric motors of 1400 hp produced a maximum speed under water of 9 knots.

The maximum diving depth of the class was 150ft, and the new craft produced their own problems for submarines due to their size and technical complexity. New safety standards had to be worked in, and diving was a matter of teamwork and technical know-how.

For all their size the new submarines did not give any better living conditions than their smaller sisters. Their length and narrow beam caused them to pitch and roll unpleasantly and in the boiler room, stokers wore oilskins because

This quarter view of *K6* gives a good impression of the length and shape of the casing.

K6 on trials, with a sailing trawler astern.

of waves entering the ventilators. On occasions the seas would wash down the funnel causing flash-backs, or even flooding in the boiler room.

Before diving the submarine had to be trimmed with great care. Her large flat foredeck produced a tendency to dive and lacked lifting buoyancy. At 12 knots or more the bows would not rise to the waves but smashed their way through, throwing spray back over the bridge and superstructure. The forward 4inch gun was impossible to man in a heavy sea, and the boat was frequently forced to reduce speed, heave to, or dive. Due to this inherent lack of buoyancy forward, the critical see-saw motion of the ship diving and the fact, that most of the class had nose dived to the bottom causing damage, the class was taken in hand for alterations. *K 6* was the first of the class to be modified with the new bulbous 'swan' bowls, and to have her funnels lengthened.

The hull was divided by nine watertight bulkheads, separating the bow torpedo room, officers' quarters, the control room (which also contained the radio room), the broadside torpedo room, the boiler room, steam turbine room, diesel engine compartment and electric motor room and finally, the steering gear compartment, which was also part of the crew space.

The main hull was divided into twenty main external ballast tanks. In the lower half of the pressure hull were more main ballast tanks (these could be filled at the rate of 200 tons a minute), as well as auxiliary ballast tanks.

The class never fully achieved their planned objectives, since the German fleet stayed in harbour. Instead the *K*'s were used on patrols, exercises with the fleet, and sorties off the enemy coast.

In the space available it is not possible to list all the disasters that the class suffered. They were involved in sixteen major incidents, and frequent operational problems. One sank on trials, three were lost after collisions prior to embarking on exercises, another disappeared, while yet another sank alongside the wall in harbour. The loss of life was appalling, but kept secret because of the war. However, for the full story of the class, I can recommend the paperback *The 'K' Boats,* by Don Everitt.

Detailed drawings for the class are drawn on two sheets and available from the David MacGregor plans service.

1 *K12,* with 'swan' bows, flashing up.

2 The after section of *K3.*

3 An unusual overhead shot of *K5,* clearly demonstrating the layout in plan view. *CPL W/8/001*

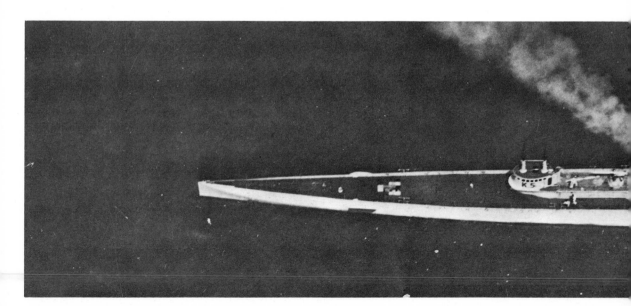

1

3

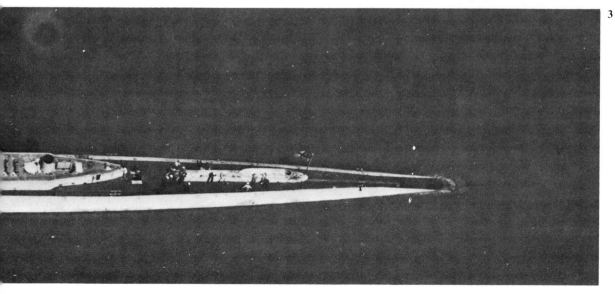

2

K5 with heightened funnels and enlarged bulbous bows.

A bow view of *K26.*
All other photos IWM

K26, the ultimate development of the *K* class.

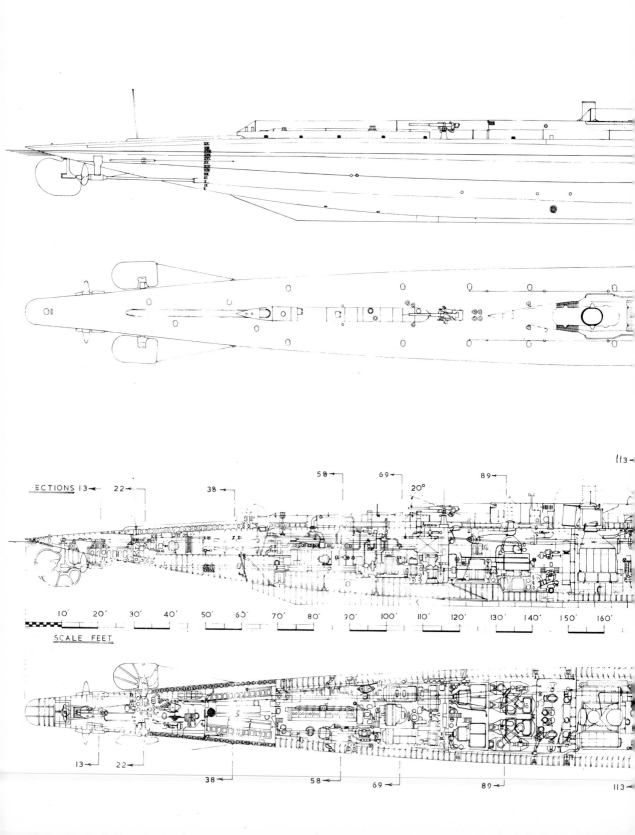

SECTIONS 13◄ 22◄ 38◄ 58◄ 69◄ 20° 89◄ 113◄

10' 20' 30' 40' 50' 60' 70' 80' 90' 100' 110' 120' 130' 140' 150' 160'

SCALE FEET

13◄ 22◄ 38◄ 58◄ 69◄ 89◄ 113◄

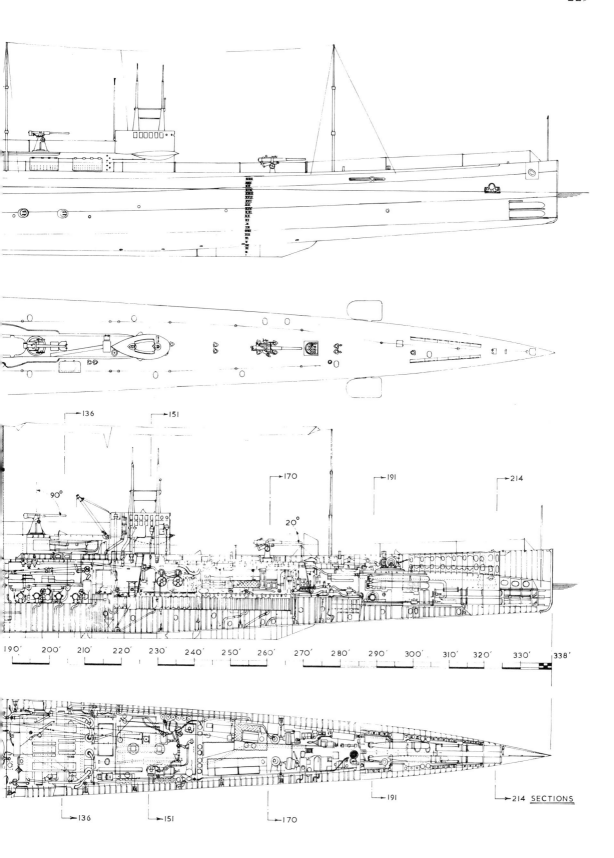

THE BEGINNINGS OF SOVIET NAVAL POWER
G5 CLASS MTBs

By PRZEMYSLAW BUDZBON

TKAs *64* and *84* (both Series 7) of the
Fourth Division (probably the Baltic
Fleet).
Boris Lemachko Collection

Both the Czarist and the Soviet Navies have paid great attention to small, fast torpedo craft. After the exploits of Lieutenant (later Admiral) Makarov's steam driven torpedo boats in the 1877-78 Russian-Turkish War, the Russians in the period 1878-89 created a fleet of at least a hundred small torpedo boats. In 1905 the 'Committee of Coastal Defence of the Russian Admiralty' decided to build motor launches (with imported gasoline engines) of the 'Nicholson' type. In the years 1906-12 a flotilla of 10 such boats, each armed with a single trainable torpedo-tube, was in commission with the Baltic Fleet.*

During the First World War, Britain, Italy and other powers developed various classes of motor launches or motor torpedo boats (MTBs). The Russian Navy did not build her own because of the shortcomings of Russian industry, which was not able to produce such sophisticated machinery as a marine petrol engine. However in 1916-17 the Imperial Navy had received about thirty US-built subchasers (a modified version of British MLs). One of these boats, *No 324* from the Black Sea Fleet, was converted into a MTB by fixing a 15inch torpedo-tube diagonally on the boat's deck. On 12 July 1917 the MTB *324* tried to attack enemy vessels in the Bosphorus but was shelled by Turkish shore batteries and was forced to abandon the attack.

Soviet experience with MTBs started in a rather negative way. At dawn on 17 July 1919 Lieutenant A W Agar (RN) on his 40ft *CMB 4* sank with a single torpedo the Soviet cruiser *Oleg* anchored off Kronstadt. On the night of 18 August 1919 the British launched a strike against Soviet warships in Kronstadt, but this carefully prepared action was not an absolute success. Only three (of eight) CMBs were able to penetrate the harbour and launch their torpedoes. The old cruiser *Pamyat Azova* (serving as a depot ship) was sunk and the battleship *Andrey Pyervozvannyi* was damaged, while the main targets — dreadnought *Petropavlovsk* and armoured cruiser *Rurik* — remained untouched. Four CMBs were sunk or fell into Soviet hands in a damaged state.

Other British CMBs operated against the Red Army in 1919 at the Dvina River and the Caspian Sea, being handed over to the local 'White' flotilla and finally two of them were captured in 1920 by the Soviets.

*A sole survivor of this class named *SK 1* still existed in the Baltic in 1941 employed as a school tender.

THE 1926 NAVAL PROGRAMME

By the end of the Civil War the Red Fleet was in an appalling state. Seven years of war had left the Soviets without a single vessel in the Black Sea, the Arctic and the Far East. Only in the Baltic did the remains of a fleet survive, but in a wretched condition without serious military potential. The dockyards and other facilities were wrecked beyond repair.

The 10th Party Congress (March 1921) discussed the rebuilding of the fleet and it was intended to construct new ships, but the industrial situation made this impossible. The new leaders were faced with an enormous and difficult task: to begin with, Soviet leaders had to remedy the disorganization of the economy and to build up new branches of industry. However the Soviets were able to put a few existing warships back into service and restore the Baltic and the Black Sea Fleets. At the end of 1923 they had 2 dreadnoughts, 1 cruiser, 8 destroyers, 9 submarines, 20 minesweepers and 4 training ships in active service.

The reconstruction of Soviet industry gave some positive results by the mid-1920s, mainly thanks to the strenuous efforts of the whole Soviet people. This encouraged thoughts of a return to naval shipbuilding in the Soviet Union.

The 'Revvoyensovyet' (Revolutionary War Soviet), under the leadership of the 'People's Commissar of War and Naval Affairs', Michail Frunze, started to work on the shipbuilding programme at the beginning of 1925. Works resulted in the first five-year naval programme which was approved by the 'Soviet of Work and Defence' on 26 November 1926. The 1926 Naval Programme authorised 12 submarines, 18 guard ships and 36 MTBs which were to be completed by the middle of 1931. Although necessary funds were provided (64 million roubles for naval expenditure in the fiscal year 1926/27 — twice the 1925/26 figure) the practical realisation of even such a small programme involved enormous difficulties of a technical nature. The Soviets had to overcome the lack of experienced naval engineers and skilled workmen, deficiency in technology and know-how and finally problems caused by the low quality of Soviet industrial products.

FIRST SOVIET MTBs

When the hostilities finished the Soviets had a few captured British CMBs to study. The bitter lesson of Kronstadt was still fresh in their minds, so the naval authorities early in 1923 entrusted to the 'CAGI' (Central Aero-Hydrodynamic Institute) a preliminary design of a fast MTB. Her characteristics based on those of the Thornycroft CMB were as follows:

Radius: 150 kilometers
Speed: 100 km/h (55 kts)
Armament: two 18inch torpedoes in troughs, one MG
Crew: 3 men
Hull: two versions — one aluminium, one wood.

Three months later the 'CAGI' had presented the preliminary design but further works were stopped owing

The inspiration for the 'G-5s' the Thornycroft CMBs (coastal motor boats). Seen here are Nos 98 and 112 at speed. *CPL W/8/002*

to lack of neccessary funds and suitable technical facilities.

More serious work started in the beginning of February 1925 when the 'Revvoyensovyet' had begun studies on the first naval programme. The 'CAGI' was provided with additional specifications of future Soviet MTBs:
1. Navigable in a sea Force 3.
2. Hull with watertight bulkheads.
3. Equipment permitting the boat to be lifted.
4. Bullet proof conning tower (CT) and machinery space. The design was undertaken by the 'CAGI' team under the leadership of A N Tupolev, the well-known aircraft engineer. His team was the best and most experienced in the Soviet Union.

However, only information concerning the 'ANT-3' design of MTB was released, the number sequence indicating the existence of two earlier ones. The first, 'ANT-1', was probably the one finished in April 1923, while work on 'ANT-2' lasted from February to May 1925 when they were abandoned in

favour of the 'ANT-3' design. The latter was approved and construction of the prototype started in August 1925 at the 'CAGI' shop in Moscow. Construction took 20 months mainly because of the technical difficulties mentioned earlier. Most troublesome was the finding of suitable engines, production of which had still not been mastered by Soviet industry. In addition the Soviets faced a lot of difficulties in placing their orders abroad. Finally the prototype received two 525bhp 'Wright-Typhoon' engines, and shafts were produced in the Leningrad 'Bolshevik' factory. After completing the 'ANT-3' was placed on a railway truck and transported to Sevastopol. She was launched there on 17 March 1927 and received the name *Pervenec* (The First One), as she was both the first MTB of entirely Soviet construction and the first warship launched by the Soviets.

The construction of *Pervenec* closely followed that of British CMBs carefully examined by the Tupolev team. The Thornycroft

hull form was adopted although constructed of aluminium-like metal. The boat was the size of a Thornycroft 55ft CMB and was armed with a single 18inch torpedo. Two petrol engines placed forward had a total power of 1050bhp, which enabled a considerable increase in speed as compared with CMBs.

Trials of the *Pervenec* started on 30 April 1927. The Soviet naval authorities took great interest in the results: even the C-in-C of the Soviet Naval Forces, R A Muklevich*, took a part in trials. Importance was attached to the comparison between manouvrability and speed of the *Pervenec* and Thornycroft CMBs, two of which had been operational with the Red Fleet. Trials were officially finished on 16 July 1927. Although an official statement recorded that results had been satisfactory in all respects, the long list of compulsory improvements necessary indicated a lot of teething troubles for the new Soviet weapon.

As the *Pervenec* was a poor sea boat, the Tupolev team made every effort to improve her sea-worthiness. Work on a new design coded 'ANT-4' started in May 1927, being based on the 'ANT-3' with the following major changes:
1. Re-designed hull forward to prevent pitching and to make the boat dry.
2. Smaller CT to reduce topweight.
3. More careful design of construction joints to prevent corrosion.
4. New electric wiring system.
5. Two torpedo troughs.

The 'ANT-4' was laid down in October 1927 and the boat named *Tupolev* was launched on 3 September 1928, in Sevastopol. She had better lines than the *Pervenec* so a speed of 50kts was attained with two 525bhp 'Wright-Typhoon' engines despite a 12% increase in displacement. A new CT and more reasonable disposition of weights gave the lower centre of gravity so needed, but although the boat proved useless in a Force 3 sea her

*Ranks abolished after the Revolution were to be restored on 22 September 1935.

characteristics more closely followed the specified ones as compared with 'ANT-3'.

Trials of the *Tupolev* were carried out in a hurry since the terms of the 1926 Naval Programme left no time for refinement of the construction. In order to save time the preparation of series construction of the MTBs began in January 1928, before the prototype boat could be tested.

THE 'SH-4' CLASS

The 1926 programme went very slowly: the capacity of Soviet industry proved to be inadequate for building modern warships in a reasonable time. Only seven guard ships of the *Uragan* class were laid down and they were still on their slips at the beginning of 1929, and it was similar in the submarine arm. Most promising was the construction of MTBs which accelerated and entered into series production by the end of 1928. In this situation the 'Soviet of Work and Defence' decided to lengthen the building times authorised in 1926 and at the same time to coordinate naval programmes with the five-year plans of the whole of the Soviet economy. On 4 February 1929 the new programme was approved, sanctioning all ships of the 1926 estimates, plus 3 destroyers, 10 submarines and additional MTBs. In addition, funds were provided for the necessary reorganisation and expansion of the shipbuilding industry.

The first standard MTB of the Red Fleet was completed on 1 October 1928 in Leningrad. The first division consisting of 6 boats was commissioned a month later with the Baltic Fleet. An additional 24 units were ordered, 18 of which were to be ready in the autumn of 1929 and the last 6 by the Spring of 1930. However only 16 boats were completed by the end of 1929 and few of them formed the Black Sea Fleet's division of MTBs. Revision of the 1926 programme had advanced the construction of standard MTBs which were known later as the 'Sh-4' class. 53 of them were completed by the end of 1932 and 2 boats were completed in the

CHARACTERISTICS OF SOVIET AND BRITISH MTBs

Name	PERVENEC	TUPOLEV	CMB 121	CMB 80c
Design	ANT-3	ANT-4	40ft	55ft
Displacement	8.91 tons	10 tons	5 tons	10 tons
Length (oa)	17.33m	16.82m	13.72m	18.29m
Beam	3.33m	3.33m	2.59m	3.35m
Draught			0.76m	0.91m
Power	1050bhp	1050bhp	275bhp	900bhp
Speed (trials)	54kts	50.4kts	37.25kts	41.19kts
Torpedoes	one 18inch	two 18inch	one 18inch	one 18inch
MGs	2	1	2-4	4
Hull		aluminium		double mahogany

first months of 1933. With experimental units this made the number of MTBs in commission 59, distributed between the Baltic Fleet, the Black Sea Fleet and the Naval Forces of the Far East where 12 MTBs had been transported by rail from the Baltic in May 1932 followed by 12 more from the Black Sea in 1933.

The construction of 'Sh-4' boats closely followed the 'ANT-4' design. Their characteristics were as follows:

Displacement 10.9 tons, 12.8 tons (full load)
Length (oa) 18.08m
Beam (moulded) 3.33m
Draught —
Machinery two 525bhp 'Wright-Typhoon' petrol engines or two 800bhp 'Isotta-Fraschini' petrol engines
Speed 44 to 50kts on trials (depending on engines), sea speed 35 to 40kts, economical speed 25kts
Radius 250 miles at economical speed
Torpedoes two 18inch Mk 07 in troughs
MGs one 7.62mm DA
Crew 6 men

The 'Sh-4' class formed the backbone of the Soviet MTB forces in the early 1930s. However, careless treatment of engines and lack of maintenance caused the rapid wearing out of all boats of this class. Their maximum speed fell below 30kts and by the end of the 1930s they were used as subchasers (24 small DCs were carried in troughs), guard ships of the 'NKVD', or as training ships; some served as naval harbour launches, and only three of them were in commission in July 1941.

1 A very poor but historically valuable shot of *Pervenec* during trials in 1927. Note the hull form similar to the Thornycroft CBMs and the prominent CT. *Author's Collection*

2 *Tupolev* during trials in 1928. Note the cruiser *Chervona Ukraina* in the background. *Author's Collection*

'G-5' - DESIGN AND PROTOTYPES

'Sh-4' boats, besides design faults, caused some difficulties to both builders and users. Firstly, they were powered by foreign-built petrol engines, import of which added greatly to the costs of construction; secondly, imported engines were highly sophisticated and needed to be handled carefully and to be well maintained by highly skilled personnel which were not available in the Soviet Navy in the late 1920s; thirdly, the boats were armed with obsolescent 18inch torpedoes.

After the design of the 'Sh-4' class had been completed the 'CAGI' started to work on an improved version of the standard MTB, coded 'G-5' (*Glissiryushchyi No 5* — 'hydroplane No 5'), the 'ANT' designation being reserved for aircraft designs only to avoid confusion. Specifications furnished by the 'Revvoyensovyet' called for a boat of similar size and lines to the 'ANT-4' but armed with two 21inch torpedoes and powered by petrol engines of Soviet origin. The 'G-5' design was to become standard construction in the following five-year naval programme.

The 1933-38 Naval Programme was approved by the 'Soviet of Work and Defence' on 11 July

1

2

3

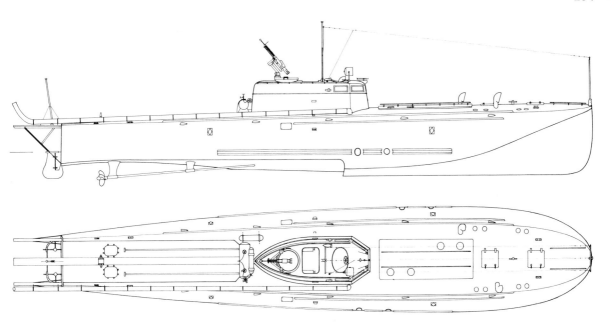

An early boat of Series 7 armed with one 7.62mm DA MG. Later boats of this series had one 12.7mm DK MG. The torpedo ram in the starboard trough is shown in the position of maximum extension aft. This boat generally resembled MTBs of the 'Sh-4' class.

Numerous Series 7 boats from the Baltic and Black Sea Fleets were completely worn out by the end of the war. Some of them were completely overhauled and this opportunity was taken to rearm boats with one 12.7mm DShK MG on DP mounting and one 7.62mm ShKAS MG on a small forecastle mounting.

Boats of Series 8 were similar except the 'TT-4' smoke screen generator abaft the CT.

Series 10: early boats of Series 11 were similar except the DShK MG instead of DK one as in the drawing.

1933. There were to be 12 destroyer leaders, 87 destroyers, 363 (later reduced to 165) submarines, and 195 MTBs (including experimental boats) delivered by the middle of 1938. Although a large sum of money had been spent on new shipyards and factories, the achievement of such an enlarged

programme was beyond the capability of Soviet industry. There were 177 submarines, 176 MTBs (including experimental boats) and only 2 destroyer leaders and one destroyer completed by the end of 1937.

According to the terms of the new programme the prototype boat of the 'G-5' design had to be ready in 1933. Although Soviet built petrol engines were still not available in 1932, the prototype named G5 was laid down in the 'CAGI' shop, in order to finish her to the naval authorities' requirements. The boat received two 1000bhp Isotta-Fraschini petrol engines and her trials in the Black Sea were finished by December 1933, when her hydrodynamics characteristics, speed and manoeuvrability had been tested. The G5 attained a speed of 65.3kts (for short periods) without armament and a full capacity of fuel, and a speed of 58.0kts at full load. She also proved to be a better sea boat than the Tupolev.

The first series boat received two Soviet 'GAM-34' petrol engines of 675bhp each, so this machinery was tested at the trials of the first standard boat — not prototype — which was finished in January 1934. Results were less promising than these of the G5 due

to the lower power and quality of Soviet production engines. The boat attained a maximum speed of 45kts at full load.

'G-5' — TECHNICAL DESCRIPTION

The 'G-5' class was comprised of Series 7,8 and 9 completed during 1934-36, Series 10 produced in 1937 and Series 11 which completed the class in 1945.

Hull. Boats of all series had standard hulls of Thornycroft form, but improved in the bow section. The hull was rather beamy with a single step formed by the fore body, built with a sharp angle of chine running from the step to the stem and formed above the legend waterline a turtle-back forecastle deck, and the slightly convex after part curved down to employ the 'Lürssen effect'. The hull of aluminium construction had a collision bulkhead forward and a second watertight bulkhead about 7m aft. There were two parallel torpedo troughs running from the midship bulkhead to the transom. The troughs were covered by the deck amidships. A large engine hatch was placed forward together with two hatchways which led to both the machinery space and the fore peak.

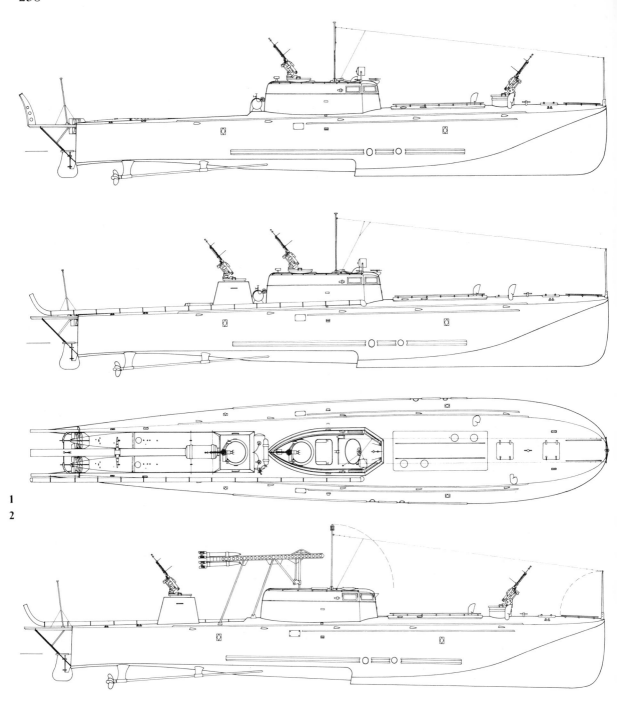

1 Series 11: the final stage of 'G-5' class MTB. Such boats were completed late during the war.

2 Series 11 (missile boat): about 20 MTBs of Series 10 & 11 were armed with 6 double rail-launches for 'ROFS-132' missiles. Boats so armed were used for bombardment of shore targets, although according to Soviet sources some of them were successfully fought in a few engagements with enemy boats. When the missiles were ready to fire, both masts were stowed horizontally and both MGs dismounted.
This silhouette was drawn according to information supplied by Mr Boris Lemachko.

Conning tower. A small CT was sited amidships: it was 4m long and of such reduced height that personnel had to work in a sitting position when inside. In the fore part of the CT all steering and navigation equipment was located and when in action the torpedo ram and fore part of troughs occupied the CT aft. There were three hatches on the CT roof: the forward one was for the commanding officer, who had a steering wheel inside the CT, the torpedo dial sight on the fore part of the roof and the 9inch searchlight to the right. A plexiglass screen was mounted forward in boats of later series. The middle hatch was used as a companionway to the inside of the CT and the machinery space. The after hatch was fitted for a MG mounting.

Machinery. Two GAM-34 petrol engines of A Mikulin design developed from the AM-34 aircraft engine design which itself was based on Isotta-Fraschini engines. Mass production of the GAM-34 engine had started in 1934, the GAM-34BS version having the following main characteristics: 720bhp, short time rating 850bhp at 1770rpm; overall dimensions — length 2.5m, beam 1.0m. Some boats built late in the war were powered by two 'Lend-Lease' Packard 4M-2500 engines.

Engines were mounted in the fore part at the machinery space between the collision bulkhead forward and the midships bulkhead aft. There were two ways into the machinery space: one through the hatchway on the foredeck and the second through the CT. Two vents, one on each side, supplied air for the engines and the machinery space. Exhausts were positioned on the legend waterline and boats of later series had an additional one or two exhausts running right aft. The port engine was mounted farther aft than the starboard one and there was no auxiliary engine for manoeuvring so the lowest possible speed was about 18kts and this made boathandling rather difficult and many collisions occured. Furthermore, the petrol engines resulted in many losses due to fire and explosions.

Boats were equipped with two gear boxes, two shafts, two bronze propellers (diameter about 670mm) and two rudders. Sea speed of these boats was around 40-48kts depending on the engines, but the boats proved no value in a Force 5 sea. Radius was 210-220 miles at economical speed, 80-90 miles at full speed. Fuel capacity at least 15-18 cubic metres.

Armament. Two 21inch torpedoes in troughs were launched in the same manner as in Thornycroft CMBs, tail first from the stern. The boat turned sharply as soon as the torpedo entered the water, but this greatly reduced the chances of a successful attack and exposed the boat to much greater risk of being hit by the enemy.

The torpedo was launched by a cordite-propelled ram fitted with an aluminium bell-head cap, which fitted against the torpedo head. The cordite chamber, ram and bell-head were mounted in the CT aft. There were rails in the troughs on which the torpedo rested on its side lugs. These were extended beyond the stern of the boat to avoid the possibility of the head of the torpedo striking the end of the trough or the boat's stern. At sea, securing screws were arranged at the bottom of the trough to hold the torpedo in its place.

Boats of Series 11 had troughs adapted for both torpedoes or depth charges. The boat could carry one torpedo and 12 small (36 kg) DCs or 24 DCs without the torpedo. Instead of torpedoes or DCs four Mk 08/39 or Mk 26 mines could be carried by means of holders placed aft.

Boats of all series were armed with 12.7mm DK or DShK and/or 7.62mm DA or ShKAS MGs on special rotating mountings. Machine guns were mounted immediately before an action and were kept below during long passages to prevent corrosion. They were mounted usually on the after CT hatch while an additional MG mount was a cylindrical one placed at the fore machinery space hatch or one placed at the fore machinery space hatch or one one placed above the troughs aft.

In the mid 1930s the 'DRP' missile launchers were mounted on some G-5 class boats from the Black Sea Fleet MTB Brigade, but they were soon removed as lacking accuracy. Work on the 'DRP' tube-launched missile was discarded for rail-launched ones, which were to be known later as 'Katyusha'.

The 'Katyusha' was developed in the 'Missile Scientific Research Institute' in mid 1939 and was successfully tested in 1941. In 1942

SERIES	7 & 8	9	10 & 11
Displacement (tons)	14.03	14.85	16.26
Length (oa) metres	18.85	18.85-19.10	18.85-19.10
Length (lw)	17.30	17.30	17.30
Beam (max)	3.50	3.50	—
Beam (moulded)	3.33	3.33	3.40
Draught (max)	0.60	0.65	0.82

SERIES	7 & 8	9	10	11
Engine	GAM-34	GAM-34B	GAM-34BS	GAM-34BS-F
Short time rating	2 x 675 bhp	2 x 800 bhp	2 x 850 bhp	2 x 1000 bhp
Speed (trials)	45 kts	49 kts	53 kts	56 kts

USUAL DISTRIBUTION OF MG ARMAMENT

SERIES	7	8 & 9	10			11		
Fore								
CT	DA*	DK* DK	DK	ShKAS	DShK	DShK	DShK	DShK
Aft					DShK			ShKAS

*could not be used for AA fire

1

the *TKA 86* of the G-5 class received a launcher for the 'ROFS-82' missiles. The twelve-missile rail launcher was constructed in the 'Kompresor' factory, the naval launcher being based on the design of the mobile army one. The first missile boat of the Soviet Navy — *TKA 86* — was first in action against enemy positions near Novorossisk in December 1942.

In 1943 some G-5 class boats received launchers for the 'ROFS-132' missiles. According to Soviet sources about 20 boats from the Black Sea and Pacific Fleets* were converted in this manner and they were used mainly for the bombardment of enemy positions. The one launcher consisted of 6 double rails and was mounted above the after part of the CT. Twelve missiles could be carried and there is no evidence of the carriage of reloads nor of the possibility of reloading at sea. The launchers were fixed in traverse and therefore aimed by handling the whole boat, while the angle was adjusted by a hand operated device.

Equipment. There were two small folding masts — one forward and a mainmast — on all boats. The foremast was placed on the stemhead. The mainmast was placed abaft the CT on Series 7 boats or on the CT between the commanding officer's and the middle hatches on others. Wireless aerials were suspended between masts, while the mainmast was also used as a signal mast. A navigation light was placed on top of the mainmast in some boats. Top lights were mounted on the CT abaft the MG hatch, with port and starboard lights on both sides of the CT. An electric siren was positioned on the port side of the CT, and on boats of earlier series it was hand powered.

A great number of Series 9 boats onwards had the 'TT-4' smoke generator sited on the deck immediately abaft the CT, smoke being passed along a pipe running in a space between the middle torpedo rails to the stern. A smoke screen pipe protruded from the end of the middle torpedo rails console. Boats equipped with stern exhausts had smoke transported through the exhaust pipe to the stern.

Mooring facilities consisted of one single and two double bollards forward, two cable chocks and two double bollards aft. Four lugs, two on each side, enabled the boats to be lifted ashore, on rail lorries or on depot ships. All G-5 and Sh-4 class MTBs of the Pacific Fleet were transported on rail lorries across the whole of Asia.

Crew. Each boat was manned by 6 men (or 7 when two MGs were carried). They were: commanding officer, of the rank of Lieutenant; one other officer; wireless operator; two motor mechanics; and one or two MG gunners. They had to be young and brave men, in order to withstand the effect of two high-speed engines in a metal hull.

G-5 — PRODUCTION

Series construction of G-5 class MTBs began in 1933 while the last boat of this class was commissioned in 1945, if not later. About 300 boats were produced at the Rybinsk and Zelenodolsk yards on the Volga and in Leningrad at the Marti and Sudomekh yards. The greatest output of these shipyards took place during 1934-36 when 152 boats were finished. They were followed by 20 MTBs in 1937, but the planned number of 193 boats for the 1933-38 five-year programme was not attained by the middle of 1938.

By the end of 1937 the Soviet Government had created the 'Peoples' Commission of the Navy' which immediately started work on Stalin's programme of expanding the Soviet Navy to the strength of traditional naval powers. Although no official naval estimate was approved, 3 battleships, 2 battlecruisers, 10 cruisers, 45 destroyers, 91 submarines and a great number of minor vessels were commenced during 1938-41 in annual 'programmes' approved by the 'Central Committee of the Party'. Russia planned to have 19

*The Naval Forces of the Far East were named the Pacific Fleet in 1935.

1 TKA *42* (Series 8) seen from the CT of
another MTB.
Boris Lemachko Collection

2 TKA *125* (Series 10) of the Black Sea
Fleet.
Jerzy Micinski Collection

2

battleships and battlecruisers, 20
cruisers, 153 destroyers and
destroyer leaders, 341 submarines,
514 MTBs and 105 subchasers in
active commission by the middle of
1943.

To reach the planned MTB
strength by the middle of 1943,
boats should have been completed
at an approximate rate of 65 per
year but only 92 units (including
experimental boats) were
commissioned during 1938-41. Eight
of them were of the new D-3 design
which started a completely new
MTB construction policy with their
wooden hull, dropped torpedoes,
better accommodation and ability to
stay at sea in Force 6 conditions.
Although this new class had been
developed, a high 1933/39 building
rate for the G-5 class boats
indicated a continuation of the G-5
construction policy.

Because of the general strain
upon the Soviet shipbuilding
industry during 1939-41,
construction of both G-5s and D-3s
had to be slowed down. On 22 July
1941 the Soviet Navy had a total of
269 MTBs in commission and 254
of them belonged to the G-5 class.
Only 39 boats of this class were
commissioned during hostilities
while about 120 units of the D-3
class entered service. Faced by the
German threat and having limited
means the 'Stavka' — Soviet
Supreme Command — had chosen
the better MTB design. Production

of G-5 boats was continued during
the war at a very slow rate and
probably very few of them were
commissioned after hostilities had
ceased.

Together with four boats sold to
Republican forces during the
Spanish Civil War, there were
about 297 boats of the G-5 class
completed by the middle of 1945.

G-5 — SUMMARY OF WAR SERVICE

During the late 1920s the Soviet
naval authorities had initiated a
general discussion of both the
tactical and strategic values of small
warships' policy. This had a lot in
common with 19th century Admiral
Aube's 'Jeune Ecole', but was
adapted for the needs of modern
warfare. The MTB fleet, the
strongest in the world, was regarded
as the 'dashing weapon of a
proletarian navy' and Soviet

commanding officers placed great
store by its use.

The first time MTBs of Soviet
origin saw action was during the
Spanish Civil War, the Soviets
having sold four G-5 boats of Series
7 to the Republican Forces. They
were misused as subchasers however
and achieved no notable results.

The Soviet MTB fleet was
organised into divisions consisting
of 12-18 boats which were
numbered in a '10-up' pattern. For
example the 1st MTB Division of
the Baltic Fleet had 18 boats
numbered in sequence: TKA 11, 21,
31,. . . 91, 101, 111, . . . 181, while
boats of the 2nd Division were
numbered TKA 12, 22, 32, etc.
Three or four MTB Divisions
comprised an MTB Brigade.
According to this system boats
commissioned in different fleets had
the same number at the same time.
When one boat was lost, any

TOTAL PRODUCTION OF 'G-5' CLASS MTBs

SERIES	7,8 & 9	10	11	Approximate annual rate
Period				
1933	1			
1934-36	152			50
1937		20		20
1938-39			76	50
1939-41			5	2
1941-45			39	10
Total	153	20	120	

replacement boat received the number of her predecessor. Some MTBs built late in the war by public subscription bore names as well as numbers, such as *Yunyi Tambovskiy Pionyer (TKA 73), Trudyashchiyesya Artyema (TKA 133), Moskovskoy Remeslyennik Trudovych Ryezorv (TKA 105)* (names chosen from G-5 class boats only).

At the beginning of the war the Soviet Navy had a fleet of 269 MTBs although half of them remained completely inactive during hostilities, as they belonged to the Pacific Fleet. Boats from the Baltic, Northern and Black Sea Fleets — 134 of them, later increased by 166 of Soviet construction and an additional 55 US-built of Lend-Lease purchase — together with submarines and naval aircraft were the most active of all operational Soviet naval forces. According to the book *Kursami Doblesti i Slavy*, published in Moscow in 1973, Soviet MTBs destroyed or damaged at least 250 enemy warships and merchantmen of 200 000 tons total. A more reliable source, the book *Boyevoy Put Sovietskovo Voyenno-Morskovo Flota* published in Moscow in 1974, gave the number

as 53 warships and 24 transports sunk by all Soviet surface warships (presumable MTBs) during the war. Additionally, 12 sinkings were reported by the Soviets for the Pacific Fleet MTBs. On the other hand, German sources gave a number of only 30 Axis vessels sunk by Soviet MTBs during the war. Despite these differences the outstanding courage of Soviet MTB crews cannot be denied; they fought bravely and with some success but with heavy losses to themselves.

During the war the Soviet Navy undertook numerous amphibious operations. As no specialized craft were built in pre-war years the Soviets were forced to use all available vessels, even subchasers, minesweepers and MTBs, and G-5 class MTBs were used as landing craft. One boat could carry at least 14 men although seated less than comfortably in the troughs. In five particular assaults 117 MTBs were used as landing crafts but with heavy losses.

According to Soviet sources, 57 MTBs were lost in action against enemy vessels. However, this figure does not include boats sunk through stranding, mines, collision, air attack, scuttling, fire or

explosions. Approximate total losses were at least 130 which includes both Soviet-built and Lend-Lease MTBs. Almost 60% of this figure were G-5 class MTBs. Boats of this class took the most active part in Soviet MTB fleet operations during the war and suffered the heaviest losses — about 45%* of their number (35%* for all Soviet MTBs). Another 30 boats of the G-5 class were discarded during the war, due to corroded hulls and worn-out engines. At the end of hostilities the Soviet Navy had a total of 386 MTBs, about 190 of them of the G-5 class. This figure was almost instantly reduced by discarding boats of earlier series.

Boats of G-5 class last saw action during the Korean War, several of them being transferred to the North Korean Peoples' Republic. Three of them were sunk in action with USS *Juneau* and HM Ships *Jamaica* and *Black Swan* off Chumunjin on 2 July 1950.

CONCLUSION
Boats of the G-5 class represented the final stage of a Soviet MTB development which begun in 1925 under the influence of the famous CMBs. However, the Thornycroft

design was not just copied but was also improved by Tupolev's team, which successfully employed the experience gained by aircraft construction. Light, strong and simply constructed, these boats completely fulfilled the specifications which had been demanded by the 'Revvoyensovyet' in 1925. They were well suited for the Red Navy's requirements and the skill of its personnel.

US-built MTBs and war experience enhanced the development of the Soviet MTB fleet, and this meant a radical departure from the pre-war MTB construction policy. When the new boats of the P-4 and later P-6 classes begun to enter service, the old style G-5 boats became obsolete. The last boat of this class was discarded during the late 1950s and thus the story of the G-5s ended.

---

*Excluding MTBs of the Pacific Fleet.

3

Series 11 boats of the Pacific Fleet (1945). Note the cage base for a forward MG mounting and spare fuel tanks aft. **1**
Boris Lemachko Collection

A rare photo of a missile boat of the 'G-5' class, the *Moskovskoy Remeslyennik* in 1944. **2**
Boris Lemachko Collection

MTBs of Series 11. Note boat hooks on the cover of the machinery hatch. **3**
Jerzy Micinski Collection

244

1 TKA *47* (Series 11) being examined by the Germans after being captured off Libau by German E-boats on 27 June 1941. *Jerzy Micinski Collection*

2 TK *755* ? (Series 9): postwar photo probably. *Jerzy Micinski Collection*

3 TKAs *72, 82, 92* and *102* (all Series 10) from the Black Sea Fleet. *Author's Collection*

APPENDIX 1. SOVIET-BUILT MTB FLEET DURING THE PRE-WAR PERIOD.

Year	Sh-4 class	G-5 class	Total
1927			1
1928	6		8
1929	24		26
1932	53		57
1933	55	1	60
1936	32	153	190
1937		173	
1939	10	249	263
1941	3	254	269

APPENDIX 2. STRENGTH OF THE SOVIET FLEET ON 22 JULY 1941

Battleships	3
Cruisers	7
Destroyers	59
Submarines	218
MTBs	269
Escort Vessels	22
Minelayers	18
Minesweepers	80
Minor Vessels	240

Appendix 3. SOVIET MTB FLEET DURING THE WAR.

Station	B	A	P	BS	C & D	Total
In commission 22 July 1941	48	2	135	84		269
Commissioned during the war	133	4		23	6	166
Old boats recommissioned	3		16	2	3	24
Transfers	+6		−6			
Total number of Soviet-built MTBs in commission	180	16	151	103	9	459
Lend-Lease boats	12	31	54	12		109
Total number of Soviet MTBs	192	47	205	115	9	568
War losses	61	14	1	54		130
Discarded or decommissioned as MTBs	27	3		19	3	52
Total losses	88	17	1	73	3	182
In commission after the war**	104	30	204	42	6	386

APPENDIX 4. G-5 CLASS BOATS DURING THE WAR.

Station	B	A	P	BS	C & D	Total
In commission 22 July 1941	42		135	77		254
Commissioned during the war	12			21	6	39
Transfers	+6		−6			
Total number of G-5 boats	60		135	92	6	293
War losses	24		1	48		73
Discarded	14			17		31
Total war losses	38		1	65		104
In commission after the war**	24*		134	27	6	191*

B	— The Baltic Fleet
A	— The Northern Fleet
P	— The Pacific Fleet
BS	— The Black Sea Fleet
C & D	— The Caspian Flotilla & The Danube Flotilla

**i.e. 9.5.1945 for B, A, BS, C & D and 2.9.1945 for P.
*Together with two boats returned by the Finnish Navy in September 1944.

APPENDIX 5. PRINCIPAL SOURCES (PUBLISHED ACCOUNTS).

1. G Ammon & S Byeryeznoy, 'Pyervye Sovyetskiye Torpyednye Katyera', *Sudostroyenye*, 11/1976.
2. I Ananin, *Korabli nashey yunosti*, Leningrad, 1974.
3. *Boyevoy Put Sovyetskovo Voyenno-Morskovo Flota*, Moscow, 1974.
4. S Breyer, 'Die Schnellboot-Entwicklung der sowjetischen Kriegsmarine', *Marine Rundshau*, 1/1970.
5. W Galkowski, *Rodowod katiuszy*, Warsaw, 1972.
6. A Grigoryev, 'Pyervyi otryad russkih torpyednyh katyerov', *Sudostroyenye*, 4/1967.
7. V Ivanov, *Oruziye pobyedy*, Moscow, 1975.
8. A Larionov, 'Torpyednye katyera', *Modyelist Konstructor*.
9. J Meister, *Soviet Warships of World War II*, London, 1977.
10. V Shlomin, 'Sovyetskoye korablyostroyeniye v kanuni Vyelikoy Otchestvyennoy Voyny', *Sudostroyenye*, 2/1972.

OPERATIONAL HISTORY

Attilio Regolo was the first cruiser of the class to enter service, on 14 May 1942, followed by *Scipione Africano* on 18 February 1943.

A single fleet was formed on 1 April 1943, from the larger war units which had originally been split into two fleets. The fleet was named the Naval Battle Force (*Forze Navali da Battaglia*), and the Commander-in-Chief, Vice-Admiral Bergamini, with his flag on the battleship *Littorio,* took over from Vice-Admiral Iachino. At that time *Regolo* and *Scipione* were attached to the destroyer group because of their similar characteristics. (The Naval Battle Force, divided between La Spezia, Genoa and Taranto, consisted of 6 battleships in two squadrons, 10 cruisers in three squadrons, 21 destroyers in one group of six flotillas).

Next *Pompeo Magno* joined the fleet on 24 June 1943. At the time of the armistice on 8 September 1943, *Regolo* was serving at Genoa, and *Scipione* and *Pompeo* were at Taranto where, together with the light cruiser *Luigi Cadorna,* they formed the Light Cruiser Squadron *(Gruppo Incrociatori Leggeri)*. At the same time two units, *Giulio Germanico* and *Ottaviano Augusto* were in an advanced stage of preparation. A memorandum from Strategic Naval Command (*Supermarina*) of 14 January 1943 mentioned that they would enter service in the course of that year, and that *Cornelio Silla* and *Caio Mario* would be ready the following year. The latter, with her hull completed, and used as a floating fuel store in the port of Genoa, would be replaced by *Ulpio Traiano,* sunk at Palermo on 3 January 1943. This would effectively bring the units in operation up to seven.

The remaining four units of the class were demolished on the stocks between July 1941 and August 1942, and the salvaged materials used to complete the other units. After this decision, due to the scarcity of ferrous materials, the *Capitani Romani* were reduced to eight units. I shall recount the operational history of each one, giving priority to the three most active units.

Capitani Romani
PART 2
by ELIO ANDO

The light cruiser *Attilio Regolo* and destroyer *Mitraglieri, Italian Navy Official, from the 1973 Calendar; drawing by the author*

ATTILIO REGOLO

From her arrival in the fleet on 8 September 1942, this light cruiser carried out 20 war missions, 1 mine-laying mission, 4 transits, 1 special mission and 14 exercises. On the evening of 7 November 1942, flying the ensign of Rear-Admiral Gasparri, commander of the destroyer group, she left the port of Palermo together with the destroyers *Mitragliers, Ascari, Pigafetta, Da Noli* and *Zeno* and the First World War destroyer *Fabrizi,* to place a mine barrage (S 8) to the south of Sicily. On the return journey, the destroyer *Corazzione* having joined the formation, while the units were steaming in two lines ahead in case of attack from the air, *Regolo* was torpedoed at 10.24 by the British submarine *Unruffled* and lost her bows. As she was in good condition below the waterline, and there was the possibility of manoeuvring her with the two propellers, she was taken in tow. A further torpedo from the British submarine *United* had no effect since the submarine was under attack at the time, and *Regolo* arrived back in Palermo on the morning of 9 November.

She was restored to normal service with new bows, and at the armistice she was at Genoa, attached to the Eight Squadron which joined the Naval Battle Forces which joined the Naval Battle Force in the Tirrenean Sea in the early hours of 9 September. Vice-Admiral Bergamini took them out to sea while waiting for clarification of the armistice conditions and at first headed straight for La Maddalena (Sardinia.) He was superior to Commander Notarbartolo, and had struck the flag of Captain Garfalo, Commodore of destroyers, who had been recalled to La Spezia the previous day.

After the battleship *Roma* was sunk at 16.11 hours by German Do 217 K-2 bombers armed with the rocket-propelled and radio-controlled. Fritz X bombs, *Regolo,* with the destroyers *Mitragliere, Carabiniere* and *Fuciliere,* and the destroyer escorts *Pegaso, Orsa* and *Impetuoso,* hastened to help the survivors. Only 622 out of the 1948

men on board *Roma* were saved, and 26 of those died later from injuries they sustained. Captain Marini of *Mitragliere* took command of all the units cut off from the Naval Force. He knew nothing of the armistice agreements or of the situation in the Italian bases, and so allowed the destroyer-escorts freedom to manoeuvre. He made no attempt to head for the Italian ports and, with *Regolo* and the destroyers, uncertain who represented the enemy and unaware of whether they were likely to encounter German or Allies, determined only to prevent his ships from being handed over. Therefore he made for Port Mahon in the Balearic Islands, where he was interned. The destroyer-escorts reached one of the smaller of these islands independently. *Orsa* chose internment and subsequently joined the other units at Port Mahon. Because of the uncertainty of the situation *Pegaso* and *Impetuoso* decided to scuttle. (At the end of the war, the behaviour of the two commanding officers, Commander Imperiali di Francavilla and Lieutenant Commander Cigala Fulgosi, was considered by the Commission of Marine Enquiry in accordance with the laws regarding military honours).

After 16 months of enforced idleness and uncertainty during which the faith of 1300 officers and seamen in their country was severely put to the test, the units left Port Mahon for various Italian and Allied bases. *Regolo* made for Algiers, arriving on 19 January 1945. She then joined the 7th Squadron at Taranto. Up to the end of the war she carried out three sorties. She then remained idle for a long strtetch at La Spezia and was stricken from the list on 26 July 1948. She arrived at Tolona on 1 August 1948 with the registration R4 and was handed over to the French who renamed her *Châteaurenault*. She was finally stricken in 1962.

Attilio Regolo leading the destroyers *Mitraglieri, Fuciliere* and *Carabinieri* returning from Port Mahon, Minorca, 23 January 1945.

Regolo with bow blown off after torpedo attack, 11 November 1942. In the background the destroyer *Mitraglieri* lays down a protective smokescreen.

Pompeo Magno at Malta, 10 October 1943. The ship has adopted typical Allied camouflage.
IWM

POMPEO MAGNO

The *Pompeo Magno* saw less than three months active service before the armistice, but carried out 17 war missions, 3 of which were transits and 4 exercises. She was serving at Taranto with the Light Cruiser Squadron (*Gruppo Incrociatori Leggeri*) together with *Scipione;* Rear-Admiral Galati was in command, with *Cadorna* flying his flag. The units of the Naval Battle Force stationed at Taranto were under the command of Rear-Admiral Da Zara, who summoned his officers, admirals and commanders on the morning of 9 September to pass on Vice-Admiral Bergamini's message with which he was in complete sympathy: it was important to consider the proud reluctance of everyone to sail for a British base in obedience to the king's orders. The phrase included in the instructions for leaving, '. . . the armistice clauses exclude the transfer of ships and the lowering of flags' was supposed to remove any doubt as to the procedure to follow. Only Rear-Admiral Galati asked to go ashore

and his request was granted. He considered that sailing for Malta was too much to demand of his conscience.

At 1700 hours all the units left their moorings for Malta. German fighter bombers attacked them during their passage but inflicted no damage. Most of the units were then transferred to Alexandria on the 14th, and *Pompeo* remained, attached to the 8th Squadron. She left the British base on 4 October for Taranto, once more assigned to the Light Cruiser Squadron.

Up to the end of the war she carried out 123 missions: 53 transporting equipment and Italian nationals, 22 transporting equipment and Allies, one special one, 13 exercises and 34 transits. After the war she was sent to La Spezia, and was stricken on 1 May 1948 and classified FV1. On March 1951 she was renamed *San Giorgio,* and after being rebuilt at the Tirreno de Genova shipyards she went into service again on 1 July 1955 as a destroyer leader. In 1964 she was modernised and became a training ship for the Naval

Academy (*Accademia Navale*). She is expected to fulfil this role until 1987.

SCIPIONE AFRICANO

From her entry into service she was stationed between Genoa and La Spezia, where she received orders to move on to Taranto, crossing the Straits of Messina (between the Italian peninsula and Sicily) at night, before Sicily was occupied by the Allies and passage in this important strait became difficult. She left at 06.30 hours on 15 July 1943 and put into Naples during the evening where she took on board a radio set for communication with fighter planes and a Metox set for the interception of radar transmissions. She left Naples on the 16th at 18.15 hours.

Shortly after 0200 hours on the 17th, in the Straits of Messina, she picked up over her radar, about six miles from her bows, four British motor torpedo boats, the MTBs *260, 313, 315* and *316*.

Scipione, under the command of Captain De Pellegrini dai Coi,

After the war *Pompeo Magno* was renamed *San Giorgio* and twice extensively rebuilt, finally mounting four 127mm/38s, three 76mm/62s, two triple A/S torpedo tubes, and an automatic depth charge mortar and new CODAG machinery. Currently used as a schoolship she is expected to remain in service until 1987.
This photo was taken in 1968.

increased her speed to over 40 knots, preparing to attack at the same time as the enemy. She engaged in a fast and bloody action which even now is difficult to reconstruct in detail. The cruiser emerged unscathed from the encounter. Damage sustained by the British MTBs consisted of: a) official Italian version: one MTB blown up, one caught fire, one sunk, and the fourth managed to escape; b) official British version: MTB 316 lost with all hands, MTB *260* sustained slight damage, and MTB *313* and *315* were unharmed.

These two conflicting estimates show how difficult it is for those involved in a tactical action, particularly if it takes place at night, to evaluate the events. Anomalies arise such as when *Scipione* mentions being showered with pieces of machinery from the blown up MTB while the British story speaks of 'a table . . .' from the MTB *305*(?) which was not even on the scene. The mystery still remains unsolved, even though the official historians of the two navies

exchanged their respective versions after the war.

A few minutes after the encounter, *Scipione* inadvertently came into the firing line of German coastal batteries which had opened fire even though the Italian commanders had reported their passage that night. *Scipione* however was unharmed, and arrived at Taranto on the 18th at 09.46 hours.

From 4 to 17 August she took part in four missions together with the light cruiser *Cadorna* in the Gulfs of Squillace (Calabria) and of Taranto, for the purpose of laying anti-invasion mine barrages. Up to 8 September she carried out 24 missions, 5 mine-laying, 5 transits, 1 special mission and 13 exercises.

At 0600 hours on 9 September Strategic Naval Command ordered *Scipione* and the corvettes *Scimitarra* and *Baionetta* to leave for Pescara from Taranto, Brindisi and Pola respectively, at top speed

Baionetta was the first to arrive at 2105 hours on the 9th. She took on board Marshal Badoglio, Head of the Government, and Vice-Admiral De Courten, the Navy Minister. Next, at the Ortona at 0100 hours on the 10th, she took the king and his retinue on board. *Scipione* arrived outside Pescara at about 0000 hours, joined *Baionetta* at 0700 hours on the 10th and escorted her to Brindisi. During the trip she radioed all the most important intercepted messages to the *Baionetta,* in order to keep the king and political leaders informed of developments in Italy. On 29 of the same month *Scipione* transferred to Malta with Marshal Badaglio, Vice-Admiral De Courten and the British General MacFarlane on board. The 'long' armistice was signed on board the battleship *Nelson,* so called because it was to apply until the peace treaty was agreed.

The flag of Captain Garofalo of the Light Cruiser and Destroyer Squadron was struck aboard *Scipione,* and from 1 February 1944 until the end of the war she was

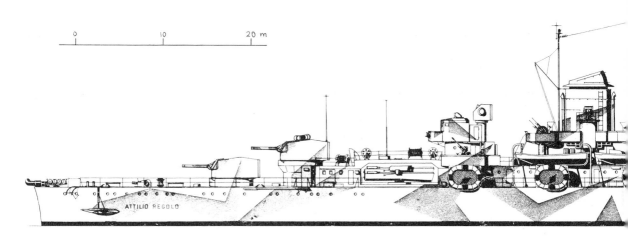

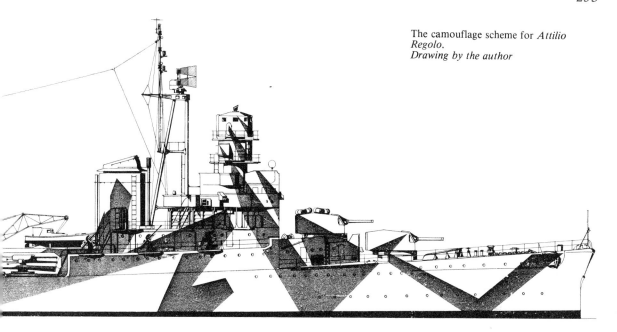

The camouflage scheme for *Attilio Regolo*.
Drawing by the author

Attilio Regolo at Malta, spring 1945

associated with the 7th Squadron. During this period she undertook 139 missions, 62 transporting equipment and Italian nationals, 42 transporting equipment and Allies, 3 special missions, 7 escort missions and 25 transits.

She was serving at La Spezia at the end of the war and was stricken on 9 August 1948. Designated *S7* on 15 August in the port of Tolone, she became the French *Guichen* and remained in active service until 1961.

CAIO MARIO

As a hulk, she was turned into a floating fuel store at La Spezia. She was sabotaged and subsequently seized by the Germans at the armistice. In April 1945 she was found sunk in the port.

CORNELIO SILLA

She remained inactive in the port of Genoa where she was seized by the Germans. She was sunk, severely damaged by an Allied air attack, in July 1944. 84% of the hull had been completed. Her engine equipment, together with that of the stricken *Paolo Emilio,* was taken on board the aircraft carrier *Aquila* which was being fitted out at Genoa.

GUILIO GERMANICO

On 8 September 1943 she was at Castellammare de Stabia about 94% complete, together with other units. Steered by her second in command, Lieutenant Commander Baffigo, she repelled an initial attack by German troops, with all the other forces in the shipyard, The Germans returned in force three days later and siezed the unit. Lieutenant Commander Baffigo was taken to Naples and shot. *Germanico* was sunk by the retreating Germans on 28 September.

She was salvaged after the war and designated *FV2* and from 1 March 1951 was renamed *San Marco* while waiting to be refitted. She re-entered service about five years later on 1 January 1955. In April of the following year she was classified as a destroyer leader. She remained in active service until 1971, when she was finally scrapped.

OTTAVIANO AUGUSTO

On 8 September 1943 this cruiser was close to completion in Ancona. Parts of her AA machine guns were taken to strengthen the defence of Monte Conero. She was sunk by Allied air attack on 1 November 1943.

ULPIO TRAIANO

This unit was fitting out in the port of Palermo on 3 January 1943 when, between 0200 and 0300 hours British underwater assault troops placed explosive charges on the hull. She sank at 1758 hours, split in two.

CONCLUSION

The results obtained from these small, fast, well-armed cruisers were unreservedly excellent. Captain De Pellegrini dai Coi wrote in his report, when referring to the night encounter with the British MTBs: '. . . all arms, guns and machine guns opened fire with such precision and violence that it would have filled me with amazement if I had not already been aware of the ship's potential . . .' All the units that entered service reached consistently high speeds with full displacement — *Scipione* achieved bursts of 43 knots in the course of the above encounter.

Their late entry into the fleet denied them the war service which would have brought them the distinction their qualities deserved. They would have proved themselves especially useful in homogeneous formation, either attacking enemy targets, or in the defence of convoys to North Africa.

1 *Pompeo Magno* laid up in reserve, La
Spezia 1946.

2 *Scipione Africano* in Taranto harbour,
5 May 1944.

3 View aft from the bridge of *Scipione*,
1944.

4 Bridge of *Scipione*, 1944.

2

3   4

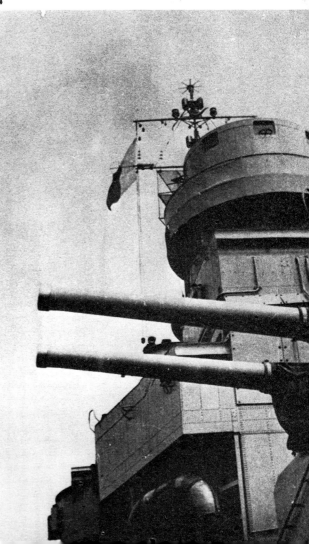

256

1 The quad torpedo tube mount of
Scipione. Note the operator's position.

2 *Ottaviano Augusto* capsized at Ancona
after aerial bombing 1 November 1943.

3 Port Mahon, Minorca, September 1943.
Attilio Regolo and the destroyers
Mitraglieri, Carabiniere and *Fuciliere*
interned.
*Photos from the Collections of E
Bagnasco, F Bargoni and the author.*

TABLE 3
Equivalences of ranks between English and Italian Navies 1940–45

RN	RM	
Admiral of the Fleet	Grande Ammiraglio	
Admiral	Ammiraglio d'Armata	
	Ammiraglio designato d'Armata	
Vice Admiral	Ammiraglio di Squadra	(A.S.)
Rear Admiral	Ammiraglio di Divisione	(A.D.)
	Contrammiraglio	(C.A.)
Commodore (1st or 2nd class)	—	
Captain	Capitano di Vascello	(C.V.)
Commander	Capitano di Fregata	(C.F.)
Lieutenant-Commander	Capitano di Corretta	(C.C.)
Lieutenant	Tenente di Vascello	(T.V.)
Sublieutenant	Sotlotenente di Vascello	(S.T.V.)
Midshipman	Guardia marina	(G.M.)

Note. Officers of Corpi Tecnici (Genio Navale, Armi Navali, Commissari, Medici) wear the same stripes, but on different colours and with the denomination as in the Army: . . . Generale, Colonnello, Tenente-Colonnello .

Equivalent grouping of ships between English and Italian Navies 1940-45

RN	RM (Regia Marina)
Fleet	Flotta
,,	Armata
,,	Squadra
Squadron	Divisione
—	Gruppo
Flotilla	— (squadriglia)
Division	Squadriglia
Sub-division	Sezione

3

2

The battle of
Tsu-Shima
by
N J M Campbell

4

DAMAGE TO THE RUSSIAN SHIPS

In considering the damage caused to the Russian battleships, that inflicted on the *Borodino* class is of most interest. At times during the voyage they were overloaded with coal to an extent which impaired their stability and it has been stated that at Madagascar, if heeled 8° they would not right themselves. An officer's diary found in the *Orel* records that on 9 March, 1905 the *Orel* displaced 16 800 tons with 2450 tons of coal aboard and her draught was 32ft 6in aft. The trim was subsequently altered and on 28 April with 2052 tons coal, of which 1150 tons were in the bunkers, 200 tons on the quarterdeck, 215 tons on the gundeck in bags and 220 tons in compartments, the draught was 30ft 3in aft. Rozhestvenski's order of 14 October, 1904 lays down that, in order to preserve a safe metacentric height at sea, the maindeck gun-ports were to be closed, coal used from lower bunkers was to be replaced by that from upper locations and stores were to be stowed as low as possible.

The diary ceases before the end of the voyage, but it is quite certain that at Tsushima the *Orel* was not loaded to the extent quoted above. When she arrived at Maizuru in Japan, her draught was 27ft 6in fore and 29ft 4in aft. Some water had undoubtedly come aboard since the beginning of the battle, and coal and ammunition had been used, so that there will be no very

great error in taking the *Orel's* mean draught at Tsushima as 28½ft 6in-29ft and it is probable that the other ships of the class were loaded to a similar extent. This, though well over the nominal intended figure, was not abnormally great for the ships as completed, and would give a displacement of over 15 000 tons and a metacentric height of 2½ft. This last figure was quite inadequate for the actual armour protection at 28½ft 6in-29ft mean draught. At this loading the 7½inch belt would be submerged by 12-18in amidships, and the upper edge of the 6inch upper belt at main deck level, would be only 3½-4ft above water in a calm, and well immersed at intervals in the rough seas of the Tsushima battle. Above this amidships, there was only the 3inch armour for the battery of 3inch guns which was broken by the gun-ports. Forward the 5¾inch belt would be a few inches below the waterline and the 4inch upper belt 4½-5ft above, and except for patches on the bow upper-deck 3inch guns, there was no 3inch armour.

Careful examination of the British and German naval attachés' reports and of many photographs, shows that the *Orel* was probably hit by five 12inch, two 10inch, nine 8inch, 39-6inch and 21 smaller shells, or fragments, of which two 12inch, five 8inch, 28-6inch and 11 smaller or fragments were on the port side. The damage was generally similar to that of the Port Arthur ships in the Yellow Sea battle. There were many large holes in the unarmoured sides including

one 10ft x 8ft by a 12inch on the port side below the fore funnel, but relatively little damage inboard. The port foward 5¾ inch armour had been hit obliquely by a 12inch which left an elongated 'splash' with circumferential cracks, but otherwise there were only three 6inch hits on the side armour below the maindeck. Two fair-sized holes in the unarmoured side aft, one by an 8inch and one by a 6inch, extended below the axis line of the 3inch guns in the maindeck battery. The left fore 12 inch gun had been hit by an 8 inch and about 7ft of the muzzle broken off. In the after 12 inch turret the roof had been forced down over the left gun-port by an 8inch shell, which restricted the gun's elevation, and there were marks of a 10inch shell having burst or more probably broken up on the turret side armour. The port fore and starboard middle 6inch turrets had been jammed by 8inch hits on their armour and much damage done to the adjacent deck. In the latter turret, ammunition had exploded inside, causing considerable damage. The starboard aft 6inch turret had been damaged by a 12inch shell obliquely striking the support. Splinters had entered the conning-tower from two 6inch hits, one on the side and one on the roof.

Coal, which had been used as additional protection, and stores were stowed above the waterline in many places, but no very serious fires had occurred.

From this relatively moderate damage sustained by the *Orel*, it

The extensive splinter damage to the *Aurora* from high explosive shellfire.
CPL W/8/003

has often been held that very many hits were made on her three sister-ships which were sunk, and which are mentioned more frequently in accounts of the battle, as being scored by the Japanese. With regard to this last point, for much of the time many of the Japanese targets were not identifiable with any certainty, and in considering the number of hits on the sunken ships it must be noted that the Japanese expenditure of heavy shells was not very great. In the battle of 27 May, including the few rounds fired against Nebogatov on the 28th, Togo's division fired:

446—12inch (*Mikasa* 124,
                Shikishima 74,
                Fuji 106, *Ashai* 142)
 50—10inch (*Kasuga* 50)
284— 8inch (*Kasuga* 103, *Nisshin*
                181)

This is considerably less than his division fired at the Yellow Sea: 603— 12inch, 33 — 10inch, 307 — 8inch. Similarly, omitting the action with the *Ushakov* on the afternoon of the 28th, Kamimura's six armoured cruisers fired 915 — 8inch at Tsushima, while the four with him at Ulsan expended 958.

It is probable that Japanese gun-laying had further improved by the date of Tsushima, but conditions of sea and visibility were not at all good as compared with those at the Yellow Sea, and although ranges were never as long as in the earlier part of the Yellow Sea battle, they were seldom less than the closest attained in the later period of that battle, except against the damaged *Suvarov*. Conditions at Ulsan too, were better than at Tsushima, and for a considerable time the ranges were not widely different. The supposition that very many hits with heavy shells were made on all the three *Borodino* class that were sunk, leads to an improbably high percentage of hits. It is not believed that this figure exceeded 10 per cent for the 12inch and appreciably less for the 8inch, which would give 45—12inch hits.

The number of rounds of 6inch and 3inch fired at Tsushima were:
5748—6inch by Toga's division
          (*Shikishima* 1395)
4046—3inch by Toga's division
          (*Shikishima* 1272)

3716—6inch by Kamimura's
          division (excluding
          action against
          the *Ushakov*)
3480—3inch by Kamimura's
          division

These figures are greater than those in the previous battles (Togo's division at Yellow Sea: 3592 — 6inch, 2142 — 3inch: Kamimura's four armoured cruisers at Ulsan 3667 — 6inch, 2327 — 3inch, — but all damage reports on surviving Russian and on Japanese ships in this war indicate that the effect of 6inch shells was not important and that of 3inch usually negligible.

With these facts in view the evidence (necessarily limited by the virtual absence of survivors) regarding the loss of the *Borodino, Alexander,* and *Suvarov* can be considered. As described in the account of the battle, the *Borodino* was sunk as the result of a magazine explosion, which was preceded by serious ammunition fires. Although a good many hits had been made on her, there is no need to suppose that the number from heavy shells exceeded that on the *Orel*.

The *Alexander* was reported as being badly on fire, but there is no mention of ammunition fires. Her bows were very much damaged and a hole on the port side forward was said by one witness to be 20 ft across. Continued flooding from these injuries forward, which would be difficult to stop in the rough seas of Tsushima, combined with flooding on the main deck from holes above the belt or damaged gun-ports, could soon reduce her stability to vanishing point. Although there is no evidence on this matter, hits on the waterline armour, though unlikely to pierce, may well have displaced the plates and caused further flooding on the slope of the lower armour deck. It is thus easy to see how a limited number of 12inch shells striking on or near the waterline forward could have led to the *Alexander* capsizing, and again there is no need to assume a number of heavy hits in excess of those on the *Orel* . Two 12inch HE shells striking at nearly the same place would be capable of producing a hole large enough to be described as 20 ft across in the unarmoured side plating.

The *Suvarov* which was engaged at short range by both Togo's and Kamimura's divisions during the battle, doubtless had considerably more hits from heavy shells than her three sister-ships. Her fate is described in the account of the battle, and until the final torpedo attack, she seems to have kept well afloat though with a list. Previous to the torpedo attack at 17.05 it would appear that steering troubles and violent fires were the reasons why the *Suvarov* did not return to the line. The fires in her were more extensive than in other Russian ships and, as previously noted, though apparently starting in the chart-house and doubtless being initially fed by surplus woodwork, wooden boats and excess paint on steelwork, must have subsequently included coal carried above the waterline, and smaller gun ammunition. The explosion noted in the battle account at about 16.30 was clearly from ammunition. One of the Admiral's staff, Semenov, who was wounded in the battle and taken off with Rozhestvenski, recorded notes of the earlier part of the action. He states that part of the roof of the after 12inch turret over the left gun was torn off and bent up, but the turret continued firing. Later the roof was blown right off the after turret, which ceased fire, and the fore 12inch turret was also silent. A shell came through the fourth 3inch gun-port on the port side and penetrated the armour-deck, and water poured onto the mess deck.

Although her fighting value was entirely destroyed by gunfire, this does not seem to have had a very great effect on her ability to stay afloat, and the sinking of the *Suvarov* was due to torpedoes of which one 18inch and from two to four 14inch hit.

The precise loading of the *Osliabia* is not known, but her metacentric height did not much exceed $2\frac{1}{2}$ft. There was no vertical armour for the first 55 - 60 ft forward, where protection was provided by the armour deck and for a further 60 ft the belt did not extend far above the waterline.

The *Imperator Nikolai I* in Japanese hands as the training ship *Iki*. CPL W/8/004

According to survivors the shell that hit forward at about 14.18, caused flooding of a compartment under the fore-turret, the foremost 6inch shell-room, fore torpedo-flat and dynamo-room. Stopping the leaks was impossible in the rough seas. The shell that pierced the side armour, presumably the 5inch uper belt, went into the tenth coal bunker and caused the flood of a magazine. The effect of these and other hits soon produced a great enough list for water to enter holes above the armour and the ports in the unarmoured 3inch battery, and within an hour from the start of the battle the *Osliabia* went down. The fore turret had been hit by three large projectiles, the first of which damaged the glacis and the third entered by a port and killed many of the turret crew.

The Japanese party which boarded the *Sissoi* after her surrender reported that the forward torpedo-flat was full of water and the bows somewhat depressed. A hole from shellfire was noticed below the waterline on the port side forward of the fore bridge. The torpedo hit aft had wrecked the rudder and apparently hit the after steering room, but use of a collision mat had reduced the inrush of water. Damage above the waterline was described as 'fairly considerable' and it was thought possible to tow her. The Russians had, however, opened the sea cocks in the engine room and she sank. Russian reports indicate rather more serious damage than the above, including a dangerous fire on the battery deck and two 12inch guns out of action. The number of large calibre hits is given as 12 in one account.

The *Navarin's* remarkable end is described in the account of the destroyer attacks at night. According to survivors she had been holed four times on the waterline during the day, twice by 12inch shells aft, in addition to other hits.

The *Nakhimov* is frequently mentioned as a target in Japanese reports but her damage from gunfire does not seem to have been serious. The torpedo hit was too far forward to sink her quickly, and flooded the first three compartments.

When examined the *Nikolai* was found to have been hit about 10 times. One hit and one that burst on the water alongside were probably 12inch, two 8inch, two 6inch and the rest not identified. The left 12inch gun had been put out of action by a shell bursting immediately below it and a 12inch shell had hit the edge of the forward port 9inch embrasure, scoring the gun and doing much damage to the shelter deck and bridge. An 8inch and a 6inch shell had hit forward, causing some flooding when under way.

There were only two hits on the *Apraxin,* one of which on the after turret had badly scored the gun, and the *Seniavin* was untouched except for splinters. It is said that the 10inch guns in both ships showed signs of weakness. The *Ushakov* was hit by a large shell forward on the 27th which reduced her speed, and there were apparently two other hits. On the 28th the training gear of the fore turret failed, and her increasing list made training impossible. Although scuttled, it seems likely that she would soon have sunk from the effect of the Japanese shells.

The *Asama,* one of the Japanese ships hit by heavy shellfire at Tsushima. *IWM*

DAMAGE TO THE JAPANESE SHIPS

It is impossible to give any figures for the total number of rounds fired by the Russian ships, though if the *Nikolai's* expenditure of 100 — 12inch and 261 — 9inch is any indication, the rate of fire of their heavy guns exceed that of their opponents. The damage caused to the Japanese is, however known in detail. The *Mikasa* was hit more than 40 times, including ten 12inch and 22 — 6inch. Of the 12inch hits the most notable were:

14.14 cut hole in roof on No 3 casemate, wounded nearly all the gun crew and exploded ten 3inch rounds nearby. The 6inch gun in No 3 casemate was still able to fire.
14.20 below fore bridge, great hole in shelter deck, one fragment into conning tower and others into fore bridge, which narrowly missed Admiral Togo.
14.25 pierced 6inch side armour

17in below the main deck and under No 1 casemate. The shell entered a full coal bunker, and until the hole was plugged much water came in.
14.40 hit lower coaming of No 7 casemate and cracked 6inch armour plates nearby.
16.15 pierced 6inch side armour near main deck level and below No 7 casemate. A large hole was made and armour was also displaced. The shell went into a full coal bunker, and as with the 14.25 hit, much water came in at first. The casemate floor was bulged up by the burst, and this restricted the training of the gun.

The most important 6inch hit was that at 18.26 which entered the port of No 10 casemate and burst on the 6inch gun saddle, putting the gun permanently out of action. One 6inch shell pierced the roof of No 3 casemate, another burst on the lower coaming of No 5, displaced an armour joint and disabled the gun crew, although the gun was uninjured. A third pierced the roof of No 11 casemate without damaging the gun.

From the point of fighting efficiency, the most serious damage was the premature in the right fore 12inch gun. A shell had burst in the muzzle at 16.07 but the gun appeared unaffected and firing continued. At 18.04 there was another premature at the 28th round of the day. The upper half of the jacket was broken, a little in front of the shell chamber, and the wires exposed and about 12 strands cut. The gun was completely out of action and the recoil gear damaged. The fore part of the turret roof was displaced and had to be temporarily secured. The left gun was also affected but reopened firing at 18.40. Apart from this and the 6inch gun put out of action at 18.26 as noted above, the only serious armament damage was to No 8 6inch gun which had a jammed breech-block at the 20th round and was not repaired until next day.

The *Shikishima* was hit by one 12inch, one 10inch and including grazes, a three 6inch and four 3inch. The 12inch hit was at 15.18 on the lower edge of No 6

casemate. Some of the armour was broken and the ammunition hoist wrecked. All the gun crew were killed or disabled but the gun was undamaged. This shell actually burst in a cabin on the main deck under the casemate. The other hits were unimportant except that water came in through a hole from an unexploded 6inch near the waterline on the starboard quarter, and as in the *Mikasa* the worst injury was from a premature in the right fore 12inch gun. This occurred at 16.15 at the 11th round of the day, and the effect was very similar to that in *Mikasa* except that it was more violent. About 5 ft of the front end of the jacket was wrecked, wire came out and the saddle split open. The recoil gear was also wrecked, as was part of the turret roof. The left gun was also out of action for a time.

Including grazes the *Fuji* was hit by two 12inch, three 6inch, two 3inch and five unidentified shells. The only important damage was from the 12inch hit on the after barbette shield at 15.00. This pierced the 6inch armour by the right gun-port, and passed along ther gun before bursting on an overhead beam just in front of the upper loading position. A 4 in rear plate was blown overboard and much of the roof blown off. A charge half in the gun caught fire and eight quarter-charges in the upper loading position also ignited, but six HE shells were unaffected. The casualties were eight killed and nine wounded. The pressure pipe to the right upper loading ram was cut and the water shooting out is said to have been of great use in quenching the flames. The right gun was scored and for that reason was not fired again, although Kure Arsenal subsequently thought it safe. When the shell hit, the right gun was about to fire its 13th round. The left gun was in action again within 40 minutes and fired 23 more rounds, its last shot apparently sinking the *Borodino*.

For some unknown reason the number of hits on the *Asahi* is not given in the Japanese reports. The damage is however recorded in detail, and it can be deduced from this that she was hit about six times. Of these two were 6inch, one 3inch and three unidentifiable. There were no serious injuries.

The *Kasuga* was hit by one 12inch, one 6inch and one unidentified shell which did not affect her fighting power, but the *Nisshin* had six 12inch, one 9inch, two 6inch and apparently four smaller or unidentified hits. As mentioned in the account of the battle three of her 8inch guns had been cut in two by 12inch hits. A British officer who examined *Nisshin* later thought that the guns might have been broken by prematures but Japanese accounts are quite definite that they were hit. Apart form the guns, neither turret was out of action although the fore turret was also hit by a 9inch shell at 16.05 which sent splinters into the conning-tower and wounded Vice-Admiral Misu. At about 15.00 a 12inch shell pierced the 6inch belt on the port side about 1 ft below water and burst in a coal bunker and a 12inch shell also struck the 6inch armour 3 ft above water without penetrating, during the battle.

The *Izumo* was hit by five 12inch, one 10inch or 12inch and three 6inch or unidentified shells. The 12 hits were mostly aft and no vital damage was caused. The 12inch hit at 19.10 pierced the decks down to the armour deck along which it slid, without bursting. On its way it pierced the casing of a boiler-room and if it had exploded, might have put all the middle boilers out of action.

The *Azuma* , including shells that burst alongside on the water, was hit by seven large projectiles, mostly 12inch, four 6inch and about four 3inch. At 14.20 a fragment from a 12inch bursting very near the side, cut 2 ft off the muzzle of No 7 — 6inch gun and not long afterwards another 12inch hit the 6inch armour of this gun's casemate which was pierced and much damage done, the gun mounting being wrecked, while a 3inch gun on the shelter deck above was also destroyed. At 14.50 the right aft 8inch gun was hit and put out of action by a 12inch shell which also made a large hole in the quarter deck.

The *Tokiwa* was hit by one large shell and seven smaller, mostly 3inch, and the *Yakumo* by one 12inch and six others, of which three or four were 6inch. No very important damage was caused to either ship, but as mentioned in the account of the battle the *Asama* was severly injured. She appears to have been hit by three 12inch, two 9inch and about seven smaller shells. The 12inch hit at 14.28 was in the captain's cabin on the starboard quarter, and shook the *Asama* sufficiently to disable the steering on the fore bridge. The two 12inch shells at 15.00 also hit on the starboard side aft and caused much damage. They struck about 5ft above water, and led to serious flooding. A 9inch shell also struck the upper deck and burst in the captain's cabin, and another burst on the after 8inch turret at the lower armour edge, only making a dent. A 6inch hit, at the base of the after funnel at 16.10, seriously affected the boiler furnace draught for 20 minutes until repairs were completed.

Including shells which burst on the water alongside, the *Iwate* was

264

1 The *Peresviet* sunk at Port Arthur.
CPL W/8/006

2 The *Mishima* was captured at Tsushima (as the *Admiral Senyavin*) without serious damage.
CPL W/8/005

3 Battle damage to the *Askold*.
CPL W/8/007

4 The *Retvisan* sunk at Port Arthur.
CPL W/8/008

hit 17 times, made up from two 12inch, three 8inch, two 6inch, one 4.7inch, five 3inch and four unidentified. No serious damage was caused, except that two 8inch shells striking on the unarmoured side a little above water caused flooding of two lower deck compartments.

The total of heavy shell hits (8inch to 12inch) by the Russians was thus 47, of which all but 10 or so were 12inch, a respectable figure in view of the battle conditions, and the disaster to their fleet.

The Russian 12inch AP shell had a small wet guncotton burster and holed 6inch armour on six occasions during the battle. All these shells appear to have burst with as much effect as could be expected, but only the hit on the *Fuji's* after barbette shield was potentially disastrous. The difference between the success of the Japanese at Tsushima and at the Yellow Sea is often said to be due in part to the improvement of their fuses which made the shells less liable to burst outside thin plating. This may perhaps account

for the rapid disabling of the *Suvarov,* but it is not supported by the state of the *Orel,* in which most shells had exploded on striking the hull plating, and prematures still occurred. Neither the Japanese so-called AP with a 5 per cent burster of picric acid (Lyddite) or the HE with a 10 per cent burster of the same explosive, would have had much effect on any but the thinnest hard-faced armour, but the heavier shells could be disastrous to unarmoured areas. Much of the Japanese success was due to their good fortune in causing the magazine explosion in the *Borodino* and in hitting the unarmoured hull near the waterline forward with heavy shells in the *Osliabia* and *Alexander.* These two ships were as vulnerable to this as could well be desired, particularly in the rough seas of Tsushima and with complements little trained in damage control.

According to information obtained in 1906, the *Mikasa* at Tsushima fired HE from the right 12inch guns and AP from the left, but at under 5000 yards AP only.

The 3in guns were only manned and used inside 4500 yards. The range was obtained initially by a Barr & Stroud rangefinder, but this was not used once the action began, until a cease-fire occurred. Salvos of 6inch shells were employed for ranging and, at moderate ranges, the range was twice obtained in three salvos. It was often impossible to distinguish the *Mikasa's* shells during the action, and when this happened firing was temporarily stopped and begun again with 6inch ranging salvos. In the *Mikasa* the gunnery lieutenant spotted the fall of shot, when possible, from the fore-bridge and passed the corrected range to the guns via the conning tower, and a sub-lieutenant was stationed in the fore-top. Five methods of communicating the range were used, apparently Barr & Stroud transmitter, loudspeaking telephone, voicepipes, messengers with megaphones and hand-worked range dials.

Both Admiral Togo and the *Mikasa's* captain were on the fore-bridge during the action, and this station was favoured by other Japanese flag officers, except Vice-Admiral Misu who used the conning-tower as did most of the captains.

In conclusion a few comparisons with the Battle of Jutland fought 11 years later. The three British battlecruisers blew up after a total of about seventeen 12inch or 11inch hits, an average of 5-6 each. The British observer in the *Asahi,* Captain Pakenham, who had seen the *Borodino* blow up, was Rear-Admiral in the *New Zealand,* and had the further experience of having the ship astern of him and the one two ahead blow up within 23 minutes. The *Grosser Kurfürst, Lützow, Derfflinger* and *Seydlitz,* four ships far better protected and more battleworthy than any at Tsushima, all suffered serious damage from heavy shell hits in the forward part of the hull which led to extensive flooding, fatal in the *Lützow.* Finally, one may wonder how much the successful Japanese mine attack on the *Navarin* influenced Jellicoe's fear that the German fleet might try something similar if closely pursued.

CVLs
The US INDEPENDENCE class
By NORMAN FRIEDMAN

USS *Cowpens* (CVL-25), 17 July 1943,
shows the configuration of the converted
Cleveland class light carriers as
completed. Her electronic suit comprises
an SC-2 medium-range air search antenna
on her foremast and a long range SK on
a stub mainmast; the lattice foremast also
carries an SG for surface search and a YE
aircraft homing beacon. This essentially
duplicated the suit of *Essex* class fleet
carriers.

During World War Two both the US and Royal Navies built two distinct series of fleet carriers: standard *(Essex, Indomitable)* and 'light' (US *Independence,* RN *Colossus).* In both navies the latter was a wartime expedient which was, however, continued after the initial emergency had passed. Thus the US *Saipan* class and various British types culminating in HMS *Hermes.*

However, the US and British programs were very different in practice, and even in detailed motivation. What is remarkable about the US program is that it very nearly died several times (and indeed was pressed only due to the President's personal intervention), yet the second series of US light fleet carriers (CVL) was approved before service experience with the

first ones had proven the concept. Indeed the unsatisfactory character of the entire CVL concept is suggested by the brevity of the postwar careers of all eleven ships built.

The origin of the CVL is to be found in the size of the US cruiser program, and the President's fear of insufficient carrier strength. As of August 1941, the US Navy had on order 32 *Cleveland* class 10 000 ton light cruisers, as well as eight *Baltimore* class 13 600 ton heavy cruisers and six *Alaska* class 'large cruisers' (12 inch guns). There were also eleven *Essexes* on order, but they were not scheduled for completion until 1944. It seemed to the President that surely some flight decks could be had more quickly by converting two of the light cruiser

hulls already on the stocks. At this time President Roosevelt had just succeeded in pushing through the very austere conversion of a merchant ship into the first US escort carrier (USS *Long Island*); that job had taken only about three months. Clearly the President felt that a similar conversion could be applied to a light cruiser hull; he was not interested in such complexities as hangar deck arrangements or elevators.

The Bureau of Ships could afford no such ideas. Its problem was a tendency — too familiar from more recent military programs — to 'gold plate', to strive for perfection when the requirement was really for some kind of carrier in minimum time.

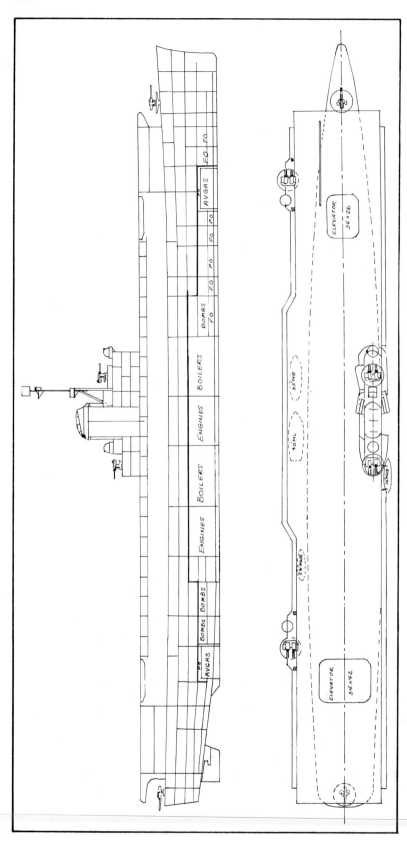

The President's views on carrier conversion gained considerable strength after Pearl Harbor; investigations were made not merely of *Cleveland* conversions, but also of *Baltimores* and even *Alaskas*, although the latter was soon abandoned. The first CVL conversion, USS *Independence* (CVL 22, ex USS *Amsterdam*, CL 59) was ordered on 10 January 1942; the order for design work had been given eight days earlier. Admiral King examined the conversion plans and on 3 February recommended two more, which became CVL 23/24 (ex CL 61 and CL 76). Later CL 77 and 78 became CVL 25 and 26; and four ships not yet laid down as cruisers (CL 85, 79, 99, 100) were reordered as CVL 27-30. All were initially designated in the fleet carrier (CV) series; the CVL designator was not applied until 15 July 1943.

All were built by the New York Shipbuilding Corporation of Camden New Jersey, which did a good part of the detail design. New York Ship was responsible for a good part of US wartime cruiser construction: all three *Alaskas*, four out of fourteen *Baltimores*, both *Worcesters*, eight out of twenty-nine Cleveland-Fargos, not to mention many cancelled ships.

Design work began at a BuShip conference on 3 January 1942; it was based on the September design, drastically reworked. If the island were eliminated entirely, much of the problem of hangar deck obstruction could be avoided, and it would be necessary to balance off a heavy starboard side (island) weight. In addition, the problems of forward elevator size and hangar deck sheer could be avoided:

'In order to avoid cutting elevator openings in the main deck plating, it appears feasible to install an additional deck to serve as the hangar deck about 3 or 4 feet above the present main deck and to extend only between elevators. The clear height between this deck and the underside of the flight deck girders will be about 17ft 4in (17ft 6in in an *Essex*) . . .'

BuShips based its carrier design, which is shown here, on an abortive

Cowpens, 17 July 1943, Starboard side.

10 000 ton carrier of 1938. The cruiser hull form presented problems. For example, the sheer in the hangar (which would be former cruiser upper deck) would make plane-handling difficult (as in contemporary C-3 CVE conversions) and the fine hull form forward would preclude the installation of a large enough elevator (26ft x 34ft forward, compared to 42ft x 34ft aft) to handle anything larger than fighters with their wings folded. This was a serious defect; US operating procedure was to zone the flight deck into landing, parking, and takeoff areas, using the forward elevator to move aircraft around the parked planes forward of the barrier. If the forward elevator could be used only for fighters, the new carrier would have little flexibility. Another flight deck problem was short length: although BuShips had tried for 580ft, only 550ft had been achieved; yet BuAer expected take-off runs over 350ft 'due to the addition [in aircraft] of armor leak-proof tanks, and other military essentials'. At this time catapults were not as yet considered acceptable as the standard means of carrier take-off. The narrow cruiser hull would support only a very narrow hangar, further constricted by the uptakes; and it seemed to the Bureau of Aeronautics that the narrow flight deck itself would probably create excessive turbulence.

An already badly constricted flight deck could not support very much of an AA battery; it had to be accepted from the outset that the new carrier would rely on her aircraft and her consorts for heavy AA protection against high-level bombers. She would be armed with AA machine guns (four quadruple 40mm Bofors, two on the island, one forward and one aft on the portside of the flight deck) against dive and torpedo bombers. This is very much analogous to current practice: the escorts carry the area defense missiles, the carrier is given a Point Defense system (SEA SPARROW). Finally, the carrier would have single-purpose guns (in this case two 4inch/50 of the type mounted in the old 'four-pipe' destroyers) to protect her from light enemy surface forces.

This design, completed in September 1941, drew universally adverse comment from the technical Bureaux; its own designers, the Preliminary Design Branch of BuShips, felt that

'. . . it would upset the orderly construction of this [Cleveland] series of cruisers, and would produce small, costly aircraft carriers of limited effectiveness little, if any, earlier than the large aircraft carriers of the *Essex* class now building'.

The General Board, the senior Navy council, rejected the

President's idea on 13 October; but he was not to be put off. In a 25 October memorandum he asked the Chief of Naval Operations to

'Please ask for a new study on the conversion into aircraft carriers of two of the 10 000 ton light cruisers now building.

I recognize the reasonableness of the General Board report . . .

However, I do not agree with the statement that the conversion of such a ship could be made little, if any, earlier than completion of the big carriers of the *Essex* class now building. All you have to do is look at the dates of prospective commissioning of the latter.

Also the reason, if sound, would not operate if we were to consider taking ships which are now 25 to 30 per cent completed.'

Probably the President was thinking in terms of his recent experience with the CVE program. The General Board still thought in terms of the rather sophisticated carrier sketched by Preliminary Design, and argued that lead times both for design and for the delivery of new material for a partially completed cruiser, would mean that

'Even under the most favorable possibilities of such conversion, an assignment to the whole project of high priority would result in the delivery of the finished ship only about three months prior to the

	Commisioned	Decommissioned	Fate
CVL 22 INDEPENDENCE	14.1.43	—	Expended at Bikini
23 PRINCETON	25.2.43	—	Lost 24.10 44
24 BELLEAU WOOD	31.3.43	23.1.47	To France 9.53-9.60
25 COWPENS	28.5.43	1.47	Stricken 11.11.59
26 MONTEREY	17.6.43	11.2.47	15.9.50-5.1.56 Stricken 1.6.70
27 LANGLEY	31.8.43	1.47	To France 1.51-3.63
28 CABOT	24.7.43	11.2.47	27.10.48-21.1.55 To Spain 30.8.67
29 BATAAN	17.11.43	11.5.47	13.5.50-9.4.54 Stricken 1.9.59
30 SAN JACINTO	15.12.43	1.47	Stricken 1.6.70
48 SAIPAN	14.7.46	30.30.57	27.8.66-14.1.70 Stricken
49 WRIGHT	9.2.47	15.3.56	11.5.63-25.7.70 Stricken 1.12.77

	INDEPENDENCE CVL 22	SAIPAN CVL 48
Standard	11,000	14,500 tons
Trial	14,220	17,800 tons
Length (LWL)	600	664 ft
Beam	71	76.7 ft
Draft (Trial)	23-1	28 ft
Power	100,000	120,000 SHP
Trial Speed	31.6	32.5
Endurance (15 kts)	13,000	13,000 nm
Flight Deck	544 x 73	618 x 84 ft
Hangar Deck	324	388 ft
Elevators	42 x 44	42 x 48 ft
Air Group: F6F	12	18
(Typical) SBD	9	12
TBM	9	12
Gasoline (gallons)	120,000	140,000
Side Belt	5" on 26 STS	4" on 25 STS
Armor Deck	2"	2.5"
Quad 40mm	2	5
Twin 40mm	9	10
20mm	5 (twin)	16 (twin)

NOTES:
Under 'Fate' a pair of dates indicates second commission and decommission. *Bataan* and *Cabot* were converted to an ASW configuration in 1950-1951. All surviving CVLs were reclassified Aircraft Transports (AVT) 15 May 1959, although none served in that role. *Wright* was converted to a command ship (CC 2); *Saipan* was to have become CC 3 but the conversion was stopped when she was 64 percent complete and she became the communications relay ship *Arlington* (AGMR 2) instead. *Cabot* is now (1978) active as the Spanish *Dedalo*.

USS *Monterey* (CVL-26) being completed at the New York Shipbuilding Corporation, June 1943. At the time of her inclining experiment, *Monterey* had her armament but not her radar aboard. The structure on her flight deck is a weight shuttled across it to determine her metracentric height and displacement from the resulting list. Note the extent to which uptakes had to be led out-board, and also the structural supports for bridge work.

CONFIDENTIAL
CV-26
TOPSIDE ARRANGEMENT STARBOARD SIDE AT TIME OF INCLINING EXPERIMENT
NEW YORK SHIPBUILDING CORP., CAMDEN, N.J.

completion of the first carrier of the *Essex* class.'

There was, however, an escape clause. In its analysis of the delay in completion of a cruise conversion, BuShip had observed that

'The question of time for conversion is also affected by the conversion design. The Bureau prepared [its] preliminary study with the object of obtaining the maximum airplane capacity and the closest approach to present aircraft carrier standards for aviation features . . . ([It] did not consider that smaller capacity or lower standards would be justifiable in view of the expense and military value of the ships to be converted in their original role as cruisers. If, however, it were decided to accept a smaller flight deck, smaller plane capacity, and less effectiveness in air operations in other respects — somewhat along the lines of the converted AVGs [CVEs], — the conversion could, of course, be completed more quickly.'

That was exactly the President's point; and what was remarkable was that rather better features could be achieved in the end, as the cruiser hulls were blistered to gain stability against added topweight.

With hangar deck dimensions unconstrained by the narrow cruiser hull form, both elevators could be the full 42 x 44ft in size. On the other hand, there were still topweight constraints: the new carrier would have only a single H-II catapult, as on escort carriers, rather than the H-IV of the larger fleet carriers. In fact, a second H 2-1 catapult (and a tenth twin 40mm mount) was installed aboard the first ship of the class, *Independence,* in March 1944; weight compensation required was the elimination of eighteen 20mm guns and a reduction in torpedo stowage to eighteen torpedoes. By 1945 all surviving ships had both catapults; but they were still short of the catapult capacity of an *Essex*. For example, an H 2-1 required a wind over deck of 22.5 knots to launch an F7F-4N *Tigercat* twin-engine night fighter; the comparable figure for the H 4 was 4 knots. The post-war AJ-1 *Savage* medium bomber required 34 (19) knots and so was effectively barred from the light carriers. These problems had to be considered in conjunction with the relatively small flight deck available, only 544ft x 73ft.

By 6 January a 315 ton blister had been adopted to solve stability problems which in the September 1941 design had required 400 tons of ballast. Fuel storage actually increased as compared to an unconverted cruiser, since the blister, filled to the waterline, added 635 tons, of which only 225 had to be sacrificed to aviation gasoline stowage.

A rather exotic configuration was contemplated at first: a bridge under the forward end of the flight deck, and a long horizontal smokepipe leading aft under the flight deck to its after end. The flight deck would not, however, be totally unobstructed: it would still have a radar mast, which would serve as kingpost for a big airplane crane, since there would be no openings in the side of the hangar deck large enough to hoist aircraft aboard (as in an *Essex*). Meanwhile experience with the first escort carriers had shown that a bridge projecting above the flight deck was essential; by March 1942, a small CVE-type island had been adopted.

This was built entirely outside the hull and so did not encroach upon the hangar. The uptakes were led up alongside the hangar deck; even so, BuAer would later comment (in connection with a new CVL design) that

'Possibly the most general adverse comment regarding aircraft operations in the CVL 22s is the narrow hangar. This is due to the multitude of vent ducts and uptakes which pierce the hangar deck inboard of its outer boundary and to the fact that the flight deck supporting bents were not landed outboard of the hangar deck proper, i.e. on the blister. It is strongly recommended, therefore, that the maximum possible hangar width be achieved on this new class by:
(a) Running all uptakes and vent ducts as far outboard as practicable.
(b) Widening the hangar by moving the bulkheads outboard to include the blisters.

One unusual problem in the conversion was the cruiser side armor. It was a type (Class A) difficult to weld or cut and so unsuitable for connection to the new blisters. In order to save time, the first two ships were completed entirely without side armor; the remaining ships had thicknesses similar to those adopted in the cruisers, but Class B instead of Class A. Side armor added about 360 tons to the ship's displacement (3in of draft) and could be expected to cost about a quarter knot, which was a minor expense compared to the knot or knot and a half lost through increased displacement and blisters.

Designed armament, in February 1942, was two 5inch/38 (at each end), eight twin 40mm, and ten 20mm. Not long afterwards the forward 5inch gun was replaced by a quadruple Bofors; and in fact only the first ship of the class, *Independence,* went to sea with any 5inch guns at all. Anti-aircraft guns were far more important; the 5inch aft was replaced by a second quadruple Bofors, and by September 1943 the authorized battery was two quadruple and nine

twin Bofors, and 22 20mm. In connection with installation of the second catapult an additional twin Bofors was mounted, and the 20mm battery reduced to four weapons.

The result of all this was a small carrier which could operate with the new large carriers beginning to come into service in 1942-43. The nine *Independences* did not in fact enter service much before the *Essexes;* but on the other hand they were started in 1942, not in 1941; and they did represent the equivalent of perhaps four extra fleet carriers. They also presented new tactical possibilities; for example, a CVL in a Task Group could supply local air cover while the bigger carriers launched their strikes against a distant target.

What seems remarkable in retrospect is that new CVLs were ordered before those already building had been tested at sea. The CVL category came to have a life of its own. Thus in July 1943 Admiral King, who was by then both CNO and Commander-in-Chief, US Fleet, wrote the Vice CNO that

'In December 1945, after allowing for reasonable attrition, it is estimated that the Navy should have about eighteen CV type carriers in commission. The CVL building program will be completed in January 1944, at which time it is estimated that seven of the original nine CVLs will be in commission, allowing two for normal attrition.

It is desirable to bring the number of CVLs up to the original nine as soon as practicable. The present concept of the most profitable use of these small carriers is to brigade one each with two CVs in a carrier division, the CVL being complemented wholly with fighters. Thus the ratio of CVL to CV should be as one to two.

It is desired that a study be made to include additional replacement CVL class carriers in the shipbuilding program in order to maintain the required ships of the class at the original nine, and to provide for a continuing program thereafter. It is recommended that these replacement CVLs be

USS *Monterey* (CVL-26) at sea. The light carriers were relatively little modified in wartime. By 1945 several, including *Monterey,* had SP fighter-director radars in place of the previous SC-2 secondary air-search sets, and additional twin Bofors gun aft. The photograph does not clearly show the catapults forward.

The light carriers *Saipan* (CVL-48) and *Wright* (CVL-49) were the postwar culmination of CVL development. Here *Saipan* carries Marine troop-carrying helicopters in an early test of 'vertical envelopment' theory. She has a largely postwar radar suit: the 'Zenith-search' SG-6 and the standard SPS-6C air search set forward, with the wartime SP fighter-control radar; aft is SR. The tall topmast aft carries HF/DF of a wartime pattern. Her YE homing beacon is mounted on her foremast. *Wright* is shown as an ASW carrier, March 1955, her deck loaded with Grumman AF ASW aircraft. She has much the same electronic suit as her sister.
USN, by courtesy of Robert Carlisle

1

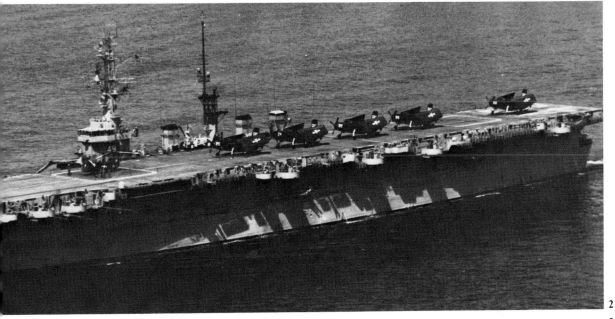

2

3

somewhat larger than the CVL 22 class with the following minimum characteristics:

Flight Deck 610 x 80ft
Hangar Deck 400 x 60ft
Elevators Two (at least 42 x 44ft)
Aircraft
Complement 40 or more
Speed 31-32 knots

Although it is not intended that any of the CA 68 (Baltimore) class cruisers be converted to CVLs, it appears that an arrangement could be worked out with approximately the above characteristics using the CA 68 or similar hull and power plant if such an expedient proved advantageous in working out the design.

It is desired that the practicability of transferring some of the tonnage now allocated to the DE building program in order to carry out the above proposals be included in this study.'

This was the basis of the Saipan (CVL 48) design, a light carrier which would rectify the more glaring faults of the earlier light carrier conversions without excessive growth and hence excessive cost. Both ships would have to be built at New York Shipbuilding, where they would occupy cruiser slipways. There would, therefore, be delays in the completion of cruisers already on order: CL 147 a large anti-aircraft cruiser (later cancelled) would be completed 1 February 1947 rather than 30 December 1946; and the new (rapid fire) heavy cruiser Des Moines (CA 134) would have to be shifted to another yard (three month delay in her completion). As for the continuing program, BuShips interpreted that to mean new CVLs to be begun in 1946. This would cause few problems.

Congressional authorization had been given for 21 000 tons of combatant ships over and above those already on order; two new 13 000 ton carriers would require an additional 5000, which would require the cancellation of four destroyer escorts. If King really wanted four new carriers (two more for 1946), twenty-four destroyer escorts would have to go. In fact, of course, so many destroyer escorts would soon be cancelled that these problems would become academic.

A crude design was ready by the end of August. It employed a Baltimore class hull, blistered for improved stability, so as to achieve a completed ship in minimum time. There were other changes: BuAer demanded a heavier flight deck, to accommodate 20 000 pound aircraft and heavier arresting gear; and the elevators were also enlarged. BuOrd wanted more light AA and some 5inch guns, but could not have them. On the other hand, it was possible to provide half an inch more of deck armor, an inch more on the sides, and better subdivision. The latter included four (rather than two, as in the Independences) boiler rooms, 'which will afford increased reliability of the machinery plant and better limitation of flooding in case of underwater damage'. However, there could be no hope of providing conventional anti-torpedo protection in so small a ship. The thicker protective deck 'is carried forward over magazines and gasoline stowage at the third deck level instead of stepping down to the first platform level forward as in the CVL 22 class. The main side belt is carried forward with its top at the third deck level. This change in armor arrangement affords a necessary increased protected volume for ammunition, control spaces, etc, and increased protected buoyancy. In order to permit this change without increased weight, the thickness of vertical armor has been reduced from 6inch or equivalent in the CA 68 class to thicknesses equivalent to those in the CV 9 [Essex] class . . .'

By November, an improved hull form had been adopted, and the blisters eliminated; it is not clear what delay in construction had to be adopted; very possibly the use of the heavy cruiser machinery in a new hull represented a considerable time saving. Other changes included an improved island similar to that being installed on the new escort carriers (Commencement Bay, CVE 105, class), and a heavier light AA battery — albeit without 5inch guns.

Two ships were built to this design, Saipan and Wright. Both were ordered on 18 September 1943, before any contract plans had

been drawn but after the idea of replacement light fleet carriers had been approved. They were the last US CVLs, although the CVL idea was to be revived several times in the 1950s in reaction to the growth of the attack carriers.

It is difficult to evaluate the American light fleet carriers. All appear to have been successful in combat, although clearly they were easier to sink than were their larger counterparts: Princeton did succumb to a single bomb hit, but then again she had nothing like the deck protection of an Essex. Independence survived a torpedo hit off Tarawa in November 1943. It appears that King's view of their operational value was realistic; but all were rushed into reserve at the end of the war — except for Independence, the largest modern US warship to be tested against nuclear weapons at Bikini in 1946.

Of the others, Cabot was recommissioned to operate as training carrier at Pensacola, a role in which her relatively low operating cost may have been important. She alternated with the later Wright and Saipan. Another post-war role was ASW, the lighter carrier acting as flagships of Hunter-Killer groups. They were somewhat deficient in this role, for example in fuel capacity. There were also, of course, conventional carrier operations, but the small decks of the CVLs cannot have been entirely satisfactory. In any case, none survived the mid-fifties in service, and the two recommission in the sixties had a rather different role, which does not belong here.

Two were transferred to France, where they appear to have functioned satisfactorily as light carriers; and now one is left in service, in the Spanish Navy — the sole carrier survivor of the wartime US task forces remaining in commission anywhere in the world.

Data for this article was taken from Preliminary Design and BuShips Wartime Correspondence files and from the files of the General Board (US Navy Operational Archives). I am especially grateful to Charles Wiseman (NAVSEC), who made Preliminary Design files available; and to Mrs Gerri Judkins of the Operational Archives.

JAPANESE B TYPE SUBMARINES AT WAR 2
by PIERRE HERVIEUX

THE I-40 CLASS (TYPE B2)

This was the second class of B type (scouting) submarines ordered under the 1941 Emergency War Programme and was an improved version of the first B type (*I-15*). Although of the same dimensions as the *I-15* class the tonnage of these vessels was slightly increased. The performance figures for this class were exactly the same as those for *I-15* and the armament was identical. As in the previous class the catapult and hangar were situated on the foredeck, and the 5.5in gun placed abaft the conning tower.

During the war several units had the seaplane hangar and catapult removed and replaced by a 5.5in gun. At the beginning of 1945 the *I-44* had the 5.5in gun aft, the hangar and catapult removed. She was then equipped to carry four Kaiten submarines. A further eight units of this class, planned under the 1942 programme, were descarded when that programme was cancelled.

Individual Fates

I-40 built by Kure Navy Yard, launched in 1942, commissioned in July 1943.

She did not sink or damage any ship, was sunk by the American destroyer *Radford,* off Makin Island, 25 Nov 1943.

Particulars	
Displacement:	2230 tons (2624/3700 tons normal, surface/submerged)
Length:	108.66mm (oa) 356.50ft
	102.41m (cwl) 336ft
Beam:	9.29m 30.50ft
Draught:	5.18m 17 ft
Machinery:	2 shaft Diesel/electric motors
	HP 11 000/2000 = 23.50/8 knots
Armament:	1-5.5inch, 2-25mm AA (1 x 2) guns
	6-21inch (bow) TT and 17 torpedoes
	1 aircraft
Complement:	About 100

I-41 built by Kure Navy Yard, launched in 1943, commissioned in Sept 1943.

She damaged the American light cruiser *Reno* (1942, 6000 tons), in the Pacific, 13°46N/131°27E, 3 Nov 1944.

I-41 was sunk by aircraft from the American carrier *Anzio* and destroyer escort *Lawrence C Taylor,* east of Philippines, 18 Nov 1944.

I-42 built by Kure Navy Yard, launched in 1943, commissioned in Nov 1943.

She did not sink or damage any ship, was sunk in the Pacific, off Palau, by the American submarine *Tunny,* 23 March 1944.

I-43 built by Sasebo Navy Yard, launched in 1943, commissioned in Nov 1943.

She did not sink or damage any ship. Was sunk in the Pacific, by

the American submarine *Aspro,* 280 miles east south east of Guam, 15 Feb 1944.

I-44 built by Yokosuka Navy Yard, launched in 1943, commissioned in Jan 1944.

She did not sink or damage any ship and was sunk by the American destroyer escort *Fieberling,* off Okinawa, 10 April 1945.

I-45 built by Sasebo Navy Yard, launched in 1943, commissioned in Dec 1943.

She sank the American escort *Eversole* (1943, 1350 tons), in the Pacific, 10°10N/127°28E, 28 Oct 1944.

I-45 was sunk by the American destroyer *Whitehurst,* east north east of Surigao Strait, 29 Oct 1944.

THE I-54 CLASS (TYPE B 3)

This third class of B type submarine was an improved version of the previous *I-15* and *I-40* classes of submarine. Of the same dimensions but slightly different tonnage. this class again mounted far less powerful engines than the *I-15* and *I-40* classes. In fact the same engines were fitted to the B type of submarines as to the C type. The engines were of only 4700/1200 hp as against 12 400/2000 and 11 000/2000 hp in the *I-45* and *I-40* classes. Thus the speed was reduced from 23.50/8 knots to 17.50/6.50 knots in this class. In other details and appearance this class was similar to the *I-15* and *I-40* class. Performance was to a certain extent bettered in this class as the radius of action was increased to 21 000 sea miles at a surface cruising speed of 16 knots and 105 sea miles at 3 knots submerged. Endurance and diving depth, however, remained the same at 90 days and 325ft. As with the *I-15* and *I-40* classes this class carried the seaplane hangar and catapult in front of the conning tower. In addition a Type 22 radar set was fitted on top of the seaplane hangar.

In the summer of 1944, *I.56* and *I.58* had the 5.5inch gun removed and fittings made to the hull casing aft of the conning tower to enable them to carry four Kaiten submarines. In March 1945 both ships were refitted to carry 6 Kaitens.

Particulars

Displacement:	2140 tons (2607/3688 tons normal, surfaced/submerged)
Length:	108.66m (oa) 356.50ft
	102.41 (cwl) 336ft
Beam:	9.29m 30.50ft
Draught:	5.19m 17ft
Machinery:	2 shaft diesel/electric motors
	HP 4700/1200 = 17.50/6.50 knots
Armament:	1-5.5-in, 2-25mm AA (1x2) guns
	6-21-in (bow) TT and 19 torpedoes
	1 aircraft
Complement:	About 100

A number of ships ordered for this class had not been laid down when they were cancelled in 1943 to make way for more urgent ship-types. Amongst these were *I.62*, *I.64* and *I.66* ordered the 1941 Supplementary Programme and 14 others ordered under the 1942 Modified Programme. Eighteen units of an improved *I.54* class, to be known as B4 type, were ordered under the 1942 Modified Programme but had not been laid down when they were cancelled in 1943. They were to have been of 2800 tons surface (normal) and with the same dimensions as the *I.54* class. They would, however, have

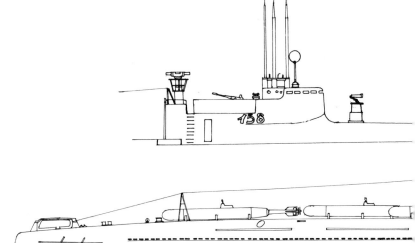

The Japanese submarine *158*.
IWM by courtesy of Anthony J Watts

carried more powerful engines giving them a speed of 22.5 knots. Armament was to have been one 5.5inch and two 25mm AA guns and eight 21inch torpedo tubes, for which they would have carried 16 torpedoes.

Individual Fates

I.54 built by Yokosuka Navy Yard, launched in 1943, commisssioned in March 1944.

She did not sink or damage any ship, was sunk by the American destroyer escort *Richard M Rowell*, 70 miles east of Surigao Strait, 25 Oct 1944.

I.56 built by Yokosuka Navy Yard, launched in 1943, commisssioned in June 1944.

She damaged the American *LST695* (1943, 1653 tons), with a conventioanal torpedo, east of Leyte, 08°31N/128°34E, 24 Oct 1944.

She damaged the American *LST695* (1943, 1653 tons), with a conventional torpedo, east of Leyte, 08°31N/128°34E, 24 Oct 1944.

She also damaged the American escort aircraft carrier *Santee* (1939, 12 000 tons), with a conventioanal torpedo, east of Leyte, 09°45N/126°42E, 25 Oct 1944.

I.56 was sunk by the American destroyers *Heermann, McCord, Collett, Mertz, Uhlmann* and aircraft from carrier *Bataan,* east of Okinawa, 18 April 1945.

I.58 built by Yokosuka Navy Yard, launched in 1944, commissioned in Sept 1944.

She damaged the American destroyer *Lowry* (1944, 2200 tons), with a Kaiten, in the Pacific, 19°30N/128°00E, 27 July 1945.

She sank the American heavy cruiser *Indianapolis* (1931, 9950 tons), with conventional torpedoes, east of Luzan, 12°02N/134°48E, 30 July 1945.

On 10 August 1945, 260 miles north east of Luzon, *I.58* launched two Kaitens. The American destroyer escort *Johnnie Hutchins* avoided them. On 12 Aug 1945 two more Kaitens were launched against the LSD *Oakhill* and the DE *Thomas F Nickel,* east of Okinawa, both missed.

I.58 was surrendered at Kure and moved to Sasebo where she was later sunk off Goto Island by the US Navy on 1 April 1946.

THE
IRANIAN
SAAM
CLASS

By JOHN JORDAN

Faramarz, 1972, with old pennant number.
C & S Taylor

By the early 1960s the destroyer as a type had completed its post-war evolution into a large, ocean-going ASW- and AA-capable vessel with the ability to operate singly or in combination with similar ships against submarines, in addition to the more traditional role of protecting larger and more valuable units. The four *Saam* class ships ordered by Iran from Vosper-Thornycroft and Vickers in 1967 marked a break in this development, in that they returned to the earlier concept of the fast, hard-hitting destroyer designed for surface attack on shipping and shore.

Philosophy of the design
Three factors made the design possible. The first was the development of the Olympus marine gas-turbine with a rating in excess of 22 500 hp — a great advance on the AEI G6 turbine

(7500 hp) fitted in the *County* and *Tribal* classes. This made it possible for the gas-turbine to become the main source of power instead of merely a boost turbine used in conjunction with conventional steam turbines. Diesel engines for cruising could therefore be added in a CODOG (Combined Diesel Or Gas) arrangement which considerably simplified gearing. The degree of confidence Iran was showing in the Vosper design is underlined by the fact that the Royal Navy, which was in the forefront of marine gas turbine development in the West, had only just begun the experimental installation of a similar COGOG (Combined Gas Or Gas) plant in the frigate *Exmouth,* and that this installation was only completed in the same month that the last ship of the *Saam* class was laid down, July 1968. To give the *Saam* high speed and to keep the transmission

simple one Olympus TM2A and one Paxman 16-cylinder diesel were linked to each shaft, giving a maximum of 48 000 hp (40 kn) on the gas turbines and 3800 hp (17.5 kn) on the diesels.

The second factor was the advent of a new generation of weapons and fire-control systems which were more powerful than their predecessors but were smaller and lighter and did not therefore require such a large ship to carry them.

The third factor was the reduced complement, resulting partly from the lower manning levels associated with gas turbines and the higher degree of automation implicit in the new generation of weapon systems, but also from the increased reliability accruing from each of these developments and the consequent reduction in maintenance. Moreover, because of the particular operational requirements envisaged for these

ships (requirements which were more than adequate to fulfil Iranian ambitions in and around the Persian Gulf at that time) they were designed to be away from base for relatively short periods, thus reducing on-board maintenance to an absolute minimum. The burden of maintenance was shifted to the back-up port, where unit replacement methods associated with both gas turbines and modern electronics would ensure faster repairs than would have previously been possible.

The result was a complement of just 135 men, compared with about twice that number required in the average destroyer or large frigate building for the major Western navies. Dimensions could therefore

be reduced to 94.5 m length (oa), 10.5 m beam, and about 3.5 m draught, with a displacement of 1100 tns (a) standard (1300 full load) — figures which are very similar to corresponding ones for the Type 14 ASW frigates of the *Blackwood* class, which cannot be said to compare with the Iranian ships in either speed or fire-power.

CUTTING CORNERS

As the Mk 5 destroyer project which gave birth to the *Saam* class was a private design, the Vosper designers were able to able to reduce weight and cost — which at £6½ million was about two-thirds the price of similarly equipped vessels built to the standards demanded by Western navies — by

a careful consideration of how far these standards were applicable to the role envisaged for these particular ships. They considered that the standards of shock-resistance laid down by the Admiralty were unnecessarily high, being based on the high probability of near-misses from an older, and less accurate, generation of weapons. Savings were also made by lowering the standards of engine mountings considered essential to reduce under-water noise in a vessel whose primary function was ASW. As a defence against submarine attack the class was to rely on high speed and the manoeuvrability bestowed on them by their KaMeWa controllable-pitch propellers.

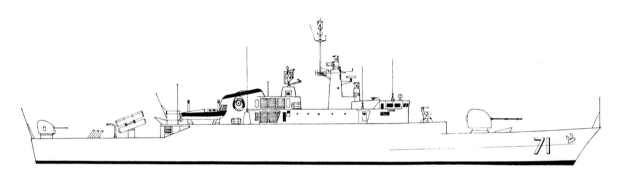

Midships superstructure of *Saam*.
John Jordon

ARMAMENT

A variety of possible weapon 'packages' was envisaged for the original Mk 5 design. A heavy gun, a smaller automatic gun, short-range AA missiles, surface-to-surface missiles, an AS mortar, even a helicopter such as the WG13 Lynx complete with telescopic hangar, could be accommodated, the only limitation being that armament weight should not exceed 9 per cent of deep displacement. Fire-control systems by HSA (Netherlands), Contraves or Elettronica San Giorgio (both Italy) could all be incorporated in the design. British firms, accustomed to concentrating on large and heavy high-performance systems for the Royal Navy, were slow to see the market for small, up-to-date ships that was beginning to open up among the second- and third-class navies of the world, which had previously been content to buy up second-hand cruisers and destroyers of World War II vintage.

It is interesting that the Iranians should have preferred a surface-to-surface variant of the Mk 5 design to the standard ship, which was an ASW version, carrying a 4.5inch gun and a single 40 mm, a helicopter and a Limbo AS mortar and which, incidentally, received no orders. For the *Saam* class as built display a better match of what the Americans would term 'platform' and 'payload' characteristics than any of the other projected variations.

High speed, manoeuvrability and sea-keeping characteristics comparable to those of a *Leander* class frigate constitute the 'platform' side of the design. The major elements of the 'payload' side are the Vickers 4.5inch Mk 8 and the Italian Sea Killer surface-to-surface missiles.

The Vickers Mk 8 was not designed primarily as an AA weapon. It has an elevation of only 55 degrees compared to 80 for the Mk 6 which it was designed to succeed, and the rate of fire — 20 rounds per minute — shows no increase over its predecessor. In the AA role it concentrates rather on a high degree of accuracy and very short reaction times — the mounting is ready to open fire unmanned within 15 seconds. Both these features make the gun a high performer in surface engagement, particularly against FPBs. Increased reliability results from a simpler feed system with moderate speeds and accelerations, using a central vertical hoist in conjunction with a new multi-purpose shell and fuse, which can be set for direct impact, proximity and air-burst overland. The gun itself is a 55 cal model based on the British Army's Abbot gun and is fitted with muzzle brake

BUILDING DATES

	Pendant No.	Builder	Laid down	Launched	Completed
SAAM	71	Vosper-Thornycroft	22/5/67	25/7/68	20/5/71
ZAAL	72	Vickers Barrow	3/3/68	4/3/69	1/3/71
ROSTAM	73	Vickers Newcastle	10/12/67	4/3/69	26/5/72
FARAMARZ	74	Vosper-Thornycroft	25/7/68	30/7/69	28/2/72

Zaal, May 1977 after her 1976/77 refit.
C & S Taylor

and fume extractor.

The first two ships to be completed, *Saam* and *Zaal,* carried the older Mk 5 model as a temporary measure, but this has now been replaced by the Mk 8 during a recent refit at Devonport.

The Sistel Sea Killer Mk 2 missiles were fitted in Naples after the completion of builders' trials and work-up. It is a medium-range missile — 25 km plus — designed to be mounted on anything down to an FPB. In the *Saam* class it is carried in a quintuple launcher aft. Once the booster is jettisoned the missile is gathered into the beam of the fire-control radar which, combining with a radio-commanded radio altimeter, guides it to its target. Optical tracking and radio command can be substituted in the event of excessive interference.

Two anti-aircraft systems are carried. The first is the Seacat missile, which is fired from a light-weight 3-round mounting specially designed for smaller craft. The missile has a range of about 5 km and is guided by a simplified optical director. The other is the Oerlikon-Bührle GDM-A twin 35 mm mounting, which is electrically-controlled and fully stabilised. The gun itself is 90 calibres long, can be elevated to 85 degrees and has a rate of fire of 550 rounds per minute. It is linked to radar fire-control but can also be operated manually.

All four of these weapon systems are controlled by two Contraves Sea Hunter 4 radars sited on and beneath the foremast. The Sea Hunter 4 is remarkable in having both search and tracking antennae mounted together on a single lightweight stabilised mount. After the search radar acquires the target, tracking is automatic.

Surface warning and long-range air search is provided by the Plessey AWS-2 scanner, a stabilised aerial with associated IFF built to stringent weight limits. It is mounted, in typical Vosper fashion, forward of the large funnel to protect it from the hot gases emitted by the gas turbines. Detection probability for air targets is claimed to be 90 per cent at ranges of 60 nm and altitudes of 35 000 ft. The radar also provides consistent automatic tracking of targets once detected.

The only anti-submarine weapon carried is the well-tried triple Limbo mortar, target information being provided by a hull-mounted sonar which at high speeds retracts into the hull and is covered by doors to protect it against excessive pressures.

All weapons and sensors are integrated in a computerised operations room, and all machinery is operated from a similar centralised control room with full instrumentation.

CONCLUSION

There is little indication in present world naval building programmes that there will be any further development of the fast destroyer as a type. Construction seems to be polarising towards large, ocean-going ASW vessels on the one hand and small, fast FPBs armed with SSMs on the other. This however, must not be allowed to take credit away from Vospers for producing such a revolutionary, and handsome, design by questioning established principles of shipbuiding practice and by utilizing the very latest technology. After all, this is how the first destroyer was born.

Saam forecastle and bridge.
John Jordon

NEMESIS
The First Iron Warship
By DAVID K BROWN

Iron ships began in modest fashion with canal barges built in Staffordshire from 1787 onwards. In 1821 the first iron steam ship, the *Aaron Manby,* sailed on her maiden voyage from London to Paris. After that there was a very gradual increase in the use of iron ships for river and coastal work. Iron hulls, being much lighter than wooden ones, were more suitable for shallow water work, and in these confined waters, the one great disadvantage of the iron hull did not matter. Until the Astronomer Royal, Sir George Airey, developed and published his work on correcting ships' compasses for the effect of the iron hull, ocean-going iron ships were not possible.

Airey published his work in 1839 and immediately there was a rush to build iron ships. Brunel altered the plans of the *Great Britain* from wood to iron and the Admiralty ordered its first iron ship, the *Dover* in February 1839, but the credit for the first order for a real warship goes to the Honourable East India Company which ordered the *Nemesis* from Lairds early in 1839. She was laid down in August 1839, launched in November and carried out trials in December the same year, being completed the following month. Principal particulars were:

Length 184 ft (overall). Beam 29 ft. Depth 11 ft. Tonnage (bm) 660.

Paddle wheels 17 ft 6 in diameter. 16 floats each 6 ft 9 in x $14\frac{1}{2}$ in.

Engine: Forrester's Vauxhall Foundry, Liverpool, 2-cylinder. Bore 44 in. Stroke 48 in. 120 nominal hp.

Her draught with 12 days' coal,

water and provisions for a crew of 40 for 4 months, and 3 years' ship and machinery spares was only 6 ft. For river work, she was able to operate at a draught of 5 ft and this gave her a great advantage over comparable RN wooden paddle gunboats, which had draughts of around 13 ft. Only part of this difference was due to the lighter iron hull; much was due to the surveyor's insistence on a sharp V-form hull.

Nemesis was built almost entirely of iron, the main exceptions being the gunwale of oak 4 in x 10 in, the deck of 3 in fir, and four 1 in square beams supporting the bitts and the forward gun. The great beams supporting the paddle boxes were of oak, 12 in square. Wood was also used for the knee, rudder, paddle boxes and cabin bulkheads.

The midship section was almost rectangular, 29 ft x 11 ft, with the bottom curved down 6 in and joining the sides in a 3 ft radius bilge. The form was parallel-sided throughout the machinery spaces and bunkers, tapering to fine ends. Augustin Creuze, a graduate of the first school of Naval Architecture, notes with an air of surprise that the shape was remarkably fair and that no difference could be detected between the two sides of the vessel.

There were six watertight bulkheads, the first to be fitted to a warship. Originally, there were only small hand pumps in each compartment and major flooding had to be drained from one compartment to another, via stopcocks, before being pumped out in the engine room. After a grounding, this peculiar

arrangement was replaced by suction pipes to each compartment.

A partial bulkhead, with an arched opening, was fitted between the engine and boiler rooms to give transverse strength without impeding access.

To improve the sailing qualities, *Nemesis* was given two modern drop keels each 7 ft long. These could be extended 5 ft below the flat bottom. These keels operated in iron trunks 12 in wide extending to the deck and were worked by a small windlass with an endless chain. The trunks both ended on bulkheads, which they helped to support, an example of Lairds' care in detail design. When the keels were down, a corresponding 5 ft extension piece of iron was lowered from the rudder. The ship's officers reported that these drop keels were most valuable in going to windward and in keeping the ship steady.

Her original armament was one 32 pdr muzzle-loader at each end but this was increased by the addition of two 6pdr on each side and, later still, by a fifth 6pdr and a rocket launching tube on the large bridge deck between the paddle boxes.

Nemesis was fitted with compass correctors similar to Airey's, but unlike the Company's other ships, they were not installed by him and so her compass was never very accurate. When crossing the Indian Ocean it was found that the compass read true when heading North or South but there were large errors when going East or West. It was probably this defective compass which caused *Nemesis* to run on to The Stones, off St Ives, during her

maiden voyage. She hit a sharp rock at about 8½ knots which pushed in the fore foot 3 in and split it over a further 8 in. Seven feet further aft the keel was indented but not penetrated. The main damage was at the turn of the bilge, by the forward bulkhead, where the shell was forced against the bulkhead which pierced it, the lower bulkhead plate also being broken.

The damage was confined to the area actually struck by the rock, since the rivets remained firm. *Nemesis* was able to borrow a powerful pump in Penzance and continue to Portsmouth for repairs. A shoe was rivetted over the forefoot and two new plates were fitted. Plants which had only been bent were straightened in the furnace and replaced. Altogether, 3 cwt of new material was used and this, together with labour, brought the repair cost to £30. Mr Laird said that with the right equipment, as installed at Birkenhead, the cost would have been about £20. Laird wrote to their Lordships in March 1840 suggesting that a full Admiralty survey be carried out while *Nemesis* was in Portsmouth Dockyard. This job was given to Augustin Creuze, who later published his report in the Journal

of the United Services Institution. It was the first of many favourable reports on the *Nemesis* which the Admiralty were to receive.

She left Portsmouth on 28 March 1840 with 60 men on board (later her increased armament led to a crew of 90) and crossed the Bay of Biscay at 7-8 knots, burning 11 tons of coal each day. After crossing the Equator, Captain Hall tried disconnecting one paddle wheel, running under sail and the lee wheel. This seemed quite satisfactory and the ship achieved 6½-7 knots at 12-15 tpm making little or no leeway. A trial with both cylinders worked from one boiler was a failure because of insufficient steam being generated. Nearing South Africa the rudder extension fell off and a new one was made. Lee boards were also made and tried, reducing leeway under sail alone by half.

This careful experimentation was typical of the Master, William Hutcheon Hall, who had entered the Navy in 1811 and been made Master in 1923. He made a very thorough study of steam engines and, as a result, was lent to the HEI Co to command the *Nemesis*. His performance in that ship was so outstanding that the Admiralty obtained an Order in Council to

enable him to become a Lieutenant on 8 January 1841. He was later allowed to count his time in *Nemesis* for seniority in the RN and became a Commander in 1843 and a Captain the following year.

Hall later invented a patent anchor and introduced iron bilge tanks, and became a Fellow of the Royal Society in 1847. He retired as a Rear Admiral in 1869 with a KCB, and died nine years later. His exceptional career showed that it was possible to rise right through the ranks of the 19th century Navy given merit and, perhaps, a lot of luck. His knowledge of steamships came just at the right time, when this branch of the RN was growing rapidly.

The most exciting and technically interesting part of the voyage came after leaving South Africa. On 16 July, near Algoa Bay, the barometer started to fall, eventually sinking to 28 in; a strong wind from the NNW freshened to full gale and the sea was high and heavy. This area is still regarded as a dangerous one as the ocean swell gets much steeper in entering shallow water. The paddle boards had been removed and *Nemesis* was under sail alone when at 3 am on the 17th a tremendous sea struck the port quarter and she broached

o. The starboard wheel broke and crack started on both sides of the ship at the corner of the square opening for the beam supporting the after end of the paddle boxes. These cracks ran all through the plates below the sheet strake and partly through the sheer strakes. Initially, the cracks were about $2\frac{1}{2}$ ft long and the plates were bulged, sketches of the damage suggest that the initial failure was under compression.

The first concern was for the broken paddle wheel. The damaged sector was hooked up with a boat anchor and brought on board. The removal of the floats had weakened the wheel and it was also thought that it should have had an additional ring of stiffening (fitted in later ships). This practice of unshipping the floats was a common one since it reduced the drag under sail. It was a dangerous habit, though, since if a storm sprang up it would not be possible to replace the boards in a rough sea and hence steam power would not be available.

On the 18th the wind moderated and the ship was able to make 4 knots on the port wheel alone. Three days later the starboard wheel was repaired just as the wind freshened once again. Some planks were put around the stern to keep the sea out and the after 32pdr was dismounted and lowered into a coal bunker. The cracks, now $3\frac{1}{2}$ ft long, were patched on the 22nd with an iron plate outside, bolted through to planks inside the hull.

In the new storm the cracks extended a further 18 in in five hours. Wooden cross braces were put inside between the frame, to prevent the broken plates from over-riding and the frames either side of the cracks were joined with long bolts to take the tensile loads. These repairs held out until Nemesis reached the shelter of Delagoa Bay, where further repairs were made. By this time the cracks were 7 ft long (in a total depth of ship of 11 ft). Long timbers were obtained from a local slave trader.

From these timbers, three wooden stringers 23 ft long were cut and fitted inside the frames each side. The spaces between the shell and the stringers was filled with timber. The cracked plates were removed and the new ones rivetted in place. The designs of these early iron ships were often attacked (eg Fairbairn INA) because of the lack of iron stringers on the deck.

A rough calculation shows the neutral axis to have been about 5 ft above the keel giving a reasonable balance of stress. The inertia of the section was about 10 000 in 2 ft 2 in giving a compressive stress of about 1/3 the ultimate for wrought iron when balanced between wave crests of height equal to 1/20th of her length. Her overall strength is proved by the fact that she could withstand a further storm with cracks extending over 7 ft of her 11 ft depth.

During the remainder of the voyage to the Far East, Nemesis continued to be plagued by a wildly inaccurate compass and also had her speed much reduced by heavy fouling on her uncoated iron bottom. Reports from P & O liners, a few years later, showed that barnacles up to 9 in long could grow in a single voyage to India. Fouling was the one problem which was never abated during the iron ship era and it remains an expensive nuisance to this day.

Once arrived in China, Nemesis lived the normal, exciting life of a gunboat of the time of the 1st China War. She was the first ship to pass the Bogue Forts, she surveyed the Canton River, took part in actions against Amoy, Ningpo and Woosung. A book on her first commission by Hall and Bernard gives a fascinating picture of Imperial Britain at work, both good and bad.

Only one of these actions was of technical significance, that of the bombardment of Whampoa in February 1841. 'Nemesis was struck several times, but fortunately only one man was wounded. One of the large shots passed completely through the outer casing of the steam chest and was very near to penetrating the steam chest itself. Besides receiving several shots in the hull she had her spars and rigging a good deal cut up . . .'

Hall and his engineer Pedder kept the ship running and frequently in action until 1843, when the commission was over and she returned to Bombay to refit. She required much less maintenance than did wooden ships on similar work and fears that gunfire would shake out her rivets, or that she would rust away, were quite unjustified. On docking at Bombay it was said:—

'The Nemesis has been for some time past in our docks, and I have carefully examined her. She displays in no small degree the advantages of iron. Her bottom bears the marks of having been repeatedly ashore; the plates are deeply indented in several places, one or two to the extent of several inches. She had evidently been in contact with sharp rocks, and one part of her keel plate is bent sharply up, in such a way that I could not believe that cold iron could have been; indeed, unless the iron had been extremely good, I am sure it would not have withstood it without injury. Her bottom is not nearly so much corroded as I expected to have found it and she is as tight as a bottle.'

Hall returned home and reported to the Admiralty on 22 November 1843. He told their Lordships that he much preferred a well-built iron ship to a wooden ship. He said that Nemesis was frequently hit, by up to 14 shots in one action. These hits caused no serious problems and were easily repaired. The effect of splinters was about the same or not as much as from a wooden hull.

Admiral Sir George Cockburn was to tell the Select Committee on Estimates in 1847, that Hall's report, together with those from Bombay and Portsmouth Dockyards, were the main factors in the Board's decision to build a large number of iron ships for the RN during the mid-1840s.

Considering that Nemesis suffered continually from fouling and from compass error, and that she had suffered a near-catastrophic structural failure, other merits must have been very conspicuous. It was perhaps fortunate that most of her actions were fought in the fresh waters of the Chinese rivers, where neither fouling nor compass errors were serious.

NEW WARSHIP TITLES
Conway Maritime Press

CONWAY MARITIME PRESS LTD, 2 NELSON ROAD, GREENWICH, LONDON SE10 9JB

CAMERA AT SEA 1939 - 1945 edited by the staff of 'Warship'

A remarkable collection of the very best photography of the war at sea — ships, weapons, equipment, personnel and action shots, many never before published. The photos are reproduced large for maximum detail, and the book includes 16 pages of full colour. The captions were written by well-known contributors to 'Warship' including Aldo Fraccaroli, Antony Preston, Alan Raven, John Roberts and Larry Sowinski.
192 pages (12¼" x 8"), 274 photos. Casebound with full colour jacket. June £12.00 (plus 75p postage)

BATTLECRUISERS By John Campbell

The first in a series of 'Warship Specials' - in the same format as a single issue of *Warship*, they employ the same combination of an authoritative text and a high proportion of illustration. *Battlecruisers* covers both British and German ships of the WW1 period, their design and service history, including the most detailed information on battle damage ever published.
72 pages (9½" x 7¼"), 55 photos, 30 line drawings. July 1978 £2.50 (plus 30p postage)

SUPER DESTROYERS edited by Antony Preston

This, the second 'Warship Special', covers the big destroyer leaders built between the wars for the navies of Britain, Germany, France, Italy, Japan and the USA. *72 pages (9½" x 7¼"), 70 half-tones, 30 line illustrations. September 1978 £2.50 (plus 30p postage)*

FORTHCOMING

SCALE MODEL WARSHIPS edited by John Bowen

In the same series as the highly successful *Scale Model Sailing Ships*, this book adopts the same approach and format, with 9 highly skilled modelmakers each discussing particular aspects of the hobby, from research sources, through the construction of the hull, decks and superstructure, to gun mountings and deck fittings. There are specialist chapters on working models and radio control, miniatures and plastic models. *192 pages (9½" x 7¼"), 150 photos and 120 plans and diagrams. Casebound with full colour jacket. October 1978 £7.50 (plus 50p postage)*

BATTLESHIP DESIGN AND DEVELOPMENT 1906 - 1945 by Norman Friedman

Many books have been devoted to the history or technical details of battleships, but this is the first layman's guide to the design process, the factors which governed the development of capital ships, and the reasons *why* battleships were built in a particular way: essential reading for anyone seeking a deeper understanding of the most impressive warships in history. *160 pages (10" x 8"), over 150 illustrations. Casebound with full colour jacket. November 1978 £8.50 (plus 50p postage)*

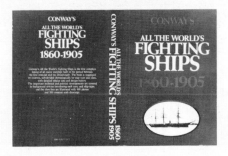

CONWAY'S ALL THE WORLD'S FIGHTING SHIPS 1860 - 1905

The first complete listing of all major warships built in the period between the first ironclad and the *Dreadnought*. The book is organised by country, sub-divided chronologically by ship type and class, with detailed tabular data and design history. The important technical and political developments are covered in background articles on major navies and ship types and the class lists are illustrated with 400 photos and 500 constant scale drawings. *384 pages approx. (12" x 8½"). Casebound with jacket. January 1979 £18.95 for first three months of publication, £24.00 thereafter (plus £1 postage)*

Warship Photograph Service